Cuba in a Global Context

Contemporary Cuba

UNIVERSITY PRESS OF FLORIDA

Florida A&M University, Tallahassee
Florida Atlantic University, Boca Raton
Florida Gulf Coast University, Ft. Myers
Florida International University, Miami
Florida State University, Tallahassee
New College of Florida, Sarasota
University of Central Florida, Orlando
University of Florida, Gainesville
University of North Florida, Jacksonville
University of South Florida, Tampa
University of West Florida, Pensacola

Cuba in a Global Context

International Relations, Internationalism, and Transnationalism

Edited by Catherine Krull

FOREWORD BY LOUIS A. PÉREZ JR.

UNIVERSITY PRESS OF FLORIDA
Gainesville / Tallahassee / Tampa / Boca Raton
Pensacola / Orlando / Miami / Jacksonville / Ft. Myers / Sarasota

Copyright 2014 by Catherine Krull
All rights reserved
Printed in the United States of America on acid free paper

THE PUBLICATION OF THIS BOOK WAS FUNDED IN PART BY A GRANT
FROM QUEEN'S UNIVERSITY, KINGSTON.

This book may be available in an electronic edition.

21 20 19 18 17 16   6 5 4 3 2 1

First cloth printing, 2014
First paperback printing, 2016

LIBRARY OF CONGRESS CATALOGING-IN-PUBLICATION DATA
Cuba in a global context : international relations, internationalism, and
transnationalism / edited by Catherine Krull ; foreword by Louis A. Pérez Jr.
pages cm — (Contemporary Cuba)
Includes bibliographical references and index.
ISBN 978-0-8130-4910-6 (cloth: alk. paper)
ISBN 978-0-8130-6217-4 (pbk.)
1. Cuba—Foreign relations—1959–1990. 2. Cuba—Politics and government—1959–1990.
I. Krull, Catherine, editor. II. Pérez, Louis A., 1943– III. Series: Contemporary Cuba.
F1788.C81585 2014
972.9106'4—dc23   2013029229

The University Press of Florida is the scholarly publishing agency for the State
University System of Florida, comprising Florida A&M University, Florida Atlantic
University, Florida Gulf Coast University, Florida International University, Florida
State University, New College of Florida, University of Central Florida, University
of Florida, University of North Florida, University of South Florida, and University
of West Florida.

University Press of Florida
15 Northwest 15th Street
Gainesville, FL 32611-2079
http://www.upf.com

Contents

Foreword vii
   Louis A. Pérez Jr.

Acknowledgments xi

Introduction: Cuba in a Global Context 1
   Catherine Krull

PART I. INTERNATIONAL RELATIONS

1. Disaster, Disease, and Environmental Degradation: U.S.-Cuban Cooperation as a Bridge to Reconciliation 27
   William M. LeoGrande and Marguerite Rose Jiménez

2. A Model Servant: The Revolutionary Armed Forces and Cuban Foreign Policy 44
   Hal Klepak

3. Cuba's Monumental Children: Operation Peter Pan and the Intimacies of Foreign Policy 58
   Karen Dubinsky

4. The Role of the Courts in Shaping U.S. Policy toward Cuba 75
   Stanley J. Murphy

5. Cuban-Chinese Relations after the End of the Cold War 89
   Carlos Alzugaray Treto

6. "Complicated and Far-Reaching": The Historical Foundations of Canadian Policy toward Cuba 109
   Asa McKercher

PART II. INTERNATIONALISM

7. The Cuba-Venezuela Alliance and Its Continental Impact 127
   Max Azicri

8. Santeria Commerce and the Unofficial Networks of Interpersonal Internationalism 144
   Kevin M. Delgado

9. The Promise of Globalization: Sustainable Tourism Development and Environmental Policy in Cuba   160
   Ricardo Pérez

10. The Heart of the Matter: The Impact of Cuban Medical Internationalism in the Global South   176
    Robert Huish

11. Cuba's Revolutionary Agro-Ecological Movement: Learning from the Experience of Food Sovereignty   192
    Efe Can Gürcan

12. Postcards from Abroad: The Cuban Special Period through Spanish Eyes   208
    Ana Serra

PART III. TRANSNATIONALISM

13. Transnationalism and the Havana Cigar: Commodity Chains, Networks, and Knowledge Circulation   227
    Jean Stubbs

14. Through the Eyes of Foreign Filmmakers: Contradictions and Paradigms of Cuban Cinema after the Revolution   243
    María Caridad Cumaná

15. Cubans in Spain: Transnational Connections and Memories   257
    Mette Louise Berg

16. Oral History and Constructions of Racial Memory   271
    Yvette Louis

17. Cubans without Borders: From the Buildup to the Breakdown of a Socially Constructed Wall across the Florida Straits   287
    Susan Eckstein

18. Ernesto Che Guevara, Dispositions, and Education for Transnational Social Justice   302
    John D. Holst

List of Contributors   319
Index   325

Foreword

On January 1, 1959, a popular rebellion in Cuba ousted a repressive military dictatorship to the general approval and acclaim of all. As the revolutionary processes deepened, as the scope of reform expanded and crossed thresholds never before breeched, as the new prime minister, Fidel Castro, challenged long-established premises about property and privilege in Cuba, the revolution changed its course and changed in character. Within the space of twenty-four months, Cuba was transformed into the first Marxist-Leninist state in the Western Hemisphere, aligned fully and unabashedly with the Soviet Union—all this occurring ninety miles from the United States, in a region traditionally proclaimed a North American sphere of influence, in a country historically secure as a U.S. client-state. "No sane man undertaking to govern and reform Cuba," the Central Intelligence Agency puzzled, "would have chosen to pick a fight with the U.S."—a comment very much of the conventional wisdom of the time. So, too, was the prevailing notion that the Cubans would be incapable of sustaining a project of such radical reach in defiance of North American power.

More than fifty years later, the *comandantes* who rose to power in 1959 remain in power. Certainly, the Cuban revolution has not aged well. It bears the infirmities and afflictions that have accumulated in recent decades, in part the result of withering—and unrelenting—sanctions by the United States, in part due to the continuing consequences associated with the collapse of the Soviet Union, and in part due to internal mismanagement and miscalculation.

But it is also true that the Cuban revolution continues to retain its resonance as an experience of enormous historical significance. The policies and personalities of the revolution have had an impact of global dimensions as Cuba has projected a presence in the world entirely out of proportion to its size and resources. "How does one tell the story of a country whose history is far larger than its size?" asks the narrator in the film *Los cubanos: Bretón es un bebé* (2008).

One effort occurred on the fiftieth anniversary of the triumph of the revolution. It was an entirely appropriate occasion to organize an international conference on the Cuban revolution, to convene an international gathering of scholars to take measure of what must be considered one of the transcendental events of twentieth-century Latin America, a process of momentous national consequences and far-reaching international repercussions. This was not merely one more commemoration of one more anniversary of the Cuban revolution. Rather, it represented a project designed to gather together informed participants to look back, of course, but also to look forward. In May 2009, an estimated four hundred scholars, researchers, writers, artists, filmmakers, musicians, and members of the public at large registered for the conference "Measure of a Revolution: Cuba, 1959–2009," hosted by Queen's University in Kingston, Ontario. Participants included scholars from Cuba, Canada, the United States, and Europe, and represented a variety of disciplines, diverse methodological approaches, and a wide range of research subjects. Many of the essays in this volume have their origins in the highly successful Queen's University conference. Others were solicited specifically to complete the breadth of analysis warranted by serious study of the multiple complexities of the Cuban revolutionary processes.

The conference provided the occasion to take stock of the Cuban revolution, reflect on its objectives, examine its achievements, consider its prospects, and contemplate its legacy, but most of all to foster dialogue and promote collaborative engagement among scholars of Cuba. Rare indeed have been the opportunities during the last fifty years for scholars of Cuba—from the island and outside—to assemble in such numbers to exchange views, share information, and engage one another in discussion and debate.

Organized around nearly fifty panels, the Kingston conference included several plenary sessions and a number of workshops and round-table sessions. The program also contained poetry readings, musical performances, dance programs, films, poster exhibits, and a book fair. Panelists and speakers addressed a variety of subjects, ranging from matters of race, gender, and sexuality to youth culture and aging; from architecture, public housing, and urban planning to the environment and sustainable development; from issues related to public health, civil society, and human rights to the economy in its multiple facets, including agriculture, sugar production, foreign investment, and trade; and to migration, education, and the arts.

The essays in this book represent the state of the art of scholarship and, indeed, offer a perspective on the range of interests that has characterized the field of Cuban studies. Organized in broadly defined categories of international relations, internationalism, and transnationalism, the essays are themselves representative of multinational perspectives, offering the insights of scholars from within Cuba and from Canada, Europe, and the United States. The essays serve also as something of a generational bridge, bringing together in one book perspectives of senior scholars working together with junior colleagues. Almost all the essays have a sense of immediacy, addressing issues both current and urgent, ranging from environment to religion, from health care to immigration, and from Cuba's foreign relations with friends like China, Venezuela, and Canada to those with its imperial enemy the United States.

These essays are informative in their own right, and also offer multiple perspectives that are often obtainable only by way of interdisciplinary collaborations. Their diversity matches their quality. At least as important, together they provide a valuable overview and serve as signposts pointing the way to new avenues of inquiry and new approaches to old issues. In many ways, the essays speak to each other as much as they speak to the reader. They serve also to underscore the value of methodological collaboration, demonstrating how interdisciplinary conventions can act together to inform the scholarship of all. These are important—and timely—scholarly contributions to the field of knowledge on Cuba.

The community of scholars and students of Cuba are deeply indebted to Professor Catherine Krull for her continuing commitment to the scholarship on Cuba. Her indefatigable efforts in organizing the successful 2009 Queen's University conference provided a felicitous venue for scholars of Cuba to meet and engage one another. Her effort in assembling this volume guarantees that much of the scholarship summoned for the conference will have a larger audience and a permanent presence in the scholarly literature. We are all in her debt.

Louis A. Pérez Jr.

Acknowledgments

The genesis of this book lies in an international conference on Cuba at the fiftieth anniversary of its revolution held at Queen's University in 2009. Organized by Soraya Castro (Havana University), Louis A. Pérez Jr. (University of North Carolina at Chapel Hill), Susan Eckstein (Boston University), and me (Catherine Krull, Queen's University), it included approximately 226 presenters from more than a dozen countries, including 52 from Cuba. But although this book's intellectual base resides in this conference, this project looks more closely at Cuba's global issues—its international relations, and internationalist or transnational/diasporic dimensions—and its contributors, some of whom did not attend the conference, have brought decided depth to the issues that they discuss. This depth adds gravitas not only to their own subjects but, collectively, has added decidedly to the intellectual rigor and scholarly exegesis of the volume as a whole.

To this end, I would like especially to acknowledge the efforts of three friends and pre-eminent scholars of Cuba who have been essential to this project from beginning to end, integral in terms of their time, advice, and knowledge: John Kirk (Dalhousie University), Louis A. Pérez Jr., and Jean Stubbs (University College London). Their insight and counsel has been integral to the development of this book. Each knows how much I am in their debt, and I want them to know how much I appreciate all that they did. I am also grateful to Soraya Castro for the many discussions on Cuba's international relations while we organized the conference and edited a special issue of *Cuban Studies*, both of which played a part in shaping my ideas for this book. I am also indebted to Rob Clark who so patiently and efficiently contributed to editing the chapters as initially submitted.

And although the publication of a new book is cause for celebration, this occasion is also marked with sadness and loss. Before its completion, renowned Cuban scholar Professor Max Azicri passed away. It is a considerable honor and privilege to include his final paper in this book.

I would like to acknowledge the institutional support that I have received throughout the process of preparing this book. At Queen's University, John Dixon (Vice-Provost International), Alistair McLean (Dean of the Faculty of Arts and Science), Rob Beamish (Sociology Department Head), and Bonnie Stewart (Research Services) were especially supportive. And, as with most of my academic work, I cannot emphasize how critical the never-ending support from Wendy Schuler has been. I also received invaluable support from Havana University, especially from Cristina Díaz López (Vice-Rector of International Relations), Ileana Sorolla Fernández (Director, Center of International Immigration Studies (CEMI), Milagros Martínez Reinosa (Senior Adviser to the Vice Rector of International Relations and Executive Secretary, Department of Caribbean Studies), and Carmen Castillo Herrera (Assistant to the Vice Rector of International Relations). While preparing this manuscript, I had visiting research fellowships at the Institute for the Study of the Americas, University of London (July 2011–June 2012) and the Center for Latin American Studies, University of Florida (January–June 2012). Their respective directors, Professor Maxine Molyneux and Professor Philip Williams, both provided places for scholarly contemplation, concentrated writing, and most important, engagement with intellectually inspiring colleagues, all of which have made this volume stronger. I am also grateful for the support that I have received from the staff at the University Press of Florida, and especially acknowledge the support and superb efforts of Associate Director and Editor-in-Chief Amy Gorelick. I am also appreciative of the time and useful feedback that the anonymous reviewers gave to this book. Of course, financial support for this project has been crucial. The Social Sciences and Humanities Research Council of Canada (SSHRC) has been particularly generous in this regard.

Cuba's rich and complex story has long fascinated me, and I consider myself incredibly fortunate to have had the opportunity to engage with a number of Cubans who have enriched my life, both professionally and personally. Among them are my dearest friends and their families: Sonia Enjamio (recently deceased), Lourdes Pérez Montalvo, Inés Rodríguez, Vivien Rocaberti, Alberto Jones, Vanessa Chicola, Aldo Peña, Camillo García, and Alberto Roque Guerra. Their endless patience with me as I grappled with understanding Cuba from a "Cuban perspective" is not only very much appreciated, but has been integral in shaping me as both an individual and a scholar. Finally, a number of scholars need mention for contributions varied and important: Karen Dubinsky, Susan Lord, Jennifer Hosek, Pedro Pérez Sarduy, Cathie McIllwaine, Mette Berg, Phil Brenner, Hal Klepak, Yolanda Prieto, Jorge Duany, Helen Safa, John Dumoulin, Carmen Diana Deere, Deborah Weissman, Efrain Barradas, Lillian Guerra, Teresita Vicente Sotolongo, Lynda Jessup, Christoph Singler, Anja Bandau, Annette Insanally, Nadine Fernandez, Mélanie Josée Davidson, Ivis Gutiérrez, Laureen Snider, Caridad Cumana, Sylvia Bawa, Janelle Hippe, Cynthia Wright, Melanie Newton, Paulina García del Moral, Jennifer Dutra, Julie James, Ana Ruiz, Zaira Zsarzsa, and Katelyn Merritt. They have had and continue to have a significant influence on my intellectual journey.

And as with any of my accomplishments, my family has been central. My children Matt/Monica, Lindsey/Dan, and Asa, and granddaughter Maria, continue to fill my life with joy. I also draw inspiration from my amazing mom, who has had to rebuild her life after the death of my father. She continues to touch our lives in spectacular ways, showing us that life indeed can have inordinate purpose even in the face of great loss. And, as always, I owe much to my husband, Brian, who made it possible for me to get this book completed at a time when life was incredibly complicated and demanding. His interminable patience and optimism, unwavering love, and steadfast belief in me has enriched my world in ways I never imagined possible.

Introduction

Cuba in a Global Context

CATHERINE KRULL

For more than half a century Cuba has occupied a unique position in global affairs, with a steadfast prominence that at first glance might seem unlikely for a small, developing island country nestled in the Caribbean. Indeed, Cuba has long had a significant, highly active place not just in the foreground of international relations—where Cubans found themselves at the center of the three-decade Cold War geopolitical struggle between the United States and the Soviet Union[1]—but also, equally importantly, within the constructs of internationalism (the promotion of increased economic and political cooperation amongst nations) and transnationalism (people-to-people rather than government-to-government relationships). These constructs of international relations, internationalism, and transnationalism are not only intertwined but also central to the country's revolutionary project.

The Context

Cuba's prominent international position began with the successful revolution led by Fidel Castro in January 1959, and it arose particularly because of that achievement and the subsequent determination of the Castro government to bring about a complete economic, social, and political transformation on the island. There was also a Cuban determination to support other revolutionary regimes and oppose what Havana saw as increasing American hegemony in the developing world, which even led to military intervention to help defend socialist Angola against U.S.-supported anti-Marxist guerrillas between 1975 and 1991.

Even after the Cold War ended in 1990–91, Cuba remained in a perilous position as the U.S. government reinforced its policies designed to strangle the revolutionary government economically in hopes of engineering a regime change to something approaching the American model.² Throughout, the Cuban people on the island have generally supported the aims of the revolution politically—those who opposed it ideologically and had the opportunity to leave largely departed. Cognizant of the dire situation in which the vast majority of Cubans had languished before January 1959, when the United States supported a succession of pro-American dictatorial regimes on the island,³ the Cuban people proved willing to continue backing revolutionary—and sometimes very unrevolutionary—economic and social efforts to build a new society.

Suffused by reactive Cuban nationalism, the continuing U.S. embargo after 1991, supported by only a few U.S. allies, appears only to have strengthened Cuban resolve. The determination to continue building a different economic, political, and social system from that of the United States underscores Cuba's continuing strategic position in global affairs—although Marxist prescriptions for the economy are to some extent being supplanted by market-driven approaches. For instance, since 2008, the Cuban government has allowed private farmers to work plots of fallow public land; eliminated a range of subsidies, including food rations; permitted limited private trade, including the selling of used cars; and expanded the purchase of some heretofore controlled consumer goods, like computers and cell phones. Moreover, more than 500,000 state workers—10 percent of the workforce—were laid off by the end of March 2011. To alleviate unemployment, the government proposed new regulations that would enlarge the cooperative sector and encourage private-sector employment, and subsequently there has been a relative explosion in the number of restaurants. These and other efforts were designed to stimulate the economy, though their impact is as yet uncertain.⁴ Nonetheless, determined to be accepted as a sovereign people governing themselves in their own best interests, even if they make mistakes in doing so, Cubans refuse to prostrate their country before their exceedingly powerful neighbor.⁵

By the same token, in the realm of internationalism the long-lasting success of the Cuban revolution and the country's activist foreign policy, which includes the defense of Marxist Angola, have seen support for Cuban ideals and practices emerge among developing countries in the Caribbean, Latin America, Africa, and Asia. For the same reasons these phenomena have spurred continued American opposition.⁶ But support for revolutionary Cuba never did abate in the wider world, in Britain, Western Europe, Canada, Australia, and New Zealand, despite these countries' diplomatic and military connections to the United States.⁷ Both capitalist and social-democratic governments have offered support for reasons of economic and political self-interest; and because at least some of their perceived national interests are dissimilar to those of the

United States, they share the Cuban desire to conduct foreign and economic policies as sovereign states unwilling to genuflect to U.S. dictates. Such practical desires only add to Cuba's continuing international importance.[8]

As for the transnational experience, yet another dimension of Cuban global importance exists in that the island's culture, including elements that are not necessarily revolutionary, has made its way across borders—including to the United States—where it is embraced by a range of individuals.[9] The cultural exchange goes far beyond the ubiquitous image of Che Guevara on posters and T-shirts and, importantly, it does not run in just one direction. Given modern communications, travel, and permeability of the fabric of culture, the cultural achievements of some parts of the developing world, of Europe, of Canada, and of other countries have also influenced Cubans.[10] Moreover, beginning in the early 1990s, a new Cuban diaspora has taken shape; unlike the post-1959 migration, which was political in nature and built émigré communities largely in the United States, the recent diaspora is primarily economic; its members largely endorse Cuba's revolutionary social achievements, and increasing numbers of them are settling in Western Europe and Canada.[11] These émigrés have helped build a blossoming cultural exchange between Cuba and other places. And facilitating this exchange might be the January 1, 2013, relaxation of travel restrictions on Cubans who wish to travel abroad and return to the island. For Cuban citizens on the island, Havana will lift both exit visa requirements and the need for letters of invitation from organizations or individuals in the destination country. Now, most Cubans—except for members of certain specific professional groups crucial to the state and economy, like the military—need only show their passport, national identity card and, if necessary, a visa from the country they intend to visit. As long as they did not leave via the U.S. naval base at Guantánamo, émigrés who left illegally after 1990—including high-profile athletes and doctors—can freely return and then leave again. Cubans should now be able not only to travel abroad but to work outside Cuba and return home when they wish.[12]

None of this is to say that Cubans, or those elements of the wider world that have been and are still willing to work with the regime and embrace its culture, have not chosen a bumpy path to follow. The collapse of the Soviet Union and its empire, and the concurrent breakdown of the socialist trading bloc after 1991, produced a major economic crisis in Cuba. Exports to Cuba and much-needed foreign currency reserves fell precipitously; and at the same time imports, especially food imports, declined markedly—a situation made more difficult by U.S. legislation in 1992 and 1996 that tightened the economic blockade of the island. Consequently, Cubans confronted the so-called Special Period in Time of Peace.[13] Lasting for several years—with ripples still being felt today after three powerful hurricanes struck Cuba in the autumn of 2008—the Special Period was marked by petroleum scarcity, food shortages, reduced construction materials for housing, and increased ill health among some parts of the populace, such as the elderly and people with chronic diseases such as diabetes.

From time to time, too, the Cuban government's tough handling of political dissent has chilled relations with other powers. Thus, the Cuban government's March 2003 arrest and imprisonment without charge of seventy-seven nonviolent "prisoners of conscience" saw the European Union (EU) impose restricted political sanctions on Cuba, limiting high-level government visits and the role of EU diplomats in Cuba's cultural events during a period of five years.[14] Still, more than fifty years after Fidel Castro's forces entered Havana in triumph, Cuba's global position—in terms of the constructs of international relations, internationalism, and transnationalism—remains strong. The ongoing Cuban-American negotiations begun by President Barak Obama and President Raoul Castro and announced in December 2014 are beginning the difficult process of normalization between the two states on a basis of equality.

Part I. International Relations

The representative chapters in part I of this book assess various global dimensions of Cuba's international relations, in particular the traditional pursuit of external politics: foreign policy. To a degree, of course, the internationalism of culture, humanitarianism, and social policies permeates the political element of international relations. But above all else, from 1959 onward, Cuban foreign policy was designed to assert both the legitimacy of the revolutionary government and the sovereignty of the revolutionary state. U.S. opposition to the post-1959 Cuban polity was one of the most notable and severe responses to this course of action. Yet, other than the United States and some of its diehard allies, a vast number of countries went on to establish formal relations with Cuba; and a few, such as Canada and Great Britain, have acknowledged revolutionary Cuba's legitimacy and sovereignty from the moment the new revolutionary regime took power.

In Cuban foreign policy circles, the United States remains the pre-eminent consideration—even though from the U.S. viewpoint Cuba may not be a prime concern.[15] Still, eventual improvement of Cuban-American relations is probably inevitable given the political eclipse of Fidel Castro in 2006—he was the lightning rod of antirevolutionary Cuba for U.S. politicians from John F. Kennedy to George W. Bush and for the Cuban émigré community in South Florida.[16] In fact, a different leadership in Havana along with a more Americanized Cuban community in the United States might prove to be the material for constructing a new relationship across the Florida Straits. The Obama-Castro December 2014 breakthrough is an important step. Just how that new relationship could take its first steps is the focus of this book's first chapter by William LeoGrande and Marguerite Rose Jiménez. The Cold War–era buildup of nuclear arms led some international-relations intellectuals to propose reducing tensions by de-escalating the arms race and ancillary crisis issues.[17] In a general sense, they endorsed a confidence-building approach that, first, would diminish the ambiguities about how antagonists acted toward one another and, second, would build assurances about any nonthreatening conduct. LeoGrande and Jiménez suggest that Cuban-American tensions might be de-escalated through the pursuit of solutions to obvious issues of common interest: for instance, confronting disasters such as hurricanes that touch both countries, organizing medical cooperation in places like post-earthquake Haiti, and responding to environmental threats that might arise with nuclear or offshore drilling accidents in either territory. Limits to cooperation will certainly emerge as the resonance of fifty years of mistrust, but the de-escalation of Cuban-American tensions can be addressed constructively. In this context and for the foreseeable future, these confidence-building multilateral initiatives might be the focus of improving relations, an approach that will avoid direct Cuban-American bilateral contacts to preserve Washington's amour-propre about keeping a formal and official distance from the island.

A traditional weapon underpinning Cuban foreign policy—indeed, the weapon sine qua non in international relations—is military power. As Hal Klepak (chapter 2) points out, it was the Ejército Rebelde (Rebel Army) that played the decisive role in winning the revolutionary war against the dictatorship of Fulgencio Batista and, afterwards, in protecting the nascent Castro government from its enemies internal and external.[18] Its successor after the revolution, the Fuerzas Armadas Revolucionarias (FAR), Cuba's Revolutionary Armed Forces, became crucial both as a domestic aid to civil power and as an instrument of foreign policy. For more than a half century now, FAR's training, acquisition of arms, and ideological strength have provided an effective and reliable buttress for the revolutionary government. In terms of international relations, as Klepak demonstrates, FAR has had two complementary strategic functions. First, although the force is unquestionably smaller than its U.S. adversary, its capabilities and cohesion have served as a strong deterrent to a conventional U.S. attack: while it might not prevent a successful invasion, it would inflict unacceptably high U.S. casualties.[19] Second, it has been an effective instrument of state in Cuba's pursuit of an activist foreign policy, helping to train anti-American guerrilla and national liberation movements in Central and South America and Africa, and providing active military assistance to Angola against U.S.-backed political groups and apartheid South Africa during the Cold War.[20] The successful deployment of FAR to ensure the survival of the revolution and its government, society, and economy has been a highpoint of Cuban statecraft. As Klepak argues, in the future, whether or not there is an amelioration of Cuban-American differences, "FAR will clearly still be working to create the best possible opportunities for bridges to be built."

Karen Dubinsky offers an innovative assessment (chapter 3) of one of the first U.S. anti-Cuban actions. Immediately after the revolution, working with anti-Castro elements on the island and the Roman Catholic Church between 1960 and 1962, the Central Intelligence Agency (CIA) engineered the departure of more than 14,000 Cuban children to Miami—unaccompanied by their parents.[21] Convincing these parents, who were not supporters of the revolution, that the new regime intended among other things to send their children to Soviet Russia for indoctrination, the CIA and its confederates looked to embarrass and weaken the new Cuban government. Subsequently, as the Cold War rift between Havana and Washington deepened, many Cuban parents were not able to join their offspring, and about one-half of the children sent to the United States found themselves in foster care or in orphanages throughout the country.

In a deft analysis of this long-simmering issue, Dubinsky maintains that "the alleged separation of children from political citizenship is one of the mainstays of our world." Raising the question of family unity as a residual Cold War issue, she goes on to draw a connection with the more recent and highly publicized Cuban-American dispute over the Elián González affair in 1999–2000. A key to the issue, she finds, rests in language. In Cuba, in what became known as Operation Peter Pan, the use of the word *Peter*, she writes, "implies English-speaking, U.S.-government, CIA manipulation." In Miami the term more likely to be used for the operation is *Pedro*—which "connotes Spanish-speaking, Cuban parents making their own immigration decisions about what, and where, was best for their children." In the end, quite simply, the needs of children were subordinated to meet competing political ideologies. Both Washington and Havana used the fate of children in part to underscore their separate foreign policies one against the other—deploying the children, their mothers and fathers, and the Cuban nation as diplomatic weapons to reinforce their own national self-perceptions (a situation echoed in the case of Elián González).

American hardline policies against Cuba have a legal basis—at least as far as U.S. courts have been concerned. Thus, in addition to what presidents and the Congress have done or might do to ameliorate differences with Cuba, the U.S. legal system has played—and will play—a major role in determining how the law interprets the Cuban-American relationship. Spectacular U.S. legal attacks on Cuba are well known: the 1992 Torricelli Act, which tightened the existing Cold War blockade; and the 1996 Helms-Burton Act, which looked to apply U.S. embargo law extraterritorially to foreign enterprises that traded with Cuba and to penalize foreign companies operating on property formerly owned by Americans and expropriated by the revolutionary regime.[22]

As Stanley Murphy (chapter 4) perceptively shows, any political détente between Havana and Washington might be slowed by an extensive network of legal decisions that will not necessarily be abrogated by improved relations. Tellingly, many of these decisions come from judges who have no firsthand experience with Cuba but, somehow, understand supposedly "widely accepted truths" about Cuban realities—"truths" that are really political opinions. Nonetheless, their decisions touch on, among other issues, the rights of Cuban and American citizens to travel from one country to the other, academic freedom, the banning of school textbooks, and (an echo of Dubinsky's exegesis regarding Elián González) child custody. U.S. legal decisions concerning the revolutionary regime include a "Cuba factor"; and as Murphy explains, the task of removing the existing network of Cuba-centered laws will be a lengthy one. More problematic for improved future Cuban-American relations, he says, "The Cuba factor in U.S. court cases creates the possibility that judges will reshape existing principles of law, redefine settled legal rights and obligations, and inject their own political preconceptions into their decisions."

While the American question has abiding importance for Havana, Cuban foreign policy has endeavored to seek friendly relations with other powers great and small to safeguard the revolution through political and economic means. Such a strategy remained essential during the Cold War, especially when difficulties in the Cuban-Soviet relationship emerged after the Cuban Missile Crisis of 1962.[23] In this context, especially in the post–Cold War era, Communist China has been a focus of Cuban diplomacy in the effort to circumvent the economic pressures of the ongoing U.S. embargo and to find a political ally among the charmed circle of Great Powers. As Carlos Alzugaray (chapter 5) points out, the Cuban government has worked assiduously to ensure that the People's Republic has become one of its principal strategic allies. This process has been two-way: for a variety of interwoven economic, ideological, and political reasons, Cuba has emerged as one of Beijing's major allies in the Western Hemisphere.

The roots of this relationship were planted during the Cold War, despite the Sino-Soviet rift that developed after 1964, which led Cuba to take a critical position vis-à-vis China over Angola and during the 1979 Sino-Vietnamese dispute. But by the 1980s, both the post–Mao Zedong leadership in Beijing and Fidel Castro and his advisers saw the advantages of closer collaboration, something made more poignant for Havana after the collapse of the Soviet Union and the onset of the Special Period.[24] Suffused by ideological similarities—Cuba and China were soon among the very few "socialist" countries in the new international order—both governments could only profit from finding a basis for friendly relations. While the island provides China with safe and secure access to its resources and with a site for investment, Cuba also stands as a bridge for the expansion of Chinese political and economic relations with other Latin American states. Conversely, the Cubans look to Chinese investment in oil, mineral extraction, and more to help their economy; politically, a firm relationship with the People's Republic provides Havana with additional diplomatic weight to balance against American inroads. With its ideological foundation, the Sino-Cuban relationship is one of mutual advantage and mutual respect, a combination that seems likely only to strengthen in the future. Then too, Cuban foreign policy has always been pragmatic. Not all of Cuba's economic and political friends have been ideological soul mates, and Cuba developed warm associations with capitalist powers even before the end of the Cold War. Canada is one of the most prominent among the range of friendly powers in Europe and the Americas that have constructed steady, long-lasting, and mutually beneficial relationships with Cuba. But unlike those friendly European countries like Great Britain that are separated by an ocean from the United States, Canada has a geographical position and lesser power status that have made it especially important in the development of Cuban policy: like Cuba, it is the closest of American neighbors. Along with the benefits of its relationship with the United States, Canada shares with Cuba the burdens of living next to a western superpower that does not always agree with its foreign policy. Thus, despite its military alliances with the United States and the importance of the U.S. economy to Canadian trade, Canada is one of the few countries in the world that immediately recognized the revolutionary regime in 1959. As Asa McKercher (chapter 6) reveals, the reasons were both economic (the same reasons whereby Canada traded with Communist China after its revolution) and strategic: Ottawa's unwillingness to have its foreign policy dictated by Washington. Here lay a fundamental shared interest of Canada and Cuba. As sovereign states, both powers expected and demanded to be treated as such by the United States and every other power.

Canada and Cuba had been trading partners since the nineteenth century. After 1959, despite the growing Cuban estrangement from the United States, the Cuban Missile Crisis and what it portended for NATO, and the U.S. economic embargo, Ottawa and Havana found a common interest in continuing trade: Canada because it saw a viable market, and Cuba because of the necessity of building the revolution. Out of the economic relationship there emerged a political relationship. Although the Canadian government at the time of the revolution was led by the Progressive Conservative Party, Prime Minister John Diefenbaker was a strong nationalist who sometimes quarreled with the Kennedy administration. It followed that Cuba was an issue on which Canada's sovereignty could be marshaled. And in the twenty years of Liberal Party governments that followed, most especially under those led by Pierre Trudeau (1968–84), Canadian-Cuban relations warmed considerably.[25] Although the relationship waxed and waned after the mid-1980s with a rotation of Conservative and Liberal ministries—the human rights issue in Cuba has been problematic at times—Canadian trade with, tourist travel to, and investment on the island have increased. Diplomatic relations have never been broken by either side, and important cultural exchanges have emerged and developed.

Part II. Internationalism

Parallel with the international relations construct of Cuba's global position is its internationalism variant. *Internationalism* gained prominence after the devastation of the First World War, with its proponents arguing that the best way of achieving worldwide peace would be by pursuing cooperation among nations.[26] Accordingly, while Cuba has strong political and economic relations with a number of powers in the developed and developing world, in many instances these relationships have been enhanced and strengthened by conscious intergovernmental efforts to increase cooperation. Following this perspective, Max Azicri (chapter 7) examines the solidification of the Cuba-Venezuela alliance since the late 1990s. The advent of Hugo Chávez as Venezuelan president in February 1999 provided the Cuban leadership with a natural ally who shared not only their strong opposition to the United States and its policies but also a desire to protect national sovereignty by finding its own responses to social, economic, and political problems.[27] Although the two countries are dissimilar in their structure and political systems—for instance, Venezuela is a major petroleum-producing country with concomitant oil wealth—their leaders have created a regional partnership that goes beyond the confines of narrow political and economic foreign policy. For example, well-trained Cuban medical professionals sent to work in Venezuela, which lacks adequate health care, are paid for by exports of Venezuelan oil to Cuba. But as Azicri demonstrates, Cuban-Venezuelan internationalism has a strong impact on more than the citizenry of the two countries. It served, importantly, as a catalyst for expanding internationalism in the Caribbean and Central and South America by the creation of the sixteen-member Petrocaribe group, whose members can purchase Venezuelan petroleum by bartering commodities. More significant, Fidel Castro and Chávez provided the impetus for the creation of the Alianza Bolivariana para los Pueblos de Nuestra América (ALBA) in 2004.[28] In contradistinction to the neoliberalism of U.S.-led globalization, ALBA exists as a venture in regional economic integration centered on notions of social welfare, bartering, and reciprocal economic assistance rather than on trade liberalization in the manner of the North America Free Trade Agreement.

Internationalism's strength devolves from its avowed intention to build cooperation beyond the political and economic interactions of government and other leaders. Thus, as Kevin Delgado illuminates (chapter 8), Cuban internationalism is not just a phenomenon experienced by the political and economic elites. Using his own activities as a backdrop—in Cuba, in 2000, he studied sacred Afro-Cuban drumming with a leading musician—he uncovers "the unofficial networks of interpersonal internationalism." Important for him is Santeria, a belief system that combines West African religion—brought by slaves imported to Cuba to work on plantations—with Roman Catholic and aboriginal traditions.[29] Some Cubans, because of their professions (for instance, in the tourist industry) have access to both the convertible peso (CUC) used by foreigners visiting Cuba and to foreign currencies; acquiring these monies helps these Cubans mitigate the material scarcities they sometimes face. But because a large number of foreign visitors are interested in Santeria rituals, *santeros*, the practitioners of the religion, receive CUCs and other currencies in return for allowing foreigners to observe or partake in their ceremonies or, like Delgado, learn from santero masters. The Cuban government is supportive of this exchange. Accordingly, "Santeria commerce" has developed, whereby increasing numbers of foreigners and the santeros have constructed "unofficial networks of interpersonal internationalism." While not always devoid of problems—fraudulent Santeria rituals arise at times to separate foreigners from their money—these networks have become integral to increased cooperation among Cuban santeros, the Cuban government, and a range of foreign tourists interested in Cuba.

As tourism became essential for the survival of revolutionary Cuba after the beginning of the Special Period because it provided billions of dollars and euros for the government's foreign currency reserves, it also added to Cuba's internationalist construct. Cuba is more than a Caribbean island with a revolutionary government. Cuban planners have long understood this condition and, therefore, have marketed the island successfully in capitalist and other countries—including, recently, Communist China—that do not see cooperation with Cuba as problematical. Joint ventures with tourist firms from the capitalist world have led to the construction of resorts and hotels around the island and to a sharing of profits. Through promoting Cuba as a vacation spot with historic sites, a unique and vibrant culture (especially music), and sunny, warm beaches—promotion which began even before 1990–1991—Cuban government policy has brought millions of tourists and significant investment over the past two decades.[30] Ricardo Pérez's examination (chapter 9) of this sector centers on sustainable tourism development and environmental policy in Cuba. Little doubt exists that Havana's tourist strategies have been successful in sustaining the Cuban economy by building its market through cooperative efforts with other governments—including such developments as "Santeria commerce." Given that large numbers of Cubans are unable to be tourists in Europe and other places, this flow is one-way. Moreover, with official encouragement, the resultant people-to-people contact that sees tourists observe, meet, and talk to Cubans allows a better understanding of the revolutionary regime—and many tourists return year after year. A problem for the future will be to ensure that Cuba's crucial tourist business can safeguard its significant share of the Caribbean market as other sunny and warm islands in the region develop their own industries. Pérez's assessment is that a continued internationalist approach by the government and its foreign partners holds the answer. Given the success of these policies to date, the country's pursuit of sustainable tourist development practices, and its ability to keep existing tourists and find new ones from targeted countries, this element of internationalism will mutually benefit Cubans, foreign investors, and the travelers who visit the island.

As the Cuban tourist industry underscores, the construct of internationalism finds a basis in intergovernmental cooperation. A major social achievement of the revolution—besides the literacy campaign—has been the improved health of all Cubans. This accomplishment arose from the determined effort of the government early on to educate the population and train a skilled medical workforce, initiatives tied to seeking advances in medical and pharmacological research. The country's success on this front, compared to the years before 1959, is marked by increased longevity for men and women, lower infant-mortality rates, better control of contagious diseases, and more.[31] As Robert Huish demonstrates (chapter 10), the Cuban government has used its accrued health-care knowledge and resources to pursue a model of "medical internationalism," with two key elements.[32] First, the Cuban government sends some of its medical assets—especially skilled doctors, other medical professionals, and pharmaceuticals—for a fee to assist governments that, lacking adequate medical resources, require assistance to meet the needs of their populations. In this context, Cuban doctors have helped in Angola, Nicaragua, the post-Chernobyl Soviet Union, and scores of other countries since 1963. Furthermore, in times of international crisis—for example, in postwar East Timor after 1999 or after the 2010 earthquake in Haiti—the Cuban government willingly dispatches medical teams at no cost. The second element concerns the Cuban government's 1998 program to train doctors from other countries—usually from developing countries that lack adequate education facilities—at the Escuela Latinoamericana de Medicina just west of Havana. More than 15,000 students have come to Havana from abroad under this internationalist initiative, then returned to practice in their home countries. Medical internationalism is consequently a major success of revolutionary Cuba.

The demise of the socialist trading bloc and the advent of the Special Period ushered in a time of food shortages in Cuba as the island's post-1959 trade system disappeared. Despite the increased cost of food imports, by the turn of the twenty-first century Cuban food supplies had recovered to a significant degree through crop diversification and the building of new trading links; then three devastating hurricanes struck the island within a month in late 2008, renewing food shortages.[33] Efe Can Gürcan (chapter 11) situates Cuban efforts to attain food sovereignty within an internationalist response admittedly touched by transnationalism.[34] The endeavor entails four interconnected mainstays: cooperatively collectivizing land; socializing participatory urban agriculture; establishing agricultural free markets to ensure local access to food; and promoting the transnationalization of domestic agro-ecological movements. Beginning in 1993, the Cuban government promoted a transition from conventional and industrial farming to organic and semi-organic farming, both in the countryside and in urban gardening. With new farming methods and various domestic social groups like horticultural clubs involved in food production, the Cuban government encouraged cooperative ventures abroad, within ALBA and through domestic bodies such as the National Association of Small Farmers (Asociación Nacional de Agricultores Pequeños), which linked Cuban farmers with those in the Caribbean, Central America, and Mexico. Such internationalist action was in part a response to the global food crisis that Cuba and its developing world partners experienced firsthand and consider to be a result of neoliberal globalization since the end of the Cold War. But it also suggests the success of the internationalist construct in terms of Cuba and its global influence, even if Obama-Castro normalization takes time.

Tourism, medical diplomacy, and food sovereignty are all tangible expressions of Cuban internationalism. A more opaque and less palpable, but still important, element of that construct lies in the intellectual sphere, especially among writers and others who see revolutionary Cuba in iconic terms. Using the Cuban-Spanish dialogue as a case study, Ana Serra (chapter 12) scrutinizes the impact of post–Cold War Cuba on progressive Spanish writers, considering how Cuba symbolizes either their political desires or their frustrations with unsatisfied potential. The basis for this dialogue was established within the Cuban government's Special Period policies, beginning in 1993, which encouraged tourism, sought foreign investment, and allowed Spanish fiction to be disseminated in Cuba. Consequently, Spain became a major investor in Cuba and a place from which large numbers of tourists descended on the island. In essence, Spanish intellectuals rediscovered Cuba; and Serra deconstructs the work of two of them—Belén Gopegui and Rafael Argullol—who visited during the Special Period and wrote books that projected their own predetermined ideas onto the revolutionary state. It is not so much that Cuba, its revolution, and the successes and failures thereof are sidebars in these treatments. They are not. But for these writers, their own ideals constitute the fulcrum of their thoughts about the revolution. In addition, both writers derived different perceptions of the Cuban reality based on their backgrounds in Spain: unlike Belén Gopegui, Argullol grew up experiencing the authoritarian regime of Francisco Franco. Cuba opened up to them but, in Serra's view, Gopegui and Argullol are both like tourists who show scant respect for the judgment or understanding of Cubans living on the island. With Havana, especially, serving as "a metonymic space" for the entire country in this Spanish intellectual current, Cuba remains "a colonized space . . . on which others continue to project their own visions of the present and future of the island nation." Clearly, in some instances, internationalism has its limits.

Part III. Transnationalism

Cuba's transnational construct flows from the internationalism of its global position. As a social movement, transnationalism has emerged not only because of the increased interconnection amongst peoples rather than governments, but also because of the declining significance of borders caused by the advent of economic globalization and the weakening of social boundaries between states. Cuban transnationalism does not necessarily rest on its unique territorial expression—the island itself—and its language infused by notions of race, ethnicity, and national and cultural identification.[35] What emerges in the next six chapters is a reiteration of Cuba that counters outdated geographic notions of spatiality. It allows for the rebuilding, interpretation, and conversion of the complexities of the Cuban diapora(s) and it reinforces the transnational construct of Cuba's global position.

With this caveat at the fore, the ne plus ultra transnational commodity of Cuban visual culture is the "Havana cigar." Emanating from the geographic, racial, ethnic, and cultural confines of the island, it has become an image of Cuba around the world. Since the mid-nineteenth century the Havana has been the deluxe cigar in the world; as a consequence, competitors have arisen periodically to imitate or surpass its quality and thereby supplant it as *the* luxury cigar.[36] And what was the case before 1959 became doubly so later, given the U.S.

embargo and the exodus of a significant number of Cuban cigar manufacturers who endeavored to build a new Havana cigar industry outside of the island. As had occurred before 1959, tobacco seed, agricultural and industrial knowledge, and human capital were relocated for its duplication, a process highlighted by various Cuban diasporas tied to the political and revolutionary crises on the island. The result has been competing brands of cigars—for instance, the Cohiba—manufactured both on the island and elsewhere.

Jean Stubbs (chapter 13) assesses the transnationalism of the Havana cigar by examining "parallel chains, networks, and circuits" of production. Three Caribbean island polities—Jamaica, Puerto Rico, and the Dominican Republic—have been integral to these developments; and their efforts have generated a multifaceted, multilayered system that, legal or not, looked to profit on the reputation of the genuine Havana cigar. Significantly, the industries of the three competitors have grown and declined in step not only with Cuba but also through "their own transnational commodity and migration histories." While the Cuban Havana survives as a luxury commodity, the other challengers have fallen off, despite limited success in the Dominican Republic—at a telling social cost in that country. Ultimately, perhaps, the real transnational test between the authentic Havana and its rivals will come when the U.S. blockade ends.

An equally significant transnational visual expression of Cuba after 1959 emerged through the medium of film.[37] Indeed, in the first months of the new government, the Instituto Cubano del Arte y la Industria Cinematográficas (ICAIC) was created; and Cubans began producing documentary films relating to the new Cuba. Just as important, because of the success of the revolution and the impact of Fidel Castro's ideas and policies, pro-Castro documentary filmmakers from outside arrived on the island to record Cuban achievements. These filmmakers and others worked with Cubans—some, like the Danish filmmaker Theodoro Christensen, asking important questions about the nature of Cuban society and its problems. To a large degree, as María Caridad Cumaná (chapter 14) demonstrates in her treatment of the transnationalism of cinema, their work largely molded the understanding of Cuba and its revolution outside the island in the 1960s and after. But, importantly, despite ICAIC and other agencies, the Cuban government could not control the images put before foreign audiences. Stereotypes of Cubans issued forth, the complexities of everyday life were glossed over, and the difficulty of the work of building a new society was minimized. With a tendency to idealize the revolution, foreign films did not offer in toto an accurate image of the Cuban reality.

With the end of the Cold War, more accurate depictions of that reality began to emerge in both documentary and popular cinema, including in comedies.

This change occurred because limited financial resources increasingly forced Cubans to co-produce films with foreigners.[38] The result was work that, while assuming the positive changes brought by the revolution, also looked more closely at issues such as prostitution, marginalization, housing shortages, and family overcrowding, plus the dearth of resources for necessities such as home repair. Consequently, as a visual medium, film has played an important transnational role in interpreting the island's culture, moving from the idealism of the early years to examinations of the difficult material and spiritual problems confronting Cubans today. Significant economic, cultural, and social differences exist between these two periods, and the transformation of Cuban cinema traces the transnational expression of visual Cuba.

As the chapters by Stubbs and Cumaná reinforce, transnationalism is tied closely to immigration, emigration, people-to-people interaction, and weakened social boundaries between states. The Cuban diaspora after 1959, which settled largely in Miami, was ideologically and politically opposed to the new revolutionary government. As a consequence, two competing representations and narratives of Cuba emerged: that of the Miami Cubans and that of the Cuban government.[39] It is a disputatious and difficult antagonism—with ideological and political overtones—that has heretofore dominated the images, history, and nature of the transnational experience of the Cuban diaspora.

Mette Berg (chapter 15) is one of a group of scholars who see the Miami–Cuban government discourse as sterile and inadequate. The recent Cuban diaspora, especially after the onset of the Special Period, is unlike that after 1959. There is dissent within it, tied to differing experiences and paths; and that is generating dialogue over gender, class, race, and generations. Using the Cuban émigré experience in Spain as a litmus test, Berg demonstrates that this milieu has profoundly different voices and understandings as compared to the experience encased in the Miami–Cuban government dichotomy; and Spain becomes the historic homeland, the "mi tierra," of some expatriate Cubans to whom it is granting rights of citizenship. Her analysis reveals the complexity of a Cuban diasporic experience in Spain that, again, is far more multifaceted than might be gleaned from the Miami–Cuban government discourse.

In this process, Cubans in Spain are still Cuban—as they are in other parts of Europe, in Canada, in other places, and even in Miami—and they are not necessarily ideological adversaries of their revolutionary homeland. Both Cuba and its diaspora, Berg posits, would benefit from "a future de-territorialized Cuban nation-state, with the Cuban government reaching out to its diasporic citizens." But doing so will necessitate a reconsideration of memory, history, and what it means to be Cuban. It will involve altered politics of memory tied to compromise and tolerance instead of blame and exclusion. Before the Special Period, for instance, the Cuban government castigated émigrés as being without patriotism and lacking revolutionary fiber.

Along with gender, class, and generation, race is fundamentally important for Cuban self-identity. Indeed, race has been integral to the island's economic, political, and social development since the early colonial period, beginning in the sixteenth century when Africans were first brought to the island as slave labor.[40] Even after Cuba's independence from Spain in 1898, the legacy of slavery—segregation, discriminatory policies, and disapproving attitudes—continued for Afro-Cubans, creating problems of access to adequate housing, education, political power, employment, and social advancement.[41] Despite the constitutional equality of all Cubans after the 1959 revolution, Fidel Castro admitted in 2009: "Blacks don't live in the best houses; you find that they still have the hardest, most physically wearing and often worst-paid jobs and that they receive much less help from their family members no longer in Cuba, in dollars, than their white compatriots."[42]

Supposedly long-buried because the revolution eliminated racism on the island by the stroke of the constitutional pen fifty years ago, issues of racism are beginning to be debated more openly in contemporary Cuba. Yvette Louis (chapter 16) considers the racial question in terms of oral history and the construction of Cuban racial memory. In the transnational construct involving both self-identification and the ways in which others recognize Cubans on the island and within émigré communities, Afro-Cubans by their very numbers—almost 50 percent of the population when both blacks and mulattos are included[43]—are of decided importance. Using a critical discourse analysis, Louis examines the link between the intricacies of daily language and its ideas and power relations. Even fifty years after the revolution, both on and outside the island, the dialogue devolving from slavery echoes Fidel Castro's admission that blackness is still seen as "inferior" and whiteness as "superior." In this regard, much work is still to be done to achieve actual equality.

Turning to another transnational construct, we find that the barriers that long existed between Cubans on the island and people in émigré communities are breaking down.[44] The best example can be seen in the remittances that émigré Cubans in the United States are sending back to the island. Before the collapse of the Soviet trading bloc and the onset of the Special Period, the second-largest Latin American émigré group in the United States was Cuban. But out of the $5.7 billion in remittances sent by Latin American émigrés by 1990, only $50 million came from Cubans; moreover, few of these Cubans traveled back to the island to visit their families—a situation that resulted from both the Cuban and U.S. governments limiting contact for ideological and political reasons.[45]

Yet, by 2003, along with increased travel, Cuban remittances had climbed to something approaching $1 billion. This figure dropped during the George W. Bush presidency but came back after 2009, for two reasons. First, Havana saw increased contact between Cubans on the island and émigrés as a way to mitigate the economic crisis. Second, despite Washington's fluctuating hardline policies, both the children of the old immigrants and the newer Cuban émigrés became or remained involved in the society and economy of their *patria,* even as they have integrated into their new country. The antipathy toward the revolutionary government is largely concentrated among the original émigrés, who had influence in Washington. Raised in the United States, less attuned to Cold War nostrums about the revolution, and aware that family members live willingly on the island, their children look through less ideological lenses at Cuba as their homeland. And newer immigrant ties are less constrained by official U.S. policies in a different international milieu.

Susan Eckstein (chapter 17) examines this transition, arguing that the end of the Cold War proved to be the catalyst that allowed Cuban émigré communities to become more transnationally tied to the island. But this transnationalism is only partially explained by people-to-people contact. In the post–Cold War era, the desires of Cuban immigrants and their capacity to undertake travel to the island and share their wealth also involve changed cultural and other conditions. With altering attitudes in Havana and Washington, this element of transnationalism only enhances Cuba's global position.

To a large degree, Cuban transnationalism as expressed in the Havana cigar, the inadequacies of the Miami–Cuban government discourse, the issue of race, and other factors is a manifestation of the construct in situ. But another element of Cuban transnationalism can be conceived as "what might be." Ernesto Che Guevara holds an especial place in the history of the Cuban revolution because of his military leadership in overthrowing the Batista regime, his political work in the first years of the new government, and his early death—some might say martyrdom—in 1967 in the unsuccessful attempt to bring revolution to Bolivia.[46] Although an Argentinian, Guevara was undeniably committed to the Cuban revolution, albeit as one part of his self-professed ambition to promote the solidarity of the poor and working classes throughout the world. He has certainly become the icon of the revolution over the past half century—something seen in his ever-present image adorning T-shirts, wall posters, and other artifacts throughout the developing and developed world. Che Guevara never used the term *transnationalism* to describe his labors to construct poor and working-class solidarity in the developing world; as a Marxist, he employed the term *internationalism.* But John Holst (chapter 18) suggests that Guevara's ideas and life's work can be thought of as transnational: "internationalism and

Bolivarianism, anti-imperialism, intrinsic motivation of love and empathy, discipline, honesty, self-criticality, flexibility in thinking, audacity, a willingness to sacrifice, a rejection of privilege, and an orientation toward service."

For Holst, perhaps the best application of this transnationalism can come through using it as the basis for educational reforms in both the developing and developed world. Times might have changed since the 1960s, but the injustices that Guevara and others perceived remain. In many respects, an undemocratic, non-participatory, and non-cooperative international society still exists. In Holst's words, "transnational social justice seems less like a politically charged phrase and more like a burning necessity." But as part of the transnational construct, pursuing Che Guevara's intellectual legacy is germane to both educational institutions and non-formal education in social movements outside Cuba.

Understanding Cuba's Global Presence

Cuban foreign policy, Cuba's efforts to establish greater cooperation with friendly powers, and the people-to-people contacts that have occurred despite the policies of its adversaries, and even its own government, have combined, then, in a process that has seen the country occupy a position greater than its small size and geographical position would otherwise have merited. The revolution is admittedly incomplete; still, despite the recent reforms to its economy and travel for Cubans, and the political transition to post–Fidel Castro governance, its importance will not diminish for the foreseeable future. New domestic considerations and the advent of an evolving new international order simply provide a different setting for how and why the Cuban government, its people, émigré Cubans, and other states and people interact.

Accordingly, the three constructs have altered, and they will continue to alter. But what will not change is the role of Cubans arguing about and working to underline their very being as a sovereign people governing themselves in their own best interests. Their determination to continue building a different economic, political, and social system—whatever that might be, and whatever emerges through their own successes and failures along the way—is a constant. To that end Cuba will continue to occupy an enhanced global position.

Notes

1. See Mervyn J. Bain, *Soviet-Cuban Relations, 1985 to 1991: Changing Perceptions in Moscow and Havana* (Lanham, MD: Lexington Books, 2007); Lester D. Langley, *United States, Cuba, and the Cold War: American Failure or Communist Conspiracy?* (Lexington, MA: D. C. Heath,

1970); Joseph S. Tulchin and Rafael Hernandez, eds., *Cuba and the United States: Will the Cold War in the Caribbean End?* (Boulder, CO: Lynne Rienner, 1991). For the zenith of Cuba's geopolitical situation and its subsequent strategic problems, see James G. Blight, Bruce J. Allyn, and David A. Welch, *Cuba on the Brink: Castro, the Missile Crisis, and the Soviet Collapse* (New York: Pantheon Books, 1993); and James G. Blight and Philip Brenner, *Sad and Luminous Days: Cuba's Secret Struggle with the Russians after the Missile Crisis* (Lanham, MD: Rowman and Littlefield, 2002).

2. See, for example, Piero Gleijeses, *The Cuban Drumbeat. Castro's Worldview: Cuban Foreign Policy in a Hostile World* (London and New York: Seagull Books, 2009); H. Michael Erisman and John M. Kirk, eds., *Redefining Cuban Foreign Policy: The Impact of the "Special Period"* (Gainesville: University Press of Florida, 2006); Morris Morley and Chris McGillion, eds., *Cuba, the United States, and the Post–Cold War World: The International Dimensions of the Washington-Havana Relationship* (Gainesville: University Press of Florida, 2005).

3. See, for instance, Marilú Uralde Cancio and Luis Rosado Eiró, *Ejército soy yo: las fuerzas armadas de Cuba, 1952–1956* (Havana: Editorial de Ciencias Sociales, 2006); Irwin F. Gellman, *Roosevelt and Batista: Good Neighbor Diplomacy in Cuba, 1933–1945* (Albuquerque: University of New Mexico Press, 1973); Louis A. Pérez Jr., *Cuba under the Platt Amendment, 1902–1934* (Pittsburgh, PA: University of Pittsburgh Press, 1986).

4. "Cuba's Economy: Money Starts to Talk," *The Economist*, July 20, 2013; Collin Laverty, *Cuba's New Resolve: Economic Reform and Its Implications for U.S. Policy* (Washington, DC: Center for Democracy in the Americas, 2011); John Jeremiah Sullivan, "Where Is Cuba Going?" *New York Times Magazine*, September 23, 2012. See also José Azel, "So Much for Cuban Economic Reform," *Wall Street Journal*, January 10, 2011.

5. See Gleijeses, *Cuban Drumbeat*; John M. Kirk and H. Michael Erisman, *Cuban Medical Internationalism: Origins, Evolution, and Goals* (New York: Palgrave Macmillan, 2009); Carmelo Mesa-Lago, ed., *Cuba after the Cold War* (Pittsburgh, PA: University of Pittsburgh Press, 1993); Morris Morley and Chris McGillion, *Unfinished Business: America and Cuba after the Cold War, 1989–2001* (Cambridge and New York: Cambridge University Press, 2002); Ricardo Alarcón and Reinaldo Suárez, *Cuba y su democracia* (Havana: Editorial de Ciencias Sociales, 2004); Fidel Castro, "The Empire and the Independent Island," *Diplomacy and Statecraft* 20 (2009), 212–28.

6. Mark Abendroth, *Rebel Literacy: Cuba's National Literacy Campaign and Critical Global Citizenship* (Duluth, MN: Litwin Books, 2009); Julie M. Feinsilver, "Fifty Years of Cuba's Medical Diplomacy: From Idealism to Pragmatism," *Cuban Studies* 41 (2010), 85–104; Wolf Grabendorff, "Cuba's Involvement in Africa: An Interpretation of Objectives, Reactions, and Limitations," *Journal of Interamerican Studies and World Affairs* 22 (1980), 3–29; John Minto, "We Can Learn a Lot from Cuba," *Business Day*, June 28, 2010, www.stuff.co.nz/business/blogs/frontline/3861600/We-can-learn-a-lot-from-Cuba. For U.S. resistance, see, for instance, Philip Brenner and Soraya Castro, "David and Gulliver: Fifty Years of Competing Metaphors in the Cuban–United States Relationship," *Diplomacy and Statecraft* 20 (2009), 236–57; Lars Schoultz, "Benevolent Domination: The Ideology of U.S. Policy toward Cuba," *Cuban Studies* 41 (2010), 1–19.

7. For the British example, see Chris Hull, "Going to War in Buses": The Anglo-American Clash over Leyland Sales to Cuba, 1963–1964," *Diplomatic History* 34 (2010), 793–822; John

McDonnell, "Why Cuba Is a Beacon," *New Statesman*, February 19, 2008; Stephen Wilkinson, "Just How Special Is Special? U.S.-UK-Cuba Relations since 1959," *Diplomacy and Statecraft* 20 (2009), 291–308.

8. See Jessica Byron, "Square Dance Diplomacy: Cuba and CARIFORUM, the European Union and the United States," *European Review of Latin American and Caribbean Studies* 68 (April 2000), 23–45; Daniel P. Erikson, *Europe's Cuba Problem: The Limits of Constructive Engagement* (Stockholm: International IDEA, 2009); José Ignacio Salafranca Sánchez-Neyra, "EU-Cuba Relations," *Cuba-Europe Dialogues* 4, no. 11 (n.d.), 22–23.

9. See R. J. Ferguson, "The Transnational Politics of Cuban Music and Cuban Culture," *Bulletin of the Centre for East-West Cultural and Economic Studies* 6 (2003), 1–19; Deborah Pacini Hernández, "Dancing with the Enemy: Cuban Popular Music, Race, Authenticity, and the World-Music Landscape," *Latin American Perspectives* 25 (May 1998), 110–25; Fernando Sáez, "Culture and Revolution Transaction Strategies: A Project of the Ludwig Foundation of Cuba," *Diplomacy and Statecraft* 20 (2009), 309–21; Jean Stubbs, *The Havana Cigar: Transatlantic Migration and Commodity Production, 1850–2000* (Chapel Hill: University of North Carolina Press, forthcoming). Compare Susan Eckstein, *Immigrant Divide: How Cuban Americans Changed the U.S. and Their Homeland* (New York: Routledge, 2009).

10. See Jay Amberg Bloomberg, "Cuba's Cigar Culture Will Have to Make Room for Wine Lovers," *Cubanet*, September 2000, www.cubanet.org/CNews/y00/sep00/20e11.htm; Jacqueline Loss, "Wandering in Russian," in Ariana Hernández-Reguant, ed., *Cuba in the Special Period: Culture and Ideology in the 1990s* (New York: Palgrave Macmillan, 2009), 105–23; Louis A. Pérez Jr., *On Becoming Cuban: Identity, Nationality, and Culture* (Chapel Hill: University of North Carolina Press, 1999).

11. Holly Ackerman, "Different Diasporas: Cubans in Venezuela, 1959–1998," in Andrea O'Reilly Herrera, ed., *Cuba: Idea of a Nation Displaced* (Albany: State University of New York Press, 2007), 90–106; Mette Louise Berg, "Between Cosmopolitanism and the National Slot: Cuba's Diasporic Children of the Revolution," *Identities* 16, no. 2 (2009), 129–56; Damián Fernández, *Cuba Transnational* (Gainesville: University Press of Florida, 2005).

12. "Cuba to Lift Broad Travel Restrictions, Eliminating Need for Exit Visa," *Ottawa Citizen*, October 16, 2012; "Cuba Lifting Hated Travel Restrictions," Reuters, October 17, 2012, http://www.reuters.com/article/2012/10/17/uk-cuba-reform-immigration-idU.S.LNE89F01T20121017.

13. See Laura J. Enríquez, *Question of Food Security in Cuban Socialism* (Berkeley: International and Area Studies, University of California at Berkeley, 1994); M. Franco, P. Orduñez, B. Caballero, J. A. Tapia Granados, M. Lazo, J. L. Bernal, E. Guallar, and R. S. Cooper, "Impact of Energy Intake, Physical Activity, and Population-Wide Weight Loss on Cardiovascular Disease and Diabetes Mortality in Cuba, 1980–2005," *American Journal of Epidemiology* 166 (2007), 1374–80; Hernández-Reguant, *Cuba in the Special Period*; Julia Wright, *Sustainable Agriculture and Food Security in an Era of Oil Scarcity: Lessons from Cuba* (London and Sterling, VA: Earthscan, 2009). See also chapter 2 in this volume.

14. Amnesty International, "Cuba: Massive Crackdown on Dissent," *Amnesty International*, April 3, 2003; compare Rafael Hernández, "A Dissenting View: Dissidents and Politics in Cuba," *Counterpunch*, March 30, 2010, www.counterpunch.org/hernandez03302010.html; Joaquín Roy, "The European Union and Cuba in the Aftermath of Castro's 'Fall,'" *Jean Monnet/Robert Schuman Paper Series* 4, no. 14 (October 2004), 1–14.

15. Schoultz, "Benevolent Domination."

16. On Cuban American antipathy to Fidel Castro, see also Ann Louise Bardach, *Without Fidel: A Death Foretold in Miami, Havana, and Washington* (New York: Scribner, 2009); Robert D. Crassweller, *Cuba and the U.S.; The Tangled Relationship* (New York: Foreign Policy Association, 1971); Jessica F. Gibbs, *U.S. Policy towards Cuba: Since the Cold War* (Oxford and New York: Routledge, 2011).

17. Louis Kriesberg, "Timing and the Initiation of De-Escalation Moves," *Negotiation Journal* 3 (1987), 375–84; David Last, *Theory, Doctrine, and Practice of Conflict De-Escalation in Peacekeeping Operations* (Clementsport, N.S.: Canadian Peacekeeping Press, 1997); Jerome B. Weisner, "Unilateral Confidence Building," *Bulletin of the Atomic Scientists* 40 (January 1984), 45–47.

18. Mayra Aladro Cardoso et al., *La guerra de liberación nacional en Cuba, 1956–1959* (Havana: Casa Editora Abril, 2007); Adrian English, *Armed Forces of Latin America* (London: Janes, 1984), 195–220. See also Ernesto Che Guevara, *Episodes of the Revolutionary War* (New York: International Publishers, 1968).

19. See "Cuba Launches 'Bastion-2009' Preparing for 'Future U.S. Attack,'" *MercoPress*, November 26, 2009; Enrique A. Baloyra, "Twelve Monkeys: Cuban National Defense and the Military," *Cuban Studies Association Occasional Papers*, Paper 1, 1996, http://scholarlyrepository.miami.edu/csa/1.

20. See, for example, Edward George, *The Cuban Intervention in Angola: From Che Guevara to Cuito Cuanavale* (London: Routledge, 2005); Piero Gleijeses, Jorge Risquet, and Fernando Remírez, *Cuba y África: historia común de lucha y sangre* (Havana: Editorial de Ciencias Sociales, 2007); Piero Gleijeses, *Conflicting Missions: Havana, Washington, and Africa, 1959–1976* (Chapel Hill: University of North Carolina Press, 2002).

21. See Josefina Leyva, *Operación Pedro Pan: el éxodo de los niños cubanos* (Coral Gables, FL: Editorial Ponce de Leon, 1993); Maria de los Angeles Torres, *The Lost Apple: Operation Pedro Pan, Cuban Children in the U.S. and the Promise of a Better Future* (Boston, MA: Beacon Press, 2003).

22. On Helms-Burton, see Jeffrey Dunning, "The Helms-Burton Act: A Step in the Wrong Direction for United States Policy toward Cuba," *Journal of Urban and Contemporary Law* 54 (1998), 213–37; Shoshana Perl, "Whither Helms-Burton? A Retrospective on the 10th Anniversary," *Jean Monnet/Robert Schuman Paper Series* 6, no. 5 (February 2006), 1–14.

23. See, for instance, Jorge I. Domínguez, *To Make a World Safe for Revolution: Cuba's Foreign Policy* (Cambridge, MA: Harvard University Press, 1989); William M. LeoGrande, *Cuba's Policy in Africa, 1959–1980* (Berkeley: Institute of International Studies, University of California, 1980); Martin Weinstein, *Revolutionary Cuba in the World Arena* (Philadelphia, PA: Institute for the Study of Human Issues, 1979). Compare Hal Brands, *Latin America's Cold War* (Cambridge, MA: Harvard University Press, 2010).

24. See Jorge I. Domínguez, Omar Everleny Pérez Villanueva, and Lorena Barberia, eds., *Cuban Economy at the Start of the Twenty-First Century* (Cambridge, MA: David Rockefeller Center for Latin American Studies, Harvard University, 2004); Erisman and Kirk, *Redefining Cuban Foreign Policy*; Mesa-Lago, *Cuba after the Cold War*.

25. Compare John M. Kirk and Peter McKenna, *Canada-Cuba Relations: The Other Good Neighbor Policy* (Gainesville: University Press of Florida, 1997); Kristopher Moore, "Cuba in

the Wake of NAFTA," *Revista Mexicana de Estudios Canadienses* (new series) 8 (November 2004), 145–61; Robert A. Wright and Lana Wylie, eds., *Our Place in the Sun: Canada and Cuba in the Castro Era* (Toronto: University of Toronto Press, 2009); Robert A. Wright, *Three Nights in Havana: Pierre Trudeau, Fidel Castro and the Cold War World* (Toronto: HarperCollins, 2007).

26. See John Boli and George M. Thomas, eds., *Constructing World Culture: International Nongovernmental Organizations since 1875* (Stanford, CA: Stanford University Press, 1999); Matthew C. Price, *Wilsonian Persuasion in American Foreign Policy* (Youngstown, NY: Cambria Press, 2007). Also compare Kjell Goldmann, Ulf Hannerz, and Charles Westin, eds., *Nationalism and Internationalism in the Post–Cold War Era* (London and New York: Routledge, 2000); Cornelia Navari, *Internationalism and the State in the Twentieth Century* (London and New York: Routledge, 2000); Richard Shapcott, *Justice, Community, and Dialogue: Philosophical Hermeneutics and the Cosmopolitan Project* (New York: Cambridge University Press, 2001).

27. Aleida Guevara, *Chávez, Venezuela and the New Latin America: An Interview with Hugo Chávez* (Melbourne and New York: Ocean Press, 2005); Javier Corrales and Michael Penfold, *Dragon in the Tropics: Hugo Chávez and the Political Economy of Revolution in Venezuela* (Washington, DC: Brookings Institution Press, 2011); Eva Golinger (foreword by Saul Landau), *Chávez Code: Cracking U.S. Intervention in Venezuela* (Northampton, MA: Olive Branch Press, 2006).

28. See Government of Venezuela, "Sobre el ALBA: Selección de artículos," 2006, alternativabolivariana.org/modules.php?name=Content&pa=showpage&pid=1. Compare Larry C. Backer and Augusto Molina, "Cuba and the Construction of Alternative Global Trade Systems: ALBA and Free Trade in the Americas," *University of Pennsylvania Journal of International Law* 31 (2010), 679–752; Emir Sader, "ALBA: From Dream to Reality," *Global Policy Forum*, May 17, 2007.

29. Christine Ayorinde, *Afro-Cuban Religiosity, Revolution, and National Identity* (Gainesville: University Press of Florida, 2004); Paulino Hernández and Marta Avedo, *Santería afrocubana: sincretismo con la religión católica: ceremonias y oráculos* (Madrid: Eride Editorial, 1998).

30. Paula DiPerna, *Complete Travel Guide to Cuba* (New York: St. Martin's Press, 1979); Jorge I. Domínguez, "Cuba's Economic Transition: Successes, Deficiencies, and Challenges," in Domínguez, Pérez Villanueva, and Barberia, *Cuban Economy*, 17–47; Mark M. Miller and Tony L. Henthorne, *Investment in the New Cuban Tourist Industry: A Guide to Entrepreneurial Opportunities* (Westport, CT: Quorum Books, 1997); Rochelle Spencer, *Development Tourism: Lessons from Cuba* (Farnham and Burlington, VT: Ashgate, 2010).

31. See Julie Feinsilver, *Healing the Masses: Cuban Health Politics at Home and Abroad* (Berkeley: University of California Press, 1993); Candace Johnson, "Health as Culture and Nationalism in Cuba," *Canadian Journal of Latin American and Caribbean Studies* 31 (2006), 91–113; Howard Waitzkin, "Health Policy and Social Change: A Comparative History of Chile and Cuba," *Social Problems* 31 (1983), 235–48. See also Elizabeth Kath, *Social Relations and the Cuban Health Miracle* (New Brunswick, NJ: Transaction, 2010).

32. More generally, see P. De Vos, W. De Ceukelaire, and M. Bonet, "Cuba's International Cooperation in Health: An Overview," *International Journal of Health Services* 37 (2007), 761–76; Kirk and Erisman, *Medical Internationalism*; Feinsilver, "Cuba's Medical Diplomacy."

33. Mélanie Josée Davidson and Catherine Krull, "Adapting to Cuba's Shifting Food Landscapes: Women's Strategies of Resistance," *Cuban Studies* 42 (2011), 59–77; Carlos Jesús Delgado Díaz, *Cuba Verde: en busca de un modelo para la sustentabilidad en el siglo XXI* (Havana: José Martí Publishing House, 1999); W. A. Messina Jr., "The 2008 Hurricane Season and Its Impact on Cuban Agriculture and Trade," in *Cuba in Transition*, Papers and Proceedings of the Association for the Study of the Cuban Economy (ASCE), 2009 (Austin, TX: Latin American Network Information Center, 2009), 421–28; M. Wilson, "'¡No tenemos viandas!' Cultural Ideas of Scarcity and Need," *International Journal of Cuban Studies* 2, no. 1 (2009), 1–9.

34. Remus Gabriel Anghel, Eva Gerharz, Gilberto Rescher, and Monika Salzbrunn, eds., *The Making of World Society: Perspectives from Transnational Research* (Bielefeld: Transcript, 2008); Philip G. Cerny, *Rethinking World Politics: A Theory of Transnational Neopluralism* (New York: Oxford University Press, 2010); Luin Goldring and Sailaja Krishnamurti, eds., *Organizing the Transnational: Labour, Politics, and Social Change* (Vancouver: UBC Press, 2007); Richard Münch, *Nation and Citizenship in the Global Age: From National to Transnational Ties and Identities* (Houndmills, Basingstoke, and New York: Palgrave, 2001).

35. See Ruth Behar and Lucía M. Suárez, eds., *The Portable Island: Cubans at Home in the World* (New York: Palgrave Macmillan, 2008); Fernández, *Cuba Transnational;* Fabio Murrieta, *Creación y exilio: memorias del I Encuentro Internacional con Cuba en la distancia* (Madrid: Editorial Hispano Cubano, 2002); Andrea O'Reilly Herrera, *Cuba: Idea of a Nation Displaced* (Albany: State University of New York Press, 2007).

36. See Charles Del Todesco, *The Havana Cigar: The World's Best* (New York: Abbeville Press, 1997); Eumelio Espino Marrero, *Cuban Tobacco: Why Cuban Cigars Are the World's Best* (Neptune City, NJ: TFH Publications, 1996); Marvin R. Shanken, *Cigar Aficionado's Cigar Companion: A Connoisseur's Guide to the World's Finest Cigars* (New York: Running Press, 2005).

37. See Hector Amaya, *Screening Cuba: Film Criticism as Political Performance during the Cold War* (Urbana: University of Illinois Press, 2010); Michael Chanan, *Cuban Cinema* (Minneapolis: University of Minnesota Press, 2004), especially chapters 6–11; Cecilia Ricciarelli, *Cinéma cubain après la Révolution* (Lille: Atelier national de reproduction des thèses, 2006).

38. For instance, see Ann Marie Stock, *On Location in Cuba: Street Filmmaking during Times of Transition* (Chapel Hill: University of North Carolina Press, 2009).

39. Compare Esteban M. Beruvides, *Cuba: los crímenes impunes de Fidel Castro* (Miami, FL: Colonial Press International, 1999); Juan M. Clark, *Religious Repression in Cuba* (Coral Gables, FL: North-South Center for the Cuban Studies Project of the Institute of Interamerican Studies, University of Miami, 1985); José R. Oro, *Poisoning of Paradise: Environmental Pollution in the Republic of Cuba* (Miami, FL: Endowment for Cuban American Studies, 1992); Luis Báez, *Guerra secreta* (Havana: Editorial Letras Cubanas, 1978); Nicanor León Cotayo, *Sin ramo de olivo: las relaciones cubano-estadounidenses bajo el gobierno de Ronald Reagan* (Havana: Editora Política, 1988); Newton Briones Montoto, *Esperanzas y desilusiones: una historia de los años 30* (Havana: Editorial de Ciencias Sociales, 2008).

40. See the important study by Pedro Pérez Sarduy and Jean Stubbs, *Afro-Cuban Voices: On Race and Identity in Contemporary Cuba* (Gainesville: University Press of Florida, 2000). See also Aline Helg, *Our Rightful Share: The Afro-Cuban Struggle for Equality, 1886–1912* (Chapel

Hill: University of North Carolina Press, 1995); Kenneth F. Kiple, *Blacks in Colonial Cuba, 1774–1899* (Gainesville: University Press of Florida, 1976); Babatunde Sofela, *Emancipados: Slave Societies in Brazil and Cuba* (Trenton, NJ: Africa World Press, 2011).

41. Lisa Brock and Digna Castaneda Fuertes, eds., *Between Race and Empire: African-Americans and Cubans before the Cuban Revolution* (Philadelphia, PA: Temple University Press, 1998); Alejandra Bronfman, *Measures of Equality: Social Science, Citizenship, and Race in Cuba, 1902–1940* (Chapel Hill: University of North Carolina Press, 2004); Carmen V. Montejo Arrechea, *Sociedades negras en Cuba, 1878–1960* (Havana: Editorial de Ciencias Sociales, 2004).

42. Ignacio Ramonet and Fidel Castro, *Fidel Castro: My Life: A Spoken Autobiography* (New York: Scribner, 2009), 230.

43. See Sherri Williams, "Cuba and Color," *Ebony*, July 2008, 160.

44. For instance, see Susan Eckstein and Catherine Krull, "From Building Barriers to Bridges: Cuban Ties across the Straits," *Diplomacy and Statecraft* 20 (Spring 2009), 341–59; Yolanda Prieto, *The Cubans of Union City: Immigrants and Exiles in a New Jersey Community* (Philadelphia, PA: Temple University Press, 2009).

45. See Eckstein, *Immigrant Divide*, 133, 179, table 6.3, 203; Manuel Orozco, B. Lindsay Lowell, Micah Bump, and Rachel Fedewa, *Transnational Engagement, Remittances and Their Relationship to Development in Latin America and the Caribbean* (Washington, DC: Institute for the Study of International Migration, 2005), 16; José Alejandro Aguilar Trujillo, "Las remesas desde exterior," in *Cuba: Investigación Económica* (Havana: Instituto Nacional de Investigaciones Económicas, 2001), 71–104, 84.

46. The work on Che Guevara is legion, but see Paul J. Dosal, *Comandante Che: Guerrilla Soldier, Commander, and Strategist, 1956–1967* (University Park: Pennsylvania State University Press, 2003); Joseph Hart, ed., *Che: The Life, Death, and Afterlife of a Revolutionary* (New York: Thunder's Mouth Press, 2003); Trisha Ziff, *Che Guevara: Revolutionary and Icon* (New York: Abrams Image, *memorias del I Encuentro Internacional con Cuba en la distancia* 2006).

I

International Relations

1

Disaster, Disease, and Environmental Degradation
U.S.-Cuban Cooperation as a Bridge to Reconciliation

WILLIAM M. LEOGRANDE AND MARGUERITE ROSE JIMÉNEZ

How do countries locked in a cycle of hostility lasting half a century move toward reconciliation? One answer, suggested by scholars and practitioners alike, is through gradual, incremental steps. During the Cold War, international relations scholars seeking to de-escalate the arms race recommended confidence-building measures—actions designed to reduce uncertainty about how adversaries behave toward one another and to increase confidence that their behavior will be benign. Although applied most often in the security realm, the logic applies equally well to any area in which adversaries have the potential to harm one another.

Charles Osgood's theory of "graduated and reciprocated initiatives in tension reduction" (GRIT for short) posits a positive-feedback model of confidence building. A conflict can be de-escalated by one side taking the initiative to make a low-cost concession and communicating an expectation that the adversary should respond with a quid pro quo. If this process is successful, a series of reciprocal concessions, or a "peace spiral," can be set in motion, with each step more substantial than its predecessor, leading to a significant dissipation of hostility.[1]

A related idea, albeit more narrowly focused, is the concept of disaster diplomacy, which posits that cooperation on disaster prevention and relief can build bonds of trust between adversaries, leading to reconciliation. Disasters tend to elicit humanitarian empathy by reminding us that we are all vulnerable in the face of catastrophe, and they create an opportunity for cooperation.[2] There is no inherent reason why this dynamic should be limited to disasters. Any cooperation on issues of mutual interest ought potentially to set in motion the same dynamic of trust building.

Over the years policymakers in both Havana and Washington have shared the presumption that negotiations on small, narrow issues might lead to a diplomatic breakthrough. In 1977, when President Jimmy Carter issued Presidential Directive NSC-6 instructing his government to move toward normalizing relations with Cuba, he approved negotiating "reciprocal and sequential steps."[3] In 1994 President Bill Clinton announced a policy of "calibrated response," in which Washington would respond to incremental positive steps by Cuba with positive steps of its own.[4] President Barack Obama's pledge to pursue a new policy of engagement with Cuba began by opening a dialogue about issues of mutual interest, including migration, narcotics control, and educational exchanges.

Through half a century, the United States and Cuba, though bitter adversaries, have consistently engaged in diplomatic dialogue and reached agreements on various issues, from small matters such as fishing and maritime boundaries to major ones such as immigration. Jorge Domínguez has remarked on the surprisingly wide range of issues on which the two countries collaborate, despite their estrangement.[5] Proponents of normalizing relations with Cuba have long hoped that successful agreements like these would open the door to negotiations on the core issues that have divided Cuba and the United States since 1959. Opponents of normalization have long feared exactly the same thing. Thus they vigorously oppose any dialogue or cooperation, even in areas that would clearly benefit immediate U.S. interests, for fear that it would be the first step down a slippery slope to normalization.

The view from Havana has not been so different. At first Fidel Castro declared that Cuba would never negotiate with the United States so long as the embargo remained in place. He quickly relented, however, negotiating the release of the Bay of Pigs prisoners in 1963, an anti-hijacking treaty in 1973, fishing and maritime boundary agreements, and the exchange of diplomatic Interests Sections in 1977. Migration talks commenced (through Swiss intermediaries) at the time of the Camarioca exodus in 1965 and have since continued, albeit with fits and starts, with agreements in 1980, 1984, 1987, 1994, and 1995. At each juncture Castro tried to parlay negotiations on these lesser issues into negotiations on the core issue of the embargo. On several occasions Washington extracted concessions from Cuba by holding out the carrot of wider negotiations.

Yet despite significant successes, the two sides have never been able to translate the momentum of these tertiary agreements into real progress toward normalization. Indeed, as the history of dialogue and cooperation in several areas—disaster response, medical cooperation, and environmental protection—clearly reveals, that leap has never been possible.[6]

Disaster Response: Hurricane Cooperation

Cooperation between Cuba and the United States on hurricane tracking and prediction dates back to the early twentieth century and continued even when bilateral hostility developed after 1959. Scientists working at the U.S. National Hurricane Center and the U.S. Weather Bureau in Miami stayed in contact with their Cuban colleagues, exchanging information on developing storms, even through the dark days of the Cuban Missile Crisis. After the Bay of Pigs, Cuba retracted permission for U.S. weather planes to enter its airspace, but when Hurricane Inez struck the Caribbean in 1966, the Cubans allowed resumption of the flights.[7]

By the end of the 1960s the meteorologists on both sides of the Florida Straits had developed close professional relations. The independent nonprofit Center for International Policy held a series of meetings between U.S. and Cuban officials around the theme of hurricane preparedness. Cuban meteorologists were also able to attend training courses in Florida, which enabled them to meet their U.S. counterparts in person. "This has created a pretty close fraternity among us," observed forecaster Hal Gerrish of the National Hurricane Center. Perhaps no one better represented the transcendence of common humanity over political difference than did Lixion Avila, a Cuban American hurricane specialist working at the National Hurricane Center, whose mother still lived near Havana.[8]

Sometimes the meteorologists in Florida had a tougher time winning cooperation from their own government than from Cuba. Although Cuban officials had allowed U.S. weather planes into Cuban airspace for several decades, the State Department and U.S. Air Force refused to let the National Hurricane Center send Air Force C-130s near the island. Only the Center's two civilian planes could be used to track storms over Cuba, which limited its ability to collect adequate data. Finally, in 2003, Center director Max Mayfield convinced the State Department to authorize the Air Force to allow the use of its C-130 "hurricane hunters" near Cuba.[9]

Cooperation in hurricane tracking was not matched by cooperation on hurricane relief. When the United States imposed the trade embargo and cut off all bilateral assistance, humanitarian aid ended as well. In 1963 Hurricane Flora stalled over Cuba for four days. It destroyed half the sugar, tobacco, and food crops, left some 1,750 Cubans dead, and did an estimated $300 million in damage. Despite the severity of the storm, the U.S. government announced that it would not offer humanitarian assistance, although it did allow the American Red Cross to offer emergency supplies, food, and equipment to the Cuban Red Cross.[10] Castro angrily rejected the offer as "cynical and reprehensible." Cuba was not interested in U.S. charity. If Washington wanted to help, it should "end the economic blockade, especially at this moment." A few months later the Commerce Department denied export licenses to two private groups seeking to send clothing and powdered milk to the island's hurricane victims. Granting the licenses, Commerce said, would be "contrary to the national interest."[11]

In November 2001 Cuba was hit by Hurricane Michelle, a Category 4 storm that did $2.8 billion in damage. Washington responded by offering condolences, a disaster assessment team, and the possibility of humanitarian aid to be channeled through nongovernmental organizations. Cuban Foreign Minister Felipe Pérez Roque declined the offer, but in surprisingly polite fashion. The "kindly offer" of assistance would not be needed, he explained, but instead Cuba asked to be able to make a one-time purchase of food to replenish its reserves destroyed by the storm. Since food and medicine sales were exempt from the trade embargo, there was no legal impediment to granting Havana's request. U.S. and Cuban diplomats quickly came to an agreement on the basic terms of the sale, and the necessary licenses were granted to U.S. suppliers. The "one-time" purchase turned into a continuing commercial relationship, and by 2010 Cuba was purchasing more than $300 million worth of food annually from U.S. producers.[12]

U.S. offers of humanitarian assistance (always on the condition that the aid be channeled through nongovernmental organizations) became more or less routine thereafter, as did Cuban refusals. President George W. Bush's commitment to regime change in Cuba poisoned bilateral relations, and the Cuban Foreign Ministry angrily dismissed a 2004 offer of assistance after Hurricane Charley as a "cynical and hypocritical offer" that "ignores the damage caused over more than four decades by the economic war . . . against our country." Then, in September 2005, Hurricane Katrina gave Castro the opportunity to reverse roles. With New Orleans flooded, Cuba offered to send more than a thousand doctors to help care for the sick and injured along Louisiana's coast. Washington declined the help as unnecessary.[13]

At first it appeared that Hurricane Wilma in late 2005 might break this stalemate. As usual Washington offered to deploy an assessment team, and this time, instead of denouncing it, Castro accepted the offer, conditionally. The Ministry of Foreign Relations replied that Cuba shared the view that countries should "provide each other with mutual assistance in situations of disaster," and would welcome the team's visit. However, Castro wanted to widen the scope of the mission from simply assessing Wilma's damage to also include discussing regional cooperation on disaster preparation and relief. Cuba wanted to be treated as an equal partner, not a supplicant for assistance. "Cuba has not solicited international aid," Castro insisted in a televised interview. The Bush administration refused to engage in a broader discussion on the grounds that Havana was "not serious." Withdrawing the offer to send a team, the State Department declared that the Cubans "wanted to make this into some sort of political show."[14]

In 2008 Cuba was hit by the worst hurricane season in its history: five major storms wracked the island, inflicting some $5 billion in damage, with more than half a million homes damaged or destroyed. At first the United States simply repeated its routine offer to send an assessment team followed by disaster relief via private charities. But as the scope of the damage became clear, the U.S. position softened. Even Cuban American members of Congress, usually unanimous in their opposition to any U.S. engagement with Cuba, urged the administration to find a way to help. The Catholic Church in Miami and the Cuban American National Foundation, for years the leading Cuban American voice for a hardline U.S. policy, urged President Bush to relax the legal limits on remittances that Cuban Americans could send to relatives. Although the White House rejected the appeal to suspend the limits on remittances, it accelerated processing licenses for delivering private humanitarian assistance, which reached $10 million. More significantly, it increased the offer of bilateral assistance from $100,000 to $6.3 million, and it was willing to provide $5 million of that amount directly to the Cuban government without preconditions—an unprecedented offer.[15]

But Cuban officials could not bring themselves to take U.S. help. In one of his "reflections" a convalescing Fidel Castro wrote, "Our country cannot accept a donation from the government that blockades us. . . . The dignity of a people has no price." Instead, the Cubans countered with a request analogous to what they had done in 2001 after Hurricane Michelle—they asked that the embargo be lifted, at least for six months, so that Cuba could buy supplies, especially construction materials, from U.S. suppliers.[16] President Bush was not willing to allow such a chink in the embargo, perhaps for fear that once general commerce with Cuba began, it would be hard to stop.

President Barack Obama changed the tenor of bilateral relations, calling for dialogue and engagement across a wide range of issues. In September 2009, a Cuban official suggested to the U.S. Interests Section in Havana that Cuba would be disposed to accept hurricane assistance in the future because of the improved atmosphere, so long as the aid came without preconditions.[17] However, in June 2010 the State Department invited foreign embassy representatives to a hurricane preparedness workshop in Washington, and Cuban diplomats were excluded.

The lack of cooperation on hurricane relief represents a stark contrast to the successful cooperation on hurricane tracking and prediction. One obvious reason is that hurricane tracking involves small groups of professionals united by their common commitment to their profession and to saving lives. Not only does cooperation benefit both countries, but it also happens below the radar (pun intended) and thus has a low political cost, especially in Washington. The task of providing economic assistance to Cuba, even as disaster relief, is fraught with more political baggage, in both Washington and Havana.

Havana sees Washington trying to appear beneficent while it nevertheless continues its policy of promoting regime change through economic strangulation. Fidel Castro, in particular, proved unwilling to have Cuba appear to be chasing after Yanqui dollars—an image of Cuban subservience that had obsessed him since his first trip to the United States as Cuba's leader in April 1959. Washington, for its part, continued to worry that humanitarian aid would be misappropriated, or at the very least that Cuban American hardliners would criticize the U.S. government on those grounds.

Such fears have led policymakers in both capitals to miss opportunities. Washington could have treated Cuba's willingness to accept a disaster assessment team in 2005 as a breakthrough, and understood Havana's desire to expand the agenda as face-saving. Instead, Washington treated the Cuban proposal as a trick to gain political advantage, and responded contemptuously. Cuba could have treated Washington's 2008 offer of unconditional government-to-government assistance as a significant change in U.S. policy, which it was, and accepted the badly needed aid. Instead, it rejected the offer, in part out of pride. Washington could have accepted a temporary lifting of the embargo for the narrow range of products that Cuba needed for reconstruction, thus alleviating suffering in Cuba and perhaps establishing a precedent for better cooperation in the face of future disasters. Yet each time one side made a gesture, the other could not overcome its suspicions and respond positively.

Medical Cooperation: The Haitian Earthquake

The earthquake that devastated Port-au-Prince, Haiti, on January 12, 2010, offered an opportunity for Cuba and the United States to cooperate on a purely humanitarian mission to alleviate extraordinary human suffering. The United States moved quickly to provide emergency assistance and coordinate worldwide offers of relief. Cuba had a well-established medical mission in Haiti of four hundred doctors and paramedics who immediately began providing emergency aid to the injured, and hundreds more Cuban doctors soon joined that team.

Cooperation began with Cuba granting U.S. planes the right to fly through Cuban airspace as they evacuated the injured to medical facilities abroad. The offer garnered a public expression of appreciation from Secretary of State Hillary Clinton, and two relatively high-level diplomatic meetings ensued to discuss ways in which Washington and Havana could extend their cooperation. In January Secretary Clinton's chief of staff, Cheryl Mills (coordinating Haiti relief efforts at State), and Julissa Reynoso (from the Western Hemisphere Affairs Bureau) met in Santo Domingo with senior Cuban foreign ministry and health ministry officials.[18] Some two months later Mills met with Cuban Foreign Minister Bruno Rodríguez in New York at a United Nations donor conference. The discussion, according to Rodríguez, focused on how to rebuild Haiti's heath system. "Some cooperative activities have taken place between Cuba and the United States, in the effort to provide emergency care," he explained, and more were expected to follow.[19] Although no one at the State Department was willing to admit it on the record, U.S. relief workers on the ground in Haiti were providing medical supplies to the field hospitals that the Cuban doctors had set up. Cuban diplomats expressed annoyance that the State Department was unwilling to acknowledge the de facto cooperation on the ground.

Privately, however, the diplomats were planning significantly more extensive cooperation: the United States would build and supply a major medical facility in Haiti which Cuban personnel would staff. The two sides seemed close to agreement when Cuba asked that Washington suspend its Cuban Medical Professional Parole program, created in 2006 to entice Cuban medical personnel serving abroad to defect by offering them entry to the United States. The Obama administration refused. Cuba then proposed that Washington build two medical facilities rather than just one, and the talks fell apart. "We have not produced any agreements," lamented Jorge Bolaños, head of the Cuban Interests Section in Washington, after a third meeting, although he reaffirmed Cuba's willingness "to cooperate with any country, including the U.S."[20]

Not even the horror of Haiti's disaster was enough to defuse the bitter partisanship that Cuba had engendered in Washington. Mauricio Claver-Carone, executive director of the conservative U.S.-Cuba Democracy PAC, argued against cooperating with Havana on Haitian relief lest it open the door to improved relations. "It's absolutely unconscionable," he wrote, "to try to use tragic disasters—such as Haiti's earthquake—as a springboard for bilateral relations."[21]

Environmental Threats: Nuclear Power

Since 1959 two major environmental issues have offered opportunities for U.S.-Cuban cooperation aimed at avoiding accidents that could have a severe environmental impact on both countries: the development of nuclear power in Cuba, and the initiation of deepwater oil drilling off the Cuban coast.

In 1976 Cuba and the Soviet Union signed an accord to build a nuclear power plant at Juragua, near the city of Cienfuegos, as the first stage in a larger plan to build plants in eastern, central, and western Cuba. The aim was to meet the island's growing demand for electricity and reduce its dependence on imported oil. Construction of the first two-unit reactor site at Juragua began in 1983.[22]

After the 1979 accident at Three Mile Island, Pennsylvania, and the 1986 Chernobyl disaster in the Soviet Union, the United States was acutely sensitive to the impact that an accident at a Cuban reactor would have on South Florida. In 1988, as part of a broader safety program sponsored by the World Association of Nuclear Operators, two officials from Cuba's nuclear program, including the director of nuclear safety, visited the Duke Power Company's McGuire Nuclear Station and training facility.[23] The U.S. Nuclear Regulatory Commission (NRC) also undertook a study of the design safety of the planned Cuban reactors, and in October 1989 the State Department arranged for an NRC official and two Duke Power representatives to visit the Juragua site and discuss safety issues with their Cuban counterparts. Deputy Assistant Secretary of State Michael Kozak testified to Congress that even though U.S. policy opposed construction of the Juragua plant, George H. W. Bush's administration had opened a dialogue with Cuba on nuclear safety because "when it comes to something like nuclear safety, we did not think politics should get in the way."[24]

What appeared to be a fruitful beginning to cooperation soon proved disappointing. The United States proposed continuing the dialogue on a "case-by-case" basis. Cuba instead proposed a formal bilateral agreement on nuclear safety and cooperation. The Bush administration was unwilling to conclude a formal agreement. As a report by the General Accounting Office explained, "U.S. officials thought that the Cuban government could use a formal agreement for propaganda purposes to indicate falsely that the United States did not have concerns about the nuclear reactors."[25] Even ad hoc exchanges were subsequently curtailed.

In September 1992 Castro announced that the Juragua project was being "temporarily suspended" because Russia insisted that Cuba pay in hard currency for the equipment and technical assistance needed to complete it. The estimated cost—$400 million—was money that Cuba simply did not have. In 1995, however, Russia and Cuba announced their intention to seek Western investors for a joint venture to complete the project.[26] The prospect of renewed construction reignited fears in South Florida and gave conservative Republicans a new issue with which to pummel President Bill Clinton, who had concluded two migration agreements with Cuba, one in 1994 to end the "Balsero" crisis and another in 1995 to establish the "wet foot–dry foot policy." Clinton's willingness to negotiate with Havana convinced his congressional adversaries that he was determined to normalize relations with Cuba, his disclaimers to the contrary notwithstanding.

"We're talking about a potential Chernobyl right in our own backyards," warned Congresswoman Ileana Ros-Lehtinen (R-Fla).[27] She was able to get 131 members of the House of Representatives to sign a letter to Clinton demanding that he stop construction at Juragua by using "all instruments at your disposal to pressure the Russian government" to halt the project. In reply, Clinton reaffirmed his opposition to completion of the Juragua reactors, noting that he had expressed U.S. opposition directly to the Russians on several occasions. In addition, the administration was working hard behind the scenes to dissuade any potential Western partners from joining the Cuban-Soviet joint venture. For Ros-Lehtinen, this approach was not sufficient. "The only solution to the Juragua national nuclear plant problem," she declared, "is to destroy it in its totality."[28]

The vituperative congressional response put Clinton on the horns of a dilemma. If efforts to derail the project failed, Washington would have only two options, perfectly expressed by Harold Denton, the former NRC official who visited Juragua in 1989. "If they really are going to finish this thing, our only choices are to complain about it and not be actively involved, or try to find some way to interact with them and make sure they have as well-trained a staff as they can get." The concerns about the safety of the Juragua plant were reasonable, Denton agreed, which was all the more reason to engage the Cubans. As he told the *New York Times*, "We ought to bend the rules a little bit and allow cooperation on safety matters."[29]

The Cubans appeared willing to reopen a dialogue on nuclear safety. In early 1996 the nonprofit Center for International Policy organized a delegation of nuclear experts to visit Cuba. Cuban officials invited U.S. experts to inspect the Juragua plant as part of normal International Atomic Energy Agency (IAEA) inspections if Washington would allow it, and said that Cuba was also prepared to discuss safety issues directly with Washington. The stakes were high. A study by the National Oceanic and Atmospheric Administration (NOAA) projected that a serious accident at Juragua could spew radioactive contamination all across Florida and, depending on weather conditions, as far north as Washington, DC.[30]

In the end President Clinton did not have to make the tough choice between either engaging with Cuba to ensure the safe operation of the Juragua site or ignoring the deficiencies of the plant in the hope that someone else, perhaps the IAEA, would take care of the problems. By 2000 an estimated $750 million was needed to complete the project. Cuba still could not pay the bill, Russia was still unwilling to cover it, and no other investors stepped forward to join the consortium. In December Fidel Castro and Russian president Vladimir Putin agreed to close the project permanently.[31] Nuclear power would not be the magic solution to Cuba's chronic energy dependency after all.

Environmental Threats: Offshore Oil Drilling

The explosion of the Deepwater Horizon oil rig in the Gulf of Mexico on April 20, 2010, and the subsequent hemorrhage of 6.6 million barrels of oil from the blown-out well, focused new attention on U.S.-Cuban environmental cooperation. As the spill spread eastward toward the Florida Straits, experts began to warn that the Gulf Stream could carry the slick onto Cuba's northern beaches and even to Florida's Atlantic coast. In mid-May, almost a month after the blowout, the State Department, as required by international law, formally notified Cuba of the environmental hazard posed by the spill and began "low, technical" bilateral talks about its spread. "We provided background related to the cause of the spill, stressed that stopping the oil leak is our top priority, and explained the projected movement of the spill," said a State Department spokesman. "We also communicated the U.S. desire to maintain a clear line of communication with the Cuban government on developments." Havana gave permission for a NOAA vessel to enter Cuban waters to monitor the spill's spread.[32]

In the end Cuba's coasts were spared; but the debate over U.S.-Cuban cooperation on energy, oil, and environmental protection was just beginning. The Deepwater Horizon disaster demonstrated that a blowout could endanger coastlines hundreds of miles away. The U.S. Geological Survey estimated Cuban oil reserves in the Gulf at about 4.6 billion barrels, enough to make the island a medium-sized exporter.[33] The Cuban government had already begun to lease blocks in the commercial zone for exploration to companies in Russia, China, India, Malaysia, Vietnam, Angola, Norway, Brazil, Venezuela, and Spain. The Spanish company Repsol drilled unsuccessful exploratory wells in 2012, then leased the drilling platform to Malaysian and Russian oil companies to drill in their commercial blocks.

The Deepwater Horizon accident prompted observers to ask what would happen if a Cuban well suffered a similar accident. The answers were unsettling. "The existing trade embargo prohibits U.S. assistance for containment, clean up, drilling a relief well, or capping the well," warned Brian Petty of the International Association of Drilling Contractors (IADC), the main industry trade association. "Absolutely no U.S. resources can be committed to containment or clean up. No U.S. rigs only miles away could be mobilized for a relief well."[34]

As former oil executive Jorge Piñon explained, all the companies cooperate when an accident happens. "All they have to do is pick up the phone and contact petroleum equipment suppliers in Houston, and in a matter of hours they'd be on site." But that would not happen if the accident was at a Cuban well. "That's not the case with Cuba given the embargo, so days would go by as the bureaucratic paperwork was shifted from agency to department, and in the meantime the oil would be moving towards Key West and South Beach." Piñon argued vigorously for a proactive U.S. approach that would remove all obstacles to an immediate U.S. response in the event of a Cuban accident, including preapproval of licenses to deploy equipment, technology, and personnel; regular exchanges of scientific and technical information to enhance Cuban safety; and even joint U.S.-Cuban exercises to practice containment and cleanup of a spill. The IADC shared Piñon's recommendations.[35]

The Obama administration took small steps toward greater cooperation. In late 2009, when the IADC requested a license to send a delegation to Cuba to discuss offshore drilling safety, the U.S. Treasury Department Office of Foreign Assets Control (OFAC) initially denied it. When IADC reapplied after the Deepwater Horizon accident, the license was granted. "Senior [Cuban] officials told us they are going ahead with their deepwater drilling program," said IADC president Lee Hunt upon his return. "They are utilizing every reliable non-U.S. source that they can for technology and information, but they would prefer to work directly with the United States in matters of safe drilling practices."[36]

In July 2010, before the Deepwater Horizon well was capped, the State Department announced that U.S. companies could seek licenses "to provide oil spill prevention and containment support to companies operating in Cuba."[37] At least one company, Clean Caribbean & Americas, a nonprofit cooperative of oil companies formed to provide oil-spill assistance, received a license to provide containment equipment to foreign companies operating in Cuba, but only after months of waiting.[38] Nevertheless, it appeared possible for firms to secure licenses in advance to transfer equipment and expertise to Cuba in the event of an accident if they were foresighted enough to do so and could predict what equipment would be needed.

The low-level technical discussions between U.S. and Cuban officials during the Deepwater Horizon crisis engaged the issue of developing a bilateral protocol for cooperation in handling an accident, although no formal agreement resulted. Former senator Bob Graham of Florida, co-chair of the U.S. National Commission on the BP Deepwater Horizon Oil Spill, suggested using Mexico as an intermediary to discuss safety standards for drilling in the Gulf. "This is not a capitulation to Castro," he argued. "Rather it is something in our self-interest to ensure that anything that relates to drilling have high safety standards." Graham's co-chair, William Reilly, traveled to Mexico to encourage authorities there to take on the intermediary role. "Cuba should also be a part of that as much as possible," Reilly said. "As we move into deep waters we have every reason to be partners."[39]

But when the Department of the Interior hosted a twelve-nation conference in April 2011 on the lessons learned from the Deepwater Horizon accident, Cuba was excluded, even though Secretary Ken Salazar acknowledged that the prospect of imminent drilling in Cuban waters was "an issue of concern." Michael Bromwich, director of the Interior Department's Bureau of Ocean Energy Management, Regulation, and Enforcement, agreed that Mexico, Cuba, and the United States all shared a common interest in assuring that "the highest standards possible are observed in all of the drilling offshore." He said reaching an agreement with Cuba on safety standards "would certainly be desirable," but that "finding the mechanism to do that is tricky and needs to be explored further."[40] It must have been the domestic politics of the issue that were tricky, because there was no indication that the State Department was exploring the issue with Havana.

Coordinator of Cuban Affairs Peter Brennan did not slight the importance of the issue. "It's a priority for us," he said. "It's a national security issue." But still the administration could not bring itself to engage the Cuban government directly to formulate a coordinated response plan of the sort that the Coast Guard had developed with Mexico in the Caribbean and with Russia in the Aleutians. The "tricky mechanism" the administration settled on was to deal directly with Repsol on safety issues, and only indirectly with Cuba, under the cover of multinational initiatives. This, officials seemed to hope, would provide a margin of safety for the environment while blunting the political furor that would result from engaging the Cubans directly and bilaterally.

After meeting with Interior Secretary Salazar, Repsol promised to comply with all U.S. environmental safety standards in drilling the Cuban well, including allowing U.S. experts to inspect the drilling platform before it was deployed in Cuban waters. Repsol also opened discussions with the U.S. Coast Guard about accident response contingencies.[41] The Department of Commerce licensed the sale of a U.S.-manufactured blowout protector for the Repsol rig, and expressed a willingness to license other firms in advance to transfer equipment and expertise to Cuba in the event of an accident. Nevertheless, Washington seemed satisfied that it had the oil-spill risk under control. "I'm confident that once we get through this process, the United States will be able to respond to an accident quickly," Brennan affirmed.[42]

In December 2011, U.S. officials participated in a conference hosted by the Regional Marine Pollution Emergency Information and Training Center for the Wider Caribbean, a multilateral organization supported by the United Nations. They joined officials from the Bahamas, where the conference was held, Jamaica, Mexico, and Cuba to discuss offshore drilling regulatory standards, safety practices, and spill-containment plans. U.S. participants "were impressed with the Cuban delegation's professionalism and the country's emergency spill response plan," according to the trade publication *Oil Daily*.[43]

Industry professionals were less sanguine about the adequacy of the administration's strategy. Although Michael Bromwich from the Interior Department assured Congress that in the event of an accident, licenses would be approved "very, very quickly," Paul Schuler from Clean Caribbean, which had already run the gauntlet of getting a license, had his doubts. Coping with a major spill would require drawing on resources from dozens of companies, he pointed out. Most would not have preapproved licenses; they would have to go through the licensing process, "which, in my experience has not been quick."[44]

Even the threat to Florida's beaches was not enough to convince Cuban American members of Congress that a dialogue with Havana was justified. The way to prevent a Cuban oil spill from fouling Florida's coastline, according to Ileana Ros-Lehtinen, was to prevent any drilling whatsoever in Cuba's commercial zone. She sponsored legislation to extend the extraterritorial reach of the 1996 Cuban Liberty and Democratic Solidarity Act to punish any foreign persons or companies that invested in or assisted the exploration and exploitation of Cuba's offshore oil reserves.[45] If such legislation passed, it would discourage U.S. allies in Latin America and Europe from developing Cuba's reserves, leaving the field open to Venezuela, Russia, and China.

The Limits of Cooperation

Decades of U.S.-Cuban cooperation on issues of mutual interest have failed to set in motion a spiral of confidence-building leading to a diplomatic breakthrough on the core issues involving Washington and Havana. The theorized dynamics of confidence-building measures, graduated reduction in tensions, and disaster diplomacy have simply not worked. Indeed, in the areas of medical cooperation, hurricane prediction and relief, and environmental protection, the dynamic has more often been reversed. Bilateral antagonism has impeded the building of anything more than relatively superficial cooperation, even when both sides have a clear self-interest in cooperating.

One reason is that the logic underlying confidence-building strategies and GRIT does not translate well from its original Cold War context. Because both superpowers, despite their differences, shared an overarching interest in avoiding nuclear war, risk-reduction strategies were rational. In the conflict between Cuba and the United States, it is not at all clear that reducing tensions and moving toward reconciliation is an overriding interest on either side, let alone on both.

At key moments in the past, Cuba has subordinated its desire for normal relations with Washington to a desire to project its influence in Africa and Latin America. For the United States, normalizing relations with Cuba has been a clear goal for only two presidents, Gerald Ford and Jimmy Carter. Bill Clinton and Barack Obama hinted that they might be willing to move in the general direction of better relations, but nevertheless insisted that full normalization would await fundamental changes in Cuba's internal political and economic system. Ronald Reagan, George H. W. Bush, and George W. Bush were openly committed to regime change, not reconciliation.

Bilateral cooperation on small measures has not set in motion a dynamic leading to normal relations because there has never been a moment when both sides wanted to normalize relations on terms acceptable to the other. For gradual reciprocal actions to set the stage for diplomatic reconciliation, both sides must have the political will to reconcile.

Of late, Havana has been more interested in improving relations than has Washington. Since assuming the presidency in 2006, Raúl Castro has repeatedly offered to open a dialogue with Washington on all issues dividing the two countries. The economic benefits from normalizing relations are substantial at a time when the Cuban economy is struggling. In the areas of disaster response, medical cooperation, and environmental protection, the Cuban side has been consistently interested in extending and deepening cooperation, while the U.S. side has been reluctant. Other areas such as narcotics interdiction, counterterrorism, and migration show a similar pattern. The United States has been content to live with perpetual hostility toward Cuba because the costs have been relatively low; changing the policy entails domestic political risks that successive presidents have judged too high. Obama, while acknowledging that the policy of hostility has been futile, has been no more willing than his predecessors to break out of this impasse.

Nevertheless, the imperative of self-interest will continue to push Washington and Havana toward cooperation on issues such as these, even if the overall bilateral relationship remains strained. Hurricanes, plagues, and oil spills do not respect national boundaries, so neither country can adequately protect itself without cooperating with the other. If such cooperation cannot bridge the bilateral divide and lead to friendship between the United States and Cuba, perhaps it can at least move them from being unmitigated enemies to respectful adversaries.

Notes

1. Charles E. Osgood, *An Alternative to War or Surrender* (Urbana: University of Illinois Press, 1962), 85–134.

2. Louise K. Comfort, "Disaster: Agent of Diplomacy or Change in International Affairs?" *Cambridge Review of International Affairs* 14, no. 1 (2000), 277–94.

3. Presidential Directive/NSC-6, Subject: Cuba, March 15, 1977, National Security Archive, www.gwu.edu/~nsarchiv/news/20020515/.

4. William J. Clinton, "Remarks to the Cuban-American Community, June 27, 1995," *Public Papers of the Presidents of the United States, 1995*, Book 1, The American Presidency Project, www.presidency.ucsb.edu/ws/?pid=51547.

5. Jorge I. Domínguez, "Reconfiguración de las relaciones de los Estados Unidos y Cuba," *Temas* (Havana) 62–63 (April–September 2010), 4–15.

6. We exclude from this analysis several other arenas in which Cuba and the United States have engaged one another—immigration, narcotics interdiction, and military-to-military dialogue at Guantánamo (the so-called fence-line talks)—because they touch directly on security issues that make cooperation even more complex.

7. J. V. Reistrup, "Weather Planes Get Cuba Flight Permit," *Washington Post*, July 9, 1967; "Gales Lash Florida as Storm Regains Hurricane Strength," *New York Times*, October 3, 1966. For a more detailed description of U.S.-Cuban cooperation on hurricane monitoring, see Michael H. Glantz, "Climate-Related Disaster Diplomacy: A U.S.-Cuban Case Study," *Cambridge Review of International Affairs* 14, no. 1 (2000), 233–53.

8. See, for example, Elizabeth Newhouse, *U.S.-Cuba Conference on Hurricane Cooperation, Galveston, Texas, December 9, 2010* (Washington, DC: Center for International Policy, 2011); Tracy Fields, "International Cooperation Kept Storms from Killing Many," Associated Press, November 26, 1988; Laura Wides-Muñoz, "U.S., Cuba Find Common Foe in Storms," Associated Press, September 1, 2006.

9. Wides-Muñoz, "U.S., Cuba Find Common Foe in Storms."

10. "Flora's Toll in Haiti Put at 4,000, Half of Cuban Sugar Crop Ruined," *Washington Post*, October 8, 1963; "U.S. Ready to Help If Cuba and Haiti Ask Storm Relief," *New York Times*, October 8, 1963.

11. Tad Szulc, "U.S. Says It Will Keep up Policy of Economic Isolation of Cuba," *New York Times*, October 24, 1963; "Group Appeals to Hodges on Cuba Gale-Aid License," *New York Times*, February 26, 1964.

12. David Adams, "Storm Sows Ruin in Cuba," *St. Petersburg Times*, November 8, 2001; Christopher Marquis, "U.S. Is Reportedly Prepared to Allow Food Sales to Cuba," *New York Times*, November 15, 2001; U.S.-Cuba Trade and Economic Council, "2010–2001 U.S. Export Statistics for Cuba," *Economic Eye on Cuba*, February 2011, www.cubatrade.org/CubaExport Stats.pdf.

13. "Cuba Rejects Hurricane Aid Offered by U.S. Government as 'Ridiculous, Humiliating,'" Associated Press, August 23, 2004; George Gedda, "U.S. Unlikely to Accept Offer of Hurricane Aid from Cuba," Associated Press, September 6, 2005.

14. Anita Snow, "Castro Confirms His Government Will Let American Aid Officials Visit Island," Associated Press, October 28, 2005; "U.S. Team's Visit to Cuba Put on Hold," Associated Press, November 2, 2005; Vanessa Arrington, "Cuba Rejects Claim It Wanted to Politicize Visit by U.S. Relief Team on Hurricane Damage," Associated Press, November 3, 2005; U.S. Department of State, Daily Press Briefing, November 4, 2005.

15. Marc Lacey, "U.S. Offers Storm Aid to Cuba Only through Relief Groups," *New York*

Times, September 5, 2008; Damien Cave, "In Wake of Storm Damage, Calls to Ease Cuba Embargo," *New York Times*, September 11, 2008. Marifeli Perez-Stable, "Castros' Arrogance Gets in the Way of Help," *Miami Herald*, September 25, 2008; Karen DeYoung, "U.S. Urges Cuba to Accept Aid; Storm Relief Would Be Sent Directly to Havana Government," *Washington Post*, September 16, 2008.

16. DeYoung, "U.S. Urges Cuba to Accept Aid"; Castro is quoted in Joshua Partlow, "Hurricanes Shift Debate on Embargo against Cuba," *Washington Post*, September 24, 2008.

17. Cable 09Havana559, "Subject: Check Please! Government of Cuba May Accept U.S. Offer of Post-Hurricane Assistance," September 14, 2009 (Wikileaks). As of June 2011 no opportunity to test this possibility has yet presented itself.

18. Will Englund, "An Invasion of Mercy," *National Journal*, January 23, 2010; Manuel Jimenez, "U.S., Cuban Officials Discuss Haiti Quake Assistance," Reuters, March 19, 2010.

19. "U.S., Cuba Hold Rare Meeting at UN, with Haiti Focus," Agence France Press, April 2, 2010.

20. "U.S., Cuba Meet but Reach No Deal on Haiti Aid," Agence France Press, April 22, 2010.

21. Mauricio Claver-Carone, "Stop Trivializing Disaster," Capitol Hill Cubans website, January 6, 2009, www.capitolhillcubans.com/2010/01/stop-trivializing-tragedies.html.

22. The fullest account, by far, of the Juragua project is Jonathan Benjamin-Alvarado, *Power to the People: Energy and the Cuban Nuclear Program* (New York: Routledge, 2000).

23. "Duke Power Hosts Two Officials of Cuban Nuclear Power Program," PR Newswire, May 20, 1988.

24. U.S. House of Representatives, *Recent Developments in U.S.-Cuban Relations: Immigration and Nuclear Power*, Hearing before the Subcommittee on Western Hemisphere Affairs, Committee on Foreign Affairs, 102nd Congress, 1st Session, June 5, 1991 (Washington, DC: Government Printing Office, 1991), 24–25, 51.

25. U.S. General Accounting Office (GAO), *Concerns about the Nuclear Power Reactors in Cuba*, September 1992, GAO/RCED 92–262 (Washington, DC: GAO, 1992), 10.

26. Foreign Broadcast Information Service (FBIS), "Moncada Barracks Anniversary Ceremony Described," *Latin America Daily Report*, September 9, 1992; David Adams, "Plans for Cuba Plant Financing Go Forward," *St. Petersburg Times*, October 15, 1995.

27. "Cuban Reactor Called a Threat," *St. Petersburg Times*, June 7, 1995.

28. U.S. House of Representatives, *Cienfuegos Nuclear Plant in Cuba*, Hearing before the Subcommittee on Western Hemisphere Affairs, Committee on Foreign Affairs, 104th Congress, 2nd Session, August 1, 1995 (Washington, DC: Government Printing Office, 1995), 3, 10–11, 79–88.

29. Larry Rohter, "Cuba's Nuclear Plant Project Worries Washington," *New York Times*, February 25, 1996.

30. Peter Zirnite, "U.S.-Cuba: U.S. Thwarts Alternatives to Cuban Nuclear Power," IPS-Inter Press Service, May 10, 1996; U.S. GAO, *Concerns about the Nuclear Power Reactors in Cuba*, 13.

31. Patrick E. Tyler, "Cuba and Russia Abandon Nuclear Plant, an Unfinished Vestige of the Soviet Era," *New York Times*, December 18, 2000.

32. Paul Haven, "U.S. and Cuba Hold Talks on Oil Spill," Associated Press, May 19, 2010; Center for Democracy in the Americas, *As Cuba Plans to Drill in the Gulf of Mexico, U.S. Policy Poses Needless Risks to our National Interest* (Washington, DC: CDA, 2011), 27.

33. Christopher J. Schenk, "Geological Assessment of Undiscovered Oil and Gas Resources

of the North Cuba Basin, Cuba," U.S. Department of the Interior, U.S. Geological Survey, 2010, http://pubs.usgs.gov/of/2010/1029/pdf/OF10-1029.pdf.

34. New American Foundation, "U.S.-Cuba Engagement in the Gulf: Lessons from the Deepwater Horizon Oil Spill," panel discussion, May 26, 2010, video, cuba.newamerica.net/events/2010/us_cuba_engagement_in_the_gulf.

35. Howard LaFranchi, "International Sensitivities: What If BP Oil Spill Heads for Cuba?" *Christian Science Monitor*, June 11, 2010; Jorge R. Piñon and Robert L. Muse, "Coping with the Next Oil Spill: Why U.S.-Cuba Environmental Cooperation Is Critical," *U.S.-Cuba Relations at Brookings*, Issue Brief no. 2, May 2010 (Washington, DC: Brookings Institution, 2010); "From the President: Principle above Politics—Cuba, U.S.A. Need a One Gulf Strategy," *Drilling Contractor* (IADC), November–December 2010, IADC, www.drillingcontractor.org/from-the-president-principle-above-politics-cuba-usa-need-a-one-gulf-strategy-7528.

36. Clifford Kraus, "Drilling Plans off Cuba Stir Fears of Impact on Gulf," *New York Times*, September 29, 2010.

37. Philip J. Crowley, Daily Press Briefing, July 16, 2010, Press Release, U.S. Department of State, Bureau of Public Affairs.

38. Monica Hatcher, "Cuba Drilling Poses Spill Issue: Group Says Trade Embargo Could Hinder a Response by the U.S.," *Houston Chronicle*, September 5, 2010.

39. Mary Ellen Klas, "Sen. Graham: Gulf Oil Spill a 'Wake-up Call,'" *Miami Herald*, January 15, 2011; "Offshore Drilling: U.S. Hopes to Bring Mexico—and Cuba—into Joint Effort on Oil Spills," *Greenwire*, March 9, 2011.

40. "Standards on Cuba's Offshore Drilling," *UPI Energy*, April 15, 2011.

41. Cammy Clark, "Cuba's Oil, Our Potential Mess," *Miami Herald*, June 26, 2011.

42. Meeting with Brennan, June 17, 2011.

43. "U.S. and Cuba Discuss Offshore Oil Spill Response in Bahamas," *Oil Daily*, December 15, 2011.

44. U.S. Senate Energy and Natural Resources Committee, *Hearing: The Status of Response Capability and Readiness for Oil Spills in Foreign Outer Continental Shelf Waters Adjacent to U.S. Waters*, Lexis-Nexis Congressional Documents and Publications.

45. "Ros-Lehtinen Continues Push to Protect against Potential Cuban Oil-Drilling Disaster," House Foreign Affairs Committee News Release, January 27, 2011.

2

A Model Servant

The Revolutionary Armed Forces and Cuban Foreign Policy

HAL KLEPAK

Any political science text dealing with the role of the armed forces will tend to emphasize their central role as servants of the foreign policy of a given state. The reality is often that, but it is surely equally the case that in vast portions of the world their key roles have been focused internally as much or more than externally.

This is true in many countries but it has been, often sadly, particularly the case in Latin America. There the armed forces have often been the political arbiters between conflicting interests, parties, or groupings of any number of kinds. They have also often been the central pillar of the state or even the direct governors of that state—and usually only in a secondary way the servants of national foreign policies.

In the case of Cuba's Revolutionary Armed Forces (Fuerzas Armadas Revolucionarias, or FAR), however, over the half century of a government led by Fidel and now Raúl Castro, those forces have indeed been the direct servants of foreign policy in many and varied ways, as required by a nation and political system under siege by the most powerful country in the world, a country that sits a mere 150 kilometers away. This argument in no way denies the FAR's exceptional missions related to natural disaster preparation and relief, management of key industries and programs of the revolutionary government in a variety of economic fields, involvement in support of social projects as varied as hospitals and education, and so much more; but its missions of deterring foreign attack and supporting the government's other international objectives have been even more central not only to its structure and way of going about business, but to its members' being and way of seeing themselves.

This foreign policy role evolved over a half century, during which time FAR's flexibility was tested as Cuba's foreign policy needs changed, with the armed forces in turn responding to those changes. An analysis of this evolution and those responses will lead us here to some tentative judgments about what role the forces might also play in the future.

The Early Years of Revolutionary Consolidation

When the Ejército Rebelde entered Santiago and Havana on January 1, 1959, it may have appeared to be a small and rather ragtag affair, but it had considerable political, administrative, and even economic experience behind it, in addition to amazing military successes against the dictatorship. It had, after all, in a very difficult campaign lasting twenty-five months, just bested a large regular army backed almost without qualification by the might of the United States. During that time it had expanded the territory under its control, always termed romantically "Cuba Libre" after the insurgents' practice in the two nineteenth-century wars for independence; and it had administered that territory fully in varying periods over those two years.[1]

While it has so far proven impossible to determine with any exactness the strength of the rebel forces as of January 1, by any standards they were clearly small.[2] In the strategic sense the relatively small size was important. While Fidel did not intend after victory to maintain a large standing army along the usual Latin American model, a number of factors led to a different outcome in the long or even mid-term.

The size and political status of the former armed forces obliged Fidel essentially to abolish these military forces and retain only those officers and other ranks that had impeccable "popular" credentials. Thus Fidel and the new government could not rely on a professional corps that could be readily incorporated into the Ejército Rebelde. In addition, the nature of the reform program that the revolutionary government quickly began to implement soon led large portions of the bourgeoisie and bureaucracy to leave the island, usually in hopes that the United States would quickly rid the island of the reformers and bring back traditional upper-class rule. A percentage of them were willing to support such a move with their own efforts, including in the military field.

When these issues were combined with international factors such as a growing U.S. opposition to Fidel's experiment and the lining up of pro-U.S. governments in the Caribbean and Latin America against Havana, the need for a significant defense force and effort became ever clearer. By September 1959 the threat was real enough, and Fidel formally named his brother Raúl minister of the armed forces, promoting him to the new rank of army general. He ordered him to establish regular forces along revolutionary but nonetheless largely traditional lines. Thus were born the formally constituted revolutionary army, navy, and air forces, still existing today.

Their international role became obvious quickly. In the early months of the new government they had been vitally necessary in running newly nationalized industries, organizing the distribution of holdings of those leaving the country, facilitating the agrarian reform that had become the hallmark of the revolutionary process, and generally being placed anywhere the comandante en jefe needed someone he could trust. Now they were needed to provide, as quickly as possible, a force not only to deter (or even defeat) foreign invasion and U.S. sponsorship of armed opposition at home, but also to build, as of December 1959, a new reserve force, the Milicias Nacionales Revolucionarias, to help in both those tasks.[3]

It was not long before those jobs were to become linked to others related to the international context of the revolution. Like many other revolutionary governments before and since, Fidel's opted to break out of the increasing isolation that U.S. power was imposing on his country; and he chose to do this through a policy of assisting leftist movements elsewhere—movements that were aiming to replace governments aligned with Washington with ones more open to the survival of the Cuban revolutionary experiment.

This approach, known to some as the "export of revolution" phase in the evolution of Cuban foreign policy, stimulated and supported armed insurrection in several countries of Latin America in the early and mid-1960s, and it grew in scope as the United States succeeded in co-opting all Latin American governments except Mexico into its policy of unseating the Cuban revolution by virtually any means possible. From 1961 to 1967 Havana found itself steadily blocked from participation in inter-American institutions and eventually suspended from almost all of them, as well as its relations with all of Latin America except Mexico broken.[4] Its response—which was never termed "export of revolution" in Cuba, where the policy was seen much more as one of active defense against a determined enemy—meant that the FAR was deeply involved in training and aiding leftist insurrection in much of the region for most or all of this period.[5] Foreign guerrillas, and especially their officers, were a common sight in Cuba, and they established some of the relationships with Cuba that are still very much a part of the links with the island enjoyed by new leftist governments in the region decades later.

The strains of this task were significant at a time when Raúl Castro was also taking in and training tens of thousands of men and women keen to defend the revolution from its enemies within and without the country. The expansion of the reserves would have been a daunting undertaking even if the FAR was not already deeply involved in running the nation and its reforms, building itself up for traditional national defense roles, and training foreign guerrillas. The combination of these jobs was a challenge indeed for a force that some three or four years earlier had numbered perhaps less than three thousand personnel and had never constituted a regular armed force at all.[6]

As if this were not enough, a further massive obstacle turned out to be arming the new FAR, its even newer reserves, and to some extent its allies on the continent. The attitude of the U.S. government ensured that Havana never had a chance of obtaining arms from that country, which had been the traditional source of almost all its armaments since the first formal occupation of the island in the wake of the U.S. intervention in the War of Independence of 1895–98.[7] When Havana sought arms from Belgium and the United Kingdom, countries that had initially favored selling them to Cuba, its efforts were soon frustrated by U.S. calls on its allies to show solidarity with its effort to "contain Cuba."[8]

In this context Cuba turned to the only source of support and weapons available to it, the Warsaw Pact. By late 1960 the first highly secret accords had been signed and the very first weapons received. The military aid came just in time, as barely had the FAR been able to begin training with the equipment than the United States launched Cuban American "exiles" into the April 1961 maelstrom that came to be known as the Bay of Pigs invasion.

Fidel had been proven right in his assessment that the United States would not long stand idly by while the revolution undid the Americans' totally dominant position on the island and brought about what the new government called Cuba's "full independence." Funded, organized, and supported by the CIA, the exile force was sent forward to make a landing and seize a town from which it could then announce the existence of a new Cuban government and call on U.S. assistance to defend itself against the inevitable fidelista counterattack. When the new president of the United States, John F. Kennedy, heard of the plan, he decided to reduce U.S. direct assistance so that the campaign would appear more like an all-Cuban affair. The U.S. government withdrew major elements of U.S. naval and air support from the exiles, although considerable support remained in place.

The result was unqualified disaster as the force proved unable to seize a single hamlet and was soon bested by local militia forces and eventually by regular elements led by Fidel himself. The gamble of preparing for national defense as a priority had paid off, but no one in the FAR or Fidel's entourage believed that this was the end. It was taken as a given that the United States would not accept what Cubans call "imperialism's first defeat in the Americas" and would now turn to more direct military means to unseat the revolution.[9]

The Soviet Connection Deepens

In the months after the spring of 1961 Cuba therefore signed more accords with Moscow to beef up its naval, air, and land forces and began a process of "Sovietization" of the FAR, pursued in earnest in the early 1970s and continuing at least until the 1980s, which left the force unrecognizable as a Latin American military institution. Indeed, the armed forces probably became the most visible sign of the linkages in foreign policy that were to be the hallmark of much of Cuba's presence in the world from the mid-1960s until the 1980s.

This linkage was to be shaken by what Cubans saw as Soviet adventurism during the missile crisis of 1962 and treachery after it, and by the conservatism of that country's leadership later on—during a time when the issue of world revolution was debated. Yet it was to stand the test of time, particularly because Cuba had nowhere to turn in its desperate strategic straits and Moscow could hardly say no to a country whose strategic position so close to the United States gave the Soviets so much nuisance value in Washington.[10] Cuban support for revolution worldwide troubled Moscow—which was nervous about its central relationship with Washington during a period when the "balance of terror" had never been so obvious—just as Soviet timidity about that relationship annoyed Havana, which believed its policies to be much more truly communist than those of the self-satisfied apparatchik in the supposed motherland of world communism.

Be that as it may, the formal linkages between the two countries soon strengthened again and even stood the strains of that litmus test of socialist solidarity, the Soviet invasion of Czechoslovakia in spring 1968. When Cuba proved itself almost alone as a virtually unquestioning ally during this trying time, the USSR knew how to reward such loyalty over the following years—providing sophisticated weaponry on a lavish scale, training massive levels of Cuban airmen, sailors, and soldiers, and offering help in everything from administration to uniforms for its Caribbean military collaborators. The FAR grew again as a central pillar of that political linkage. It was essential for the revolution's survival in the face of a continued U.S. determination to end the anomaly of a socialist state in the Western Hemisphere.

From the late 1960s until the early 1980s the "alliance"—actually a grouping far less formal than that and one where Cuba was never considered seriously for membership in the Warsaw Pact, which would have been a real guarantee of Soviet direct support against U.S. attack—served each partner well; and nowhere was this relationship more important than in the military sphere. After the death of Che Guevara in 1967, Cuba became less engaged in support of leftist movements in Latin America and therefore less troubling for Moscow's relationship with the United States. Equally, Cuba's powerful position in the

Non-Aligned Movement gave Moscow much more leverage in that important body than anything else it had in its quiver of political influence. On a variety of occasions Cuba could act in ways that furthered Soviet goals without involving the USSR directly.

This possibility was most visible in Africa, where in both the Horn and Angola the Cubans were to make their mark in ways that Moscow saw as being largely positive. With Soviet influence waning in much of the third world after the late 1960s and into the early 1970s, anything troubling the Western powers in those areas was likely to be favored by the Soviets. Still, it is important not to make too much of this pattern. Havana was obviously pleased when Moscow saw its activities as helpful, but its decisions were its own and usually only obliquely related to Soviet desires. Even as ferocious a critic of the Castro government as its most senior military defector, Brigadier General Rafael del Pino, admitted that Cuban-Soviet military relations were "indifferent and at times antagonistic. . . . They [the Soviets] do not have the slightest influence on the decisions Cubans make."[11]

In any case, the military connection with the Soviet Union remained key for Cuba's access to the Soviet assistance that to a considerable extent made possible its relatively high standard of living and many of its social programs. It also helped greatly in allowing Cuba to continue to, in the words of Canada's most important Cubanist John Kirk, "consistently punch above its weight in international affairs"; for example, in its support for the Sandinista movement before and after it took power in Nicaragua in 1979.[12]

The Connection Weakens

The context of international relations was, however, steadily evolving. By the late 1970s or early 1980s the balance of terror had achieved a status of mutual assured destruction (MAD, as the strategic jargon of the day termed it), assuring Moscow that its long-awaited goal of having concrete status as a military superpower instead of one merely *par courtoisie* had indeed been achieved; yet, its overall power position relative to the United States had declined.

Soviet assistance, other than in the military field, was less and less sought after by third world countries, which had become increasingly content with their relations with former colonial powers and with the United States itself. The USSR's influence in the Middle East was continually eroding. The breakup of the unity of the communist world in the years after the beginning of the Sino-Soviet schism in 1959, then the disastrous impact of the 1968 Prague Spring, both meant that Moscow was losing ground internationally. Even more important and striking than this political retreat was the Soviet inability to markedly improve its economic production and convert itself into a power in more than merely the military and vaguely ideological sense.

When in the elections of 1980 the Republican candidate for the presidency, Ronald Reagan, campaigned on a platform of "rolling back communism," then won those elections and began to apply policies aiming at just that effect, the long-term impact would be shattering. U.S. defense budgets soon completely outstripped those of the Soviet Union, which tried unsuccessfully in the early 1980s to compete. President Mikhail Gorbachev's policies of glasnost and perestroika were attempts at answering the deepest challenges that the new context presented, but they were clearly, as history was soon to prove, too little and too late. While virtually no one saw Soviet collapse as being around the corner, it was soon clear that Moscow would do almost anything to reduce tensions with the United States at a time of deep and sustained crisis at home and in Eastern Europe.[13]

Fidel and Raúl were well aware of the evolving thinking going on in the USSR regarding defense and international commitments. As early as the 1980 U.S. presidential campaign it was clear to the Cuban leadership that the Soviet Union, except briefly in 1962, had never committed formally to a defensive alliance with Cuba in case of a U.S. attack on the island, and that Moscow was less inclined than ever to risk disturbing its central relationship with Washington for peripheral issues such as the Cuban link, however valuable it had been on occasion.

The Cuban single approach of a deterrence posture by now had been in place for twenty years. While accepting that defeating the United States was not a practical option, the Cubans could deter their neighbor by making an invasion so expensive in blood and treasure that for Washington the game would not be worth the candle. Now they had to acknowledge that they would need to maintain such a posture essentially without the Soviet factor coming into play. To do so, Cuba would need a defensive force much greater and more sustainable than in the past.

The then recent Vietnamese experience beckoned to Raúl with special clarity as a campaign based on a huge mobilized reserve force, combined with a regular force that was hard-hitting and mobile, and using the depth of the country as an essential element of the strategy. It would be the Guerra de Todo el Pueblo (War of All the People) that would henceforth deter a U.S. attack. While much of this approach could already be seen in the organization of the first revolutionary militias in 1959, and indeed in the setting up of a universal male compulsory military service system as of 1963, the scale and extent of the new reserves would represent another degree of commitment altogether. The Milicias de Tropas Territoriales (Territorial Troop Militias) were to be combined with other reserve forces to reach the staggering total of some 800,000 personnel, a figure dwarfing the military resources of any other Latin American country, even Brazil, with twenty times, or Mexico, with ten times, Cuba's population.

This approach allowed Cuba to maintain its high-level foreign policy, its commitments abroad, and its prestige at a time of reducing Soviet support and influence. Indeed, in Latin America successive governments abandoned the policy of hostility toward Cuba, and the number of their embassies in Havana steadily increased. And while the shattering defeat inflicted on Cuba in Grenada in 1983 left deep scars on the FAR, Cuba's newfound additional strength helped ensure that the Pentagon, and indeed the White House, were not tempted to attempt a repeat of that invasion in the largest of the Antilles. Indeed, by the end of the 1980s Cuban involvement in southern Africa, and to some extent in Nicaragua, was demonstrating that the island's foreign policy still had kick to it, and that it was the FAR that best represented that kick.

The Special Period

Nothing that Cuba or its armed forces had seen before could have prepared them for what was soon to come. For events in the Soviet Union and Eastern Europe were now to take a turn whose impact on the island is impossible to exaggerate. Fidel may not have seen the change coming in all its force, but as early as the summer of 1989 he said in his major annual 26th of July speech, "We can no longer say with certainty if socialist camp supplies, which arrived with the precision of a clock for thirty years, will continue."[14]

Indeed, within a year Cuba's massively important special conditions as a member of the Council for Mutual Economic Assistance (COMECON) and the international socialist division of labor were a thing of the past, and the island was soon to reel under the impact of an 80 percent drop in its purchasing power abroad and the almost total loss of its Soviet and Eastern European markets and suppliers.[15] Of almost equal importance, Cuba, as a socialist regime, would become nearly an anomaly as communism collapsed in Europe and became an almost irrelevant political force in much of the rest of the world. While China and Vietnam remained as examples of surviving communist regimes, they were far away, almost unknown in the Cuban political context, and themselves rapidly reforming their systems.

The desperate belt-tightening that Cuba underwent during its Special Period in Time of Peace, declared in the summer of 1990, could not help but massively alter the defense program because of the FAR's enormous dependence on the Soviet Union. Given the probability that the United States would now try to close in for the kill given the island's vulnerable condition, Fidel initially said that defense would have to be the one area in which Special Period cuts would not be allowed to apply. But soon he had to give up this line of thought and deal heavy blows to the FAR as well.[16]

Over the next four years Cuba cut the FAR by somewhere between two-thirds and three-quarters of its regular force strength. The FAR saw its defense budget shrink from $1,149 million (unconvertible currency pesos) in 1990 to $651 million in much devalued pesos in 1994; and its fuel consumption (essential for training but especially for a reserves-dependent deterrence policy) dropped by some 70 percent or more.[17] These reductions were body blows, and combined with the other losses—of Soviet support for acquisition of weapons and equipment, provision of spare parts, training, intelligence sharing, interesting postings and exercises, doctrine, and linkages to the world—they left the FAR deeply weakened.

As if all of this were not enough, the FAR was meanwhile given more tasks, not fewer, to complete in the context of the profound national crisis of the Special Period. At a time of such challenges, when most of the Cuban population was yielding to the temptation to engage in illegal activities, the military, consisting of persons of complete and tested loyalty, could be counted on as no one else. When this factor was added to their competence in many other fields, and not just those pertaining to national defense, the value of the institution and many of its individual personnel was great indeed. And never had it been more necessary to show the United States that Cuba could be a useful partner in areas of national security that the U.S. took seriously and with which it needed help abroad, such as countering drugs and illegal immigration.

Thus, the FAR saw additions to its usual responsibilities of providing deterrence to foreign attack, acting against the narcotics trade and illegal immigration, providing natural disaster preparation and relief, and contributing to food production through the activities of the Ejército Juvenil de Trabajo (EJT, the 100,000-person organization founded in 1973 based on the conscription system but using those personnel for essentially agricultural tasks). Now the FAR was also asked to feed itself and help feed the nation, not only through the EJT but also using regular units. It was also asked to provide well-trained administrative and business personnel from within its ranks to staff the key foreign-currency-earning industries of the nation. In addition, deterrence of foreign attack became a much more direct role as the crisis deepened and U.S. policies toward the island evolved, inexorably increasing the threat perception of the country.[18]

Then, too, in the harshest years of the Special Period the nation's food situation entered a critical stage, with widespread disease occurring against a backdrop of Cubans, and especially Cuban children, consuming insufficient and unhealthy calories. The FAR had the central job of addressing these problems.

The government had a desperate need to find industries that could stimulate exports and thus earn hard currency. It needed to manage those domestic industries (such as tourism) that had become increasingly central to any sustained recovery from the crisis, and to stave off collapse of others through improved management techniques. In all of these efforts the FAR became central. It took over both failing industries, such as sugar, and booming ones, such as mining and tourism. It sent officers to Spain and Latin America for training in the hopes of providing them with the technical skills (and loyalty to the system) to manage and expand key industries. It provided the model, techniques, and much of the personnel for expansion throughout the economy of the improved management system that it had been developing since the mid-1980s—a practice termed *perfeccionamiento empresarial*.[19]

With many policymakers in the United States now wanting to finish off Castro, Cuba also found it essential to connect with sectors in the U.S. government that would at least in some sense support the Cuban leader and his administration. These sectors existed already, and were powerful, but they needed Cuban cooperation in order to function. Among them were the armed forces, which had long argued that Cuba was no longer a threat to the United States and which were in constant touch with the FAR through Guantánamo; and the U.S. Coast Guard, which was to develop a good relationship with its Cuban counterpart in anti-narcotics operations and later in campaigns against illegal immigration.

Thus Cuba had elements of the U.S. government—especially in the security field, which could not be accused of being "soft on communism"—arguing in favor of a softer line toward Havana. And Cuba, and particularly the FAR, moved dramatically to reinforce that perception. The FAR provided effective cooperation in drug interdiction in a region where U.S. allies and friends were woefully inefficient in doing so. Cuba's geostrategic position, amidst key air routes from Colombia and northern South America northward, made its cooperation essential to effective interception. The U.S. Coast Guard and Drug Enforcement Agency made no secret of their admiration for the Cuban effort.[20] This was rare indeed in a Latin American and Caribbean context where the United States had precious few defense partners who could be counted upon for real and effective cooperation.

If this was true for anti-narcotics it was also the case for the issue of illegal immigration, which in the United States had become increasingly seen as belonging in the security domain as the 1990s wore on. The "rafter" (*balsero*) crisis of the mid-1990s, when tens of thousands of Cubans fled the economic disaster of the Special Period, obliged the United States to negotiate directly with Cuba to find a solution. In 1994 and 1995 formal accords setting up bilateral cooperation on the issue were signed by the two countries and began to come into play. Interviews with officials from both sides suggest that despite the suspension of regular bilateral talks between Havana and Washington as part of President George W. Bush's increasingly visceral anti-Castro campaign, effective cooperation remained in place and was immensely appreciated by U.S. authorities.

Thus within the U.S. debate on what to do about Cuba, the direct action of the FAR has provided a favorable assessment of the island and its government in two key areas of U.S. defense and security concerns. Hence U.S. agencies with considerable clout in key circles have brought a positive view of the country to the fore. This has not been seriously damaged by the growing defense links between Havana and some ALBA nations, especially Venezuela and to a slight extent Bolivia, Ecuador, and Nicaragua. Indeed, analysts often point to the fact that Cuba has been a moderate member of ALBA on issues that affect defense and has found ways to distance itself from Caracas on many of the more strident policies, or at least the public statements, the late President Hugo Chávez and his successor have put forward on defense matters. And the fact that the close bilateral relationship between the two countries involves only relatively minor defense links helps to make this moderation more clear.

Nevertheless, despite all these advances, the key foreign policy role for the FAR remains that of deterring attack. U.S. military assessments of the FAR emphasize that the Cuban forces have suffered enormously in recent years and that their ability to project power abroad has more or less disappeared. Yet those sources do not follow this assessment with any serious criticism of the FAR's ability to give a good account of itself in the event it were called upon to defend the island against foreign invasion.[21] Indeed, given their favorable impression of the FAR's efforts in fields of strategic importance to the United States, the tendency in the Pentagon has been to suggest the need for actual defense cooperation with the island.[22]

Contributions—Past, Present, and Future

While the Cuban armed forces have always been major partners in furthering the foreign policy of the revolutionary government of the country, that tradition was only confirmed and strengthened—not in any sense abandoned—in the vexing days of the Special Period.

In the half century following the revolution, the comandante en jefe has asked the Cuban military to do all manner of things. The armed forces have farmed, managed ministries and industries, deterred attack and fought wars, trained insurgents and been trained by Soviet specialists, expanded and contracted in size and levels of activity. Throughout, they have always responded in original ways to the demands made on what are, after all, still revolutionary armed forces and servants of a revolutionary political project to which they are themselves intimately tied and to which, as to the nation, they swear allegiance.

More traditional, however, has been their central role in providing a deterrence system protecting the government against foreign attack, a system that has worked and has stood the test of more than fifty years of threat and near-open conflict with their giant neighbor. While the United States was far from consistently keen on invading Cuba, the FAR was successful in ensuring that any debate in Washington about the wisdom of such an adventure, during all those five decades, would take place against a backdrop of widespread knowledge that an invasion of Cuba would neither be easy nor bloodless and most assuredly would not be over quickly. Analysts leave little doubt that this knowledge has been central to the ongoing willingness of the United States to allow the Cuban revolutionary experience, however detested, to continue without further direct and violent military action to unseat it. This result must surely be considered the key positive contribution that the FAR has made to national foreign policy and the survival of both the nation and the revolution.

This finding does not take away from the other contributions in the foreign policy arena that have grown of late and include—through the good work of the FAR, and in fields as diverse as drug interdiction and control of illegal immigration—the building of something akin to a real working relationship with, and favorable opinion within, key U.S. security sectors that see Havana as a worthwhile and credible partner in areas of key and sustained security interest to Washington.

Given the possibility that President Barack Obama may yet see his way clear to open up a significant dialogue with Cuba, these final elements may prove in the future to be as important as the longer-standing ones of the past. Even if Obama falls short of that promise, once the moment does come, the FAR will clearly still be working to create the best possible opportunities for bridges to be built.

Notes

1. See, especially, Raúl Castro's experience in this regard in his "Campaign Diaries," December 1956–February 1957, published jointly with those of Ernesto Guevara, as *La conquista de la esperanza: Diarios de campaña Ernesto Che Guevara y Raúl Castro Ruz 2 de diciembre de 1956–19 de febrero de 1957* (Havana: Casa Editora Abril, 2005).

2. For an early study of this issue see Neill Macaulay, "The Cuban Rebel Army: A Numerical Survey," *Hispanic American Historical Review* 43 (May 1978), 284–95. Cuban historian Marilú Uralde has been engaged in carrying out the first systematic study of this question, and has a book forthcoming.

3. See the early chapters of María del Pilar Díaz Castañón, *Ideología y revolución: Cuba 1959–1962* (Havana: Ciencias Sociales, 2001).

4. For this story, see F. V. García-Amador, *La cuestión cubana en la OEA y la crisis del sistema interamericano* (Miami, FL: University of Miami Press, 1987).

5. This perspective can be found in virtually any Cuban book on the period. An especially interesting one is found in the excellent work of Paul Dosal, *Comandante Che: Guerrilla Soldier, Commander, and Strategist, 1956–1967* (University Park: Pennsylvania State University Press, 2003), 20–22. Dosal shows that even the legendary revolutionary Che thought of the policy as being more of a defensive posture against U.S. invasion than an active exporting of the Cuban model.

6. For this earlier status, see Mayra Aladro Cardoso, Servando Valdés Sánchez, and Luis Rosado Eiró, *La guerra de liberación nacional en Cuba, 1956–1959* (Havana: Casa Editora Abril, 2007), especially 184–89.

7. See Morris Morley, *Imperial State and Revolution: The United States and Cuba, 1952–1986* (Cambridge: Cambridge University Press, 1987); and for the military aspects, the Cuban national chapter in Adrian English, *Armed Forces of Latin America* (London: Jane's, 1984), 195–220.

8. See Hugh Thomas, *Cuba: The Pursuit of Freedom* (London: Eyre and Spottiswoode, 1971), 1237–44.

9. Perhaps the best English-language work on the invasion is Peter Kornbluh, ed., *Bay of Pigs Declassified: The Secret Report of the CIA on the Invasion of Cuba* (New York: New Press, 1998). A Cuban view is given in Tomás Díez Acosta, *Octubre de 1962: a un paso del holocausto* (Havana: Editora Política, 2008), 46–47.

10. For the story of this relationship, see Yuri Pavlov, *The Soviet-Cuban Alliance, 1959–1991* (New Brunswick, N.J.: Transaction, 1993), especially 59–64.

11. Quoted in Jay Mallin, *History of the Cuban Armed Forces: From Colony to Castro* (Reston, VA: Ancient Mariners Press, 2000), 333. See also Raúl Marin, *¿La hora de Cuba?* (Madrid: Editorial Revolución, 1991), 61–62.

12. John Kirk, interview with the author, Halifax, N.S., September 2008.

13. The exception, one author who indeed did see that the USSR's collapse was nigh, was Hélène Carrère d'Encausse in her truly exceptional book *L'Empire éclaté* (Paris: Flammarion, 1979). But even she did not think the end was going to be quite so near or quite so complete.

14. Marin, *¿La hora de Cuba?* 110.

15. See Homero Campo and Orlando Pérez, *Cuba: los años duros* (Mexico City: Plaza y Janés, 1997), 41–45.

16. Fidel had originally said, "The fortifying of defense is among the priority programs of the Special Period and it is one of those sacrifices that we will inexorably have to make." Fidel Castro, *Un grano de maíz: conversación con Tomás Borge* (Havana: Publicaciones del Consejo de Estado, 1992), 148.

17. For the extraordinary drop in the defense budget, which says much about a government

fighting for its life, see the annual issues of *Anuario Estadístico de Cuba,* Oficina Nacional de Estadística, 1990 to 1996; and for Cuban budgetary figures in general, see Omar Everleny Pérez Villanueva, "La administración del presupuesto del estado cubano: una valoración," in O. E. Pérez Villanueva, *La economía cubana en 2001* (Havana: Centro de Estudios de la Economía Cubana, 2002), 19–40.

18. In 1992 the U.S. Congress passed the Torricelli Act, which greatly tightened the blockade/embargo, and four years later passed the Helms-Burton Act, which codified the whole series of measures constituting that stance and made destruction of the Castro government U.S. law rather than just policy. For a Cuban view, see Carlos Batista Odio, "Bloqueo, no embargo," in Carlos Batista Odio et al., eds., *El Conflicto Cuba–Estados Unidos* (Havana: Editorial Félix Varela, 1998), 38–48. For an international view, see Joaquín Roy, *Cuba, the United States, and the Helms-Burton Doctrine: International Reactions* (Gainesville: University of Florida Press, 2000).

19. See the different aspects of this approach in Mercedes Sánchez et al., *Gerencia: del propósito a la acción* (Havana: Editorial Arte y Literatura, 1999).

20. Nor did the British, who began a major program of cooperation with Cuba in the anti-narcotics field. Cuba became something of a model of cooperation in this regard, and further programs were set up with the French while bilateral agreements were signed and implemented with a host of countries, especially in the Caribbean. For this extraordinary story, see Francisco Arias Fernández, *Cuba contra el narcotráfico: de víctimas a centinelas* (Havana: Editora Política, 2001). For positive U.S. reactions, see my own elaboration of this issue in Hal Klepak, *Cuba's Military 1990–2005: Revolutionary Soldiers in Counter-Revolutionary Times* (New York: Palgrave/Macmillan, 2005), especially 127–31; and officially in no less a source than *U.S. State Department Narcotics Control Strategy Report, 2005* (Washington, D.C.: GPO, 2005). To put this response in context, in the 1980s Cuba was seen as a source of the problem rather than part of the solution; see Armando Ferrer Castro, *Conexión en Cuba* (Mexico City: Planeta, 1990).

21. See, for example, Christopher Marquis, "Report Downplaying Cuban Threat Back for Review," *Miami Herald,* March 31, 1998.

22. Christopher Marquis, "Pentagon Wants U.S. Military to Work with Cuba," *Miami Herald,* February 21, 1998.

3

Cuba's Monumental Children

Operation Peter Pan and the Intimacies of Foreign Policy

KAREN DUBINSKY

As common sense tells us, and political scientists are beginning to analyze, the alleged separation of children from political citizenship is one of the mainstays of our world. "The concept of the 'political,'" writes Helen Brocklehurst, "is formulated . . . as if separate from children. The contribution children may make to a community is often not recognized as political until it is invited to be so by adults."[1]

Anyone who believes that children are not political subjects has not been paying much attention to Cuba. The politics of children are inscribed in the iconography and geography of Havana, to take one example. A stroll along the city's seafront Malecón takes one past the U.S. Special Interests Section and, strategically located next to it, the "Anti-Imperialist Tribunal." This large open-air plaza was built during the Elián González crisis and was a perfect site for staging the many Cuban rallies and speeches demanding young Elián's return from his extended family in Miami to his father in Cuba. At one end of the plaza stands a statue of Cuban nationalist hero José Martí, who holds a child protectively in one hand and points an angry, accusing finger toward the United States with the other. Post-González this plaza still comes in handy. It is used for a variety of political and cultural events, so much so that it is now known, irreverently, as the *protestódromo*. There are plenty of reasons to point accusing fingers at the United States. Why, after years of political conflicts between Washington and Havana, did the custody battle over a single child occasion the construction of this permanent tribute? What makes this incident—of all those before and since—monumental?

Elián González's ill-fated journey across the Florida Straits in 1999, and the subsequent intra-familial and international debate about where he ought to grow up, represent an especially prominent instance of how children can act as lightning rods for—and thus bear the burden of—adult political conflicts. In this case, the fate of an actual child became a compelling metaphor for a fractured nation. But there is a world of symbolic children; González is just one example of how children are inseparably attached to politics. In this sense González belongs among the pantheon of children the world over who have become (mute) global icons of adult political dilemmas: the child soldier, the child laborer, the child sex worker, or the child in need in war- or disaster-ravaged countries.

Such children do not simply absorb or experience adult-initiated political issues; they also sustain them. Several centuries of history have created the figure of the child as a near-hegemonic signifier of innocence. Because we equate children solely with emotion or affect, when children symbolize a story, an ideology, a social movement, or a war, the conceit actually explains very little. But at the same time children as symbols can move emotional and psychic mountains. Elián's precursors, rather than his legacy, are my focus here. The key to understanding the commotion caused by *one* migrant Cuban child lies in the backstory—the tale of the 14,000 who went before him.[2]

This chapter takes its cue from scholars such as Ann Stoler, who have insisted that the "emotional economy" of parenting, domestic arrangements, and sexuality help to maintain political and economic authority the world over.[3] "Most formal analyses of international politics," declares political scientist Cynthia Enloe, "underestimate the varieties of power it takes to form and sustain any given set of relationships between states."[4] This chapter argues that fifty years of child migration conflicts have, just like missile crises, bombings, and assassination plots, nurtured profound animosities between Cuba and the United States.

The Creation of Cold War Orphans—The View from Cuba

Between January 1961 and October 1962, more than 14,000 Cuban children under the age of sixteen, unaccompanied by their parents, departed Cuba for Miami. "Operation Peter Pan," as the press dubbed it, was a clandestine scheme organized by the Catholic Church in Miami and Havana, working in conjunction with the CIA and anti-Castro forces in Cuba. Parents were motivated to send their children out of Cuba for several reasons. Among them were rumors (organized by the revolution's opponents) that the new government was planning on nationalizing children and sending them to the Soviet Union for indoctrination or worse. (In an extreme variant of the rumor, people were led to believe that their children would be sent to the Soviet Union and returned as tinned meat to Cuba.) The children who left Cuba were housed in camps and shelters in Miami, while their parents on the island awaited Castro's imminent demise. As U.S.-Cuban relations deteriorated, and parents were unable to rejoin their children, many youngsters—about half, or 7,000—found their way into long-term foster care or orphanages throughout the United States. In a story replete with ironies, one in particular remains glaring: parental custody rights were indeed abrogated, but not by the Cubans. As one former Peter Pan child puts it, "We ended up in camps after all. We were saved from Prague but were sent instead to naval bases in Opa-Locka, orphanages in Toledo, camps in Jacksonville."[5]

Operation Peter Pan still creates tremendous disagreements, with the lines drawn even in the terminology used. Counterintuitively, perhaps, in Cuba the affair is known by its English name, *Peter* Pan, a nickname given by a Miami newspaperman. In Miami it is now more commonly known by its Spanish name, *Pedro*. The significance of the two variations became clear to me during my research time in Miami. I learned the story first in Cuba under the name of "Peter" (and I continue to use that name), but in Miami I often found myself being corrected. I had the impression that my use of "Peter" was, at best, impolite. The puzzle lies in the politics: *Peter* implies English-speaking, American-government, CIA manipulation; *Pedro* connotes Spanish-speaking, Cuban parents making their own immigration decisions about what, and where, was best for their children. Is the context for this story the history of CIA-sponsored "dirty tricks" against Cuba? Or does it lie in the history of immigration? Can it be both?

The Cuban government's response to the escalating series of baby-snatching rumors in the early 1960s set a tone that lasted a number of years. An inventive balance was struck, in which both the perpetrators and the intended targets of the rumors were mocked. Responding to the rumor that children, like oil refineries and sugar mills, were about to be nationalized, the revolutionary government declared that this was "obviously too stupid for anyone with common sense."[6] Fidel Castro, with characteristic subtlety, laid the blame on both his opponents and those who listened to the rumors. "Those imbeciles," he said, invented this story to "trick the irrational people, because rational people would not allow themselves to be tricked." Furthermore, he had a firm understanding of who the real target was: "It is truly cruel," he said, "that they make a group of mothers the victims of their shameless actions, that a group of mothers has to suffer this fear."[7]

Symbolic babies are not the province of any particular political ideology. Yet socialist tenets about women's equality and children's political autonomy—even when they are more theoretical than practical—have historically drawn fire from critics.[8] International outcries about communist baby-snatchers followed child relocation schemes by leftist forces during the Spanish Civil War in 1937 and again during the Greek Civil War in 1948, and the Soviet Union itself had a long and well-known history of pushing the limits of Western notions of childhood.[9] The Cuban government was well aware of this complicated history. "This is not the first socialist revolution in the world," Castro stated in 1961, and "in no socialist country has there been made a law of parental authority which separates children from their parents." Revolutionary publications dutifully reproduced the legal codes of the Soviet Union and Czechoslovakia, in an effort to calm baby-snatching rumors.[10]

Thus, those who believed the rumors were constantly reproached, and that was especially true of Peter Pan parents. Those parents—at least the ones who were later able to rejoin their children in the United States—were portrayed in the familiar terms of all who departed from Cuba in those years. "Imagine," said Castro in 1971, speaking of the Peter Pan parents, "all those undisciplined, anarchic worms, without a homeland, without principles, without anything."[11] Whether those parents were bamboozled by imperialist treachery or seduced by visions of shopping malls, we end up in the same place: Peter Pan parents—always represented as mothers—were weak-minded women whose immigration decisions had disastrous effects on their families and their nation—particularly so when the fate of the children themselves was pondered. Peter Pan children always filled stereotypical roles in the Cuban imagination about life in the United States. "What happened to these children?" Castro asked rhetorically in 1971. "They were led into vices . . . transformed into gangsters, put into prostitution."[12]

The history of U.S. attempts to thwart Cuba's revolutionary government, by overt and covert means, is well known; but because of the centrality of children to the revolutionary enterprise, Operation Peter Pan occupies a particular place in this history. It would be impossible to overstate the symbolic importance attached to early revolutionary reforms of the education system, the literacy campaign, and the creation of a public system of child welfare, including day care, inside Cuba.[13] Healthy, educated, serious-minded children leap off the pages of early revolutionary publications, reinforcing one central message: children were essential to the revolution, and vice versa. In this climate, there was simply no sympathy for those parents who believed that the line between "taking care of" and "taking" was about to be breached.

Escape, Rescue, and Salvation: Peter Pan Flies to America

Cold War escape narratives were a popular feature in North American magazines of the 1940s and 1950s. Tales of escape from behind the Iron Curtain to freedom in North America usually revolved around family unification, revealing how the Cold War touched insecurities from the abstract to the intimate.

Political demonology is a complicated process, and during the Cold War enemies were created at levels simultaneously global and familial.[14] On the U.S. side of the divide, the Peter Pan story became a remarkably popular and powerful example of the escape narrative genre, particularly because *children* were added to this drama.

Invoking the language of the space race, the Miami Catholic clergy involved in the relocation and resettlement of Cuban refugee children referred to their project as "a race between the two great powers of the world for the minds of children."[15] By insisting that child saving was just as important as rocket counting, the rescuers assumed for their project, and themselves, world historic importance. The most prominent rescuer, Irish-born Father Bryan Walsh, who became the public face of Operation Peter Pan, was the director of Miami's Catholic Welfare Bureau, a social service agency of the Catholic Diocese of Miami. The agency was licensed by the state of Florida for child welfare programs. In October 1960 Walsh and his small staff were contemplating how they were going to continue their work in the face of a looming 30 percent budget cut. Some two months later he found himself at the Miami Airport waiting for the first planeload of Cuban children to arrive, having just received $1 million authorized by President Dwight D. Eisenhower for their assistance. As he recalled, "No longer were we simply a social agency concerned about a community problem. We were now sharing the worries of families we did not even know, hundreds of miles away in a life and death struggle in the Cold War."[16] Given the extraordinary powers wielded by Walsh in this tale, he could be forgiven a bit of hubris. During the twenty-three months of Operation Peter Pan's existence, the Catholic Welfare Bureau's staff increased from fifteen to more than three hundred, and Walsh oversaw a budget of several million dollars provided by the U.S. government for the care of Cuban children. More remarkably, Walsh himself acquired the power to direct immigration policy, for he was given authority to grant visa waivers to any Cuban child under the age of sixteen. As political scientist María de los Angeles Torres puts it, with considerable understatement, this program created "historically unprecedented relationships" between the U.S. government and private and religious refugee relief organizations.[17]

Operation Peter Pan, and the visa waiver program for minors, remained officially classified, but several decades later a lawsuit brought by Torres to open U.S. government archives pried loose a tiny portion of the information about it. U.S. government officials and Catholic Welfare Bureau staff worked very hard to keep this a clandestine operation, for in their view, as the director of the Federal Children's Bureau explained, publicity "would inhibit the possibility of other Cuban children coming to this country" and might also "endanger families and relatives."[18] Secrecy is central to the escape narrative, and in this case it reinforced two key themes—Cuban children were in imminent danger, and the U.S. population as a whole had a role to play in helping them.

Even when the story broke in March 1962, secrecy remained, paradoxically, an integral feature of the narrative. Heightening the drama, the Miami Diocese sent out an official photo of Walsh with a group of Peter Pan children who were photographed from behind, their faces obscured from the camera. The diocese requested that other news media follow suit, and so, through the spring of 1962, daily newspapers and Catholic weeklies across the United States featured sentimental stories about how their communities had participated in the rescue of Cuban children from communism, complete with photos of children with black bars printed over their eyes. This ongoing discourse of secrecy mixed culturally shared assumptions about the special vulnerability of children with garden-variety Cold War paranoia. It was a potent mix.

This first flurry of U.S. media interest helped to establish a lasting framework for the story, featuring three essential components: escape, rescue, and salvation. Headlines such as "Displaced Tots Know Horror of Red Cuba" took commonsense Cold War anticommunism and wrapped it around the innocent, malleable child.[19] To those across the narrow Florida Straits, the range of dangers facing children in Cuba after the revolution was staggering. Reporting on the rumors that Castro was about to revoke parental custody (*patria potestad*) and send all Cuban children to full-time day-care centers, *Time* magazine claimed that trucks were sweeping through the country picking up unaccompanied children. To those who found this surprising, *Time* reminded its readers, "As Lenin himself said, revolution is impossible as long as the family exists."[20]

Another set of rumors concerned the changes that the revolutionary government was making to the education system. One such change was the literacy campaign of 1961, during which all schools were temporarily closed and thousands of young urban volunteers were encouraged to move to the countryside to teach literacy. The campaign "caught the attention of the world," historian Richard Gott observed. Hugh Thomas declared it the "last fling of the romantic side of the revolution."[21] The Cuban visual record of the literacy campaign—preserved in such films as *La brigadista* and *Batalla por un idea*, and in a remarkable small museum in Havana—is one of wildly enthusiastic youth, many of them female, many of them black, cheering their role in eradicating illiteracy. To some parents, however, the prospect of sending their middle-class teenagers to the countryside, long imagined as primitive and unsanitary, where they might encounter promiscuous mingling between the sexes (and even the races) was yet another example of the threat posed by the new social order. "The literacy campaign," writes Roman de la Campa, "exposed Havana's white children to the rest of Cuba." Former Peter Pan child Ileana Fuentes speculates that this issue was at the heart of her parents' decision to send her away. "Perhaps," she considers in retrospect, "it wasn't so much about political oppression as it was about premature personal freedom."[22]

Even worse were the changes that the revolutionary government instituted to right the lopsided balance between the private and public education systems. The complex history of education in Cuba, the overwhelming inequalities between the private religious system and the public system, and internal rifts between church and state and among classes, races, and regions were flattened into one seemingly inescapable fact: Castro was attempting to "capture the minds" of Cuban children, forcing them to learn communism "from Kindergarten up." With no hint of irony, Father Walsh himself described Cuba's private Catholic schools as "the last refuge from indoctrination" constantly threatened by the revolutionary government.[23] Cartoons circulating in the U.S. media depicting, for example, a wild-eyed Castro reading Marx to a group of schoolchildren, who themselves are frantically trying to swim away from Cuba, helped to foster this one-dimensional understanding. "They were teaching us Marxism in school," remembers Eduardo Machado, who has written a play about his Peter Pan experience. "But my parents treated it like they were gassing us."[24]

To understand fully the perceptions of the menace of the Cuban revolution for young people, we have to remember that Americans have long had trouble granting Cubans—of any age—adult political subjectivity. The clearest answer to the question that everyone asks now about Peter Pan—Why did their parents let them go?—can be found in this attitude. Most onlookers at the time thought that the U.S. government would do what it had done in Cuba throughout the twentieth century: get rid of a regime that it didn't like. The revolution simply reinforced Washington's habit of representing Cubans, as historian Louis Pérez Jr. describes it, "as children incapable of understanding their best interests." The image of third world leaders as volatile children was a constant motif for the Eisenhower administration during a period when a world of infantilized (sometimes feminized) decolonizing nations appeared vulnerable to subversive influences.[25]

Perhaps the same attitude also helped Americans to understand—especially in light of the constant litany of horror stories—why the revolution attracted tremendous support from youth at home and abroad. The virile young men who took the reins of power in Cuba in 1959 were entering what Gott called a "geriatric" world stage: Eisenhower, Charles de Gaulle, Harold Macmillan, Nikita Khrushchev, and Mao Zedong had all been in power for years, and all of them had been born in the nineteenth century. "Everywhere," wrote an enthusiastic Elizabeth Sutherland after visiting Cuba in 1969, "Youth seems to be on the move.... Nobody is too young to be mobilized for anything." A generation of New Leftists in Europe and North America saw in the Cuban revolution an inspiring illustration of youth culture in action.[26] Growing up outside of all of this ferment, some Peter Pan children had the sense that they missed a lot. Reflecting on her parents' decision decades later, one Peter Pan adult said sadly, "They sent us away from Cuba so that we would continue to be like them."[27]

From the moment the story went public when U.S. Welfare Secretary Abraham Ribicoff issued what was termed "a national plea to American families to shelter the youngsters," Operation Peter Pan invited widespread U.S. participation.[28] One Christian publication put its pitch for foster parents in the familiar folk-language metaphor of the "Good Neighbor Policy," a name applied to Franklin D. Roosevelt's policy toward Latin America: "Many U.S. citizens traveling through Latin America have received the gracious Spanish welcome '*Esta usted en su casa*.' Now several hundred American families can return the hospitality each month, saying to Cuban children bereft of parents, 'Make yourself at home!' ... We can think of fewer better ways to 'fight communism' than to care for the children who flee from it."[29]

Americans had previously been encouraged to rescue Korean and Chinese children through donations and adoption, thus personalizing U.S.-Asian relations in terms of familial love and elevating adoption as an effective means of fighting the Cold War. After Ribicoff's appeal hundreds of families came forward to help wage what some called "a personal, everyday fight against communism."[30]

Peter Pan children came with a few liabilities. They were not cuddly babies, nor were they adoptable. The majority of them were older boys, never highly sought after in the North American adoption and foster-care system. Yet to many foster parents, the rewards for sheltering these "little refugees from atheistic communism" were great. As one Illinois foster mother explained, "Having Daniel in our home helps our own children realize how fortunate they are to be able to go to a Catholic school and the blessing it is to live in freedom." Another agreed: "Raimundo and Raul cause us to realize our own freedoms better now." A few foster parents saw in their Cuban guests an opportunity for cultural exchange. While the Miami Diocese made Spanish-speaking foster parents a priority, supply quickly swamped demand, particularly outside of Miami. One Illinois couple prepared for their foster child by taking Spanish lessons and noted that their children too enjoyed learning from their Cuban visitor. They joked, "The baby likes Lourdes so much that we thought she was going to learn to speak in Spanish." The foster parents of (future) Florida construction magnate Armando Codina enjoyed the lesson in Cuban cuisine that their young charge provided; after a while, they said, "we really got to like black beans."[31]

Far more common were stories of triumphant transitions to American culture and values. "If Cuban parents inside the tragic island are worried about their sons who came alone to America," wrote a Miami journalist, "they should have a look at the boys kneeling in the chapel or snitching sweet rolls from the dining room. On the basketball court, they looked and acted like American teenagers." The writer made that picture much more poignant by pointing out, "These same arms could be carrying rifles in Cuba, and these legs would not know basketball courts."[32]

Outside Florida, Latin American immigrants were rare, and Peter Pan children were not only a curiosity but also a heartwarming symbol of American generosity. Photo spreads from Birmingham, Alabama; Denver, Colorado; and Oswego, New York portrayed Cuban children as being "enthralled" with their first snowfall, enjoying "exotic" American foods like peanut butter, and defiantly learning to play Monopoly, "a game of rampant capitalism." One evocative photo, captioned "God has not moved," depicted a girl at her orphanage bedside, praying. Scenes like this, wrote a Virginia Catholic newspaper, "filled the patriotic American with justifiable pride."[33]

From this morass of self-congratulation emerged a chilling example of how Peter Pan children reflected glory back upon their U.S. rescuers. In a widely circulated Associated Press story Jean Wilson, a veteran Miami journalist, wrote that the children "arrived heartbroken, but hopeful that a life in freedom will make up for a life without parents."[34]

Peter Pan Grows Up

Unlike their namesake, these children did grow up. Beginning in the 1970s Peter Pan children moved beyond mute icons to develop and speak in their own voices. Their symbolic meaning continued, even intensified, but their actual experiences remain open to question. To date the only empirical study of the experiences of Peter Pan children in the United States, by journalist Yvonne Conde, is based on survey responses from a small group (442, about 3 percent of the official figure of 14,048 child refugees), all drawn from the (then) thousand-name mailing list of a Peter Pan adult group active in South Florida. Another Peter Pan chronicler, Victor Triay, based his tale of Peter Pan veterans on oral histories of a tiny (though moving) sample.³⁵ When the "children" began, about a decade later, to narrate their own lives, a remarkable range of stories emerged.

Is Peter Pan a Marxist?

Despite their early symbolic value as miniature anticommunists, some Peter Pan children took their assimilation into American culture seriously and, like many of their generation in the late 1960s and 1970s, became radicals. When they finally addressed their pasts in their own voices, *recuerdos agridulces* (bittersweet memories) came flooding forth.

A 1978 collective memoir, *Contra viento y marea* (Against wind and tide), speaks of the excitement of departure, mixed with vivid, sad memories of goodbyes at the airport. Most of the children believed their stay in the United States would be short, and many were excited that they had the opportunity to study in the North, which had been a sign of status in Cuba for many generations. Almost all of them believed that their parents had been frightened by the patria potestad rumor into sending them away. Like immigrants the world over, they explained their subsequent radicalization in terms of the gap between what they had been promised and what they encountered.

Life in the Florida transit camps—which for some children lasted years—evoked terrible memories. "We weren't allowed to complain," recalled one woman, "because after all they had saved us from Communism."³⁶ A few remembered excursions to local American Legions, where they were expected to narrate their story as anticommunist parable.

Despite all of this, at least some of them began to think more independently as they approached adulthood. By the early 1970s Young Cuban Socialist Groups began appearing on Florida university campuses, and many of the refugees joined with other Latinos in the cause of civil rights, Puerto Rican independence, and anti-imperialism. Taking their symbolic currency into their hands, Peter Pan radicals appeared in demonstrations marching under banners that read "No Todos Los Cubanos Son Gusanos."³⁷ Even more remarkably, a group of them, dubbed the Antonio Maceo Brigade, returned to Cuba in 1978. A Cuban-made documentary, *55 hermanos* (55 brothers), told their story to a mass audience in Cuba as a tale of prodigal children returning to correct the errors of their parents. That was the first time, as film scholar Marta Díaz notes, that pejoratives were *not* used in official discourse to describe Cuban immigrants. Instead, as victims of their parents (and obviously enthusiastic supporters of the revolution), they were embraced. A year later a Miami-based anti-Castro group assassinated travel agent Carlos

Muñiz Varela, a Maceo Brigade member and organizer of several such trips for returning Cuban exiles.[38]

Is Peter Pan a Republican?

By far the loudest and most public voice belonged to those Peter Pan children who told their stories as one of success, pure and simple. The success narrative positions Peter Pan children as the ultimate rags-to-riches immigrants: from child refugee to secure, well-off American in little more than a decade. The achievements of these children reflect the wisdom, indeed heroism, of those who organized the operation, and thus another part of this story is the elevation of its protagonists, especially Father Walsh, to the status of saint. According to this perspective, Operation Peter Pan was simply the right thing to do. To hold this narrative thread together, the handprints of the CIA are erased. Rather than a Cold War plot, Peter Pan is remembered as a moving tale of humanitarian child rescue.

Cynical observers might be forgiven for thinking that the success narrative was predetermined—that just as the Cubans believe all Peter Pan children grew up to become prostitutes and drug addicts, Americans have been encouraged to believe the children all became construction magnates and real estate agents. The list of professionally and economically successful Peter Pan alumni and alumnae is well known in South Florida. Among them are Codina, singers Willy Chirino and Lysette Alvarez, and numerous Miami politicians. In the 1990s Peter Pan grown-ups could brag that they were running Miami, but a decade later their political influence extended much farther as George W. Bush appointed two high-profile Peter Pan alumni, Eduardo Aguirre and Mel Martínez, to political posts in Washington. Martínez, probably the most famous Peter Pan alumnus outside Florida, was elected to the U.S. Senate in 2004, the first Cuban American to hold this position. His Peter Pan credentials became strong assets during his campaign as what he referred to as "my incredible life story" became part of virtually every speech he made. By highlighting his own dramatic escape from communism—claiming, for example, that as a child he hid from photographers when they visited his Florida boys' camp, fearing for his parents' safety in Cuba—he effectively (if inaccurately) used his childhood to bridge the Cold War and the War on Terror.[39]

The real hero of this story remains Father Bryan Walsh. Endlessly described in the media in sentimental, familial terms, Walsh clearly inspired affection from a great many of his 14,000 "children." His death in December 2001 was the occasion for massive tributes from civic, political, and religious leaders in South Florida, as well as from hundreds of Peter Pan alumni (one of whom placed his visa waiver in Walsh's casket during the father's funeral).[40]

Walsh had provided the main focus for the ongoing memorialization of Peter Pan in the United States for several decades. The practice began in 1978, when five hundred Peter Pan alumni and alumnae honored Walsh at a dinner at a Miami hotel. Banquets like that one were held occasionally through the 1980s, and annually in the 1990s. The success narrative was confirmed at such events through their exclusive location: hotel banquet rooms, with plenty of photos of wealthy revelers in Miami newspapers the next day. These events allowed for the continued circulation of the Peter Pan story through the 1980s and 1990s, when it might have otherwise disappeared from public view. Peter Pan events were also always tied to fund-raising efforts for children's charities, casting the operation in the warm glow of child rescue.

All historical memory is selective, but in this case it is staggeringly so. The public cracks in the rescue narrative—and there have been a few—disappear quickly. In 1990, for example, when Cuban dissident Ramón Grau admitted to a Miami journalist that the U.S. government had indeed manufactured and spread false rumors concerning patria potestad, the *Miami Herald* called Operation Peter Pan "a massive form of child abuse perpetrated by the U.S. government" and insisted "it's time to stop idealizing this horrible chapter of Cuban American history." A flurry of letters from grateful Peter Pan alumni refuted this charge, as did others when María Torres launched her well-publicized lawsuit against the CIA to try to force open the agency's archives. "The CIA's role, no matter how crafty or embarrassing," one letter writer said, "will have sowed a noble and justified undertaking."[41]

The painful, personal dimensions of this Cold War battle also complicate its place in historical memory. To acknowledge the role of the U.S. government in creating a climate of fear in 1960s Cuba is, in a sense, to erase Peter Pan parents or, perhaps worse, to render them in the same terms as they were portrayed in Castro's early speeches on the topic—as stooges who permitted themselves to be hoodwinked by the Yanquis. When some middle-aged Peter Pan adults opted for denial, refusing to consider that the CIA or the Cold War had any bearing on their parents' decisions to send them away, the statements register on two levels: the intimate familial and the abstract ideological. These were their (by now aging) own parents that they were talking about.

Peter Pan Returns: Elián González

The intrusive public discussion of familial intimacies that accompanied the Elián González saga helped to create a new idiom for speaking of both the past and the present. While scholars termed the González story a "magnifying glass" for immigration tensions in Miami, a host of commentators have seen in it a potent symbol for Cuban-U.S. foreign relations, the U.S. economic embargo, immigration policy, religion, and the self-presentation of Miami's Cuban American community, to name several examples.[42]

Still, on this rare occasion when a child entered the lexicon of international politics, few analysts have focused on Elián as a *child*. The story caught fire on both sides of the divide because of how it symbolized, in the body of one photogenic boy, the tensions, fractures, and separations experienced by Cuban children over decades of U.S.-Cuban hostilities. Operation Peter Pan was clearly part of this history, but so too are the countless stories of Cuban families separated by immigration. The continuing Elián González saga did more than bring the Peter Pan story back into the limelight; it also added a new layer of meaning to the place of children in U.S. and Cuban historical memory. "I was an Elián of the 1960s" was how one Peter Pan alumna described herself, as many related their stories—almost always remembering the painful dimensions—and weighed in on the proper fate of González.[43]

Peter Pan alumni and alumnae did not speak with one voice about González. Some supported his return and, as is perhaps fitting for those now in middle age, found the language of therapy, forgiveness, and familial reconciliation more compelling than the Manichean discourse of the Cold War. Elly Chovel, a leading voice for the adult Peter Pan community in Miami, decided after meeting with Elián in Miami that the boy would be better off with his father in Cuba. For her, as for many Peter Pan grown-ups, the story raised painful memories; after her meeting with Elián she was shocked to find that "nothing had changed." Even Father Walsh refused to jump on the Elián bandwagon; he declined to reveal his views on the subject other than to note his alarm at the evidence of what he termed "an emotionally disturbed child" in Miami. Speaking of the attempts of Peter Pan adults to understand their peculiar and painful childhoods, Flora González emphasizes the difficulties of analyzing individual traumas in a climate of ongoing political tensions.[44] Indeed, not many of us have two governments' foreign policies deeply invested in our childhood memories.

Elián González's story was popular because, despite its particular—and profound—tragedies, it reflected widespread social experiences. This vast public conversation authorized a popular rethinking of immigration conflicts in Cuba, especially those involving children. In the González era, migration issues—always sensitive in Cuba—emerged with a vengeance in cinema, painting, fiction, and theater. For example, Humberto Solás's film *Miel para Oshún* (2000) follows an adult child exile on his return through Cuba during the González saga. The parallels between the adult child émigré and González are established as the protagonist, Roberto, looks out his window in the Hotel Nacional on the crowd gathered in the Anti-Imperialist Tribunal outside the U.S. Special Interests Section. In the background we hear the voice of Juan Miguel González demanding his son's return. Roberto's quest is for his lost childhood as well as for his mother, who is portrayed sympathetically (if one-dimensionally) as a woman mad with grief when her son left. Juan Carlos Cremata Malberti's *Viva Cuba* (2005) is the first Cuban film that tries to narrate child migration conflicts from the point of view of a child rather than that of a retrospective adult. Focusing on the impending separation of two best friends, Jorgito and Malu, as Malu's mother has decided to leave, *Viva Cuba* is a unique attempt to imagine immigration conflicts not over the bodies of, but rather through the eyes of, children.

Peter Pan also returned in music. In one of his epic historical poems, *Jalisco Park*, the popular Cuban singer-songwriter Carlos Varela uses the imagery of an empty playground to lament the loss of childhood playmates, vanished thanks to the "calumny of Patria Potestad."

The Politics of Symbolic Children

María Torres argues that Peter Pan "manipulated" children's needs to suit competing political ideologies. "The exodus," she argues, "was not a contest over protecting children, but, rather, about competing state building projects."[45] Here I have emphasized the centrality of children *to* state-building projects. In this history Cuban children were indeed manipulated; so too were their parents and their country. But children specifically were canonized, rendered mute symbols of an extraordinarily stark conflict between nations. Foreign encounters always shape domestic identities, and U.S-Cuban conflicts have produced especially durable national self-perceptions. What could be more suited to the benevolent supremacy of Cold War America than the story of thousands of its citizens providing refuge for young victims of communism? What could provide a better anti-imperialist inspiration in Cuba than the revelation that, along with profits, resources, and the national treasury, the children too had been stolen?

The painful intimacies of these stories—Cold War dramas played out in thousands of Peter Pan families—have helped to create, and re-create, the cultural climate in which bilateral relations between the United States and Cuba have taken place over the last fifty years. When we follow the advice of political scientists such as Cynthia Enloe and widen our perspective on how nations relate to each other, we can see that the playing field of foreign policy is vast. Its protagonists might be midwestern American families impelled to fight the Cold War by "rescuing" a child, or Cuban children who suddenly found themselves almost as important as missiles in one of the great conflicts of the twentieth century. And further, we can see that the corrosive consequences of international conflicts can endure, almost endlessly.

Notes

1. Helen Brocklehurst, *Who's Afraid of Children? Children, Conflict, and International Relations* (Aldergate, UK: Ashgate, 2006), 16.

2. Many of the themes of this chapter are further elaborated in Karen Dubinsky, *Babies Without Borders: Adoption and Migration across the Americas* (Toronto: University of Toronto Press; New York: New York University Press, 2010).

3. Ann Stoler, "Intimidations of Empire: Predicaments of the Tactile and Unseen," in Ann Stoler, ed., *Haunted by Empire: Geographies of Intimacy in North American History* (Durham, NC: Duke University Press, 2006), 14.

4. Cynthia Enloe, "Margins, Silences and Bottom Rungs: How to Overcome the Underestimation of Power in the Study of International Relations," in *The Curious Feminist: Searching for Women in a New Age of Empire* (Berkley: University of California Press, 2004), 6.

5. Roman de la Campa, *Cuba on My Mind: Journeys to a Severed Nation* (London: Verso, 2000), 41. The most thorough account of Operation Peter Pan remains María de los Angeles Torres, *The Lost Apple: Operation Pedro Pan, Cuban Children in the U.S. and the Promise of a Better Future* (Boston: Beacon Press, 2003).

6. *El Mundo*, December 1, 1960, cited in Torres, *Lost Apple*, 90.

7. "Si de alguien se ha ocupado La Revolución ha sido de los niños," *Bohemia*, September 24, 1961; "La patria potestad," *Verde Olivo*, October 1961.

8. See, for example, Paul C. Mishler, *Raising Reds: The Young Pioneers, Radical Summer Camps, and Communist Political Culture in the United States* (New York: Columbia University Press, 1999), 16.

9. Dorothy Legarreta, *The Guernica Generation: Basque Refugee Children of the Spanish Civil War* (Reno: University of Nevada Press, 1984); Loring M. Danforth, "'We Crossed a Lot of Borders': Refugee Children of the Greek Civil War," *Diaspora* 12, no. 2 (2003), 169–209; Lisa Kirschenbaum, *Small Comrades: Revolutionizing Childhood in Soviet Russia, 1917–1932* (New York: Routledge, 2000).

10. "La patria potestad," *Verde Olivo*, October 1961.

11. Fidel Castro, "Fifth Anniversary of CDR," Havana, 1965; "CDR Main Event," Havana, 1971, speeches by Fidel Castro on the Latin American Network Information Center website: lanic.utexas.edu/la/cb/cuba/castro.html. See also *Fidel and Religion: Talks with Frei Betto* (Havana: Publications Office of the Council of State, 1987), 225.

12. Fidel Castro, "Women's Rally," 1971, LANIC. *Granma* repeated these charges some years later: "this monstrous and egotistical society converted them into drug addicts, gangsters, and the girls into prostitutes." "Glorificación de un crimen," *Granma*, September 19, 1986.

13. Marvin Leiner, *Children Are the Revolution: Daycare in Cuba* (New York: Penguin, 1974), 131. See also Karen Wald, *Children of Che: Childcare and Education in Cuba* (Palo Alto, CA: Ramparts, 1978); and Julie Marie Bunk, *Fidel Castro and the Quest for a Revolutionary Culture in Cuba* (University Park: Pennsylvania State University Press, 1994), 21–86.

14. Franca Iacovetta, *Gatekeepers: Reshaping Immigrant Lives in Cold War Canada* (Toronto:

Between the Lines, 2006); Ron Robin, *The Making of the Cold War Enemy: Culture and Politics in the Military-Intellectual Complex* (Princeton, NJ: Princeton University Press, 2001); Michael Rogin, *Ronald Reagan, the Movie, and Other Episodes in Political Demonology* (Berkeley: University of California Press, 1988).

15. Mary Maxwell, "The Unaccompanied Cuban Children's Program," unpublished paper, April 29, 1963, Barry University Archives, Operation Pedro Pan collection, Miami.

16. Monsignor Bryan O. Walsh, "Cuban Refugee Children," *Journal of Interamerican Studies and World Affairs* 13, no. 3–4 (July–October 1971), 395.

17. Torres, *Lost Apple*, 74–87.

18. Ibid., 233–39, 78.

19. "Displaced Tots Know Horrors of Red Cuba," *Marathon Keynoter*, February 1, 1962.

20. "And Now the Children?" *Time*, October 6, 1961.

21. Richard Gott, *Cuba: A New History* (New Haven, CT: Yale University Press, 2004), 189; Hugh Thomas, *Cuba: Or the Pursuit of Freedom* (New York: Da Capo Press, 1998), 1339.

22. De la Campa, *Cuba on My Mind*, 59; Ileana Fuentes, "Portrait of Wendy, at Fifty, with a Bra," in Andrea O'Reilly Herrera, ed., *Remembering Cuba: Legacy of a Diaspora* (Austin: University of Texas Press, 2002), 60. Melina López uses the dispute between a teenage girl and her parents over her desire to join the literacy campaign as a dramatic device in her play about Peter Pan, *Sonia Flew*, performed in Boston's Huntington Theatre in 2004. See Flora M. González Mandri, "Operation Pedro Pan: A Tale of Trauma and Remembrance," *Latino Studies* 6 (2008), 252–68.

23. "Cuban Reds Concentrate on Conquering Children," *Steubenville Ohio Register*, March 22, 1962; "Cuban Parents Desperate, We Must Get Our Children Out," *Miami Herald*, June 19, 1961; Walsh, "Cuban Refugee Children," 382. The history of relations between the Catholic Church and the revolutionary government is well told in John Kirk, *Between God and the Party: Religion and Politics in Revolutionary Cuba* (Tampa: University of South Florida Press, 1989).

24. "A Return to Cuba, a Search for Himself," *New York Times*, October 21, 2001.

25. Thomas Borstelmann, *The Cold War and the Color Line: American Race Relations in the Global Arena* (Cambridge, MA: Harvard University Press, 2001), 112–13; Vijay Prashad, *The Darker Nations: A People's History of the Third World* (New York: New Press, 2007); Louis A. Pérez Jr., *On Becoming Cuban: Identity, Nationality, and Culture* (New York: HarperCollins, 1999), 490. See also Pérez's masterful analysis of the iconography of Cuba as the classic spoiled child in decades of U.S. political cartoons, in *Cuba in American Imagination: Metaphor and the Imperial Ethos* (Chapel Hill: University of North Carolina Press, 2008); and John J. Johnson, *Latin America in Caricature* (Austin: University of Texas Press, 1980).

26. Gott, *Cuba*, 175; Elizabeth Sutherland, *The Youngest Revolution: A Personal Report on Cuba* (New York: Dial Press, 1969), 95. For the influence of the Cuban revolution on youth culture in various countries, see Van Gosse, *Where the Boys Are: Cuba, Cold War America, and the Making of a New Left* (London: Verso, 1993); Cynthia Wright, "Between Nation and Empire: The Fair Play for Cuba Committees and the Making of Canada-Cuba Solidarity," in Robert Wright and Lana Wylie, eds., *Our Place in the Sun: Canada and Cuba in the Castro Era* (Toronto: University of Toronto Press, 2009), 96–120; and Jennifer Hosek, *Sun, Sex, and Socialism: Cuba in the German Imaginary* (Toronto: University of Toronto Press, 2012).

27. *El otro lado de cristal: Un documental sobre Operación Peter Pan*, dir. Marina Ochoa, ICAIC, Havana, Cuba, 1994.

28. "8,000 Cuban Children Saved from Castro Brainwashing," *Miami Herald*, March 8, 1962.

29. "Refugee Cuban Children Need Homes," *Christian Century*, April 4, 1962.

30. Christina Klein, *Cold War Orientalism: Asia in the Middlebrow Imagination, 1945–61* (Berkeley: University of California Press), 2003; "Many to Offer Homes to Teen-Age Exiles," *Fort Lauderdale Daily News*, March 12, 1962.

31. "Cuban Children Meet Snow, Peanut Butter, English Language—and Come Through Fine," *Rockford Observer*, April 1962; "New Life for Cuban Boys—For 'Gringo' Parents Too," *Sarasota Herald Tribune*, September 16, 1962; Armando Codina, filmed testimonial on the occasion of receiving the Florida Entrepreneur Medal, Florida Merchant Builders Association, 1995, Barry University Archives.

32. "Eighty Cuban Boys in Miami: A Day in Their New Life," *Miami Herald*, March 8, 1962.

33. "Young Refugees Here from Cuba," *Pueblo Star Journal and Sunday Chieftain*, March 25, 1962; "Eight Thousand Unaccompanied Children from Cuba," *Catholic Virginian*, March 16, 1962.

34. "Operation Pedro Pan: A New Life for Cuban Children," *Miami Daily News*, May 27, 1962.

35. Yvonne Conde, *Operation Pedro Pan: The Untold Exodus of 14,048 Cuban Children* (New York: Routledge, 1999); Victor Triay, *Fleeing Castro: Operation Pedro Pan and the Cuban Children's Program* (Miami: University Press of Florida, 1998).

36. Grupo Areíto, *Contra viento y marea* (Havana: Casa de las Américas, 1978), 34, 40.

37. Ibid.

38. Marta Díaz Fernández, "Representación de la emigración en el cine cubano contemporáneo," paper presented at the Latin American Studies Association Conference, Montreal, 2007; Louis Adrián Betancourt, *¿Por qué Carlos?* (Havana: Editorial Letras Cubanas, 1981).

39. See *Miami Herald* coverage of Martínez's Senate election campaign in 2004, for example, as well as his campaign DVD "Mel Martínez for U.S Senate," Barry University Archives, Pedro Pan Collection, Individual Files.

40. "Msgr. Walsh Remembered," *Florida Catholic*, January 3, 2002.

41. "The Dark Side of Peter Pan," *Miami Herald*, November 29, 1990; "Pedro Pan's Heroes," *Miami Herald*, January 3, 1998.

42. Alex Stepick, Guillermo Grenier, Max Castro, and Marvin Dunn, *This Is Our Land: Immigrants and Power in Miami* (Berkeley: University of California Press, 2003), 2. Among the volumes of Elián commentary, see especially Lillian Guerra, "Elián González and the 'Real Cuba' of Miami: Visions of Identity, Exceptionality, and Divinity," *Cuban Studies* 37 (2007), 1–24; Sarah Banet-Weiser, "Elián González and 'The Purpose of America': Nation, Family and the Child-Citizen," *American Quarterly* 55, no. 2 (June 2003); Ann Louise Bardach, *Cuba Confidential: Love and Vengeance in Miami and Havana* (New York: Vintage, 2003); Miguel A. De La Torre, *La Lucha for Cuba: Religion and Politics on the Streets of Miami* (Berkeley: University of California Press, 2003); "Saving Elián," PBS Frontline, February 6, 2001.

43. "I Was an 'Elián' of the Early '60s," *Boston Globe*, February 3, 2000.

44. "Pedro Pan Exiles Finding Their Past," *Miami Herald*, December 4, 2000; "The Passion of Elián," *Washington Post*, April 7, 2000; "Meet Miami's Moderates," *Salon*, April 7, 2000; González Mandri, "Operation Pedro Pan."

45. Torres, *Lost Apple*, 22.

4

The Role of the Courts in Shaping U.S. Policy toward Cuba

STANLEY J. MURPHY

Although legislative and executive actions provide the first definition of U.S. national policy toward Cuba, the courts are often where the ultimate contours of that policy are drawn. Virtually every statute, regulation, or executive action related to Cuba leads to the filing of a lawsuit or lawsuits, and the decisions in those cases have a substantial impact on the nature of the relationship between the two countries. In their decisions on cases related to Cuba, U.S. courts often appear to be more deferential to political judgments than they are in other litigation. When relations with Cuba are at issue, routine legal actions become complicated. Established legal principles are no longer quite so settled, controlling case precedent becomes less important, and previously firm legal standards show a newfound flexibility.

The effect of Cuba on the U.S. courts became apparent after 1959, survived the end of the Cold War, and continues today. In the new era of the Cuban revolution a succession of U.S. presidents and congresses, along with a variety of state and local agencies in Florida, propounded a volatile, evolving, and sometimes self-contradictory series of statutes, regulations, and executive actions regarding Cuba. Starting with legal challenges to restrictions on travel to Cuba, the influence has evolved to the point of having a bearing even on cases dealing with matters of purely U.S. domestic law. From the selection of elementary school library books to child custody decisions, from criminal trials to intellectual property protection—if Cuba becomes part of the issue, U.S. courts are apt to behave strangely. Although not always determining the outcome of a case, the Cuba factor can influence both the arguments of the parties involved and the court's analysis. In the process this factor may have an unintentional, lasting impact on broader areas of U.S. law in which the island neighbor is not an issue. The impact has been particularly unsettling in cases affecting the well-established constitutional rights of U.S. citizens to travel, to academic freedom, and to censorship-free access to information.

The Right to International Travel

In 1958 the U.S. Supreme Court decided that the right to travel internationally was a constitutionally protected freedom akin to the enumerated guarantees of the First Amendment.[1] In *Kent v. Dulles* the Court ruled that the U.S. State Department violated the constitutional rights of two U.S. citizens who were denied passports because they were suspected of being sympathetic to, or members of, the Communist Party. They proposed to travel not to Cuba, but to Europe and Turkey. The question raised in *Kent v. Dulles* was the extent to which the Secretary of State could restrict the ability of U.S. citizens to travel internationally. The Court held that the right to travel in and out of the country was protected by the Constitution. Although that right could be limited on occasions such as war or epidemic disease, simple disapproval of a traveler's politics or ideology was not a legal basis to restrict his or her right to travel.

The Court held that the right to travel abroad was essential to the ability of journalists, educators, and ordinary citizens to educate their readers, their students, and themselves on the issues of the day and to make "sounder decisions at home." Justice William O. Douglas, writing for the majority, explained: "Freedom of movement across frontiers in either direction, and inside frontiers as well, was a part of our heritage. Travel abroad, like travel within the country, may be necessary for a livelihood. It may be as close to the heart of the individual as the choice of what he eats, or wears, or reads. Freedom of movement is basic in our scheme of values."[2]

The distinct role of Cuba in U.S. courts began to emerge after the termination of diplomatic relations between the United States and Cuba in 1961. Shortly afterwards the State Department prohibited the use of U.S. passports for travel to Cuba. When U.S. citizen Louis Zemel applied to Secretary of State Dean Rusk for permission to use his passport to travel to Cuba, his application was rejected. Zemel filed suit, and when his case went before the Supreme Court, he lost.[3]

Zemel "wished to make the trip to satisfy [his] curiosity about the state of affairs in Cuba and to make [himself] a better informed citizen."[4] A majority of the divided Supreme Court held that this was an insufficient reason, and that the Secretary of State could prohibit this type of travel by U.S. citizens to Cuba. Although it had only recently invalidated similar restrictions in *Kent v. Dulles*, the Court believed that different rules applied in the case of Cuba.

Zemel's request came shortly after the Cuban Missile Crisis, but the Court did not base its decision on any particular hazards to travel by U.S. citizens or concerns that Zemel would have faced any immediate dangers in Cuba. Rather, it was a generalized threat to U.S. security that justified the ban: "That the restriction which is challenged in this case is supported by the weightiest considerations of national security is perhaps best pointed up by recalling that the Cuban missile crisis of October 1962 preceded the filing of appellant's complaint by less than two months."[5]

Without explaining why Zemel's travel to Cuba was relevant to the then-resolved missile crisis, the Court described a general political rationale for the restriction: "Cuba is the only area in the Western Hemisphere controlled by a Communist government. It is, moreover, the judgment of the State Department that a major goal of the Castro regime is to export its Communist revolution to the rest of Latin America. The United States and other members of the Organization of American States have determined that travel between Cuba and the other countries of the Western Hemisphere is an important element in the spreading of subversion, and many have therefore undertaken measures to discourage such travel."[6] The Court acknowledged the need to distinguish this decision from *Kent v. Dulles*, in which it had reached the opposite conclusion just a few years earlier. To explain the apparent disregard for recent precedent, the majority of justices held that the two cases had important differences. First, in *Kent v. Dulles* the travel rights of individual U.S. citizens were being restricted because of their personal political beliefs, whereas in *Zemel v. Rusk* the travel prohibition applied equally to all U.S. citizens irrespective of their political beliefs. There was no invidious effort to apply an ideological test to the use of a U.S. passport by a specific and politically suspect traveler. Second, according to the U.S. Department of State, Cuba was a force for antagonistic political influence in the hemisphere. The prohibition of travel to Cuba was somehow justified as an antidote to the influence of the new Cuban government in the Americas.

The *Zemel* decision was not unanimous. Several members of the Court believed that the general prohibition on Cuban travel was directly contrary to the Court's 1958 decision in *Kent v. Dulles*, and represented a serious retreat from the constitutional protection of the freedom to travel abroad. Justice Douglas, writing this time for the losing side, stated:

> We held in *Kent v. Dulles* that the right to travel overseas, as well as at home, was part of the citizen's liberty under the Fifth Amendment. That conclusion was not an esoteric one drawn from the blue. It reflected a judgment as to the peripheral rights of the citizen under the First Amendment. The right to know, to converse with others, to consult with them, to observe social, physical, political and other phenomena abroad as well as at home gives meaning and substance to freedom of expression and freedom of the press. Without those contacts First Amendment rights

suffer. That is why in *Kent v. Dulles* ... we said that freedom of movement has "large social values."

The ability to understand this pluralistic world, filled with clashing ideologies, is a prerequisite of citizenship if we and the other peoples of the world are to avoid the nuclear holocaust.[7]

Justice Douglas believed that the presence of a politically antagonistic government could not justify limiting the right to international travel. This constitutional freedom "presupposes a mature people, not afraid of ideas.... The First Amendment leaves no room for the official, whether truculent or benign, to say nay or yea because the ideas offend or please him or because he believes some political objective is served by keeping the citizen at home or letting him go. Yet that is just what the Court's decision today allows to happen."[8] *Zemel v. Rusk* eviscerated *Kent v. Dulles*. It upheld the prohibition on travel to Cuba, and became the basis—both explicit and implicit—of many subsequent court decisions that departed from established legal principles when Cuba was at issue.[9]

Academic Freedom

The injection of Cuba into cases of academic freedom has altered the legal understanding of that doctrine. Academic freedom as an enforceable legal interest began to take shape in response to governmental intrusions on the academic community during the McCarthy era of the 1950s. The doctrine, which had to that point been articulated principally by university faculty and faculty organizations—such as the American Association of University Professors (AAUP)—began to take on a legally recognized substance in *Sweezy v. New Hampshire*.[10]

In that decision the Court ruled on the protection from governmental intrusion into open inquiry and debate by members of the academic community, finding that this protection was a matter of critical national interest. It held "the essentiality of freedom in the community of American universities is almost self-evident. No one should underestimate the vital role in a democracy that is played by those who guide and train our youth. To impose any strait jacket upon the intellectual leaders in our colleges and universities would imperil the future of our Nation.... Scholarship cannot flourish in an atmosphere of suspicion and distrust. Teachers and students must always remain free to inquire, to study and to evaluate, to gain new maturity and understanding; otherwise our civilization will stagnate and die."[11]

Academic freedom as a legally enforceable right became a principle embedded in U.S. law. Some ten years later, during the Vietnam War controversy, the Court rejected the state of New York's requirement of "loyalty oaths" from faculty and employees of public colleges. In *Keyishian v. Bd. of Regents of State University of New York*,[12] the Court extended its decision in *Sweezy* and held that academic freedom was embedded in the First Amendment:

> Our Nation is deeply committed to safeguarding academic freedom, which is of transcendent value to all of us and not merely to the teachers concerned. That freedom is therefore a special concern of the First Amendment, which does not tolerate laws that cast a pall of orthodoxy over the classroom. "The vigilant protection of constitutional freedoms is nowhere more vital than in the community of American schools." The classroom is peculiarly the "marketplace of ideas." The Nation's future depends upon leaders trained through wide exposure to that robust exchange of ideas which discovers truth "out of a multitude of tongues, [rather] than through any kind of authoritative selection."[13]

In both *Sweezy* and *Keyishian* the Court ruled in favor of individual faculty members and against intrusions by the government. And then along came Cuba.

Cuba as a Factor in Academic Freedom Cases

Academic freedom is an issue in several important cases related to Cuba in which the *Sweezy* and *Keyishian* concept of academic freedom has been significantly eroded. The United States and the state of Florida have both taken steps to limit the rights of academic researchers, faculty, and students to travel to Cuba as part of their educational work. Undeterred by injury to the interests of academic freedom, the courts have largely upheld these restrictions. The Cuba effect on these cases is evident in both the vocabulary of the argument and the decisions of the courts.

In the case of the U.S. government, in 2004 the U.S. Treasury Department Office of Foreign Assets Control (OFAC) significantly reduced the types of licensable academic and educational travel to Cuba. A coalition of academics, researchers, and students sued to invalidate the new regulations, arguing that the restrictions violated the academic freedom rights of faculty and students in U.S. colleges. In 2007 the U.S. District Court, and in 2008 the U.S. Court of Appeals for the District of Columbia, upheld the OFAC regulations. These courts held that, even if the plaintiffs had some injury to their academic freedom rights, the OFAC restrictions were a permissible regulation of foreign affairs by the executive branch of government.[14] Both courts relied heavily on the earlier Supreme Court rulings in the Cuba travel cases, *Zemel v. Rusk* and *Reagan v. Wald*, which had already established a special place for Cuba in U.S. constitutional law.

In the case of Florida, the state government has enacted a statute, known as the Florida Travel Act, prohibiting faculty and students of state-supported universities from using institutional funds for travel to Cuba.[15] The prohibition extends to funds from all sources, including private foundation grants and federal and state funds. Although the law on its face applies to academic travel to countries on the U.S. State Department's list of "state sponsors of terrorism," it is clearly directed toward Cuba.[16] In 2006 faculty and researchers at Florida public universities and the Faculty Senate of Florida International University challenged the law, contending that the statute was a usurpation by the state of Florida of the power of the federal government to control foreign affairs and also an unconstitutional impairment of their academic freedom. Ultimately the district court decided that the Florida law did invade the province of the federal regulation of international relations, but did not violate the First Amendment. The court ruled that, although Florida could legally prohibit the use of purely state funds for this type of academic work, it could not similarly limit non-state monies.[17]

The state of Florida appealed this ruling to the U.S. Court of Appeals for the Eleventh Circuit in Atlanta, which hears appeals from Florida, Alabama, and Georgia. Because a large portion of Cuba-related litigation has been based in Florida, that court has exerted the principal influence on the judicial role in determining national policy toward Cuba. The appeals court reversed the district court, holding that Florida could legally prohibit faculty and students at its public universities from using funds from private sources such as foundations.[18] The court was untroubled by the reality that virtually every public university in Florida and elsewhere requires that all private grants pass through institutional accounts. Similarly, the policy of almost all private foundations is to award grant funds to the researcher's institution, rather than to the individual scholar. In 2012 the Supreme Court refused to review the decision of the Eleventh Circuit. The practical effect of the ruling is that, absent fundamental changes in institutional or foundation policies, faculty and students at Florida's public universities face substantial financial obstacles to their Cuba research.

As with the unsuccessful challenge to the 2004 OFAC regulatory amendments, the decision in the Florida Travel Act case not only reflects the erosion of the doctrine of academic freedom that began in Cuba-related litigation, but it may also have a far broader impact on the future scope of academic freedom protections.

School Library Books: The Removal of *Vamos a Cuba*

In both Cuba and the United States, books about Cuba have had trouble staying on school library shelves. The 1954 edition of *Geographia de Cuba* by Cuban author, environmentalist, and geographer Antonio Núñez Jiménez was removed from Cuban public schools under a dictate of the Batista regime. Perhaps because the author of the book did not conform to the prevailing political orthodoxy, government education officials forbade the book's use in public schools. In Batista's Cuba no effective legal challenge was possible.[19]

More recently another book on the people and geography of Cuba has been removed from public schools, this time from the elementary school libraries of the Miami-Dade County public schools in Florida.

The Cuba effect on U.S. court cases reached new heights in the strange case of *Vamos a Cuba* in which the Eleventh Circuit, in a ninety-page decision on a vote of two assenting judges to one dissenting judge, approved the removal of a children's book about Cuba from public school libraries in Miami. The decision starts with a quotation from Franz Kafka, which provides an initial clue to the odd prism through which the court viewed this case. That the court cited Kafka, whose own work was banned for years from the libraries in his native Prague, as authority for removing books from a school library is, well, Kafkaesque.[20]

History of the Litigation

The case had its beginnings when the Miami-Dade County School Board purchased a series of children's travel books for elementary school libraries. Intended for ages four through eight, the books described in simple words and pictures some basic aspects of children's lives in different countries. The series included books on many countries, including China, Egypt, Brazil, Vietnam, Colombia, France, and Cuba. All the books were about thirty pages long and used the same formulaic descriptions of life in each country: what children like to eat, the clothes they wear, and the music and games they like. It was only the Cuba book, *Vamos a Cuba*, that caused any trouble.

A parent of a student in the Miami-Dade County public schools saw *Vamos a Cuba* in the library at his child's school. Identifying himself as a former political prisoner in Cuba, the parent complained that the book did not describe what he believed to be the harsher realities of modern Cuban life: child prostitution, long prison terms for political dissenters, forced farmwork for all children, and rigid food rationing. Even the cover photograph of smiling children in school uniforms reminded him of Hitler youth groups.[21] The school board decided to remove the Cuba book from the libraries of all the schools in the system. The American Civil Liberties Union (ACLU) joined with others to file suit to require the school board to return the book to the school libraries.

Finding that the removal of *Vamos a Cuba* was likely motivated by political animus, rather than by any material inaccuracies in the book, the federal district court in Miami ordered the school board to return the books to the libraries.[22] The school board appealed, and in 2009 the Eleventh Circuit reversed the federal district court and upheld the removal of the book.[23] The court invoked a far less demanding standard of review and made strenuous efforts to distinguish this case from established precedent in other schoolbook cases.

As a general rule, appellate courts are required to give great deference to a district court's findings of fact, particularly those on the motivations of the parties to the litigation. Ordinarily, findings of fact are to be reversed only if they are clearly erroneous, but when it came to *Vamos a Cuba* the Eleventh Circuit departed from this routine rule of appellate law and decided to use the rarely applied "constitutional fact" standard of review. Under this unusual doctrine the Eleventh Circuit unshackled itself from the ordinary constraints on its authority, substituted its judgment for that of the district court on the motives of the school board, and was thus able to reverse the district court's decision.

The "constitutional fact" standard of review doctrine was developed by the U.S. Supreme Court in two defamation cases in which the Court ruled that the very highest standards of proof were required before liability could be imposed for public expression.[24] Both decisions sought to increase the First Amendment's free speech protections, but now, paradoxically, the same "constitutional fact" doctrine was used in the case of *Vamos a Cuba* to diminish those very protections.

The Law on School Library Books before *Vamos a Cuba*

There have been many cases in U.S. courts defining the legal obligations of public schools on the selection and removal of school library books and textbooks. Much of this litigation has involved claims that some books were too sexually explicit, were offensive to particular political or religious inclinations, or promoted some other type of disfavored viewpoint. To reverse the district court and uphold the removal of *Vamos a Cuba* from the school libraries, the Eleventh Circuit had to distinguish this schoolbook case from a substantial body of established law. Just as in cases involving the right to travel and academic freedom, the injection of Cuba as an issue seemed to loosen the strictures of controlling precedent.

In *Board of Education v. Pico*[25] the Supreme Court decided that a New York school board acted unconstitutionally when it removed from high school and junior high school libraries nine books that had been found to be "objectionable" and "un-American" by a conservative political group.[26] In *Pico* the Court held that, although school officials had great latitude in selecting the books they acquire for their libraries, those books, once acquired, could not legally be removed because of a political or viewpoint disagreement:

As noted earlier, nothing in our decision today affects in any way the discretion of a local school board to choose books to *add* to the libraries of their schools. Because we are concerned in this case with the suppression of ideas, our holding today affects only the discretion to *remove* books. In brief, we hold that local school boards may not remove books from school library shelves simply because they dislike the ideas contained in those books and seek by their removal to "prescribe what shall be orthodox in politics, nationalism, religion, or other matters of opinion." Such purposes stand inescapably condemned by our precedents.[27]

Thus, a central issue in such cases was the motivation of the school officials. The district court judge in Miami decided that the removal of *Vamos a Cuba* was likely motivated by the political viewpoints of the board, and hence was illegal under the *Pico* standard. The Eleventh Circuit disagreed, holding instead that the book was removed because it gave the false impression that in Cuba "everything is hunky dory."[28]

The *Vamos a Cuba* Appeal Changes the Law

The Eleventh Circuit held that two types of factual errors justified removal of the book: direct misstatements on relatively minor matters and, more importantly, errors of implication and omission. The supposed misstatements included some confusion about whether Cuban maracas are made from gourds or pumpkins (the Spanish edition says "maracas hechas de calabazas"[29]), which part of a palm tree is used to build houses, and whether the prehistoric murals near Vinales are paintings of or by ancient people. More objectionable were the omissions of what the Eleventh Circuit believed to be the cruel realities of the lives of Cuban schoolchildren. The court held that "the book presents a false picture of life in Cuba, one that misleadingly fails to mention the deprivations and hardships the people there endure."[30] Most offensive to the court was the book's introductory statement: "People in Cuba eat, work, and go to school like you do."[31] The court was so concerned about this mundane statement (which also appeared in some of the companion books about life in other countries) that the majority opinion repeated it fourteen times.

Because this appeal was from a preliminary injunction and not a final decision, the evidentiary record was incomplete, with little direct evidence in the court record on what turned out to be the central issue in the case: the present realities of children's lives in Cuba. To fill in this evidentiary gap and support the linchpin of their decision, the two judges in the majority relied on their own personal knowledge of contemporary Cuban life: "The book did not tell the truth. It made life in Cuba under Castro appear more favorable than every expert who testified for either side at the hearing knows it to be, more favorable than the State Department knows it to be, more favorable than the district court knows it to be, *and more favorable than we know it to be.*"[32] Deciding any type of case because an assertion on a material fact differs from how the judges "know it to be" is an extraordinary departure from the dispassionate perspective commonly expected of the courts. Although judges' life experiences inevitably influence their legal approach, it is rare for that assumed personal knowledge to be cited as a basis for a decision.

Vamos a Cuba is a small and superficial picture book, written for children aged four to eight. It is not *Origin of the Species*. The problem is that the Eleventh Circuit's decision on this little book will have a far broader impact on what had been a well-settled area of First Amendment law. The established protections for authors, librarians, teachers, and students are now diminished. In Florida, Alabama, and Georgia,[33] all schoolbook controversies, very few of which will have anything at all to do with Cuba, will now be judged by this new standard. A book can be challenged and removed if it contains factual inaccuracies. Mistakes either of direct statement or of omission, or even errors of implication, will suffice. Not many books in elementary school libraries—or for that matter in the Library of Congress—can meet that test. This is troubling news for those trying to keep Darwin on school library shelves.

Child Custody

The Eleventh Circuit, the same court that approved the removal of *Vamos a Cuba*, also ordered the return of Elián González to Cuba in 2000. Elián's mother had died in her effort to come to Florida with her young son, who was rescued and placed in the care of relatives in Miami. His father remained in Cuba. Ordinarily children of this age and in these circumstances would be returned automatically to the surviving parent, no matter where that parent lived. This, however, was no ordinary child custody case. Cuba was involved. Those who objected to the boy's return to Cuba into the custody of his father argued that Elián's life under the Cuban political system would be so manifestly worse than his future in the United States that the courts should depart from the usual principles of child welfare law and keep the boy here for political reasons. In its decision the court described its own predisposition about Cuban life:

> We acknowledge, as a widely-accepted truth, that Cuba does violate human rights and fundamental freedoms and does not guarantee the rule of law to people living in Cuba. Persons living in such a totalitarian state may be unable to assert freely their own legal rights, much less the legal

rights of others. Moreover, some reasonable people might say that a child in the United States inherently has a substantial conflict of interest with a parent residing in a totalitarian state when that parent—even when he is not coerced—demands that the child leave this country to return to a country with little respect for human rights and basic freedoms.[34]

In spite of this ostensibly widely accepted truth, the Eleventh Circuit grudgingly upheld the decision of the Immigration and Naturalization Service (INS) to return Elián to his father.

To some observers it was in the case of Elián González that the Cuba factor reached its inherent limitation. During the oral argument before the Eleventh Circuit, one of the judges spoke of his distaste for the political circumstances in Cuba and implied that, because of this belief, he was reluctant to return the child to live there with the father. In response an attorney for the INS pointed out that the court's decision could have significant consequences for thousands of children of U.S. citizens living abroad. If political tensions or hostilities between governments were permitted to intrude upon child welfare decisions here, the same influence might well be visited upon U.S. families in other countries. Perhaps the court's ultimate decision to return Elián to his father's custody was shaped by the recognition that decisions in Cuba-related cases could have a broader, potentially global, impact.

Although the Elián González decision might seem to have only a limited effect on areas of concern outside Cuba, two aspects of the case do have a potential for larger consequences. First, it is very rare for what is essentially a child custody case to find its way into federal court. When such a case does, it is almost always in the context of a dispute between parents who are living in different countries. Here, the custody fight was between a competent father and an entire political community. That the dispute was ever even seriously considered by the Eleventh Circuit is evidence of the potency of the Cuba effect. Although the court ultimately permitted the boy's return to Cuba, its decision forms a precedent for the argument that, even in the absence of any legitimate concern about the fitness of a parent, the political system in another country could serve as a basis for separating a child from his family.

The Impact of the Cuba Factor

U.S. policy toward Cuba is largely determined by the legislative and executive branches of government, but it would be a mistake to overlook the role of the judiciary. Long after OFAC regulations are withdrawn and acts of Congress are repealed, a residual Cuba factor may well influence decisions in U.S.

courtrooms. The Cuba factor in U.S. court cases creates the possibility that judges will reshape existing principles of law, redefine settled legal rights and obligations, and inject their own political preconceptions into their decisions. Litigants need to recognize and address this problem, but doing so is a particularly difficult undertaking when judges are willing to rule based on how they "know [life in Cuba] to be" and on the basis of "widely accepted truths" about Cuban realities.

The impact of the Cuba factor is that the resulting court decisions potentially have a much broader effect on U.S. law. Established protections of the right to international travel, the contours of the doctrine of academic freedom, the insulation of schoolbook selections from ideological influence, and long-recognized principles of family law have been reshaped.[35] The residual effect of these decisions is likely to linger long after an improvement in the U.S.-Cuban relationship.

Notes

Grateful acknowledgment is made for the assistance of Dylan Reeves (Haskell Slaughter Young & Rediker LLC of Birmingham, Alabama) and Catherine McCord Bailey (McCord & Martin of Gadsden, Alabama). This discussion of the courts as an important component of the shaping of U.S. policy toward Cuba evolved from the author's presentation at Queen's University, Kingston, Ontario, Canada, which appeared in *Temas*, 59, Havana, July–September 2009.

1. Kent v. Dulles, 357 U.S. 116 (1958).

2. *Kent*, 357 U.S. at 126. (relying on Zechariah Chafee, Three Human Rights in the Constitution of 1787 [1956]).

3. Zemel v. Rusk, 381 U.S. 1 (1965).

4. *Zemel*, 381 U.S. at 23 (internal quotations omitted).

5. *Zemel*, 381 U.S. at 16.

6. *Zemel*, 381 U.S. at 13.

7. *Zemel*, 381 U.S. at 23, 24 (internal citations omitted).

8. *Zemel*, 381 U.S. at 26.

9. *Zemel* was followed by Reagan v. Wald, 468 U.S. 222 (1984), in which the Court upheld continued regulatory restrictions on Cuba travel by the U.S. Treasury Department.

10. 354 U.S. 234 (1957).

11. *Sweezy*, 354 U.S. at 250.

12. 385 U.S. 589 (1967).

13. *Keyishian*, 385 U.S. at 603 (internal citation omitted).

14. Emergency Coal. to Defend Educ. Travel to Cuba v. U.S. Dep't of Treasury, 545 F.3d 4 (D.C. Cir. 2008).

15. "Act Relating to Travel to Terrorist States," Fla. Stat. §§ 1005.08 & 1011.90(6). Not to be confused with the Florida *Sellers of Travel* Act, Fla. Stat. § 559.929, which attempted to place extraordinary financial burdens on the OFAC-approved travel agencies arranging licensed

travel to Cuba. The latter statute was invalidated by the U.S. District Court in Miami as an impermissible intrusion by Florida into the federally preempted domain of international affairs. Order Granting Motion for Summary Judgment, *ABC Charters v. Bronson*, No. 08-21865, 2009 WL 1010435 (S.D. Fla. 2009). More recently Florida enacted a statute forbidding certain contracts between the state and companies having business relationships in Cuba. Prohibition Against Contracting with Scrutinized Companies, Fla. Stat. § 287.135 (2011) (*as amended by* 2012 Fla. Laws ch. 196 ([May 2012]). The law was challenged by a Florida subsidiary of a Brazilian international conglomerate (another of whose subsidiaries did construction work in Cuba). A U.S. District Court in Miami granted a preliminary injunction against the enforcement of the statute, holding that the law unconstitutionally invaded the province of the federal government. The court noted that this law was another example of the "long history" of "[T]he State of Florida and its municipalities . . . enacting legislation aimed at Cuba." Odebrecht Constr., Inc. v. Prasad, No. 12-cv-22072-KMM, 2012 U.S. Dist. LEXIS 90982, at *5–6 (S.D. Fla. June 29, 2012). The district court's preliminary injunction against enforcement of the law was affirmed by the Eleventh Circuit. *Odebrecht Constr. v. Sec'y, Fla. Dep't Transp.*, No. 12-13958, 2013 U.S. App. LEXIS 9175, at *56 (11th Cir. May 6, 2013).

16. At the time the State Department list included Cuba, Iran, North Korea, Sudan, and Syria.

17. Faculty Senate of Fla. Int'l Univ. v. Roberts, 574 F.Supp.2d 1331 (S.D. Fla. 2008). In the earlier decision on the same case, a different judge also rejected the plaintiffs' argument on federal preemption. Thus, although both decisions rejected the academic freedom claim, the plaintiffs did prevail at least partially in the second round.

18. Faculty Senate of Fla. Int'l Univ. v. Winn, 616 F.3d 1206 (11th Cir. Fla. 2010). The plaintiffs asked the U.S. Supreme Court to review this decision on the grounds that, through this statute, the State of Florida has unconstitutionally usurped the power of the federal government to regulate international relationships. The Court sought the view of the United States on the case. Faculty Senate of Fla. Int'l Univ. v. Florida, No. 10-1139, 2011 U.S. LEXIS 3797 (U.S. May 16, 2011). The U.S. Solicitor General wrote that although the Florida statute " . . . conflicts with federal law and thus is preempted" and "undermines" the federal system of international sanctions, the Court should nonetheless decline to review the Eleventh Circuit's decision. Amicus Brief, 2012 U.S. S. Ct. Briefs LEXIS 2210, May 24, 2012. On June 25, 2012, the Court denied the plaintiffs' request to review the case, thus allowing the Eleventh Circuit's decision to stand. 2012 U.S. LEXIS 4859.

19. A political challenge was, however. In 1959 a second edition of the Núñez geography book was published and returned to Cuban school libraries. Núñez's academic, environmental, and civic education interests are continued today by the Fundación Antonio Núñez Jiménez in Havana.

20. The decision begins with a partial quotation from one of Kafka's letters: "Kafka advised a friend that 'we ought to read only books that bite and sting us. If the book we are reading doesn't shake us awake like a blow on the skull, why bother reading it in the first place?'" ACLU v. Miami-Dade Cnty. Sch. Bd., 557 F.3d 1177, 1182 (11th Cir. 2009). Kafka's message would have been clearer, more complete, and certainly more appropriate to a book-removal case if the court had continued with the next sentence in Kafka's letter: "So that it can make us happy, as you put it? Good God, we'd be just as happy if we had no books at all." Kafka to Oskar Pollak, January 27, 1904.

21. Explaining the rationale for the reaction against the school uniform photographs, the court wrote, "The Hitler Youth wore uniforms, too, and that uniform was symbolically connected to that which many people abhor about the Third Reich." ACLU v. Miami-Dade Cnty. Sch. Bd., 557 F.3d at 1223 n 18. The strong response to photographs of Cuban children wearing school uniforms, as ostensible evidence of a new, oppressive regime, ought to have been tempered somewhat by the fact that long before 1959, many Cuban schoolchildren in both public and private schools wore uniforms. The Eleventh Circuit, because it ruled on the case at a preliminary stage and without benefit of a full evidentiary record, was perhaps unaware of this fact and thus the objectors' outrage on that issue was given more credence than was warranted.

22. ACLU v. Miami-Dade Cnty. Sch. Bd., 439 F.Supp.2d 1242 (S.D. Fla. 2006).

23. ACLU v. Miami-Dade Cnty. Sch. Bd., 557 F.3d 1177 (11th Cir. 2009).

24. In *New York Times, Co. v. Sullivan*, 376 U.S. 254 (1964), and *Bose Corp. v. Consumers Union of the United States*, 104 S. Ct. 1949 (1984), the Court required that the ultimate finding of actual malice in a libel case must have an independent review in the appeals process. For a thorough discussion of the history and application of this doctrine, see Henry P. Monaghan, "Constitutional Fact Review," 985 COLUM. L. REV. 229 (1985).

25. 457 U.S. 853 (1982).

26. The removed books included *Slaughterhouse-Five*, by Kurt Vonnegut Jr.; *The Naked Ape*, by Desmond Morris; *Best Short Stories of Negro Writers*, edited by Langston Hughes; *Black Boy*, by Richard Wright; and *Soul on Ice*, by Eldridge Cleaver.

27. *Pico*, 457 U.S. at 871, 872 (internal citation omitted).

28. ACLU v. Miami-Dade Cnty. Sch. Bd., 557 F.3d 1177, 1227 (11th Cir. 2009).

29. *Vamos a Cuba* (Chicago: Heinemann Library, 2001), 28.

30. ACLU v. Miami-Dade Cnty. Sch. Bd., 557 F.3d at 1225.

31. *Vamos a Cuba*, 5.

32. ACLU v. Miami-Dade Cnty. Sch. Bd., 557 F.3d at 1225 (emphasis added; internal citation omitted).

33. The geographic jurisdictional contours of the Eleventh Circuit.

34. González v. Reno, 212 F.3d 1338, 1353 (11th Cir. 2000) (*citing* U.S. Dept. of State, 1999 Country Reports on Human Rights Practices: Cuba [2000]) ("[The Cuban Government] continue[s] systematically to violate fundamental civil and political rights of its citizens.").

35. The same argument could be made for the Cuba effect in other areas of law. Long-standing litigation over Cohiba cigar and Havana Club rum trademarks and commercial rights, and the criminal prosecution saga of the "Cuba Five" cases, may be other examples. Other countries, international businesses, and economic organizations with which Cuba has established or has prospective relationships may have their own concerns about the unusual treatment of Cuba issues by U.S. courts. That treatment may thus have a broader impact on the interests of other nations, and their citizens and affiliated businesses in the future than is apparent now.

5

Cuban-Chinese Relations after the End of the Cold War

CARLOS ALZUGARAY TRETO

In the relatively short period of twenty years since the end of the Cold War, China has become one of Cuba's main strategic allies. Simultaneously, the Caribbean nation has turned into one of the Middle Kingdom's most significant partners in the Western Hemisphere. From a political standpoint, Cuba and China share two important traits: their political leaders openly proclaim that they are endeavoring to build a socialist economic system with "national characteristics"; and their communist parties have exercised basically unchallenged ideological and political hegemony ever since the victories of their respective revolutions in 1949 and 1959.

Nevertheless, in 1989 few experts would have predicted such an expansion and consolidation of relations between the two countries. Cuba and China are on opposite sides of the planet. They are completely different in terms of population and territory, and their national, political, and cultural identities contrast significantly. Moreover, despite an auspicious beginning to their relations in the 1960s, for the better part of twenty years, from the mid-1960s to the early 1980s, Havana and Beijing often found themselves on opposite sides of major international issues.[1]

How and why, then, did Cuba and China become such close allies after the end of the Cold War? From my standpoint, answering this question entails approaching the subject from historical and political points of view and dividing the chronology into four periods: a synopsis of relations before 1989; a summary of the main steps taken by both governments to improve their interactions between 1989 and 2001; a presentation of the situation since 2001; and an analysis of the interests and preferences that have determined the present state of Cuban-Chinese connections.

Background: 1959–1989

Historically, the relationships between Cuba and China go back to the nineteenth century, when the Spanish colonial regime started to import Chinese laborers (coolies) as replacements for the diminishing numbers of African slaves working in the cane fields. Between 1847 and 1874, 150,000 male Chinese laborers were imported into Cuba. At the turn of the century a new wave of Chinese immigrants arrived in Cuba from California. The legacy of a fairly significant population of Chinese immigrants can still be felt today all over Cuba, but especially in Havana's Chinatown. Citizens of Chinese origin were represented in a range of historical and cultural activities. For example, one of the most significant Cuban painters of the twentieth century, Wilfredo Lam, was biracial, born to Chinese and African parents in Sagua la Grande, in central Cuba, a town that had very strong Chinese influences from the mid-nineteenth century.

Although separated by ten years, the victories of the Chinese and Cuban revolutions were part of the same broad historical processes taking place fifty to sixty years ago in the third world. Driven by individual historical trajectories, however, both events were interjected into the context of the Cold War—defined as the ideological and geopolitical conflict between capitalism, led by the United States, and socialism, led by the Soviet Union, that spanned several decades of the twentieth century. That clash was particularly acute in the global South, or underdeveloped world, after the Second World War.[2]

At the time, revolutionary leaders in both Havana and Beijing proclaimed themselves to be inheritors of the 1917 Russian Revolution. The triumph of the Chinese People's Liberation Army over the Guomindang led by Chiang Kai-shek (Jiang Jieshi) and that of the Cuban Rebel Army over the Batista dictatorship relied on similar guerrilla tactics identified with Mao Zedong's and Che Guevara's writings. Both revolutionary processes were confronted immediately by sharply hostile policies from administrations in Washington; in both cases, as it had done with the Soviet Union, the U.S. government withheld diplomatic recognition to deny their legitimacy.[3] It is no surprise that both China and Cuba adopted strongly anti-imperialist positions, which Beijing maintained until the 1970s.

From its establishment in 1949 the Chinese People's Republic (PRC) endeavored to develop relationships with Latin America and the Caribbean. Most countries in the region, however, followed the U.S. lead, maintaining diplomatic ties with the Republic of China's Nationalist government in Taipei and refusing to recognize Beijing as the rightful representative of the Chinese people.[4] The first real breakthrough came on September 1, 1960, in the First Declaration of Havana, a document Jorge Domínguez considers to be Fidel Castro's "first formal call for revolution in the Western Hemisphere."[5] Speaking at the Plaza de la Revolución, the then prime minister of the Cuban revolutionary government proclaimed, among other things, that Cuba would break its links with Taiwan and establish ties with the government of the PRC. Shortly thereafter, on September 28, 1960, the two countries established diplomatic relations.

Cuban-Chinese relations developed rapidly from that moment on. Responding to Cuba's recognition, the PRC provided political backing and economic and military aid. For example, the first hundred Cubans trained to pilot the Soviet-supplied MiGs were trained in China. In return, Cuba staunchly supported China's aspiration to replace Taiwan as a permanent member of the United Nations Security Council. This support became more important when Havana joined the Non-Aligned Movement at its inaugural summit in Belgrade in 1961, becoming simultaneously a founding member and the only Latin American member country at the time. That step turned Havana into a key player in third world politics, which would be the natural field of Chinese leadership in the international communist movement.

There is no doubt that, as Simon Shen writes, "leaders from both sides shared a similarly radical approach, such as political voluntarism, mass mobilization, anti-elitism and bureaucracy, and advocating moral incentives, to propel their respective societies towards communism."[6] In his excellent essay on Cuban-Chinese relations from 1959 to 1966, Cheng Yinghong—quoting from the memoirs of Chinese ambassador to Cuba Wang Youping—points out the intimate relationship that developed between the diplomat and Cuban leaders.[7] As the quasi-official *China Daily* reported, both countries exchanged high-level visits, with President Osvaldo Dorticós and Che Guevara visiting China.[8] Groups of young Chinese and Cubans studied abroad in Havana and Beijing, respectively, as did, for example, Professor Xu Shicheng, one of China's foremost Latin American specialists, who took courses at the University of Havana in the 1960s.

As Cheng Yinghong concludes from Chinese sources, "from 1960 to 1964, Sino-Cuban relations were much closer and more intimate than many observers had assumed. The Cuban leaders' frequent unannounced visits to the Chinese embassy, and the personal ties between Chinese diplomats and senior Cuban officials, are indicative of the close relationship. Economic and technological cooperation between the two countries went far beyond mere exchanges of rice for sugar, and the close relationship lasted much longer than has often been suggested."[9] The close, intimate relations that developed during the early 1960s began to deteriorate as a result of the "Sino-Soviet split," as historians have called the sharp struggle between the Soviet and Chinese communist parties over the direction of the international communist movement.[10] For Cuba, as for Vietnam, which at the time was facing U.S. military aggression, the fact that the two largest socialist countries would spend more time and effort struggling with each other than against the West had risks as well as benefits. While sympathizing with China's criticism of Soviet détente with the United States, and while taking advantage of the split to increase their autonomy, the Cubans saw the domestic dangers of both parties' divisive policies.

Norwegian historian Odd Arne Westad provides an outstanding explanation of the dilemma:

> The dynamic of Cold War confrontation in the 1960s and 1970s depended to a high extent on the policies of the new revolutionary states. Cuba and Vietnam challenged not only Washington in defense of their revolutions; they also challenged the course set by the Soviet Union for the development of socialism and for Communist intervention abroad. . . .
>
> The Cuban and Vietnamese challenges to the Cold War would have been impossible without the early 1960s Sino-Soviet split in the international Communist movement. That Mao Zedong—himself, as he was fond of pointing out, the head of a Third World country—could claim to speak of Marxist-Leninist theory with an authority that he denied the Soviets, meant more room to maneuver for Marxists elsewhere. Mao's claim of criticizing Moscow from the *left* was particularly useful for Third World revolutionaries—even if very few of them wanted to adopt Chinese models of development or follow the vagaries of Chinese foreign policy—because it implied that they, too, could claim to have found ways of speeding up socialist construction. The Sino-Soviet split opened up great opportunities and great dangers for Communist parties in the Third World; it made it possible to tack between the two self-proclaimed centers of Communism and get support from both, but it also signaled an internal split in many parties, which in some cases reduced them to political irrelevance (if not infantility).[11]

Westad quotes Fidel Castro's appeal for socialist unity in a March 13, 1965, speech: "We small countries, which do not entrust ourselves to the strength of armies of millions of men, which do not entrust ourselves to the strength of atomic power—we small countries, like Vietnam and Cuba, have enough instinct to calmly see and understand that no one more than we, who are in a special situation 90 miles from the Yankee empire and attacked by Yankee planes, are affected by these divisions and discords that weaken the strength of the socialist camp."[12] That Havana remained neutral in the Sino-Soviet split produced tensions in Cuban-Chinese relations from 1964–65 on. China feared that the Cuban Communist Party had no other option than to align itself more closely with the Communist Party of the Soviet Union, as demonstrated by the visits that Fidel Castro made to Moscow in 1963 and 1964, the participation of Raúl Castro in a meeting of communist parties in Moscow that same year, and Chinese exclusion from a meeting of Latin American communist parties in Havana in 1965.[13]

According to Cheng Yinghong, Mao Zedong was fully aware of the situation, which he explained in a meeting of the Central Committee of the Chinese Communist Party in 1964: "In Cuba they [the Cubans] listen to half and reject half; they listen to half because they can't do otherwise, since they don't produce oil or weapons."[14] China could not offer Cuba the same level of economic and military support as the Soviet Union, and it tried to compensate for its weaker position by using its propaganda machinery. It knew perfectly well that ideologically its Cuban comrades were more sympathetic to the Chinese views. Wang, the Chinese ambassador in those years, put it this way: "China did everything it could to accommodate Cuba, but it could not match the Soviet Union in supplying oil, energy, and major weaponry."[15]

The island's leadership wanted to avoid the consequences that the divisions between its allies would have on the Cuban Communist Party, which was founded in 1965 after a difficult process of uniting several revolutionary organizations that had participated in the struggle against Batista: the 26th of July Movement, the Popular Socialist Party (old Communists), and the March 13 Revolutionary Directorate. It could not therefore allow the Chinese tactic of compensating for its lack of resources with a propaganda campaign carried on inside Cuba.

Consequently, the Cubans went beyond maintaining neutrality, striving to mediate in the conflict. On several occasions Fidel Castro himself, Che Guevara, and other high-level party and government leaders made attempts to facilitate reconciliation between their two main allies. But China was not interested. The last attempt took place in February 1965, when Guevara cut short a visit he was making to several countries in Africa, in preparation for his internationalist expedition in the Congo, and joined Emilio Aragonés and Osmani Cienfuegos, two of the most important party leaders at the time, to fly to Beijing.[16] Guevara was obviously chosen because of his close ties with the Chinese leadership. In a statement about the Sino-Soviet split, he had said, "the Sino-Soviet quarrel is, for us, a sad development, but because the dispute is a fact, we tell our people about it, and it is discussed by the party. Our party's attitude is to avoid analyzing who is right and who is not. We have our own position, and as they say in the American films, any resemblance [presumably of Cuba to either contestant] is purely coincidental."[17] Guevara's mission failed. This time, Mao Zedong, who had received him on previous occasions, declined to do so. Guevara met instead with Liu Shaoqi and Deng Xiaoping, head of state and general secretary of the Communist Party, respectively. A month after the visit, Fidel Castro made his major speech of March 1965. In it he openly criticized the Chinese authorities for trying to distribute propaganda favorable to their positions among officers of the Cuban Revolutionary Armed Forces.[18]

Although there was never a formal rupture of party and government relations, the events described here inevitably led to a freeze, especially after the unleashing of the Cultural Revolution in China and the strong alliance of Cuba with the Soviet Union in the 1970s. In the second half of the 1970s, as China began its rapprochement with Washington, periods of open hostility occurred, as in the case of the interventions of Cuba and China on opposite sides, first in the Angolan conflict and later in the Sino-Vietnamese armed clashes at the end of the decade.

During the Angolan conflict in 1975–76, Cuba sided with Agostinho Neto's MPLA government in Luanda, supporting it militarily against attacks from South Africa and the other two liberation movements, UNITA and FNLA; China directly aided the FNLA and was wooed by U.S. Secretary of State Henry Kissinger to be more active in defeating Neto and the MPLA. In *Conflicting Missions*, his outstanding and well-researched text about the confrontation between Havana and Washington in Africa, Piero Gleijeses demonstrates that the Chinese withdrew their support for the FNLA as soon as it became evident that Pretoria had invaded Angolan territory from Namibia, and thereafter refused to cooperate with the United States as long as South Africa was involved in the conflict. Nevertheless, when the UN Security Council reprimanded South Africa for its invasion, the Chinese delegate, although refusing to vote, lashed out at "Soviet social imperialism and its [Cuban] mercenaries," accusing them of "towering crimes" against Angola. Gleijeses points out: "His diatribe could not obscure a basic fact: in Angola, Beijing had been on the side of South Africa's clients, and the well-publicized departure of Chinese instructors in late 1975 could not dispel the smell of collusion with the apartheid state."[19]

The second incident took place in 1979, when armed conflict broke out between China and Vietnam. Cuba immediately sided with Hanoi, and Fidel Castro condemned Beijing in the harshest terms, blaming Deng Xiaoping personally.[20]

After these verbal clashes, relations between the two countries were cool but remained normal. Michael Erisman indicates that "these political tensions in the Sino-Cuban relationship generally had little negative impact on trade issues," as demonstrated by the fact that "the island had by the end of 1990 emerged as the PRC's most important trading partner in all of Latin America," with a volume of $561.9 million in both directions, which made the Chinese position in the Cuban market very similar to that of the Japanese.[21]

The rapprochement process began in 1983, when both parties and governments started to exchange mid-level delegations, but it did not pick up speed until 1989, coinciding with the end of the Cold War between the USSR and the United States. In the first half of the 1980s some of the issues that had separated Cuba and China began to subside, especially the question of support for opposite sides in southwest Africa. The Chinese leadership realized that Cuba's position in the third world was strong. On the other hand, Havana had always considered Beijing a very important economic partner. As relations with the Soviet Union started to deteriorate with the advent of *perestroika*, China became a natural option.

Initial Steps toward Consolidating a Relationship, 1989–2001

The period of consolidation was initiated in 1989 when both foreign ministers visited each other's capitals. These visits are seen as the initial steps toward the full resumption and normalization of relations between the two socialist countries. What is interesting about this period is the intense exchange of high-level visitors that took place immediately afterward and continued for the next ten to twelve years.[22]

The meetings began in May–June 1989, with Foreign Minister Qia Qisheng's visit to Cuba as part of a tour of Latin American and Caribbean countries. He was received by President Fidel Castro. Later that year Foreign Minister Isidoro Malmierca visited China and met with President Jiang Zemin. These two exchanges were relevant at the time not just because China was facing isolation due to the Tiananmen Square incidents but also because of the economic and social crisis taking place in Cuba after the fall of the European socialist regimes.

That initial foray was followed two years later by a delegation of the National People's Congress (the equivalent of Parliament) and the Standing Committee, led by Vice-Chairman Chen Muhua, which visited Cuba at the invitation of the Cuban National Assembly of People's Power (NAPP). They held meetings with Fidel Castro, Vice-President Carlos Rafael Rodríguez, and Juan Escalona, president of the NAPP. Then, between July 1, 1991, and April 7, 2001, at least twenty-eight visits of dignitaries took place between the two countries.

Several of these trips were particularly notable. In July 1991 Carlos Rafael Rodríguez made an official visit to China. He was received by Jiang Zemin, general secretary of the Chinese Communist Party, in the first formal contact between the two political organizations. Then, from August 3 to September 9, 1991, José Naranjo, a minister without portfolio in the Cuban government, went to China. This visit was important not only because of its duration—more than a month—but also because Naranjo was at the time Fidel Castro's chief of staff and was thus an official who would not normally visit a foreign country by himself unless he was carrying out important tasks in the name of the president. The November 1992 visit to Beijing of Carlos Lage, vice-president in charge of the Cuban economy, signaled the reestablishment of major economic cooperation relations between both governments.

In 1993 and 1995, respectively, both heads of state, Jiang Zemin and Fidel Castro, exchanged official state visits, raising bilateral relations to their highest levels. From then on, practically all sectors of both countries, including the defense and the state security ministries and the communist parties, established direct links and began the practice of conducting bilateral negotiations in each other's capitals every year.

We can draw several conclusions from these continuing exchanges. Obviously, both sides intensified the interactions between their principal officials during the last decade of the twentieth century. Practically all major officials of both countries visited the other, in some cases more than once. These exchanges laid the groundwork for the future. In some cases, such as that of the ministries of foreign affairs, coordination and cooperation talks continued annually.

For the Cuban and Chinese communists the disappearance of the Soviet Union and the Eastern European socialist countries clearly meant different things. For Cuba's part, the country recognized the need to search for new allies. For China, Cuba continued to be very important politically, as a third world country with which it shared common principles. This was demonstrated in the wake of the Tiananmen events of 1989, when Fidel Castro was one of the major world leaders who expressed understanding for the Chinese government's stance. In those years it was evident that China offered Cuba not only a political alliance but also important economic possibilities due to the manifest success of Chinese reforms. If China welcomed the news that the Cuban leaders would extend the red carpet to their foreign minister in June 1989, when many Latin American and Caribbean countries cancelled his visit, for Cuba it was of paramount importance that President Jiang Zemin decided to make his first official visit to Cuba in 1993, the worst moment after the breakup of Cuba's traditional ties with the Soviet Union, which had been until that time its main economic, political, and military ally.

Relations 2001–2011

The twenty-first century was marked by an unprecedented intensification of economic links and by the continuation of a very intense political relationship, as demonstrated by three presidential visits made from China to Cuba.[23]

Commercial relations have drawn heavily on the precedent established when Cuba established diplomatic relations with China in September 1960. At the time the two countries initiated a "clearing account trade" system, in which the exchange of products was determined by annual quotas. The first Five-Year Trade and Payment Agreement was signed that year and was subsequently renewed every five years. Over three decades bilateral trade remained relatively stable, and in 1990 Cuba was China's largest Latin American trading partner. The collapse of the Soviet Union had a severe impact on Cuba's capacity to export sugar and other products, and on January 1, 1996, following the legalization of U.S. dollars in Cuba, the clearing account system was replaced by cash-liquidation trade.

The Cuban government showed remarkable ingenuity and creativity in its response to the crisis, opening a number of sectors to foreign investment while remaining committed to the fundamental structures of a socialist economy. Cuba and China once again became important markets for each other's products, with bilateral trade exceeding pre-crisis levels. Trade became relatively complementary, with China importing raw sugar and nickel from Cuba and exporting machinery, dry beans, transport equipment, and light industrial products in return. China reported bilateral trade figures of $2.29 billion in 2007, $2.27 billion in 2008, $1.55 billion in 2009, and rising to $2.43 billion in 2012.

A 2008 state visit by President Hu Jintao came at a critical time for Cuba, as it was a concrete affirmation of the strength of the bilateral relationship. During the visit the two countries signed accords postponing for ten years repayments of unspecified trade debts that Cuba had accumulated through 1995, and extending for five years a $7.2-million line of credit that China granted in 1998. President Hu also donated $80 million toward Cuba's hospital modernization program.[24]

After 2000, bilateral trade grew to the extent that China became Cuba's second-largest trading partner. As the Economist Intelligence Unit reported, "China has emerged as an important strategic ally [of Cuba] in recent years, with extensive economic and military cooperation, including substantial credit guarantees that have had a strong impact on the cost and availability of external financing."[25]

A number of Chinese enterprises have established branch offices in Cuba. Some of these offices focus on the export of Cuban primary products, such as nickel and sugar, to China, though they are increasingly incorporating medical and biological products into their portfolios. Other offices oversee the import of Chinese products into Cuba and the integration of investments into economic development projects.

Chinese investment in Cuban oil prospecting and production is an important recent development, as alternative energy sources such as coal and hydroelectricity harbor little potential on the island. The termination of Soviet oil supplies after the disintegration of the USSR in 1991 forced Cuba to start paying world prices, seriously hampering economic growth and draining foreign purchasing capacity. In 2004 fuel imports cost Cuba $1.31 billion, a significant figure relative to the size of Cuba's economy.[26]

Since the early 1990s Cuba has gradually opened petroleum exploration to foreign investors, and the industry has consequently expanded rapidly. Oil and natural gas fields were discovered in a 112,000-square-kilometer marine area under Cuban jurisdiction in the Gulf of Mexico. The area has been divided into fifty blocks, each spanning about two thousand square kilometers. Foreign capital and technology have been introduced through joint venture contracts, which are operating in seventeen blocks, each with an average exploration cost of $50 million. In March 2004 the Chinese enterprise Sinopec signed the "Memorandum on Blocks No. 1, 2, 3 and 4" with the National Petroleum Company of Cuba (CUPET), and in January 2005 the Shengli Oilfield Administration Bureau (a division of Sinopec) signed with CUPET a "product-sharing contract for prospecting in and exploiting three blocks."

For the Cuban population the impact of Cuban-Chinese trade is quite obvious. Stores throughout the island sell Chinese electric fans, televisions, stoves, and refrigerators at a cost below average world prices, and almost every Cuban family owns more than one Chinese-brand appliance. Stimulated by the government's "Energetic Revolution" campaign, many people have replaced their inefficient Soviet-era refrigerators with energy-efficient appliances from the Chinese manufacturer Haier. Many have also replaced their electricity-intensive lighting with energy-saving Chinese light bulbs. By mid-2009, 1,572 fuel-efficient cars from the Chinese manufacturer Geely had been shipped to Cuba, and more than 1,000 buses from the Chinese company Yutong had replaced the aging retrofitted trucks and trailers known as "camel buses." Demonstrating their linguistic flexibility, many Cubans now use the word *Yutong* interchangeably with "public bus."[27]

While trade is crucial to Cuban-Chinese relations, exchanges and cooperation in the fields of social research, education, performing arts, science, sports, and tourism have also expanded substantially. In the early 1960s China and Cuba had established several agreements for cooperation in culture and postal services, but the initiative tapered off during the subsequent two decades. A September 1987 agreement on cultural exchange revived interaction in these areas and provided the basis for a more detailed plan signed during Hu Jintao's 2004 visit.

Setting the stage for President Hu's arrival, in September 2004 the president of the Chinese Academy of Social Sciences (CASS), Chen Kuiyuan, led a delegation to Cuba for the first Cuban-Chinese Forum on Social Science. The event, held in collaboration with the Cuban Ministry of Science, Technology, and the Environment (CITMA), focused on the role of the social sciences in advancing more effective socioeconomic development policies and international collaboration. In September 2005 CITMA Vice-Minister Lina Domínguez led a Cuban delegation to a reciprocal forum in Beijing. The participants exchanged opinions on the evolution of socialism in Cuba and in China, a discussion they continued in the third CASS-CITMA forum in Havana in April 2008, and in a consultation meeting in Beijing in December 2010.[28]

Academic exchange between the two countries dates back to the early 1960s, when 150 Chinese students were sent to Cuba to study Spanish. Suspended in the mid-1960s, the program resumed again in 1984. In November 2004 the two countries established scholarships to support the exchange of thirty Cuban students for twenty Chinese students per year. The program was expanded in 2006 to one hundred scholarships each way, and the Cuban government expressed its willingness to host 1,260 Chinese senior middle-school graduates from central and western China. During his 2008 visit to Cuba, President Hu delivered a speech at Tarará Student City, home to some three thousand Chinese students, in which he confirmed China's intention to send five thousand students to Cuba by 2011 to help create a human platform for sustainable bilateral cooperation. In support of these initiatives, both countries have organized three meetings between Cuban and Chinese university presidents held in Havana (2002), Beijing (2004), and Havana (2006).

State-to-state cooperation has allowed China to build educational exchanges and capacity in priority areas. In 2007 the China Scholarships Council funded twelve thousand young Chinese to study overseas; four hundred of these went to Cuba to study medicine and tourism, and in 2008 that number doubled. As a senior representative of the council explained, the program was strategically designed to maximize human impact: "the Chinese students we send to Cuba to study medicine are overwhelmingly from the western provinces of China, because that is where our central government is trying to develop infrastructure and social programs. So these doctors will return from Cuba to western China and fill an important need. In the meantime, a significant number of Cuban doctors are in western China, filling the need for the short term."[29] Medical exchange with Cuba is fresh in the minds of many Chinese in the wake of the Wenchuan earthquake in May 2008. Cuba immediately sent a medical team to assist in the most devastated areas, and on May

24 Premier Wen Jiabao visited the team, stating that its superior level of professional skill would maximize relief to the earthquake victims. The Cuban ambassador to China, Carlos Miguel Pereira Hernández, also praised the efforts of the medical team, stating that it was a "symbol of long-standing friendship between the two nations, and aid to each other in difficult times."[30]

In late 2002 the University of Havana established the Center for Chinese Language Training. In September 2004, three teachers were sent from China to the university to supervise a new one-year Chinese-language course through the center, and two more teachers were sent to oversee the second term. Their contracts were extended, and an additional two teachers were sent for a third term. This and other Chinese language and culture programs were reinforced by the establishment of the Confucius Institute in the heart of Havana's Chinatown, which was presented to a Chinese delegation in conjunction with President Hu's November 2008 visit.

Cuba and China believe that language training is an important component of broader technological and industrial cooperation, and technicians are usually enrolled in courses to become more familiar with each other's linguistic and cultural backgrounds. Language training has therefore been increasingly coordinated with more technical spheres of collaboration, such as scientific and technological programs. Even before the collapse of the Soviet Union three such programs had been implemented, and in March 1990 the first Joint Committee on Scientific and Technological Cooperation was established. Since then this committee has met every two years to draw up a biennial plan; in October 2003 (at the committee's sixth meeting) a plan for cooperation in health, information, and agriculture was signed. The first Symposium on Sino-Cuban Biotechnology Development and Human Health was convened in February 2004, and a memorandum of understanding promoting cooperation in this field was signed in November of the same year. The Working Group on Biotechnological Cooperation was established in May 2005, coinciding with the seventh meeting of the Joint Committee, resulting in a five-year plan for cooperation in this field. The second and third meetings of the working group were held in October 2006 and September 2008. All of these forums and meetings have promoted cultural understanding as a key component of successful technical cooperation.

Bilateral visits are often timed to coincide with preparations for broader multilateral forums, providing Cuban and Chinese officials with opportunities to preview matters of mutual concern. September 2009, for instance, was a high point of bilateral activity in the lead-up to the UN General Assembly. That month, Vice-President Ricardo Cabrisas arrived in Beijing at the head of a high-level delegation to participate in the Twenty-Second Session of the

Joint Committee on Scientific and Technological Cooperation. Cabrisas was preceded by Cuban Foreign Minister Bruno Rodríguez, who visited Beijing to hold talks with his counterpart, Yang Jiechi. Shortly thereafter, Wu Bangguo, president of China's Permanent Committee of the National People's Assembly, visited Havana to consult with Cuban National People's Assembly President Ricardo Alarcón and with President Raúl Castro himself.

Cuba has the most highly developed biotechnology and pharmaceutical sectors in Latin America, largely because the Cuban government has invested heavily in health programs, with considerable frontline medical staffing and research output. The weakness of the sector lies in its manufacturing capacity, and for this reason Chinese assistance has been important in translating Cuba's research results into products suitable for distribution through state and market channels. Conversely, Cuban technology transfer and investment has resulted in biopharmaceutical factories in Beijing (producing anti-cancer drugs), Changchun (interferon), Shandong (drugs for blood diseases), and Xinjiang—all of them manufacturing products to be sold in both China and Cuba. Cuba has expressed its desire that future Chinese investment in the sector be directed toward the manufacture of drugs in Cuba to meet demand both at home and in other Latin American countries.

Another key area of cooperation is tourism, a sector that has become a prominent driver of Cuba's economic development. In April 2007 a Cuban tourism office was established in Beijing, and in July a memorandum of understanding entitled "Operational Plan for Chinese Tourist Groups Visiting Cuba" was signed, coming into force in November of the same year. This project has permitted a number of Chinese tourist groups to visit Cuba. The numbers are not significant as yet, but could grow if direct flights are established. Owing largely to its unique natural endowments, Cuba attracts more than two million tourists per year, and Cuban tourism enterprises are making efforts to create a more accommodating environment for Chinese tourists.

The Cuban and Chinese governments have worked together to build the tourism market and establish facilities through joint ventures. On February 3, 2010, a jointly owned Cuban-Chinese hotel managed by the Spanish consortium Meliá was inaugurated in Shanghai's Pudong Financial District in the presence of the Cuban minister of tourism. This was a first in many ways: the collaboration of two socialist state enterprises, Xintian (Suntime) and Cubanacán, opened access for a private Spanish company into the Chinese market. The next phase of the project, now underway, is to complete a $1 billion holiday resort in Havana's Marina Hemingway resort.

Cuban-Chinese joint commercial ventures are often integrated with attempts to maximize technology transfer, with the aim of progressing from initial sales of Chinese products to their eventual manufacture in Cuba. For instance, shortly after the collapse of the Soviet Union, China shipped 500,000 bicycles to Cuba. The success of the initiative led to a similar export-to-production scheme for electric fans, and more recently for household appliances and heavy machinery.

Following the successful sale of Chinese washing machines, televisions, air conditioners, and refrigerators to Cuba, Hu Jintao signed sixteen accords in 2004 pledging Chinese support for the domestic manufacture of these and other goods, a promise that has materialized in a three-story production facility near Havana's Lenin Park. Similarly, the buses sold to Cuba by the Chinese company Yutong arrived together with thirty Chinese technicians, commissioned to teach their Cuban counterparts how to build them. Like the training in electrical appliances, this kind of human capital development will provide a valuable source of specialized talent as Cuba integrates into the world economy.

The world economic crisis that hit at the end of 2008 had an impact in all countries of the world, and Cuba and China were no exceptions. For Cuba the crisis only made a bad situation worse. The annual hurricane season in 2008 (from June to December) was one of the most destructive in twenty years. The storms hit the island at a moment when the country was trying to redesign its economic model, introducing necessary changes of "structures and concepts" as President Raúl Castro announced in July 2007. The process led to the Sixth Party Congress in April 2011 and the adoption of draft guidelines for the government's future economic policy.[31] This is a moment when the Cuban leadership needs to emphasize its relationships with its key economic allies, China among them.

Although the crisis had an effect on China, most experts concur that it is one of the few countries that was able to minimize the pernicious consequences. Furthermore, China's domestic economic policies in times of crisis have been designed to diminish the social costs. In the period after the crisis, the Chinese economy became the second largest in the world. This and other factors enhance Beijing's influence in the whole world. Latin America and the Caribbean is one of the regions where China has more prospective interests.[32] Although the Chinese government avoids clashing directly with the United States in its spheres of influence, and Latin America and the Caribbean have traditionally been defined as Washington's backyard, China has been making important strides and has vital geopolitical objectives in this region.

This context has made it possible for Cuban-Chinese relations not only to continue as before but also to prosper in certain ways. The enhancement of relations after the beginning of the crisis was underlined almost immediately with the state visit of President Hu Jintao to Cuba at the end of November 2008. During that visit more than ten bilateral agreements were signed between the two countries as part of the accords reached in the Twenty-First Session of the Joint Intergovernmental Commission on Economic and Technical Cooperation, which took place in Havana shortly before Hu's arrival. Among the most beneficial of these agreements for Cuba were the postponement of payments on the trade deficit until 2018 and a credit line for $7 million for another five years. There was also an accord of mutual recognition of titles. China also agreed to give Cuba a $70 million credit for the repair and refurbishing of the health facilities on the island. The political talks between Hu and former president Fidel Castro and President Raúl Castro were broadly and positively reported on in the Cuban press.

To underline Cuba's favorable attitude toward China, Fidel Castro dedicated his March 29, 2009, *reflexión* to China, calling it "the future great economic power."[33] Referring to the forthcoming London Summit of the G-20, he stated: "As one can appreciate, the influence of the People's Republic of China in the London meeting will be enormous from the point of view of the economic crisis. This had never occurred before when the power of the United States was supreme in this field." He followed up this message the next day with another contribution in the same vein, echoing a DPA (Deutsche Presse Agentur) news dispatch from London, which argued that China would demand a greater role in world economic governance for the developing countries.[34]

The Future of Cuban-Chinese Relations

The history and contemporary development of China-Cuba relations bode well for the future. The main reasons for the estrangement between the two governments in the 1960s have disappeared. In the years since then, China has become the second-largest economy in the world and now exercises global political influence second only to that of the United States. It can be argued that no major international economic or political problem can be solved without Chinese participation and cooperation.

Cuba has been able to survive as an independent socialist state, very similar to China in many ways and with an unprecedented regional standing in Latin America and the Caribbean. One of the main reasons for Cuba's "soft power" has been its ability to survive while fighting against the U.S. economic blockade. In this light, as Cuba's ambassador to China recently put it, "The relationship between Cuba and China has been and will continue to be of decisive significance. . . . Cuba and China have reached increasing consensus."[35]

The two countries share similar ideologies and values, and both have pursued socialism with locally adapted characteristics. Each continues to advocate multipolarity in global affairs while opposing hard-power politics and external intervention, providing a strong basis for political cooperation. It is the hope of both countries that their approaches to collaboration and technology transfer will advance a more locally beneficial and reasonable mechanism of international engagement.[36] Furthermore, both leaderships have adopted the position of letting bygones be bygones, avoiding references to the fifteen to twenty years of disagreements. On this basis, the firmness of the bilateral political relationship can never be sufficiently underlined.

The intensifying political, cultural, scientific, and commercial dimensions of Cuban-Chinese relations have brought about an important economic transformation as new areas of collaboration, such as medical services and education, emerge. These are now key features of Cuba's export portfolio and were integral to the rapid rise in bilateral trade to $2.29 billion in 2007.[37] The diversification of trade signifies a major change in the relationship, which for many years saw China exporting to Cuba significantly more than it imported, with the deficit financed by Chinese loans.

In early 2008 Raúl Castro formally took office as Cuba's head of state, quickly demonstrating his considerable experience and pragmatic approach to economic restructuring. He has begun to implement reforms that steer certain productive sectors toward a market economy model—in the area, for instance, of agricultural production and in the management of enterprises to encourage economic vitality and efficiency. This process of restructuring will generate business opportunities for Chinese enterprises in numerous sectors. This process was ratified at the Sixth Party Congress, with Hu Jintao warmly congratulating Raúl Castro on his election as first secretary of the Central Committee of the Cuban Communist Party.

In terms of territory, population, economy, historical traditions, and cultural identity, the differences between Cuba and China are so great that it would be impossible for Cuba to duplicate the Asian giant's development model, as some have suggested it should do.

Nevertheless, several aspects of the reform processes introduced in China are extremely important for Cuba to emulate if it is to achieve Raúl Castro's objectives as articulated in the guidelines adopted at the Sixth Congress.[38] Among these are the enhancement of productive forces as a means of achieving socialist goals; the principle that socialism is built according to the specific characteristics of each country; the pragmatic reformulation of economic policy; more effective use of monetary-commercial relations through the socialist market economy; and the monitoring and refinement of newly introduced measures to address any unintended outcomes of the reform process.

Principles such as these have enabled the Chinese leadership to lift 300 to 500 million people out of poverty in a relatively short time, to create a middle class of some 180 to 200 million, and as a result to endow the country with significant social stability. These achievements have not been free of negative consequences, but it must be acknowledged that there is no perfect society, and that the leaders of the Chinese Communist Party are the first to admit these difficulties.

In the more immediate term, Cuba also has much to offer China. The country's oil industry represents a key opportunity for Chinese firms, which are encouraged by the discovery of potentially large reserves in the Gulf of Mexico. The rapid development of the Chinese economy has dramatically increased its demand for oil, leading the Chinese government to implement strategies to secure multiple supply sources. Because Cuba would benefit from China's demand for oil, there is enormous room for bilateral cooperation in this field. Due to its lack of exploration and production capacities, Cuba needs help in finding and accessing its oil reserves. For some years Sinopec has carried out onshore oil exploration in the west of Cuba, and the Cuban government now wishes to cooperate with Chinese oil enterprises that are capable of ultra-deepwater drilling to explore and exploit offshore oilfields.

Just as China's demand for oil is increasing, so too is its demand for nickel. Cuba is endowed with major nickel deposits and is an important world supplier, creating another significant nexus for mutually beneficial development. The two countries have reached an agreement on strategic cooperation in this field, and further measures to facilitate the export of Cuban nickel ore to China are under exploration.

Significant room exists for boosting bilateral economic and trade relations. As the Cuban ambassador to China stated in September 2008, "today, what is important to Cuba is to push and support the participation of Chinese enterprises in the Cuban market. It means not only increasing joint investment in well-known fields, but also promoting investment and cooperation in modern technology, import substitution, renewable electricity sources, telecommunications, transportation, infrastructure facilities, and other sectors. At the same time, Cuba will increase investment in China, especially in health services and biological products manufacturing."[39] One important factor in Havana's new economic policies, which might be very important for its relations with China, is the emphasis that Raúl Castro has placed on the need to control Cuba's external debt.

Following these ideas and principles, relations between Cuba and China will continue to develop and increase in both the economic and political fields. For Cuba, China is a strategic ally, especially because of its world role, but also because of its increasing economic strengths. For China, Cuba is a vital link with Latin America and the Caribbean. Cuba has established a number of alliances in the region—with Venezuela, Brazil, Argentina, and other countries—which can only benefit Beijing. The geopolitical and ideological implications of Cuban-Chinese relations can never be sufficiently emphasized. Recent developments have demonstrated that Cuba exercises a very active and influential foreign policy, especially in Latin America and the Caribbean, a region where its interests coincide with those of Beijing.

It is difficult to envisage that the U.S. government could ever pressure China into abandoning Cuba. Furthermore, the normalization of Cuban-U.S. relations would not damage China in any way.

Notes

1. "Sino-Cuba Relations," *China Daily*, November 11, 2004; website of the Ministry of Foreign Affairs of the People's Republic of China, www.fmprc.gov.cn.

2. Eric Hobsbawm, *The Age of Extremes: The Short Twentieth Century* (London: Michael Joseph, 1994), ch. 16; Odd Arne Westad, *The Global Cold War: Third World Interventions and the Making of Our Times* (Cambridge: Cambridge University Press, 2005).

3. Moscow was not able to establish diplomatic relations with the United States from 1917 until 1933, during the Franklin Delano Roosevelt administration. Washington maintained relations with the Nationalist government in Taiwan after 1949 and did not officially recognize the People's Republic of China until 1979. The Eisenhower administration broke diplomatic relations with Cuba in 1961 and no administration since has reestablished relations.

4. See Xu Shicheng, "El desarrollo de las relaciones sino-latinoamericanas," lecture, Higher Institute of International Relations, Ministry of Foreign Affairs, Havana, Cuba, June 15, 2005.

5. Jorge Domínguez, *To Make the World Safe for Revolution: Cuba's Foreign Policy* (Cambridge, MA: Harvard University Press, 1989), 27.

6. Simon Shen, "Romanticization for Domestic Debate: Online Chinese Perceptions of Cuba and Implications for Cuban-Chinese Relations," paper presented at the Latin American Studies Association Congress, Toronto, October 2010, 2. The author is associate professor in the Faculty of Arts and Sciences at the Hong Kong Institute of Education.

7. Cheng Yinghong, "Sino-Cuban Relations during the Early Years of the Castro Regime, 1959-1966," *Journal of Cold War Studies* 9, no. 3 (Summer 2007), 78–114; Wang Youping, *My Career as Ambassador in Seven Countries* (Nanjing: Jiangsu Renmin Publisher, 1996), 85–87, as cited by Cheng several times (original in Chinese).

8. Cheng, "Sino-Cuban Relations," 113.

9. Ibid.

10. For a brief description of this split, see Archie Brown, *The Rise and Fall of Communism* (New York: HarperCollins, 2009), 318–24.

11. Westad, *Global Cold War*, 158.

12. Quoted in Westad, *Global Cold War*, 176.

13. Zhu Wenchi, Mao Xianglin, and Li Keming, *Latin American Communist Movement* (Beijing: Contemporary World Press, 2002), 319 (original in Chinese).

14. Mao, quoted in Stuart Schram, ed., *Chairman Mao Talks to the People* (New York: Pantheon Books, 1974), 198, quoted in Cheng, "Sino-Cuban Relations," 101.

15. Quoted in Cheng, "Sino-Cuban Relations," 88, 101–2.

16. Piero Gleijeses, *Conflicting Missions: Havana, Washington and Africa, 1959–1976* (Chapel Hill: University of North Carolina Press, 2002), 104–5.

17. Quoted in Cheng, "Sino-Cuban Relations," 98; from Herbert L. Matthews, *Revolution in Cuba: An Essay in Understanding* (New York: Charles Scribner's Sons, 1975), 78.

18. Cheng, "Sino-Cuban Relations," 98, 105–6.

19. Gleijeses, *Conflicting Missions*, 345.

20. Yinghong Sheng, "Sino-Cuban Relations and the Future of Cuba after Fidel Castro," *History Compass* 5, no. 2 (2007), 729.

21. H. Michael Erisman, *Cuba's Foreign Relations in a Post-Soviet World* (Gainesville: University Press of Florida, 2000), 139.

22. The compiled data are based on reports in *China Daily*, *Granma* (Havana), and other official media in both countries.

23. The following section draws from (adapting and updating) Mao Xianglin, Liu Weiguang, Carlos Alzugaray Treto, and Adrian H. Hearn, "China and Cuba: Past, Present, and Future," in Adrian H. Hearn and José Luis León Manríquez, eds., *China Engages Latin America: Tracing the Trajectory* (Boulder, CO: Lynne Rienner Publishers, 2011).

24. "Cuba's Repayment of Debt Deferred," *China Daily*, November 20, 2008, www.chinadaily.com.cn/cndy/2008-11/20/content_7221725.htm.

25. Economist Intelligence Unit, "Country Profile: Cuba 2008," 16; see store.eiu.com/product/30000203CU.html.

26. Ibid., 50.

27. *Xinhua*, November 17, 2008, news.xinhuanet.com/world/2008-11/17/content_10370729.htm.

28. Yuan Dongzhen, "The Third Cuban-Chinese Social Sciences Seminar Convened in Havana," *Journal of Latin American Studies* 3 (2008), 74 (original in Chinese).

29. Interview with the author, July 5, 2007.

30. "Premier Wen Jiabao Visits Cuban and Japanese Medical Teams," Ministry of Foreign Affairs of the People's Republic of China, May 28, 2008, www.fmprc.gov.cn/eng/zxxx/t459401.htm; Carlos Miguel Pereira Hernández (Cuban ambassador to China), Speech on the 48th Anniversary of the Establishment of Diplomatic Relations between Cuba and China, Cuban Embassy in China, September 26, 2008.

31. Raúl Castro Ruz, "Trabajar con sentido crítico, creador, sin anquilosamientos ni esquematismos," Discurso en el acto central por el LIV aniversario del asalto al Cuartel Moncada, Camagüey, July 26, 2007, published in *Granma*, July 27, 2007. For the English translation, see 21stcenturysocialism.com/article/ral_castros_camagey_speech_01517.html. For the Spanish-language version of the guidelines, see: www.cubadebate.cu/wp-content/uploads/2010/11/proyecto-lineamientos-pcc.pdf.

32. Mitch Moxley, "China avanza sobre América Latina," IPS Spanish service, August 24, 2010, reproduced in Rebelión digital newspaper, www.ipsnoticias.net/nota.asp?idnews=96200.

33. "China, la futura gran potencia económica," *Reflexiones de Fidel*, March 29, 2009, Cubadebate website, www.cubadebate.cu/reflexiones-fidel/2009/03/29/china-futura-gran-potencia-economica/.

34. "China en los cables internacionales," *Reflexiones de Fidel*, March 30, 2009, www.cubadebate.cu/reflexiones-fidel/2009/03/30/china-cables-internacionales/.

35. Carlos Miguel Pereira Hernández, Speech on the Forty-Eighth Anniversary of the Establishment of Diplomatic Relations.

36. Mao Xianglin, *Studies on Cuban Socialism* (Beijing: Social Sciences Academic Press, 2005), 320–21.

37. Carlos Miguel Pereira Hernández, "Current Socialist Building in Cuba," *Journal of Latin American Studies* [Institute of Latin American Studies, Chinese Academy of Social Sciences] 30, no. 2 (2008).

38. For the main documents approved at the Sixth Congress of the Cuban Communist Party (Spanish version) see www.cubadebate.cu/noticias/2011/05/09/descargue-en-cubadebate-los-lineamientos-de-la-politica-economica-y-social-pdf/.

39. Carlos Miguel Pereira Hernández, Speech on the Forty-Eighth Anniversary of the Establishment of Diplomatic Relations.

6

"Complicated and Far-Reaching"
The Historical Foundations of Canadian Policy toward Cuba

ASA MCKERCHER

Over several weeks in early 1962 Canada and the United States argued publicly over Cuba. Speaking to reporters in Vancouver, Arthur Schlesinger Jr., an aide to U.S. president John Kennedy, charged Canada with aiding and abetting Cuban revolutionary activity throughout Latin America. A few days later, while addressing an Organization of American States (OAS) summit, U.S. Secretary of State Dean Rusk raised Canada-Cuba trade as a source of concern. Firing back in the House of Commons, Canadian Prime Minister John Diefenbaker declared that Canada would not be pressured into adopting policies with which it did not agree. In private the issue of Cuba was just as divisive. When Rusk followed up his public rebuke of Ottawa by pressing the Canadian ambassador in Washington to urge his government to support the U.S. embargo, the two men argued bitterly for several hours. Alarmed by this sniping, Howard Green, the Canadian foreign minister, ordered a review of Canada's Cuba policy.[1]

The resulting report began by observing, "The implications of our relations with Cuba, particularly in terms of U.S.-Canada relations, are complicated and far-reaching. Our policy has frequently been misunderstood and occasionally distorted both at home and abroad." Even though Ottawa and Havana had different political and economic ideologies, and despite Canadian officials' doubts about the direction of Cuban domestic and foreign policy, Canada found little reason to abandon its normal relationship with the Caribbean nation. A complicating factor was the United States, a power that had long tried to dominate Cuba. Given both Washington's strong desire to overturn the Cuban revolution and the economic and military importance of the United States to Canada, Ottawa's independent stance toward Cuba was remarkable. By following its own course and avoiding "'knuckling under' to U.S. pressure," the Canadian government made it "clear that our policy was not calculated essentially as a mere demonstration of independence for its own sake regardless of the merits of the case." Rather, Canadian policy toward Cuba was based on the principle that

Ottawa should maintain normal relations with any other country, regardless of ideology, differences in political outlook, or the wishes of Canada's chief ally.[2]

Doubtless a paper tracing a similar view of policy toward Cuba could be produced in Canadian government circles today. As scholars of Canada-Cuba relations observe, Diefenbaker laid the "foundation" of the "special relationship" between the two countries, and "the pattern first established by Diefenbaker—to treat Cuba as a 'normal' state"—has held for more than fifty years.[3] While it may beggar belief to label Diefenbaker—the archetype of a fusty, conservative politician—a trendsetter, he did indeed lay a basis for Canadian relations with revolutionary Cuba. Over the at times vociferous objections of Washington, Diefenbaker maintained economic and diplomatic ties with Havana. At the same time he and other Canadian officials looked on with evident concern at Cuba's new system of government and its actions in foreign affairs. As a comparison of Canadian policy toward Cuba in the Diefenbaker era and in more contemporary periods makes clear, the contours of the normal relationship between Canada and Cuba have changed little over time.

After the Revolution

Following the victory of Fidel Castro's 26th of July Movement in January 1959, Canada was quick to recognize the new government in Havana. It did so eight days after the dictator Fulgencio Batista fled the country. Although Canadian diplomats in Cuba held reservations about some of Castro's actions during his first months in power, generally Ottawa looked favorably upon the revolution.[4] In autumn 1959, after revolutionary reforms had begun to be implemented, a new Canadian ambassador arrived in the Cuban capital with instructions that read "We have no outstanding political problems with Cuba" and "as the [representative] in Cuba of a friendly country you . . . will, therefore, display as much patience and understanding as are compatible with your functions and seek ways to reconcile Canadian political and economic interests with a revolution which cannot be stabilized until the deep grievances that produced it have been redressed." For Ottawa the legitimacy of the revolution was clearly not in doubt. What worried officials in the Canadian foreign ministry was that "the inexperienced revolutionary government of Dr. Fidel Castro is undertaking very ambitious new social and economic programmes which have already begun to produce serious reactions at home and abroad." Thus, at this early date, although Canada had concerns about instability in Cuba and the Western Hemisphere, no major upsets in Canadian-Cuban relations were being predicted.[5]

Nonetheless, over time additional concerns developed among Canadian government observers. An embassy cable from early 1960 pointed out, "We do not know whether Castro is a Communist or not. That is to say, we do not know whether . . . he follows the orthodox Marxist ideology." Still, the Cuban leader appeared to be "closely entangled with Communists, here and abroad. If we are right, the precise label on Castro as a person makes no difference. Castro as an executive of the State acts like a full Communist."[6] The issue of categorizing Cuba's government continued to vex the Canadian Embassy in Havana. A report from spring 1961 declared, "The ideological label that should be affixed to Castro's Cuba may still be somewhat obscure but the nature of his regime is not difficult to discern: it is [a] ruthless dictatorship," one that "is establishing a highly nationalized and planned economy on the basis of the experiences of the Sino-Soviet bloc nations." In addition to these telltale domestic actions, Cuba was clearly moving closer toward Canada's Cold War enemies. "By whatever name they may be called," the report concluded, "these are unmistakably the characteristics common to communist countries."[7]

Yet the exact label to be applied to the Cuban system of government ultimately mattered little. In 1962 Canada's undersecretary of state offered an overview of Ottawa's position on Cuba to Canadian delegates at a joint Canada-U.S. economic summit. Expecting, correctly, that the Cuban issue would emerge as a point of debate with the U.S. delegates, he stated that his government "acknowledges the Communist commitments of the present Cuban regime in both its domestic and external policies," but that this "ideological orientation" did not provide sufficient grounds for breaking diplomatic or economic relations. Crucially, when Cuba's government moved to nationalize foreign-owned firms, Canadian economic interests were protected and dealt with in a nonconfrontational manner.[8] Therefore the Canadian government watched the implementation of Castro's nationalist program and other socialist reforms with interested dispassion rather than anger. For Canadian policymakers, Cuba was just another state, even if communist. Although Canada and Cuba were ultimately on opposite sides of the Cold War divide—indeed, at the height of Cold War tension in the early 1960s—officials in Ottawa did not see any reason why either ideology or Cuba's own domestic policies should prevent the maintenance of good bilateral relations.

With the end of the Cold War in 1989–91, affixing a label to the Cuban government as a guide for policy completely lost relevance. André Ouellet, Canada's foreign minister in the mid-1990s, stated plainly, "It is time to turn the page on Cuba. The Cold War is over."[9] The recent reforms implemented by Cuban prime minister Raúl Castro have been welcomed in Canada. Before departing for Cuba in early 2012, the Canadian minister responsible for the Americas noted that she saw "a very significant process of economic reform and liberalization in Cuba," although she lamented that "political change is not what the Cuban leadership had in mind."[10] Cuba's domestic policies are important to Canada, but they are not a defining factor of Canadian policy.

Still, during the Cold War Cuba's alignment with the Soviet Union and other communist states did trouble the Canadian government. Although Diefenbaker reacted to the failed U.S.-backed invasion of Cuba at Playa Girón in April 1961 by warning the U.S. ambassador in Canada that he disagreed sharply with the intervention, he nevertheless warned the Cuban ambassador, "There was one Cuban export with which the world and particularly Latin America could do without and that was the effort to export the Cuban Revolution in the form which it has now taken."[11] In public he chided Cuba's government for showing "manifestations of a dictatorship which are abhorrent to free men everywhere," but he saved his full opprobrium for Moscow. The Soviet Union's support for Havana "revealed beyond doubt the extent to which international communism is prepared to go in consolidating its foothold in Cuba, a bridgehead from which the penetration of the whole of Latin America could be launched."[12] Diefenbaker's view of Cuba was seen through a Cold War lens but, again, even Cuban alignment with the USSR provided little reason to curtail normal relations. Indeed, at a NATO summit held a month after the Playa Girón invasion, Diefenbaker's foreign minister informed his colleagues that Ottawa shared Washington's concern "about the evidence of Castro's increasing orientation toward the Soviet bloc." But, he thought, there seemed to be little "conclusive proof" of Cuba's "complete adherence" to the Soviet side.[13]

Although Canadian officialdom was content to let the Cuban government go its own way on domestic politics, the Cold War atmosphere meant that Canada did become an increasing critic of Cuba's foreign policy. Summing up elements of foreign policymaking "behind the Sugarcane Curtain" in an October 1962 memorandum, Undersecretary of State Norman Robertson cast a woeful eye toward the increasing Cuban ties to the Soviet Union, the People's Republic of China, and the countries of Eastern Europe. Looking in particular to the expanding Soviet military presence on the island as a cause of apprehension, Robertson nevertheless expressed the belief that "there seems to be no substantial reason for terminating our present normal diplomatic relations with Cuba."[14] Canada deplored Cuban foreign policy but, again, this aversion did not provide grounds for cutting ties to the island.

Only two weeks after Robertson finished his report the Cuban Missile Crisis brought the world to the brink of nuclear war. Famously, or infamously, Diefenbaker initially refused to back Kennedy's brinksmanship. As one scholar argued, "Underlying Canadian-American interaction during the missile crisis were profoundly different perceptions of Fidel Castro's Cuba."[15]

Diefenbaker's actions, however, were the result of issues within Canadian-U.S. relations—sovereignty and the question of consultation during a military emergency being chief among them—and his refusal to alert Canada's military forces stemmed from a distaste for Kennedy and not from any bonhomie for Castro. Throughout the crisis, Canadian diplomats were unstintingly critical of Cuba. At several points the Cuban ambassador was called into Canada's Department of External Affairs to be harangued for his government's actions, which posed a "grave threat to the security of the Americas, including Canada." In Havana the Canadian ambassador lodged several protests with the Cuban foreign minister. Unlike their response to the Bay of Pigs, Canadian officials, except for the prime minister, viewed Washington's response to the crisis as "a necessary response to clear provocation."[16] So, just as Cuba had very little to do with either U.S. or Soviet decision making during those thirteen days of October, so too was Diefenbaker's initial decision not to back the United States based upon his grievances with Washington and not upon any appreciation for Havana's position.[17] But even this grave crisis was not enough to prompt Canada to abandon its ties with Cuba.

Nor were Cuba's ties to the Soviet Union the only aspect of Cuban foreign policy that troubled Canada. Canadian diplomatic posts throughout Latin America often issued warnings about the appeal of the words "Viva Castro" or cautioned that the "Cubans are both activists and a symbol making them a grave danger to Latin American political stability."[18] Concerns were also raised in the mid-1970s about Cuba's activism in Angola, where Cuban armed forces intervened in support of a leftist liberation movement. This intervention came midway into the "golden age" of relations between Canada and Cuba, a period that coincided with the premiership of Pierre Elliott Trudeau, who expanded bilateral contacts between the two countries and, in 1976, became the first Western leader to travel to Havana. Yet that visit took place under a cloud, and despite the friendly rapport between Trudeau and Castro, their meetings with one another, at least when the issue of Angola was broached, became, as the prime minister reported to the House of Commons, "brutal and frank."[19] Shortly after returning from his trip, Trudeau wrote Castro to complain about the presence of Cuban troops in Angola. "The resolution of the basic political problems of that country," he argued, "and the achievement of permanent stability, will be hastened by the removal of all elements of foreign involvement." As in the Diefenbaker era, there was worry over Cuban efforts to export its revolution. Despite Trudeau's sunny disposition, then, "after Angola nothing was ever the same in Canadian-Cuban relations." Indeed, a similar pattern played out in the early 1980s, when Cuban support for left-wing movements in Nicaragua and El Salvador led to an exchange of sharp letters between Trudeau and Castro.[20]

Frostiness with Cuba as a result of that country's foreign policy was, then, a constant. In the wake of the spat between Ottawa and Havana over Angola, James Hyndman, Canada's envoy in the Cuban capital, argued for a rapprochement. Encouraging improved bilateral contacts, high-level visits, and increased aid, he opined, would serve "not only our direct commercial and political interests, but also our wider interest in moderating Soviet influence in Cuba" and fostering Cuba's "reintegration within the Latin American community and normalisation with the USA."[21] Little came of Hyndman's efforts. Instead, the prevailing attitude in Ottawa reflected the sentiment of a paper produced in 1981. Citing "Cuba's orthodox Communist government, its close economic and political dependence on the Soviet Union, its activities in Africa and its interference in Central America and the Caribbean," the paper concluded that "the naturally hostile relationship between the United States and Cuba places severe restraints on the development of closer relations."[22]

This attitude carried over when Progressive Conservative Party leader Brian Mulroney became prime minister in 1984 and moved Canada closer to the United States. Even so, at no point were Cuban actions abroad or Cuba's relations with other countries seen to provide sufficient grounds for Ottawa to sever bilateral relations. The pattern in place since 1959 held: Canada treated Cuba as a normal country. Its disapproval of Cuban foreign policy over the years was no different, say, from equally dim assessments of U.S. policy in Southeast Asia or U.S. relations with odious right-wing regimes.

With the end of the Cold War, the anxiety shown over Cuban foreign policy declined, although one can imagine the Canadian government being at least somewhat concerned with Cuba's promotion of ALBA, the Bolivarian Alliance for the Peoples of the Americas, a grouping of nations committed to economic policies that are in stark contrast to Canada's support of neoliberalism. Since the late 1980s, beyond championing international organizations such as the World Bank and the International Monetary Fund, successive Canadian governments across the political spectrum have vigorously pursued free trade. Economic imperatives have long driven Canada's engagement with Latin America and the Caribbean and, as of late 2013, Canada has more free trade agreements in the Americas than with the rest of the world combined. "Canada promotes open doors to trade and responsible investment," affirmed Diane Ablonczy, Canadian minister of state for the Americas, in late 2011, adding "open markets with our neighbours are a priority for us."[23] Whereas Ottawa champions private-market–based economic globalization—the capstone being the now-stalled effort to negotiate a Free Trade Area of the Americas—Havana, with its partners in ALBA, stands diametrically opposed to such neoliberal notions. Further, in an effort to protect its sovereignty, the Cuban government places controls on the actions of foreign investors. As in the Cold War, Canada and Cuba still find themselves on different sides of an ideological divide.

Humanitarian Concerns and "Constructive Engagement"

Differences over foreign and economic policy aside, one area in which Cuban actions have deeply upset Canada—more so, it seems, than on any other issue—has been human rights. While bilateral disputes on this question have been prominent in contemporary Canada-Cuba relations, even here the roots can be traced back to Diefenbaker. Like many Western observers, Canadian officials deplored the "revolutionary trials" and resulting executions of members of the Batista government that took place within the first few months of the revolution.[24] Hackles also rose in early 1962, when the Cuban government put on trial those members of the invading force from the Playa Girón attack who had been taken prisoner. A vocal champion of human rights, Diefenbaker ordered Canada's foreign office to raise humanitarian concerns through both the Cuban ambassador in Ottawa and the Canadian ambassador in Havana. When an aide pointed out that, with one exception, those on trial were not Canadians, Diefenbaker responded that he still held an interest in seeing fair trials as well as the avoidance of death sentences for any of those found guilty. "If Castro took exception to this," he said, "we could break off trade with Cuba."[25] Perhaps only an off-the-cuff remark, this comment nevertheless showed the depth of feeling that Diefenbaker, and successive prime ministers, have had with regard to Havana's respect for Western-defined human rights.

Since the end of the Cold War, humanitarian concerns have only increased as an issue on the bilateral agenda. Jean Chrétien, the Liberal Party prime minister from 1993 to 2003, was very much a successor to Trudeau, both in his outlook on many political issues and in his desire to seek increased ties with Cuba. Like that of Trudeau, his premiership was divided between a good and then a tense period of relations. Under considerable pressure from U.S. critics to curtail Canada's trade to Cuba, Chrétien courageously refused, instead advocating for treating Cuba as a normal country. One proviso was that Canadian officials would urge Havana to implement reforms. The collapse of the Soviet Union and of Soviet-backed regimes in Eastern Europe showed that the communist world was not static. Canada's diplomats and politicians began to do what they had never done before: insist that Cuba change. Addressing the OAS General Assembly in 1994, Christine Stewart, Chrétien's secretary of state for Latin America, averred, "It is in all our interests, individually and as an organization, as well as in the interests of the people of Cuba, that we support a process of change in Cuba that is positive and orderly."[26]

To bring about this change, Ottawa pursued a policy known as "constructive engagement," which became the watchword of Canada-Cuba relations during the late 1990s, although, in truth, since 1959 the Canadian approach has favored engagement. Through increased bilateral contacts, Ottawa has hoped, in the words of Lloyd Axworthy, Chrétien's second foreign minister, to "provide Cuba with the assistance and support that will be needed if a peaceful transition is to occur with full respect for human rights, genuinely representative government institutions, and an open economy."[27] The human rights issue proved especially thorny, though, particularly given that it served as a lightning rod for critics of constructive engagement. Ultimately Canada's advocacy of human rights led to a chill in relations between Havana and Ottawa.

Famously calling for putting some "northern ice" into the Canada-Cuba relationship in 1998 after a raucous meeting with Fidel Castro, Chrétien ordered a review of his country's Cuban policy, delayed official visits to the island, and condemned Cuba in annual UN votes on human rights. Commenting on the jailing of several political dissidents, he complained, "Cuba sends an unfortunate signal to her friends in the international community when people are jailed for peaceful protest."[28] Signs of a thaw in the relationship were evident in 2002, when a Canadian trade mission led by a government minister traveled to Havana, but the jailing of dissidents the following year prompted the foreign minister to reprimand the Cuban ambassador. Ottawa also gave its support to a resolution calling for the OAS to take noneconomic moves to pressure Cuba over its human rights record.[29]

This chill, and its connection to humanitarian concerns, did not dissipate and indeed showed little sign of fading under the Conservative prime minister Stephen Harper. Peter Kent, Canada's secretary of state for Latin America and Africa from 2008 to 2011, put it bluntly: Cuba "is a dictatorship, any way you package it."[30] Despite such heated rhetoric Harper's government did not alter the shape of the bilateral relationship. As with Cuba's communist orientation during the Cold War, the Cuban government's position on human rights had not been a sine qua non for normal relations with Canada. In sharp contrast to Kent's comments, in January 2012 Diane Ablonczy, who took over his ministerial portfolio, promised not to "take a lecturing approach" with her Cuban counterparts on human rights. "There's a lot of debate around these things," she continued, "and there's a lot of caution too. But Canada, as an investor in Cuba, with lots of people-to-people contact, wants to play as positive and constructive a role as possible."[31] The Harper government's approach bears a notable resemblance to that of its Liberal Party predecessors. Speaking at the Canadian Foundation of the Americas in 1996, for instance, Christine Stewart noted that Canada desired "a peaceful transition to a genuinely representative government," one that "fully respected internationally agreed human rights standards. And we look forward to Cuba becoming an open economy. However, we differ from the United States on how to reach these objectives. We have chosen the path of engagement and dialogue; the United States has picked isolation."[32]

Trade Relations: Isolation, Engagement, Dialogue

Comparisons between U.S. and Canadian policy toward Cuba are striking because they differ so markedly in terms of the divide between isolation and engagement. They are also conspicuous given that the U.S. factor in Canadian-Cuban relations has been ubiquitous. Canada's close ally and closest trading partner, the United States is also Cuba's sworn enemy. Much of Canada's Cuban policy has been determined by the United States, and scholars have referred to the existence of a "Canada-Cuba-U.S. triangle."[33] Again, Diefenbaker set the Canadian course, one that reflected fundamentally different views of international relations. As the Canadian ambassador to the United States in the early 1960s reminded U.S. diplomats, Ottawa and Washington held divergent beliefs on trade and diplomatic representation "with governments of whose systems we totally disapproved."[34]

This position was made clear to U.S. officials early on in their growing dispute with Castro. In July 1960, with their program of economic warfare beginning to take shape, several U.S. cabinet members approached their Canadian counterparts to inquire as to whether Ottawa would join Washington in an embargo. After listening to the Americans plead their case, Canadian foreign minister Howard Green responded that he was "very doubtful of the wisdom of attempting to deal with the Cuban situation by external economic pressure." Once the embargo was put in place that October, Green reported to the Canadian cabinet that he and the prime minister saw Canada-Cuba relations as "normal." Some two months later, after remaining silent on the issue in public, Diefenbaker outlined Canadian policy toward Cuba to the House of Commons. There was, he said, "no valid objection to trade with Cuba" nor was there reason to abandon "the kind of relations with Cuba which are usual with the recognized government of another country."[35]

Still, two areas of cooperation on the embargo did emerge. Soon after the revolution Canada moved to stop arms sales to the Caribbean, and hence to Cuba, later expanding this ban to specifically target Cuba and prevent sales of items with even minimal strategic and military value, such as dynamite. The latter restrictions were so potent that one State Department official tasked with coordinating the embargo praised the Canadian controls as a model for other countries to follow.[36]

Then, with the embargo about to go into effect in October 1960, the Americans asked that the Canadian government prevent the transshipment, or re-export, of goods of U.S. origin to Cuba via Canada. Commenting on this appeal, Diefenbaker remarked to an aide that he did not rule out "some degree of cooperation" with the United States. On the following day he added that "he was not inclined in favour of more than a minimum compliance" with the U.S. request. As Diefenbaker told Parliament, minimum compliance meant that Canada would not "exploit the situation arising from the United States embargo, and we have no intention of encouraging what would in fact be bootlegging of goods of United States origin."[37] While Canadian firms certainly took advantage of the absence of U.S. competitors in the Cuban market, Ottawa's policies of preventing the re-export of U.S. goods into Cuba and circumscribing the sale of strategic items remained in full force over the following decades, into the present.

Cooperating with Washington, however, did not mean approving of U.S. policy. Meeting with Kennedy in February 1961, Diefenbaker made clear that it was Canadian policy to trade with all nations. He added, though, that his government had restricted trade in strategic items, had forbidden the re-export of U.S. goods through Canada to Cuba, and was not pushing to expand Canadian-Cuban trade. Still, he cautioned that it was "perfectly true" that "when Canada disagreed with the United States on policy it would not follow the United States' lead." Diefenbaker's unstinting position came under attack from the White House, the State Department, the U.S. Congress, and the American public, but he held firm, as did successive Canadian prime ministers who faced down similar attacks from critics within the United States.[38]

Perhaps at no time was U.S. criticism of Canada-Cuba trade worse than in the 1990s. Energized by the end of the Cold War and by the strains that the collapse of the Soviet Union placed upon Cuba, the U.S. Congress passed a series of bills targeting foreign trade with Cuba: the Mack Amendment in 1990, the Cuban Democracy (or Torricelli) Act in 1992, and the Cuban Liberty and Democratic Solidarity (or Helms-Burton) Act in 1996. Against this legislation, all of which strengthened the embargo and impugned Canadian sovereignty by threatening the principle of territoriality, Canada launched angry protests and raised the specter of using the Foreign Extraterritorial Measures Act, blocking legislation that could target businessmen and businesswomen who attempted to comply with extraterritorial measures. Summing up the Canadian position, one that Diefenbaker would have defended, Axworthy explained, "The whole embargo and the Helms-Burton bill is totally counterproductive. . . . It just doesn't work."[39] Thankfully for Canada, successive U.S. presidents were unwilling to apply the extraterritorial provisions of this legislation, but the ongoing embargo, despite some loosening, would continue to underscore the differences between Ottawa and Washington over Cuba.

Apprehensive about the direction of U.S. policy, Canada has intermittently sought to mediate the Cuban-U.S. dispute, or at least Canadian officials have toyed with this idea. The mid-1960s saw a joint effort by the Brazilians, Mexicans, and Canadians to offer their "good offices" to begin a rapprochement between Cuba and the United States.[40] This trilateral overture proved futile, but failure did not dissuade Howard Green from trying again. In the wake of the failed Playa Girón invasion, a move that brought the U.S.-Cuban dispute to a new low, Green remarked to a NATO foreign ministers conference that he hoped "that the possibility of negotiation [between Washington and Havana] would not be ruled out." He then voiced this message publicly, telling several reporters that Canada would be more than willing to act as a mediator. The remark drew a sharp rebuke from Washington.[41]

Green's hope to bring about an end to the Cuban-U.S. quarrel did not die. Speaking in 1990, Mulroney's foreign minister, Joe Clark, pointed out that the Canadian government was "trying to go in and see what we can do." As he explained, "Canada can't solve the contest between Cuba and the United States, but we may well be able to create some conditions . . . to create some room where the principal actors might move."[42] Almost two decades later Michael Wilson, the Canadian ambassador in Washington, echoed this sentiment: "We have a dialogue, and that is different from the United States because they have nothing like this type of dialogue." Due to this channel of communication, Wilson said, "We have an understanding of how Cuba thinks. We also have an understanding of how Washington thinks. Cuba sees us as a North American country with which they can have some sort of dialogue. We can build a greater understanding between the two countries."[43] Hope springs eternal, and the normal relationship between Ottawa and Havana may pay dividends to any U.S. administration that intends to alter a policy of isolation that has failed for more than fifty years.

Whether or not Canada can play a role in bringing about a rapprochement in Cuban-U.S. relations, the Canadian position on Cuba has proved advantageous for both Cuba and Canada. Both countries benefited from economic, educational, and cultural ties, and although the policy of constructive engagement as pursued by Chrétien failed, "*engagement* has not."[44] Canadian engagement with Cuba, which has always been constructive, owes much to Diefenbaker. While other Canadian prime ministers could have taken the step of abrogating ties with Havana, Diefenbaker, at the height of Cold War tension and revolutionary fervor in the Western Hemisphere, had the greatest justification for choosing to isolate Cuba. But he chose not to do so. His policy, still in effect today, was to construct "a normal relationship . . . one in which both sides politely agree to disagree on certain policy questions."[45] Such disagreements—whether on Angola, human rights, or free trade—have not led to a breach between Ottawa and Havana. Travel, trade, and diplomatic links have remained intact through years of bilateral and international friction and show no signs of ending. Indeed, although Canada's current government, that of Conservative Party prime minister Stephen Harper, initially signaled that it would adopt a new strategy toward Cuba, like its predecessors it has instead chosen engagement over isolation. Whether or not this approach will result in the constructive changes that have long been championed by Canadian policymakers remains to be seen, but since 1959 Canada's approach to Cuba has been remarkably consistent.

Notes

1. Ottawa Embassy to State, no. 708, January 29, 1962, John F. Kennedy Library (hereafter JFKL), Arthur M. Schlesinger Jr. Collection, White House Files, box 3a, file Canada; "Rusk Hopeful Canada Will Join Boycott of Cuba," *Globe and Mail*, February 2, 1962; Canada, House of Commons, *Debates*, February 2, 1962, 479–80; Campbell to Robertson, memo, "Cuba—Trade Policy," March 8, 1962, Library and Archives Canada (hereafter LAC), Basil Robinson fonds, MG 31 E83, vol. 5, file 18.

2. Memorandum for the Minister, "Relations with Cuba," March 8, 1962, LAC, MG 31 E83, vol. 5, file 19.

3. John Kirk and Peter McKenna, *Canada-Cuba Relations: The Other Good Neighbor Policy* (Gainesville: University Press of Florida, 1997), 34; and Lana Wylie, *Perceptions of Cuba: Canadian and American Policies in Comparative Perspective* (Toronto: University of Toronto Press, 2010), 16.

4. For an excellent examination of the views emanating from the Canadian Embassy in the Cuban capital, see Don Munton and David Vogt, "Inside Castro's Cuba: The Revolution and Canada's Embassy in Havana," in Robert Wright and Lana Wylie, eds., *Our Place in the Sun: Canada and Cuba in the Castro Era* (Toronto: University of Toronto Press, 2009), 51–55.

5. Secretary of State for External Affairs to Ambassador in Cuba, September 25, 1959, in Janice Cavell, Michael D. Stevenson, and Kevin Spooner, *Documents on Canadian External Relations 1959* (Ottawa: Public Works and Government Services Canada, 2006), 961–65.

6. Havana to External, numbered letter L-68, January 29, 1960, LAC, Department of External Affairs fonds, RG 25, vol. 7258, file 10224-40 pt. 7.

7. Havana to External, numbered letter L-304, April 11, 1961, LAC, RG 25, vol. 5352, file 10224-40 pt. 11.

8. Memorandum for the Minister, "The Cuban Question," January 11, 1962, LAC, Howard Green fonds, MG 32 B13, vol. 7, file 10. The Royal Bank of Canada and the Bank of Nova Scotia both had a "preeminent role in prerevolutionary society," and Canadian insurance companies dominated the Cuban market; see Kirk and McKenna, *Canada-Cuba Relations*, 16.

9. Mimi Whitefield, "Saying 'the Cold War Is Over,' Canada Restores Aid to Cuba," *Miami Herald*, June 21, 1994.

10. Mike Blanchford, "Canada Welcomes Cuban Reforms on Eve of Tour by Harper's Latin America Minister," *Canadian Press*, January 8, 2012.

11. Embtel G-252, April 25, 1961, U.S. National Archives and Records Administration, Foreign Service Post files, RG 84, Box 224, file Cuba Limited Distribution, 1959–1961.

12. Canada, House of Commons, *Debates*, April 19, 1961, 3795.

13. Geneva to External, tel. 529, May 11, 1961, LAC, RG 25, vol. 5050, file 2444-A-40 pt. 1.

14. Memorandum for the Minister, "Policy on Cuba," October 5, 1962, LAC, RG 25, vol. 5077, file 4568-40 pt. 10.

15. Jocelyn Maynard Ghent, "Canada, the United States, and the Cuban Missile Crisis," *Pacific Historical Review* 48 (1979), 160.

16. Robertson to Green, memo, "Cuba at the United Nations," October 26, 1962; External to Permanent Mission, New York and Washington, outgoing message XL-106, October 25, 1962, LAC, RG 25, vol. 4184, file 2444-40 pt. 10; Campbell to Robertson, memo, "Cuba," October 30, 1962; Havana to External, tel. 218, October 31, 1962; Havana to External, tel. 217, October 30, 1962, LAC, RG 25, vol. 4181, file 2444-40 pt. 11; Kidd to Roa, letter, November 2, 1962; Havana to External, tel. 222, November 1, 1962, LAC, RG 25, vol. 4184, file 2444-40 pt. 12; and Robinson to Ritchie, memo, "Cuba," November 1, 1962, LAC, MG31 E83, vol. 6, file 13.

17. See Jorge I. Domínguez, "The @#$%& Missile Crisis: (Or What Was 'Cuban' about U.S. Decisions during the Cuban Missile Crisis?)," *Diplomatic History* 24 (2000), 305–15; and Asa McKercher, "A 'Half-hearted Response'?: Canada and the Cuban Missile Crisis, 1962," *International History Review* 33 (June 2011), 335–52.

18. Montevideo to External, tel. 24, March 2, 1962; Quito to External, tel. 15, March 2, 1962, LAC, RG 25, vol. 5030, file 1415-40 pt. 10.

19. Kirk and McKenna, *Canada-Cuba Relations*, 120. Trudeau's visit to Cuba and the issues surrounding it are ably described in Robert Wright, *Three Nights in Havana: Pierre Trudeau, Fidel Castro and the Cold War World* (Toronto: HarperCollins, 2007); Canada, House of Commons, *Debates*, February 3, 1976, 10571.

20. Head to Robinson, September 15, 1976 and, attached, Trudeau to Castro, August 10, 1976, LAC, RG 25, vol. 11431, file 20-Cuba-1-3 pt. 12; Kirk and McKenna, *Canada-Cuba Relations*, 113; Trudeau to Castro, letter, April 3, 1981, LAC, RG 25, vol. 8639, file 20-1-2-Cuba pt. 32. When Trudeau died in 2000, Castro traveled to Montreal to attend his funeral and pay his respects.

21. Havana to External, tel. 2807, December 6, 1976, and Havana to External, tel. 2, January 4, 1977, LAC, RG 25, vol. 11431, file 20-Cuba-1-3 pt. 12.

22. Memorandum for the Minister, "Cuban Request for a Courtesy Call," June 25, 1981, LAC, RG 25, vol. 8639, file 20-1-2-Cuba pt. 32.

23. "Address by Minister of State Ablonczy to the Canadian Hispanic Business Association, Ottawa," Canada, Department of Foreign Affairs and International Trade, Speech no. 2011/39, November 15, 2011; Larry Catá Backer, "From Colonies to Collective: ALBA, Latin American Integration, and the Construction of Regional Political Power," in B.J.C. McKercher, ed., *Routledge Handbook of Diplomacy and Statecraft* (London: Routledge, 2012), 325–37.

24. Havana to External, D-151, April 1, 1959, LAC, RG 25, vol. 7257, file 10224-40 pt. 6.

25. Diefenbaker to file, memo, "Telegram Received from Confederation of Cuban Professionals, Washington," March 24, 1962; and Robinson to Robertson, note, March 24, 1962, LAC, RG 25, vol. 5076, file 4568-40 pt. 9.

26. Government of Canada, "Notes for an Address by the Hon. Christine Stewart to the General Assembly of the Organization of American States," June 7, 1994. Canada's position of urging reforms in Cuba was similar to policies adopted by other countries, including the United States, a point made in Peter McKenna, "Comparative Foreign Policies toward Cuba," *International Journal* 59 (2009), 281–302; and Robert Wright, "'Northern Ice': Jean Chrétien and the Failure of Constructive Engagement in Cuba," in Wright and Wylie, *Our Place in the Sun*, 195–96.

27. Quoted in *The Soft Touch: Canada & the World Backgrounder* [Ottawa] 65, no. 1 (September 1999), 1.

28. Canada, Office of the Prime Minister, "Statement by the Prime Minister," March 15, 1999; and see Peter McKenna, John Kirk, and Christine Climenhage, "Canada-Cuba Relations: 'Northern Ice' or '*Nada Nuevo*'?" in Sahadeo Basdeo and Heather Nicol, eds., *Canada, the United States, and Cuba: An Evolving Relationship* (Coral Gables, FL: North-South Press Center, 2002), 57–72.

29. Jeff Sallot, "Canada's Trade Mission to Cuba Signals Thaw," *Globe and Mail*, November 2, 2002; Paul Knox, "Graham Protests against Cuban Trials," *Globe and Mail*, April 8, 2003; and Paul Knox, "Canada to Seek OAS Action against Cuba," *Globe and Mail*, June 7, 2003.

30. Mike Blanchford, "New Minister Sees a Future for Canada in Cuba," *Financial Post*, January 6, 2009.

31. Blanchford, "Canada welcomes Cuban Reforms."

32. Christine Stewart, "Keynote Address," in Wendy Druker, ed., *Helms Burton and International Business: Legal and Commercial Implications* (Ottawa: FOCAL, 1996), 4–5.

33. Peter McKenna and John Kirk, "'Sleeping with an Elephant': The Impact of the United States on Canada-Cuba Relations," in Morris Morley and Chris McGillion, eds., *Cuba, the United States, and the Post–Cold War World: The International Dimensions of the Washington-Havana Relationship* (Gainesville: University Press of Florida, 2005), 149.

34. Washington to External, tel. 515, February 19, 1962, LAC, RG 25, vol. 5030, file 1415-40 pt. 10.

35. Robertson, memo, "The Cuban Situation," July 13, 1960, LAC, Norman Robertson fonds, MG 30 E163, vol. 18, file Personal Correspondence 1960 pt. 2; Cabinet Conclusions, October 20, 1960, LAC, Privy Council Office fonds, RG 2, series A-5-a, vol. 2747; Canada, House of Commons, *Debates*, December 12, 1960, 700–1.

36. "Telegram from the Department of State to the Embassy in the United Kingdom, 30 August 1962," in *Foreign Relations of the United States, 1961–1963*, vol. 10 (Washington, DC: GPO, 1994), document 396.

37. Robinson to Robertson, memo, "Cuba," October 19, 1960; Memo for file, "Cuba," October 20, 1960, LAC, MG 31 E83, vol. 3, file 10; Canada, House of Commons, *Debates*, December 12, 1960, 701.

38. The theme is ever present in Kirk and McKenna, *Canada-Cuba Relations*. For Diefen-

baker, see Memorandum of Conversation, "Visit of Canadian Prime Minister Diefenbaker," February 20, 1961, JFKL, National Security Files, series 1, box 18, file Canada, General 1/61–3/61.

39. "Bush Expected to Veto U.S. Export Bill," *Globe and Mail*, November 30, 1990; Paul Koring, "Axworthy, Helms Aide Slug It Out on Cuba," *Globe and Mail*, March 7, 1998. See Heather Nicol, ed., *Canada, the U.S., and Cuba: Helms-Burton and Its Aftermath* (Kingston, Ont.: Centre for International Relations, Queen's University, 1999).

40. Mexico City to External, tel. 144, July 30, 1960, LAC, RG 25, vol. 5050, file 2444-A-40 pt. 1; and Diefenbaker to López Mateos, letter, July 17, 1960, LAC, Albert Ritchie fonds, MG 31 E44, vol. 1, file 4.

41. Geneva to External, tel. 529, May 11, 1961, LAC, RG 25, vol. 5050, file 2444-A-40 pt. 1; Washington to External, tel. 1551, May 13, 1961, LAC, MG 31 E83, vol. 5, file 5.

42. Quoted in "Canada Seeks to Thaw Frost in U.S.-Cuban Relationship," *Globe and Mail*, April 14, 1990.

43. Tim Harper, "Wilson Pushes Cuba Connection," *Toronto Star*, February 17, 2007.

44. Wright, "'Northern Ice,'" 217.

45. McKenna and Kirk, "'Sleeping with an Elephant,'" 157.

11

Internationalism

7

The Cuba-Venezuela Alliance and Its Continental Impact

MAX AZICRI

For more than ten years now—since at least 1999—Cuba and Venezuela have worked together to establish a remarkable partnership based on mutual reinforcement of sociopolitical forces and historical, ideological, and personal friendship factors cemented by geographical proximity. Although the Cuban socialist regime and the Venezuelan Bolivarian process remain systemically and structurally different,[1] the two countries have placed a claim to the Bolivarian ideal of a united Latin America free of U.S. dominance.

This closely knit partnership has had a significant domestic effect—recognizing their capacity to help each other, the countries exchange goods and services in a collaborative fashion[2]—which has been matched by a widely felt continental impact. In addition to being a source of vital resources and services to both countries, the partnership has promoted Latin American unity and other long-held objectives. ALBA, the Bolivarian Alternative for the Peoples of the Americas (changed in 2009 to the Bolivarian Alliance for the Peoples of the Americas)—the brainchild of Fidel Castro and Hugo Chávez—has been instrumental in pursuing such goals.

Since Cuba and Venezuela founded ALBA in 2004, several other countries have joined. These include Bolivia (2006), Nicaragua (2007), and Dominica and Honduras (2008) (after the 2009 coup ousting President Manuel Zelaya, the right-wing government of Honduras withdrew its membership), Ecuador, St. Vincent and the Grenadines, and Antigua and Barbuda (2009). In 2012 Suriname and St. Lucia were admitted as "guest countries." Havana and Caracas took up outreach initiatives through ALBA and other programs, and those projects continue today despite the depressed financial conditions caused by the world economic crisis of 2008–9. Relationships with Bolivia, Argentina, Ecuador, Nicaragua, and Mercosur (Common Market of the South) offer prime examples of the connections being fashioned.

Spreading Health and Oil Benefits

The regional approach included record-setting initiatives such as Cuba's Operation Miracle, which restored the sight of more than one million patients free of charge. The program started in 2005, catering only to Venezuelans, but in two years it was expanded throughout the region. By mid-2008 the project had reached thirty-two countries; low-income patients from Latin America and the Caribbean, as well as from Africa and Asia, whose vision was impaired by diabetes, glaucoma, cataracts, and other illnesses had been treated and had their eyesight restored. Havana's continuing program aims at treating from six to ten million patients.[3]

Venezuela's Petrocaribe (conceived by Castro and Chávez) was launched in 2005, with Cuba, twelve of the fifteen members of CARICOM (the organization of Caribbean countries), and the Dominican Republic signing the agreement. Later Haiti (2006), Honduras (2007), and Guatemala (2008) joined the program. Petrocaribe guarantees oil supplies to sixteen participating state-run agencies at market-value prices, with deferred payments in a twenty-five-year agreement carrying 1 (or 2) percent interest (the 2005–10 participating countries' borrowing credit was estimated at more than $4.5 billion). The sales, made directly by Venezuela's state oil company PDVSA, amount to close to 200,000 barrels per day, and the buyers can pay for the oil with commodities such as bananas, rice, and sugar.

Cuba's daily supply of 200,000 barrels of oil is based on exchanging in return more than 30,000 medical doctors and health personnel, including a number of professionals in other fields. This agreement springs not from Petrocaribe but dates back to the December 14, 2004, convention between Havana and Caracas. Havana's technical support allowed the Chávez administration to carry out its national social missions—from health and literacy campaigns and other educational projects to unemployment and peasant welfare issues to supports for mining communities and indigenous peoples and the subsidization of supermarkets. Yet another mission is administered through an organization called Mothers of the Barrio, which targets drug use and unintended pregnancies in young girls and provides help to mothers in poverty. The missions in their totality are aimed at eradicating poverty by 2021.[4]

Petrocaribe has had its problems, such as failing at times to deliver the agreed quota of oil, failing to satisfy the Dominican Republic's demand to increase its quota, and postponing completion of the Nicaraguan refinery until 2018.[5] Altogether, however, Petrocaribe has provided vital help to sustainable development efforts in the area, at advantageous terms. This support has also been provided to countries outside ALBA, including Argentina and Haiti. Indeed, under Chávez's humanitarian program and starting in the winter of 2005 low-income citizens in the northeastern United States purchased Venezuelan oil and heating gas at subsidized prices, until Caracas ended the practice in 2008.[6]

The Cuba-Venezuela Alliance

Not since the Nicaraguan Sandinista revolution in the 1980s has Cuba enjoyed a level of support from a neighboring country as firm as that of Venezuela. In response Cuba stood as an unconditional Chávez supporter. The exchanges between Havana and Caracas, the long-standing close personal relationship between Fidel (and later Raúl) Castro and Chávez, and the commitment to common regional goals have been central to the bilateral alliance. Despite Chávez's death in March 2013, this relationship looks to continue under Nicolás Maduro, the new Venezuelan president and Chávez's hand-picked successor.

On December 14, 2004, when Chávez and Castro signed a joint declaration toward the creation of ALBA, they integrated the two countries following common goals and values. The agreement formalized a comprehensive exchange program that grew rapidly—setting the stage for regional ALBA projects in other countries along similar lines.

Promoting common solidarity principles, the agreement covers mutually convenient exchanges of goods and services. Among other programs, it includes Cuban doctors assisting the Barrio Adentro Mission and the Bolivarian University, training new doctors and scientists, helping to carry out other social missions, and working with regional countries to eradicate illiteracy.

The agreement establishes technological exchanges; cultural and educational programs and scholarships; increased trade through organized credits, financing, and payments; and elimination of customs fees and taxation for joint ventures. It also regulates state investment (and in Venezuela's case, private investment) in the other country, and policies for sharing transportation and aviation facilities. It also sets Cuban imports of Venezuelan oil according to market prices, but never below $27 per barrel.[7]

The Havana-Caracas alliance's hemispheric programs have been financed by Venezuela, which after a period of overpriced oil revenues witnessed their rapid fall. From $91.58 per barrel in 2008 the price of oil plummeted to $33.87 by early 2009, an almost 42 percent reduction. However, it returned to $70 per barrel by mid-2009 and rose to $74.88 some twelve months later. By February 2011 it reached $90.86 per barrel and a year later was just over $101. Given that oil revenues are central to Venezuela (they represent one-third of its gross domestic product and more than 80 percent of exports), oil price volatility causes financial uncertainty for Cuban-Venezuelan joint initiatives, including ALBA.[8]

Although Chávez has been criticized for wasting the country's wealth by pursuing ill-conceived projects, a 2007 report by the Center for Economic and Policy Research (CEPR) showed approval for his economic policy: "The performance of the Venezuelan economy during the Chávez years does not fit the mold of an 'oil boom headed for a bust.'" The economy had recovered after the domestic political situation was stabilized in early 2003 (following the 2002 anti-Chávez coup and a subsequent oil strike), with high oil prices certainly contributing to its improvement. CEPR also advised containing and reducing inflation and expenditures, and diversifying the economy away from its dependence on oil.[9]

The CEPR report was cautiously optimistic that Venezuela could manage economic hardship properly, but Brazil, Chile, and other countries overcame the 2008–9 economic crisis better than Venezuela (and Cuba) did.[10] Latin America EconoMonitor had a distressing forecast for Venezuela and the region, saying that the area "was poorly placed to handle external market shocks . . . leaving it quickly vulnerable to a joint deterioration in both real and financial external conditions [and] . . . lower commodity prices."[11] Still, Venezuela retained a high emerging global market index performance in the first quarter of 2009 with a plus 24 percent rate.[12]

Chávez enforced fiscal readjustment policies. The Bank of Venezuela was nationalized, and several infrastructures, such as seaports and airports, were seized; the federal budget was reduced, and the value-added tax was increased, but the social missions were not touched.[13] After having rescued six million people out of poverty, Venezuela still faced high inflation, food and housing shortages, infrastructure problems, and rising crime and corruption.[14]

Reversing his 2007 defeat, Chávez won the 2009 referendum then lifted reelection limits for the presidency and other offices. In 2010 Chávez's United Socialist Party of Venezuela retained ninety-six congressional seats, but the opposition gained sixty-six after receiving close to half of the popular vote. Although this was a worrisome political development for Chávez in the years leading up to the 2012 presidential election, Maduro won election in April.[15]

In Cuba Raúl Castro substituted cabinet members and other officials, signaling new forthcoming policies—Foreign Minister Felipe Roque and Vice-President Carlos Lage were replaced.[16] Among other changes, Raúl announced in 2010 the radical trimming of the "overloaded" state payroll: "No one will be simply left out in the cold, [but] unproductive or under-employed workers... [will] have to find other jobs." The policy would affect 500,000 workers, nearly 10 percent of the workforce, by mid-2011.[17] By early 2012 radical changes had taken place in Cuba, with self-employment tripling from what it had been just two years earlier. The reforms undertaken in Caracas and Havana, by improving their own countries' economic outlook, could benefit the alliance's regional outreach programs.

The Alliance's Impact in the Americas

Through ALBA and other initiatives, the bilateral partnership has marked a distinct direction for Latin America. Progressive leaders speak a similar reformist language, but their opponents characterize them as ill-founded populists. The prevailing populist sentiment agrees that when "the common person's interests are oppressed... by the elite in society... the instruments of the state need to be grasped... and used for the benefit... of the people as a whole."[18]

This idea has been dominating Latin America for some time now: "From Venezuela to Argentina many of the traditional parties... are disintegrating.... Latin Americans have grown frustrated with Washington-backed economic prescriptions like unfettered trade and liberalization."[19] Critical observers dichotomize the process as a battle for the future "between liberal democrats—of left and right—and authoritarian populists."[20] The Cuba-Venezuela alliance has promoted new initiatives such as Telesur, the hemisphere-wide, noncommercial television network set up by Venezuela, Cuba, Argentina, and Uruguay in 2005, which broadcasts anti–U.S. hegemony programming.

Bolivia

The 2005 presidential electoral victory of Evo Morales, a former coca growers' union chief, was a success story for the Latin American left.[21] On a triumphant tour with Havana and Caracas as his first stops, Morales signed cooperative agreements with Cuba in health, education, and sports, and with Venezuela in energy (diesel fuel), education, health, and other areas—all of which are being actively carried out.[22] Morales joined Castro and Chávez in Havana's Revolution Square in 2006, celebrating Bolivia joining ALBA as its third member. Morales stated, "In Cuba and Venezuela we find unconditional solidarity. They are the best allies for changing Bolivia.... There are now three of us to defend the peoples of Latin America." Castro joined in, declaring that the new alignment "makes me the happiest man in the world."[23]

The energy agreement between Caracas and La Paz signed in 2007 at the Fifth ALBA Summit was one of many programs providing financial assistance to Bolivia's army, cattle ranches, soybean cultivation, microfinance projects, urban sanitation, and oil industry, and helping to increase domestic coca production.[24] Responding to the opposition against changes taking place with ALBA's backing, Chávez offered military support if necessary to defend Bolivia's constitutional government from internal or external aggression.[25] The country's economy has been controlled by the Santa Cruz elite, but new discoveries of lithium in the Uyuni region and other salt deserts are in the hands of impoverished indigenous groups (reportedly Bolivia could become the Saudi Arabia of lithium).

Argentina

In 2006 the late Argentine president Néstor Kirchner rejected the Washington Consensus directives of the International Monetary Fund (IMF). Argentina charged the IMF with abandoning it during the 2001–2 economic crisis, causing President George W. Bush to get his lowest approval rating in the region, 6 percent in 2006. After national commodity prices achieved 8.6 percent economic growth in 2005, Argentina cleared its IMF debt in one lump sum, totaling $9.8 billion. The deal became possible after Venezuela purchased $1.5 billion in Argentine bonds. Caracas purchased Buenos Aires bonds twice, totaling more than $2.5 billion of Argentina's debt, rivaling the IMF and United States. Argentina still owes billions of dollars to private lenders.[26]

Could Venezuela continue helping others without harming its own finances? According to its Central Bank, helping neighboring countries economically in 2005–6 (during a period of high oil revenues) did not weaken Caracas's financial assets. Its 2005 economic growth reached 9.4 percent, and the balance of payment surplus was less than $5 billion (3.6 percent of GDP), with $28.9 billion in foreign currency reserves. It also lowered its inflation rate to 15.3 percent (down from 19.2 percent in 2004), although that rate was still high for Latin America.

Ecuador

Venezuela offered the president of Ecuador, Rafael Correa, $500 million in financial assistance to restructure the country's external debt. Also, Caracas sent a tanker carrying 220,000 barrels of diesel fuel as part of a fuel-swapping deal that would save Quito millions of dollars in foreign exchange.[27] But at the 2009 Mercosur summit President Correa noted the "failure of the Bank of the South [an incipient South American monetary fund] to help buffer the negative effects of the global economic crisis," adding, "If it were consolidated, its funds would have compensated for the loss of foreign investment in the region." For his part, Chávez stated that the Bank of the South "will remain 'on ice' for the moment."[28]

Nicaragua

Aid programs signed by Chávez and Nicaraguan president Daniel Ortega expanded an earlier offer to write off more than $30 million in Nicaraguan debt. A new development bank in Managua will offer loans to small businesses, and dozens of generating plants will alleviate the country's energy crisis. The planned projects also include an oil refinery and a pipeline running from the Caribbean to the Pacific to transport crude oil destined for Asia. In 2007 Chávez told a grateful Ortega, "Nicaragua can forget about fuel problems."[29]

Mercosur

At the Fourth Summit of the Americas held in Mar del Plata, Argentina, in 2005, the founding members of Mercosur (Brazil, Argentina, Uruguay, and Paraguay) closed ranks with Venezuela to oppose the Free Trade Area of the Americas (FTAA), which was endorsed by the Bush administration.[30] Countering efforts by Mexico to favor FTAA (now considered doomed), the Venezuela-Mercosur group opposed holding more meetings to discuss FTAA's problems. They stated, "The necessary conditions are not yet in place for achieving a balanced and equitable free trade agreement."[31] President Chávez pressured Mercosur to expunge its organizing principle as a neoliberal trade bloc and look for ways to satisfy people's needs instead.[32]

ALBA's Alternative to Washington's FTAA

As Cuba and Venezuela intended, ALBA has charted an alternative to FTAA, as well as to the Washington Consensus, globalization, and neoliberalism.[33] The free-market programs prescribed by the IMF and other lending institutions are a contemporary version of nineteenth-century laissez-faire doctrine.³⁴ ALBA offers a distinct developmental alternative, breaking away from privatization, free-trade agreements, and structural adjustment policies.

The joint declaration establishing the bases for ALBA—signed by Venezuela and Cuba, and agreed to by its membership—stated its founding cardinal principles. Agreeing that trade and investment should be not ends in themselves, but instruments to achieve just and sustainable development, ALBA's bilateral and multilateral interactions are based on four integrating values: complementary exchanges, cooperation, solidarity, and the protection of national sovereignty.³⁵

Although in its hemispheric projection the Cuba-Venezuela alliance profited from Chávez's towering figure, in some quarters the Venezuelan president's role caused a backlash, which has been heightened among conservatives by his open association with Cuba and endorsement of Fidel Castro. In different electoral contests Chávez was accused of interfering in those other countries' domestic affairs. He was thus used as a fear factor, a tool of pressure to make voters favor conservative candidates. Still, electoral success brought a number of center-left and leftist leaders to power all over the region.³⁶ The 2009 victory in El Salvador of Mauricio Funes, the candidate of the Farabundo Martí National Liberation Front (FMLN) and to a lesser extent that of Peru's Ollanta Humala in 2011, matched the 2007 return of Ortega to the presidency of Nicaragua. These Latin American leaders (though less ideological) represent basically the same leftist orientation that Washington had been aggressively opposing in the person of Chávez.³⁷

The elected progressive leaders' response to ALBA's programs stretches from sympathetic (but not involved) to committed partnership. Far from a progressive monolith, these leaders represent a broad spectrum having significant differences within their ranks—Cuba, Venezuela, Bolivia, and Ecuador stand at one end, with Brazil at the other. Meanwhile conservative victories in Colombia, Mexico, Chile, Costa Rica, and Honduras have to some extent offset the impact of the left's electoral successes.

The Economic Crisis and the Latin American Left

Latin American leaders have faced major problems caused by the 2008–9 global economic crisis. Damaging commodity prices, scarce lines of credit, declining foreign investment, and a depressed export-import market are particularly taxing for developing countries. Even before those economic hardships, some analysts had questioned the viability and ultimate impact of the continent's leftward movement.³⁸ Popular support can dwindle if social programs fail to deliver on their promised reformist policies—and the implementation of those projects has become extremely difficult.[39]

The G-20 allocated $6 billion for developing countries in 2009. The IMF is in charge of the monies, which is not a promising sign. To become eligible for funds the IMF demands acceptance of neoliberal programs such as the Washington Consensus. As an *Economist* analyst noted, developing and "emerging economies" have "an almost visceral dread of having to approach the IMF."[40]

Asked if his country was requesting the IMF's aid, Brazilian president Luiz Inácio Lula da Silva replied, "with a lot of pride," that "Brazil needs no money from the IMF."[41] Mexico, however, requested $47 billion from the IMF using the new Flexible Credit Line program, and Colombia asked for $10 billion under the same service.

ALBA expressed the frustration felt by developing nations over their lack of representation at the 2008 G-20 deliberations in Washington. After calling the world economic crisis the "funeral of capitalism," Ortega characterized ALBA as a vital "alternative model of development." Recognizing that ALBA should confirm its own institutional viability and legitimacy, the organization sought to strengthen its institutional structure. Some of ALBA's initiatives in the planning stage include an OPEC-style enterprise called Petroamerica (including Petrosur, Petrocaribe, and Petro Andina) to replace multinational companies with state oil companies; a Latin American parliament to replace the Organization of American States (OAS); a Food Security Fund; an ALBA bank (along with the Bank of the South), and a new currency, the "SUCRE."[42]

In addition to ALBA's member delegations, the 2009 summit held in Caracas included representatives from Antigua and Barbuda, St. Kitts and Nevis, Haiti, and Uruguay. The summit sought "an alternative to the global capitalist model," offering a freer "geopolitical, social, cultural and ideological space." Several economic and social agreements were signed, and a new ALBA Bank was approved.[43] The new ALBA Bank has an initial funding of more than $1 billion to promote economic integration and infrastructural development projects, as well as social programs, all of it aimed at eliminating the "economic weaknesses" and "economic asymmetries" resulting from globalization. But given that the Bank of the South has been on hold due to the economic crisis, the financial viability of the ALBA Bank is questionable.

President Chávez proposed breaking the hegemony of the U.S. dollar and U.S.-dominated international financial institutions using the SUCRE. After approving a food production enterprise that would provide food to the Americas, Chávez said, "We are [creating] a supranational company . . . guaranteeing food sovereignty to our people."[44] Also, 139 out of 370 projects approved at the 2010 Cuba-Venezuela Economic Union Summit were started almost immediately. And when the defense ministers of the Union of South American Nations gathered in 2009, the South American Defense Council discussed how to "promote transparency regarding... [their] defense expenditures."[45]

Cuba, Venezuela, and U.S. Policies

Cuba's standing as a country whose development model runs contrary to Washington's policies dates back more than five decades, but Venezuela moved from being a U.S. client state to an adversarial one only fairly recently, under Chávez. President George W. Bush opposed any rapprochement with Fidel or Raúl Castro, or any softening toward Chávez, Bolivia's Morales, or other leftist leaders. As for President Barack Obama's Latin American policy, the hemisphere initially looked toward the 2009 Fifth Summit of the Americas in Port of Spain, Trinidad and Tobago, to meet him and learn of his own initiatives.[46] Before the summit, it was reported, "The debate from Washington to Miami and Havana over President Barack Obama's next step toward Cuba heated up." The Cuban American National Foundation, the driving force behind most anti-Castro U.S. policies since the 1980s, reversed itself, supporting expanding relations and ending restrictions on Cuban Americans' remittances to the island.[47]

The White House announced that it would lift restrictions on Cuban Americans traveling to their homeland and on sending money to their relatives (under President Bush they could travel to Cuba only once every three years, and annual remittances were limited to $1,200); and it would resume regular immigration talks. To open up contacts, telecommunication companies were permitted to pursue licensing agreements allowing them to broadcast from the island; however, the embargo remained untouched.

Obama's changes in Cuba policy were found to fall "short of the more drastic policy adjustments" required. The Council on Foreign Relations stated, "The president's political advisers are 'not looking at this as a matter of foreign policy.'" A group favoring improved relations thought the "administration may be trying to take 'baby steps' toward building confidence" by allowing Cuban Americans to "get used to the idea" of a new policy. Fidel Castro called Obama's changes "positive although minimal."[48]

President Raúl Castro responded within hours to President Obama's policy changes, indicating that he was ready to discuss "human rights, freedom of the press, political prisoners—everything." At the summit's opening, President Obama stated, "The United States seeks a new beginning with Cuba." He added, "I know there is a longer journey that must be traveled to overcome decades of mistrust, but there are critical steps we can take toward a new day." But further change in Cuba policy waited until January 2011, when the travel ban was partially lifted. The White House approved traveling to Cuba for academic, religious, and cultural purposes, and for specific people-to-people exchanges, but not for the general public.

Addressing the Trinidad summit, President Cristina Fernández of Argentina won applause when she called on the United States to lift the embargo on Cuban trade. As others noted, however, "This is a thaw, but it is a thaw that is going to take some time."[49]

After meeting with Fidel Castro, a six-member Congressional Black Caucus delegation met with Raúl Castro. Representative Laura Richardson (D-Calif.) remarked that Fidel "wants to see change," and Representative Barbara Lee (D-Calif.) stated that Raúl Castro said, "Everything is on the table." Cuban leaders were signaling to President Obama their readiness to negotiate—the volume of commerce has made the United States Cuba's fifth-largest trading partner, with $582 million in 2007, up from $484 million in 2006.[50]

Brazilian president da Silva, who maintained good relations not only with Washington but also with Cuba and Venezuela, commented positively about Obama and also spoke on behalf of Venezuela's democracy. The Brazilian foreign minister thought that Venezuela and the United States should bridge their differences. Chávez and Obama were seen shaking hands at the Trinidad summit, and Chávez announced the appointment of an ambassador to Washington.[51]

Cuba, the only country in the hemisphere missing from the summit, garnered most of the attention. Many delegations at the diplomatic gathering voiced calls for the United States to end the Cuban embargo. A *New York Times* article reported that Latin American leaders were insisting that "the future" for Cuba-U.S. relations "is now."[52]

Since 2011 the opposition to any improvement in U.S.-Cuba relations has been centered on the Republican majority in the House of Representatives. Speaker of the House John Boehner and Representative Ileana Ros-Lehtinen, head of the House Foreign Affairs Committee (and born in Cuba), are opposed to easing U.S. sanctions—though they might encounter resistance from a few House members in their own party. At "Danger in the Andes," a forum held in Washington, DC, in fall 2010—sponsored by Ros-Lehtinen and attended by members of Congress and U.S. and Venezuelan anti-Chávez activists—those gathered rated ALBA and Venezuela, Bolivia, and Ecuador as threats to U.S. security. Participants expressed the opinion that ALBA's programs were having an unsettling influence in the hemisphere. President Chávez saw the Capitol Hill forum as a dangerous precedent that called for a careful analysis.⁵³

Key Dynamics and a Shift in Relations

The Cuba-Venezuela alliance has accomplished an unusual and successful task, both domestically and in the region (with two hundred bilateral cooperative regional projects accomplished in 2009 alone). Starting with the coming together of two like-minded leaders, followed by the formation of a unifying and solidarity-based alliance of two nations that had either undergone or were undergoing political and socioeconomic transformations, Havana and Caracas combined their resources to achieve key goals. Soon enough, the bilateral alliance's initiatives spilled over into the region. Together with Brazil, for example, they are developing a national public health-care system in post-earthquake Haiti. The alliance's message attracted other like-minded leaders, who joined regional programs. ALBA was born out of the many exchanges between Fidel Castro and Hugo Chávez. In their dialogues these two leaders shared ideas and dreams and a common vision of a united Latin America, bringing back to life the historic vision of the nineteenth-century *Libertador* Simón Bolívar.

The alliance's initial phase started with the first agreement between Havana and Caracas in 1999 and lasted until around 2009–10, when the partnership appeared to have entered a new stage. Important events spanning more than a decade had, in general, a positive impact on the domestic and regional milieu. Still, in economic terms the fall of oil prices badly damaged Venezuela's capacity to provide extensive financial resources for alliance programs, including some initiatives under ALBA, and other ventures. The world economic crisis compounded a difficult situation for both countries and the region, making them concentrate on basic economic concerns while postponing costly projects—it seemed they would, to some degree, have to wait for better economic times.

The dynamics in the relationship between Washington and the region seemed to improve with the election of Barack Obama in 2008. The years of the Bush administration were finally over. While neoliberalism as a policy of choice by U.S. and international lenders has not ended, Washington's FTAA is practically doomed. But the sense of euphoria raised by the Summit of the Americas was soon replaced by an atmosphere of restrained disappointment, heightened by Obama's limited regional policy initiatives. As President Lula lamented by the end of his term in 2010, the diplomatic antagonism that had characterized the Bush administration was now being replaced by a generalized sense that an opportunity for improving relations was being lost.

Chávez, as long as he lived, and Obama moved from acrimonious exchanges to mostly civil ones. Maduro, it seems, will follow in his predecessor's footsteps. But the expectation of better relations suffered badly with the dispute surrounding their diplomatic representatives. Toward the end of 2010 Washington revoked the visa of Venezuelan ambassador Bernardo Alvarez after Caracas refused to accept the newly appointed American ambassador, Larry Palmer, who was at home awaiting Senate confirmation. If poorly handled, the diplomatic clash could have dangerously escalated, provoking unwanted and perilous consequences.

While limited, Obama's Cuba policy changes suggest the possibility of the eventual emergence of a broader constructive phase. President Raúl Castro's rapid and affirmative response following Obama's remarks at the Trinidad summit reinforced the momentum for change, but that direction has so far not been further pursued. Yet the U.S. president has learned firsthand of the hemisphere's almost universal yearning for a Cuba that could once again be an active member of regional organizations, for an end to the U.S. embargo of Cuba, and for the restoration of normal U.S.-Cuba relations for the hemisphere's sake.

In its current depressed economic phase, the bilateral relationship needs to be reexamined, particularly in its hemispheric projection, and it also probably needs to undergo timely readjustments. Some regional programs, especially the most expensive regional infrastructure ones, might be scaled down or even put on hold. While Cuba and Venezuela might want to continue their exchanges unaltered, can Caracas—after seeing improvement in oil prices but remaining seriously hurt by the world economic recession—afford to continue financing costly regional initiatives, including those of ALBA? The Venezuelan administration has wisely accrued significant hard currency reserves, but the internal and external financial demands might prove to be too costly for the country to continue underwriting services as lavishly as it was doing in recent times.

The mildly improved regional relationship with Washington, including the steps taken through the alliance, might eventually bear fruit. Certainly, for the countries involved it remains a wish to have relations substantially improved. Reversing to a situation akin to the Bush years is unlikely, notwithstanding the potential for trouble coming from the Republican-controlled House of Representatives. Normalized relations with Washington could free the alliance's creative forces domestically and regionally—making possible continued efforts to strive for the goal of a united region that pursues sustainable development goals without having to guard itself from Washington's own self-serving objectives. The parties involved cannot expect to achieve an ideal relationship overnight; but still the characteristics of present and future hemispheric exchanges should be defined by interactions of mutual respect and a recognition of the existence of legitimate concerns for both sides (North and South). While the Cuba-Venezuela alliance must realistically assess the viability of its more ambitious objectives and, if possible, work toward an enhanced relationship with the Obama administration, when all is said and done the project has a long, productive way to go, both at home and in the hemisphere.

Notes

1. Bolivarianism, based on the vision of Simón Bolívar, combined with nationalism, populism, and lately twenty-first-century socialism, provides the ideological underpinnings of the social change process in Venezuela under late President Chávez. Max Azicri, "The Castro-Chávez Alliance," *Latin American Perspectives* 36, no. 1 (January 2009), 103.

2. Azicri, "Castro-Chávez Alliance," and Azicri, "El ALBA, iniciativa venezolana para el continente," *Temas* 54 (April–June 2008).

3. For the most authoritative account of the international dimension of Cuban medical programs, see John M. Kirk and H. Michael Erisman, *Cuban Medical Internationalism: Origins, Evolution, and Goals* (New York: Palgrave Macmillan, 2009).

4. Azicri, "Castro-Chávez Alliance," 109.

5. Jodie Neary, "Venezuela's ALBA in the Face of the Global Economic Crisis," *Upside Down World*, January 5, 2009, online; "PetroCaribe," Wikipedia, March 20, 2009, online.

6. Simon Romero, "Venezuela Suspends Heating Aid to the U.S.," *New York Times*, January 6, 2009, online.

7. "Cuba-Venezuela Agreement," *Cuba Socialista*, December 2004, online; "Preparan en La Habana audiencia sobre el ALBA," *Cuba Socialista,* January 2006, online.

8. Rana Foroohar, "The Decline of the Petro-Czar," *Newsweek*, February 23, 2009, 24–27.

9. Mark Weisbrot and Luis Sandoval, *The Venezuelan Economy in the Chávez Years* (Washington, DC: Center for Economic and Policy Research, July 2007), 21.

10. Max Azicri, "The Cuba-Venezuela Alliance: Dynamics of a Beneficial Solidarity Exchange in Hard Economic Times," paper delivered at the International Congress of the Latin American Studies Association (LASA), Toronto, October 6–9, 2010.

11. Vitoria Saddi, Italo Lombardi, and Bertrand Delgado, "Is Capital Flowing to Latin America?" *Latin America EconoMonitor*, March 16, 2009, online.

12. "Numbers," *BusinessWeek*, April 20, 2009.

13. Juan Forero, "Chávez Trims Budget to Offset Low Oil Revenues," *New York Times*, March 20, 2009, online.

14. Neary, "Venezuela's ALBA."

15. Simon Romero, "Venezuelan Elections Offer Plebiscite on Chávez's Rule," *New York Times*, September 28, 2010, A9.

16. Domingo Amuchastegui, "Raúl Shakes up His Regime; *Fidelistas* Out, *Raúlistas* In," *CubaNews*, March 2009, 4.

17. "Cuba: 500,000 Workers to Be Cut," *Caribbean Update*, May 2010, 5.

18. "Populism," Wikipedia Encyclopedia, 2006, online.

19. Juan Forero, "Populist Movements Wrest Much of Latin America from Old Parties," *New York Times*, April 20, 2006, A8.

20. "The Battle for Latin America's Soul," *The Economist*, May 20, 2006, 11.

21. Luis A. Gómez, "Evo Morales Turns the Tide of History," in Vijay Prashad and Teo Ballvé, eds., *Dispatches from Latin America* (Cambridge, MA: South End Press, 2006), 140.

22. Joaquín Rivery Tur, "Suscriben Fidel y Evo Morales acuerdo de cooperación bilateral," *Granma Internacional*, December 31, 2005, online.

23. "Bolivia Cements Trade Ties with Cuba and Venezuela, Associated Press, May 1, 2006, online.

24. Simon Romero, "Venezuela Rivals U.S. in Aid to Bolivia," *New York Times*, February 23, 2007, online.

25. "Llamado a defensa popular armada centra la atención en Bolivia," *Granma*, September 22, 2006, online.

26. Juan Forero, "Chávez, Seeking Foreign Allies, Spends Billions," *New York Times*, April 3, 2006, A1, A6; Larry Rother, "As Argentina's Debt Dwindles, President's Power Steadily Grows," *New York Times*, January 3, 2006, A1, A9.

27. Simon Romero, "Chávez Ends Busy Week Aiding Venezuela's Latin Neighbors," *New York Times*, February 24, 2007, online.

28. Neary, "Venezuela's ALBA."

29. Romero, "Chávez Ends Busy Week."

30. The FTAA "was proposed . . . to eliminate . . . trade barriers among . . . the America[s] [excluding Cuba]. Against [FTAA] were Cuba, Venezuela, Bolivia and Nicaragua. At Mar del Plata, Argentina, in 2005, no agreement on FTAA was reached. "Free Trade Area of the Americas," Wikipedia, June 14, 2007, online. Mercosur's membership includes Argentina, Brazil, Paraguay, Uruguay, and Venezuela (once ratified by Paraguay and Argentina); and five associate members: Chile, Bolivia, Colombia, Ecuador, and Peru (considered for full membership). Joanna Klonsky, "Mercosur: South America's Fractious Trade Bloc," Council on Foreign Relations, online.

31. Laura Carlsen, "Timely Demise for Free Trade of the Americas," in Prashad and Ballvé, eds., *Dispatches from Latin America*, 68–70.

32. "Mercosur goes beyond the trade liberalization measures of trade deals . . . seeking to harmonize . . . political and economic activities of the member nations. . . . [It is] a less-developed cousin of the European Union." Jason Tockman, *ZNet*, January 22, 2007, online.

33. "The opening of Latin America's economies to foreign investment and trade . . . privatization . . . deregulation . . . production . . . for export and fiscal austerity—[is] in a word, neoliberalism." Eric Hershberg and Fred Rosen, "Turning the Tide?" in Hershberg and Rosen,

eds., *Latin America after Neoliberalism: Turning the Tide in the Twenty-First Century* (New York: New Press, 2006), 7.

34. For a critique of market fundamentalism, see George Soros, *The New Paradigm for Financial Markets* (New York: Public Affairs, 2008).

35. Fernando Ramón Bossi, Secretary of the Peoples' Bolivarian Congress, "Construyendo el ALBA desde los pueblos," Third Summit of the Peoples, Mar del Plata, Argentina, November 3, 2005, *Portal ALBA*, 2005, online.

36. Max Azicri, "ALBA y el renacimiento de la izquierda en la América Latina," *Diálogo*, Summer 2008.

37. "First, Ortega in Nicaragua . . . and now Funes in El Salvador, are not keeping the radical politics of the 1980s." Blake Schmidt and Elizabeth Malkin, "In a Salvadoran Leftist's Victory a Pledge to Govern as a Moderate," *New York Times*, March 17, 2009, A5.

38. Ibid.

39. "The World Bank predicted . . . that the global economy and the volume of global trade would both shrink . . . for the first time since World War II. . . . The crisis that began with junk mortgages in the United States was causing havoc for poorer countries that had nothing to do with the original problem." Edmund L. Andrews, "Report Says Economy Will Shrink Worldwide," *New York Times*, March 19, 2009, online.

40. Mark Landler and David E. Sanger, "World Leaders Pledge $1.1 Trillion to Tackle Crisis," *New York Times*, April 13, 2009, A1, A11; "The IMF: Mission Impossible," *The Economist*, April 8, 2009, 69–70, 72.

41. "The IMF: Mission Impossible." "Brazil's role in Latin America . . . is unique—a broadly popular government of the left which pursues moderate economic policies, promotes broad hemispheric integration on the basis of shared economic and political interests." Thomas Trebat, "Brazil and the U.S.: Reflections on Lula's Visit," *Latin America EconoMonitor*, March 19, 2009, 10, online.

42. Neary, "Venezuela's ALBA."

43. Kiraz Janicke, "Summit of the Bolivarian Alternative (ALBA) Concludes in Venezuela," Venezuelanalysis.com, January 27, 2009.

44. James Suggett, "Venezuela Proposes New Regional Currency During ALBA Summit," Venezuelanalysis.com, November 28, 2009; James Suggett, "ALBA Trade Bloc Forms Joint Food Company at Summit in Venezuela," Venezuelanalysis.com, February 23, 2009.

45. Tomás Ayuso, Romain Le Cour, and Guy Hursthouse, "The Paradox of South American Integration: The Founding of a Defense Council," COHA, March 12, 2009, online.

46. Larry Luxner, "OAS: Time for a 'Dialogue' with Cuba," *CubaNews*, March 16, 2009, 1.

47. Damien Cave, "Exiles Want to Expand U.S.-Cuba Relations," *New York Times*, April 9, 2009, A15.

48. Robert Burns, "Obama Eases Some Travel, Money Curbs on Cuba, Breaking with Half-Century Policy," Associated Press, April 13, 2009, online; Sheryl Gay Stolberg and Damien Cave, "Loosening Cuba Restrictions, Obama Leaves the Door Ajar for More," *New York Times*, April 14, 2009, A5; "Now Slightly Restricted," *Time*, April 17, 2009, 12.

49. Vivian Sequera and Ben Feller, "Obama Seeks Castro Talks," *Pittsburgh Tribune-Review*, April 18, 2009, A1, A4.

50. Associated Press, "U.S. Lawmakers, Fidel Castro Meet," Associated Press, April 8, 2009; "Cuba-U.S. Trade Rises," Reuters, August 15, 2008, online.

51. Fareed Zakaria, "Lula Wants to Fight," *Newsweek*, March 30, 2009, 43; EFE, "Brasil augura aproximación Chávez-Obama," *Miami Herald*, April 10, 2009, online; Sequera and Feller, "Obama Seeks Castro Talks," A4; Francis Robles, "Chávez Offers Soothing Words and a Wry Gift to Obama at the Summit," *Miami Herald*, April 18, 2009, online.

52. Ginger Thompson and Alexei Barrionuevo, "Rising Expectations on Cuba Follow Obama," *New York Times*, April 19, 2009, online.

53. "Rechaza Venezuela foro en Washington contra el ALBA," *CubaDebate*, November 23, 2010, online.

8

Santeria Commerce and the Unofficial Networks of Interpersonal Internationalism

KEVIN M. DELGADO

In 2000, I spent four months in the Cuban city of Matanzas studying sacred Afro-Cuban drumming with legendary musician Cha-Chá (Esteban Vega Bacallao, 1925–2007). As the owner of prestigious drums sacred to the Santeria religion, Cha-Chá regularly employed several men of varying ages who were ritually "sworn" to his drums. The youngest of these men were in their twenties, and they often served as assistants during my drum lessons.

In February one of these young assistant drummers, Alejandro, frequently left our lessons early to visit his sick mother, Cha-Chá's niece. Alejandro's mother was hospitalized due to a circulation problem and subsequent infection in her leg, and for many days he reported either no progress in her condition or minor changes for the worse. At times he expressed concern that his mother would have her leg amputated or perhaps even die. One day, when we were alone, with some embarrassment Alejandro asked me if I had any antibiotics he could take to his mother. For whatever reasons, Alejandro's mother's doctors knew she needed antibiotics but could not provide the drugs given low supplies in the hospital. Dismayed, I told Alejandro I had none, but as we spoke I remembered that I did have a small tube of a common topical three-in-one antibiotic ointment (part of an almost forgotten first aid kit my mother had insisted I bring with me). I mentioned the ointment to Alejandro, explaining that it was topical, to be used externally on the skin. Alejandro thought that it might still be of help, if only for use to barter for something more appropriate. He gratefully accepted the small tube, and I was left feeling saddened that I could not do more.

When I saw him a couple of days later, Alejandro was beaming. He reported that he had given his mother's doctor my ointment and they had injected it into her leg, causing immediate improvement and a steady recovery. I was happy but puzzled. Injected a topical ointment? Surely he must have been mistaken.

No, he insisted, they had indeed injected it *into* her leg. He imitated the action of a syringe with his fingers for emphasis. Alejandro thanked me warmly. I was happy to have helped, but inwardly I reeled at the possibility that this over-the-counter, two-dollar tube of ointment I had packed as an afterthought might have saved a woman's leg.

This incident was certainly peripheral to my research, one of countless anecdotes of deprivation and invention that are now common tropes in ethnographic accounts of post-Soviet Cuba. Putting aside the question of exactly what medical treatment Alejandro's mother received, what interests me here is not the adaptive nature of the medical care but rather Alejandro's use of the Santeria religion as a location of exchange between foreigners and Cubans. Caused by the withdrawal of Soviet financial support, the Cuban government's Special Period in Time of Peace ushered in an era of austerity and uncertainty. As Cubans struggled to resolve problems caused by shortages through means both legal and illegal, the ubiquitous circulation of American dollars in an underground economy forced the government to legalize their use in 1993. Two decades later, foreign currency is still the most efficient means by which to resolve problems in Cuba. Had Alejandro been one of many Cubans to receive remittances from supportive family members living abroad, most likely he could have purchased the necessary medicine himself through the purchasing power of foreign-equivalent Cuban currency. With neither remittances nor contact with the relatively low level of tourism in urban Matanzas, Alejandro was nonetheless able to tap into a source of foreign currency and goods through his affiliation with Cha-Chá, who regularly received international visitors seeking his knowledge and liturgical expertise.

My own visits had begun in 1996, but cultural experts such as Cha-Chá occasionally received foreign visitors during the 1980s and earlier. Such visits grew exponentially during the 1990s as Cuba's post-Soviet economic crisis forced an opening of Cuban society to large-scale tourism and foreign investment. I was one of many visitors who arrived at the doorsteps of Cha-Chá and other master drummers not arbitrarily but through unofficial transnational networks based upon personal contacts, ritual associations, and religious expertise. As a result of these contacts, experiences are shared, status is transformed, and rituals, lessons, and interviews are undertaken. But, as well, currency is exchanged in unequal but mutually beneficial transactions.

I characterize these kinds of informal yet systematic and stable international networks, including those of Santeria's religious commerce, as cases of interpersonal internationalism. In so doing I alter the term *internationalism* from its common usage in the context of Cuban international relations. Almost since its inception, the Cuban revolutionary government has undertaken collaborative or unilateral internationalist projects to support what it considers worthy socialist or humanitarian causes. Proponents of these internationalist actions, and particularly of Cuba's long-standing and extensive medical training and exchange programs, marvel at Cuba's outsized ability to "punch above its weight" and have impact on the lives of doctors and patients worldwide.[1]

Supporters of such internationalist efforts characterize them as essential not only as demonstrations of Cuba's dedication to socialism and justice, but also as linchpins of the survival of the revolution because they have cultivated socialist values that have allowed the state to ask for great sacrifices from its citizenry during Cuba's Special Period.[2] But contemporary critics contend that Cuba's commitment to certain internationalist projects comes at the expense of serious domestic needs, representing a drain on Cuba's already strained economy.[3] Even with the internationalism of favorable economic agreements from supportive nations (such as Cuba's so-called doctors for oil partnership with Venezuela), the global recession that began in the late 2000s forced Cuban leaders in 2010 to cut back on long-standing domestic subsidies and propose the unprecedented elimination of hundreds of thousands of government jobs. The steady trickling of bad economic news brought uncertainty as to how lost government jobs would be offset by job creation in a fledgling private sphere—and this in turn brought renewed attention to the cost of Cuba's foreign commitments.

When I reflect on my time in Cuba researching the music of Afro-Cuban religions, the fading national memories of military internationalism or the classic examples of medical internationalism become eclipsed by earthier matters, such as the countless everyday encounters between Cubans and foreigners visiting their island—encounters that enact a variety of unofficial, interpersonal transactions toward mutually beneficial ends. In such cases the obstacle that Cubans work to overcome is their own economy, which greatly privileges foreign-value currency that Cubans cannot directly earn. Cubans are paid salaries and pensions in *pesos nacionales*, typically earning the equivalent of about US$15 to $30 per month. This low figure is made manageable due to government subsidies of free health care and education, low-cost housing, and monthly "rations" of household staples. But foreign visitors exchange their currency for what is in effect a foreign-currency-equivalent peso, the *peso convertible* (CUC). Cubans cannot earn convertible pesos as salaries but may obtain them from foreign remittances sent to the island or through firsthand contact with foreigners visiting Cuba. Many desirable goods (appliances, electronics, certain types of food, clothing, and as Alejandro's example illustrates, some medicines) are sold exclusively in government stores that accept only convertible pesos. As a result the economic and material gulf between those who possess convertible pesos and those who do not is far larger than a simple comparison of monetary value would indicate.

The dual-currency economy has profoundly altered Cuba, creating huge disparities in wealth, dividing society between Cubans with access to convertible pesos and those without. The desire for convertible pesos has led to a type of domestic or internal "brain drain," a situation whereby highly educated or skilled workers leave their jobs for tourist-industry work or private-enterprise activities, both legal and illegal. An additional result of the dual-currency economy and increased tourism to Cuba is the rise of *jineterismo*, a word describing a broad range of informal hustling and solicitation activities. Finally, within the overlapping spheres of tourism and jineterismo is the increasing commoditization of Cuban culture for foreign consumption, for which Santeria commerce may serve as but one of many examples.

The systematic element of an international network operating outside of official channels is a key component of interpersonal internationalism. Such networks, whether they are associated with Christian charity work, political activism, or Santeria culture, build and perpetuate specific alliances rather than resulting from random, one-time interpersonal encounters.[4] Generally such alliances in Cuba result in mutually beneficial exchanges, with the foreigner typically offering CUCs, material goods, prestige, and possibly transformative connections in exchange for experiences, knowledge, objects, or actions. Importantly, the foreigner holds the power of international mobility and convertible pesos, resulting in power relations that are inherently unequal. In the interpersonal internationalism of the Santeria religion, alliances and networks are not only built upon personal contacts and word-of-mouth recommendations but also strengthened by the social structure of the religion itself.

Santeria in Cuba

In international contexts, Santeria is the best-known term for a syncretic Cuban religion based upon West African beliefs; other names for the religion include La Regla Lucumí, La Regla de Ocha, and Ifá. Brought to Cuban shores in the minds of African slaves, the religion's West African worldviews and rituals were remembered and reassembled both in bondage and, to a greater extent, in the free Afro-Cuban population. While components of European spiritism and

Catholicism exist within its religious rituals, most of the religion is based upon West African elements, particularly from the Yorùbá culture of southwestern Nigeria and Benin.

Santeros (Santeria practitioners) believe that the world is alive with spiritual forces and that actions must be taken to exist harmoniously with those forces. The interaction of human agents and spiritual beings necessitates fundamental practices of the religion: divination (a systematic casting and reading of thrown objects to communicate with spiritual beings, ascertaining answers to questions or approval of actions taken); the offering of sacrifices; ancestor veneration; and spirit possession. Reflecting its West African roots, Santeria is a pragmatic religion, focused not on an impending existence after death but rather on living well on Earth and realizing personal potential and destiny. Santeros believe in a creator of the universe, but in Yorùbá tradition this God Almighty, incomprehensible in its wholeness, is characterized as distant and indifferent to the tribulations of humans (as in matters of health, happiness, finance, and relationships). For these earthly concerns practitioners appeal to the *oricha* (also *orisha*).

Oricha are ancient, anthropomorphically conceived divinities, each associated with a domain of nature and human behavior. Having once lived on earth, oricha are thought to be closer to human beings than God is, and therefore more sympathetic to human plights. Santeria initiates have a deeply personal connection with their tutelary oricha, whom they honor, worship, placate, and appeal to in several ways. In the most public communal rituals involving sacred drumming, song, and dance, the oricha themselves may be called to attend the festivities through spirit possession, temporarily "mounting" the body of an initiate to assume human form on Earth. Once down among their "children," the oricha may be honored and asked for blessings, assistance, or advice.

Surrounded by the Catholic religion, colonial-era oricha worshippers noticed parallels between the mythology and representations of the *santos* (Catholic saints) and the oricha, resulting in a complex and multilayered pairing of the two. Indigenous African religious elements of secrecy, hidden symbolism, and flexible interpretation helped Cuban practitioners to preserve, adapt, and conceal their beliefs through Santeria's history of persecution. The localized practice and oral traditions of the religion's African source meant that a knowledgeable oricha priest could reconstitute a form of the religion with a modest number of participants.

Key to perpetuating African cultural knowledge in colonial Cuba was the *cabildo*, a segregated fraternal order approved by the Catholic Church and organized under the sponsorship of a patron Catholic saint. *Cabildos de nación*—cabildos organized by African ethnicity or "nationality"—enabled the retention of ethnic-specific African culture on the island, including religious practices honoring the oricha. As slavery was phased out in the 1880s, the Afro-Cuban cabildos de nación were increasingly suppressed. Many cabildos disappeared, while others transformed themselves into family-based houses of worship dedicated to a primary African divinity and its corresponding saint. This so-called house-temple (*casa templo*), led by an experienced oricha "priest" (*babalocha* for males, *iyalocha* for females) and located within a private home, has been the standard locus of Santeria religious worship for more than a century.

The religious social organization of these house-temples holds the key to the religious networks of commerce. Individuals cannot instantly convert or simply become santeros of their own volition, but rather must undergo graduated rituals, acquire sacred objects and knowledge, and consult with the oricha. All of these steps are policed by expert practitioners. The most important ritual in Santeria is the full initiation of an individual, who receives objects sacred to his or her tutelary oricha and has the essence of the oricha "seated" within his or her head. The initiate completes a year in a restricted novice status before achieving a degree of "adulthood" within the religion. An experienced babalocha or iyalocha educates and guides the initiate through the process, becoming the new santero's godparent. This long-term if not lifetime relationship requires respect, loyalty, and deference on the part of the junior initiate. In time knowledgeable practitioners may begin to initiate individuals on their own. They sometimes break away to form their own independent house-temple communities, but often operate independently while still deferring to their approving godparent, or bring new initiates into the fold of their godparent's "house."

This pyramid-type structure, with a senior babalocha or iyalocha at the pinnacle of authority with ranks expanding downward and outward based on seniority, has been the norm in Cuban Santeria since the end of the colonial era. While formerly limited in geographic scope to a neighborhood, city, or province, the reach of some Cuban religious experts is now international. Although some santeros immigrated to other countries in the first half of the twentieth century, migrations increased at the beginning of the revolutionary government, surging according to Cuban political or economic conditions. In some cases immigrant santeros broke away from their Cuban elders and simply established independent religious houses in their new homelands. Others remained loyal to their godparents, cultivating a local or satellite independence while maintaining links to their Cuban elders as best they could.

For some santeros this deference may be driven by necessity resulting from the lack of a local community or specific ritual items or expertise. But for others Cuba serves as a mecca of Santeria authority, the ultimate source of religious genealogies and power to which all santeros can connect when tracing the legitimacy of their spiritual lineages.[5] An iyalocha in New York, Miami, or Veracruz, for example, might send or accompany her religious godchildren to Cuba to meet her own godparents or to undergo "proper" initiations with respected Cuban elders. Santeria master drummers might follow a similar pattern, as certain consecrated drums used in Santeria rituals must be "born" of existing sets and the drummers initiated into an existing drum fraternity (my U.S. teacher's fraternal alliances with Cuban master drummers is the connection that led me to Cha-Chá). The international travel involved in all of these spiritual networks is costly, but the pull of Cuba as the source of authentic culture and spiritual authority is powerful, and for many, worth the effort.

The Commercialization of Santeria

These international networks of Santeria spirituality existed on a very small scale before the revolution and continued after Fidel Castro came to power, though under more difficult circumstances. Even while it was promoting Santeria culture as folklore in national troupes, the Cuban government hardened its policies toward all religions in the early 1960s. Citizens with any religious leanings were banned from Communist Party membership and excluded from certain jobs or leadership roles. Santeros were required to register their drum ceremonies with local authorities (a policy still in place today), and government agents monitored participants, jailing santeros who dared to initiate children into the religion.[6]

Regulated and marginalized, Santeria persisted. From the mid-1960s until the late 1980s, government rhetoric and policy toward all practitioners of Afro-Cuban religions adopted a hostile yet paternalistic tone, implying that Afro-Cuban religions were primitive holdovers from an ignorant and persecuted past. The authorities believed that given time to absorb the state benefits of education and modern medical care, combined with the secular ideology and scientific rationalism of the revolution, santeros would eventually abandon the religion, transforming it into a benign, secular folk tradition.[7]

During these decades, transnational networks of santeros brought foreigners to the island for initiations, even when initiating foreigners and possessing their currency were illegal.[8] But Cuba's post-Soviet opening of the island to foreign travelers greatly increased the traffic of Santeria commerce. Because Cuba's dual-currency economy greatly privileges contact with foreigners, visitors to the island interested in Santeria provide Cuban santeros with an unusual opportunity to use their everyday religious practice to procure convertible pesos. For santeros with no connection to tourism and no source of foreign remittances, the impact of such transactions can be great. And because of the remote chance that the foreigner, pleased with the results of the encounter, may want to seriously engage with some element of the religion, the possibility of cultivating a long-term foreign client or godchild is worth pursuing for many santeros.

Foreigners who want to deepen their involvement in Santeria can undertake a variety of religious ritual actions ranging from minor spiritual consultations to full initiation into the religion. Each ritual action has a *derecho*: a ritual fee that covers not only the supplies and expenses but also the esoteric knowledge and religious status necessary to carry out the rituals. The greater the importance of the ritual action involved, the higher the derecho. The highest fees are associated with Santeria's most important ritual: full initiation into the religion. The amount of these initiation fees illustrates the magnitude of Santeria's potential commerce within Cuba's dual-currency economy.

Initiation expenses involve a broad range of ritual items and clothing, sacrificial offerings, specialized religious labor, supportive labor, and facilities. For many Cubans, initiation costs are prohibitively high—so much so that some interested Cubans never undergo initiation or delay it for years, even decades.[9] A rough average cost for a Cuban to be initiated in Cuba, expressed in equivalent U.S. dollars, is about $500 (plus or minus $200), well beyond a year's salary for most peso-earning Cubans.[10] By comparison, for an American to become initiated in the United States the cost of an inexpensive initiation is often between $5,000 and $15,000, with more costly initiations ranging from $20,000 upwards to $40,000 or more.[11] In addition to the attraction of Cuba as an authentic source of the Santeria religion, the lower costs and perceived higher quality of religious actions in Cuba motivate some foreigners to travel to Cuba for their initiations. However, as with most experiences on the island, Santeria commerce is a dual-currency system—foreigners are charged convertible pesos for the same actions and experiences that Cubans typically pay for using pesos nacionales. To become initiated in Cuba costs a foreigner roughly $2,000 to $5,000 CUC, a relative bargain for the foreigner but a huge sum by Cuban standards.[12]

The transactions in Cuba between foreign patrons of Afro-Cuban religions and Cuban religious practitioners are mutually beneficial. The foreigner undergoes religious rituals (ones perhaps unavailable domestically) for a price lower than possible in his or her home country while experiencing rituals of a perceived higher quality, authenticity, and prestige. The Cuban religious experts providing the religious rituals and experiences earn the tangible benefit of convertible pesos. In addition, the Cuban santero gains the prestige of being viewed as an authority by a foreign client, as well as the possibility of permanently expanding the network of his or her religious "house" internationally, becoming a religion-based site of interpersonal internationalism. The large sums of convertible pesos enhance the reputation of the expert santero locally by benefiting a variety of ritual specialists aligned with him or her: diviners, ritual assistants, liturgical singers, drummers, and support labor drawn from the santero's local godchildren. The prospect of earning convertible pesos generates enthusiasm on the part of all; for poorer santeros with no access to foreign remittance money, these occasional opportunities to earn convertible pesos represent a helpful windfall.

For performance experts of Santeria dance, drumming, and song liturgy, contact with foreign students produces similar results. Such students might send their own students and colleagues to Cuba with letters, currency, and goods. These individuals then return with news and letters in response, perpetuating the networks. In the case of Cha-Chá, drum lessons and sacred drum initiations for foreigners benefited not only him but also his "sworn" drummers (such as Alejandro) and other allied associates, who might also prevail upon the visitor to bring items should he or she return (medicine and clothing were the most common nonmonetary requests I received from Matanzas drummers). In addition to payment, expert teachers might also request that the foreign visitor use his or her audiovisual equipment to document the teacher's expertise to serve as a promotional work or bolster the teacher's reputation, both in Cuba and abroad.[13]

Just as tourists are widely visible in many areas of urban Cuban life, foreigners are increasingly a part of urban Santeria commerce.[14] Foreign students of Santeria religion and performance arts come from all over the globe to study in Cuba, often drawn to the prominent displays of state folkloric troupes but sometimes engaging expert individuals with no connection to the folklore or tourism industries (such as Cha-Chá). My research in Matanzas revealed a clear split between santeros with foreign clients (and often having connections to state folklore performance) and those who operated on a purely local, peso nacional level. When combined with the localized idiosyncrasies of the religion, personal jealousies, and economic crisis, access to foreigners and their currency sometimes creates conflict or accusations regarding the motivations of santeros who take foreign clients. In a sense, conflict has always been part of the religion as the local, compartmentalized practices that helped Santeria to survive persecution perpetuated non-standardized practices—with the variations subject to criticism by fellow santeros. With no single leader or Vatican-type institution to rule on orthodoxy, standardize practices, and settle disagreements, disputes are common in the religion. Even without foreign clients, rivalry and disagreement over religious issues can result in criticism, gossip, and accusation in regard to religious competence or personal motivation, pulling at the loyalties and alliances of local santeros. The potential monetary reward involved with foreign clients raises the stakes and exacerbates rivalries.

Concerning foreign initiates, rumors abound as to whether or not ritual requirements are relaxed or abbreviated in the interest of profit or to accommodate time-pressed foreign visitors. Jineterismo and fraud also exist near the margins of Santeria as the ignorance of new visitors or novice foreign santeros may be exploited for financial gain. Blurring the line between local variation and deception, accounts exist of ritual experts intentionally performing fraudulent initiations on foreigners or selling foreign clients suspect oricha for personal gain.[15] Some travelers to Cuba return to their native countries having purchased a ritual object, participated in a Santeria ritual, or even undergone some type of initiation, only to be told by local Santeria authorities that their experiences or items were the result of either incompetence or fraud.

For some observers, the penetration of the Special Period's hardships and jineterismo into Santeria's praxis exemplifies the devastating cultural effects of the dual-currency system on Santeria culture. The commercialization of the religion is now a common theme in ethnographic studies, as are the claims by many santeros that they personally are not motivated by profit but that many other santeros are so inclined.[16] Some santeros complain that international Santeria commerce has inflated the costs of rituals in general, pushing the prices of initiations or religious supplies even further beyond the reach of Cubans locked in the national peso economy.[17]

International commerce appears to cause some expert santeros to prioritize foreign clientele over the local community. In the 1990s the prefix *diplo-*, taken from Soviet-era foreign currency stores reserved for diplomats and other foreign visitors, was disparagingly affixed to Santeria terms to identify practitioners and religious practices focused on commerce with foreigners.[18] These entrepreneurs of diplo-Santeria often work with institutional support or solicit new customers who are attending public performances of Afro-Cuban culture.

But as with other elements of the Cuban economy, the Cuban government took note of foreign visitors' interest in Santeria as a religion. In response the state developed programs of Santeria religious tourism in an attempt to capture hidden international Santeria commerce. These so-called *santurismo* programs reportedly offer all-inclusive tours—some that even include full initiations into Santeria—that direct foreigners to santeros who work in partnership with the state.[19] These government-authorized santeros are an exception to the norm of international person-to-person exchanges, but in the early 1990s the Cuban government took action to bring more Santeria commerce under the auspices of the state. After years of refusing to authorize organized groups of santeros or *babalaos* (specialized Santeria divination experts), in the early 1990s the Cuban government recognized the Asociación Cultural Yoruba (ACY), supporting it with funding, granting it a renovated building across from Havana's *capitolio*, and allowing it to raise money from foreign organizations. Besides enabling it to sponsor educational, folkloric, and touristic activities, the ACY's privileged and official status allows it latitude to work with foreign groups and for its card-carrying members (7,000 strong and growing) to host visitors interested in undergoing religious activities. ACY membership cards, issued for an annual fee of 250 pesos nacionales, have become for some members a state-sanctioned guarantee of religious authenticity, one offered to foreigners who appear interested in Santeria or, for that matter, anything else.[20]

For expert practitioners in Cuba, government sponsorship is a divisive issue. ACY members (whose ranks include many highly respected babalaos) point to government recognition as acknowledgment of expertise and authenticity, its institutional wealth and international connections as evidence of the quality of its organization. Those without government approval characterize government-sponsored groups as sellouts susceptible to state influence and deferential to government political policies, a charge the ACY consistently denies.

Such conflicts are apparent in what is arguably the most prominent annual activity conducted by babalaos, the announcement of the *letra del año* (letter of the year), an annual spiritual prognostication guided by the wisdom of the oricha. The ACY enjoys an official monopoly over this important divination and announces its "reading" through government media, while a rival group of babalaos without government support conduct their own letra del año rituals (yet another group of babalaos in Miami conduct their own reading as well). Because the "letters" revealed through divination refer to Yorùbá verses that in turn must be interpreted by the babalao, great is the potential to interpret the letra's "signs" referring to health, prosperity, misfortune, or danger as metaphors applying to the Cuban government. In a 1995 paper on

Cuban NGOs, Gillian Gunn notes that government authorities had long been interested in influencing babalaos due to the latter's respect within the Santeria community. While the president of the ACY told Gunn that the organization contested the membership applications of babalaos "pliant" to government positions, such a statement concedes that government-influenced babalaos exist.[21]

In his study of the conflict over the letra del año, anthropologist Kenneth Routon argues that government involvement in the ritual pushed what was once a localized, esoteric disagreement into the realm of politics. Presenting multiple perspectives concerning the letra del año controversy, Routon concludes that "the 'official' babalaos of the ACY will always come up with a politically correct letra," one at least neutral if not favorable to the government.[22] Thus, santeros and babalaos not affiliated with the government may claim spiritual superiority vis-à-vis the ACY due to their not being subject to co-optation by the state or deferential to government positions; in short, not bending religion to accommodate state politics. But such claims are given little circulation and must compete with the wealth and international reach of the ACY and the state tourism industry. Truth be told, several unofficial organizations critical of the ACY continue to wait for government approval of their own groups so that they might take their place as state-sanctioned authorities of Santeria and its international commerce.

Human Capital and Happiness

From Santeria tourism to religious jineterismo to government-authorized ritual divinations, material need is the primary catalyst behind accelerated change in Cuban Santeria. While most case studies depict government involvement in Santeria commerce as reactive to preexisting economic activity, the government itself plays a role in commercializing not only Afro-Cuban culture aimed at tourists but also even Cuban grassroots community movements. In one such case described by anthropologist Adrian Hearn, the government's concern with generating revenue overruled the holistic nature of a proposed community project by recommending a focus on music and dance components more likely to attract tourist commerce.[23] Shaped by the government's financial need, such projects become one more node in a commerce-driven feedback loop anticipating and then fulfilling touristic desire.

By contrast, some non-Cuban santeros, students, scholars, musicians, and dancers eschew the constrictions of tourism and the artifice of official folklore to pursue personal contacts with Cuban experts—sometimes carrying only a name, other times bearing a letter of introduction—thereby creating, reactivating, or extending international religious networks. In time some of these individuals may bring others to Cuba—friends, students, colleagues, customers, godchildren—introducing new individuals to the rich culture of Afro-Cuban religion, honoring their teachers and elders, and providing a context for cultural exchange and commerce. These are unofficial international networks that result in mutually beneficial exchanges, examples of interpersonal internationalism.

There are darker, exploitative networks as well, and the degree of capitalist penetration into Cuban culture as a result of the economic crisis can be depressing for those who consider its human toll. The rise of Cuba as an international destination for sex tourism, replete with tropes of exotic desire and racist stereotypes and fantasies, represents the return of a demeaning situation that the socialist revolution had purposefully stamped out. Although some Cubans set their terms for these types of transactions and are able to transform their lives materially, it seems a moral stretch to characterize these interactions as mutually beneficial. Some encounters become relationships (which also, ironically, must be registered with the government) and may generate new interpersonal networks. Cuban-foreigner couplings may become long-term serial affairs, some based on exploitation and material need, others based on affection and love resulting in marriages and families. Nonetheless, jineterismo and international sex tourism can transform Cuban bodies into a form of human capital painfully different from the type celebrated in speeches by Cuban leaders.

In contrast to all this darkness of need, commercialism, and networks of exploitation, others interpret the global appetite for Cubans and their culture through alternative symbolism. When I chatted with musicologist Olavo Alén in Havana in 2003, he conceded that Cuba needed to import many things and that its industry did not manufacture much to export to the rest of the world. But, he noted, so many countries with great manufacturing industries, powerful nations that create remarkable products, also produce citizens that do not seem entirely happy, individuals who consume media and travel the world searching for novelty and distraction. When some of these citizens discover Cuba and its culture, they become enamored, happy. Often they come back for more. And so, Alén reasoned, through its culture Cuba was manufacturing happiness. Importer of goods, Cuba possesses a surplus of happiness to export to the world in the form of a culture that captivates individuals and brings joy to their lives. Sitting in Alén's office, I smiled, because I knew exactly what he meant.

Notes

I gratefully acknowledge funding for research in Cuba in 2000, 2003, and 2007 provided by a UCLA Dissertation Year Grant and by SDSU University Grants Program awards. I dedicate this essay to the memory of Gregory Aaron Feldman (1977–2010), a young surgeon who, among his many deeds, traveled to Cuba and Rwanda to share his medical knowledge and ease the suffering of those in medical need regardless of nationality or circumstance.

1. John Kirk, "Reflections on Medical Internationalism," *Latin American Perspectives* 36, no. 1 (2007), 139–40.

2. Isaac Saney, "Homeland of Humanity: Internationalism within the Cuban Revolution," *Latin American Perspectives* 36, no. 1 (2009), 111–23; Richard L. Harris, "Cuban Internationalism, Che Guevara, and the Survival of the Cuban Revolution," *Latin American Perspectives* 36, no. 3 (2009), 27–42.

3. James Petras and Robin Eastman-Abaya, "Cuba: Continuing Revolution and Contemporary Contradiction," 2007, petras.lahaine.org/articulo.php?p=1705&more=1&c=1.

4. For brief case studies on unofficial Christian networks connecting the United States and Cuba, see Sarah J. Mahler and Katrin Hansing, "Myths and Mysticism: How Bringing a Transnational Religious Lens to the Examination of Cuba and the Cuban Diaspora Exposes and Ruptures the Fallacy of Isolation," in Damián J. Fernández, ed., *Cuba Transnational* (Gainesville: University Press of Florida, 2003), 42–60.

5. Since the 1960s a variety of movements within the international oricha community have moved away from Cuban Santeria in favor of a more African-centered model, viewing African rather than Cuban practices as authoritative models for oricha worship. These movements result from a variety of political, national, ethnic, and personal motivations.

6. Anonymous personal communications with the author, Havana and Matanzas, Cuba, 2000, 2003, 2005, 2007. In Cuba I collected anecdotes regarding religious persecution during informal conversations rather than formal on-the-record interviews. Due to the personal nature of religious practice and varying degrees of comfort in discussing it, or government persecution of santeros, I intentionally avoid using named sources for certain anecdotes.

7. This attitude is best exemplified by a 1973 essay "Regarding Folklore" by Cuban ethnologist and folklorist Rogelio Martínez Furé, more widely republished in English in Peter Manuel, ed., *Essays on Cuban Music: North American and Cuban Perspectives* (Lanham, MD: University Press of America, 1991), 249–65. When I interviewed Martínez Furé in Havana in September 2000, he disavowed the majority of the essay, citing directives he was given at that time to articulate government attitudes.

8. Marta Moreno Vega reports that at the time of her 1981 initiation in Cuba it was illegal for Cubans to initiate foreigners. Prohibited from paying for her initiation with dollars, she covered her initiation costs by bringing fifteen pairs of contraband U.S. blue jeans to Cuba for her godmother to sell on the black market. Vega, *The Altar of My Soul: The Living Traditions of Santería* (New York: Ballantine, 2000), 215–17.

9. From within Cha-Chá's circle of drummers, Daniel Alfonso Herrera (1946–2010) exemplifies the long-term santero who waited decades to become fully initiated in 2005, something he finally accomplished in part due to the earnings generated from his foreign drum students.

10. My figure is based on discussions with santeros in Havana, Matanzas, and the United States. For a comparison of initiation cost estimates for Cubans in scholarly literature, see Katherine J. Hagedorn, *Divine Utterances: The Performance of Afro-Cuban Santería* (Washington, DC: Smithsonian Institution Press, 2001), 9; Michael Atwood Mason, *Living Santería: Rituals and Experiences in an Afro-Cuban Religion* (Washington, DC: Smithsonian Institution Press, 2002), 60, 142; and Christine Ayorinde, *Afro-Cuban Religiosity, Revolution, and National Identity* (Gainesville: University Press of Florida, 2004), 162.

11. These figures are based on my research in California. For a comparison of U.S. initiation costs in scholarly literature, see Raul Canizares, *Walking with the Night: The Afro-Cuban World of Santeria* (Rochester, NY: Destiny Books, 1993), 33; Miguel A. de la Torre, *Santería: The Beliefs and Rituals of a Growing Religion in America* (Grand Rapids, MI: William B. Eerdmans Publishing, 2004), 116; Steven Gregory, *Santería in New York City: A Study in Cultural Resistance* (New York: Garland, 1999), 90; Migene González-Wippler, *Santería: The Religion* (St. Paul, MN: Llewellyn Publications, [1989] 1994), 174, 289; Julio O. Granda, "A Materialist View of Santería and the Expenses Associated with the Initiation," MA thesis, Department of Anthropology, Florida State University, Tallahassee, 1995, 69; Hagedorn, *Divine Utterances*, 220; Joseph Murphy, *Santería: African Spirits in America* (Boston, MA: Beacon Press, [1988] 1993), 91. See also John Lantigua, "Holy Wars, Inc.," *Miami New Times*, April 9, 1998, www.miaminewtimes.com/1998-04-09/news/holy-wars-inc/.

12. My figure is based on discussions with santeros in Havana, Matanzas, and the United States. See also Hagedorn, *Divine Utterances*, 220–21; Ayorinde, *Afro-Cuban Religiosity*, 162.

13. See Lisa Knauer's essay on the transnational video dialogue between Cubans on the island and in the United States via "audiovisual remittances." Lisa Maya Knauer, "Audiovisual Remittances and Transnational Subjectivities," in Ariana Hernández-Reguant, ed., *Cuba in the Special Period: Culture and Ideology in the 1990s* (New York: Palgrave Macmillan, 2009), 159–77.

14. The unofficial nature of much Santeria commerce with foreigners makes it difficult to estimate numbers of participants with any accuracy. Writing of her Santeria research in Santiago, anthropologist Kristina Wirtz states, "Seldom did I meet a santero who did not boast of at least one foreign godchild." Kristina Wirtz, *Ritual, Discourse, and Community in Cuban Santería: Speaking in a Sacred World* (Gainesville: University Press of Florida, 2007), 152.

15. Ayorinde, *Afro-Cuban Religiosity*, 161–62; Rogelio Martínez-Furé, interview with the author, September 20, 2000, Havana; Miguel Ramos, "Diplo Santería and Pseudo Orishas," Eledá.org, 2010, eleda.org/blog/2010/12/27/diplo-santeria-and-pseudo-orishas/.

16. Wirtz, *Ritual, Discourse, and Community*.

17. Ayorinde, *Afro-Cuban Religiosity*, 162. I heard similar complaints in both 2005 and 2007, mostly in Havana.

18. Martinez-Furé, interview; Ramos, "Diplo Santería and Pseudo Orishas." Cuban ethnologist Natalia Bolívar claims the Cuban government began offering specialized Santeria spectacles for foreign tourists using diplo-santeros in the late 1970s, though by her account (including outrageous "rituals" featuring bare-breasted female dancers) these were entertainment- and folklore-driven enterprises rather than religious commerce. See Juan O. Tamayo, "In Cuba, a Clash between Religions," *Miami Herald*, January 12, 1998, A1.

19. Hagedorn, *Divine Utterances*, 9, 221–22; Rogelio Martinez-Furé, "A National Cultural Identity? Homogenizing Monomania and the Plural Heritage," in Pedro Pérez Sarduy and Jean Stubbs, eds., *Afro-Cuban Voices: On Race and Identity in Contemporary Cuba* (Gainesville: University Press of Florida, 2000), 161.

20. In 2007, a babalao introduced himself to me on the street near the ACY building (did he follow me from inside the ACY?) and offered to assist me in my research or in recommending private restaurants or rooms for rent, producing his ACY membership card to assure me of his religious legitimacy. For similar encounters, see Wirtz, *Ritual, Discourse, and Community*, 72; and Adrian H. Hearn, *Religion, Social Capital, and Development* (Durham, NC: Duke University Press, 2008), 45–46.

21. Gillian Gunn, *Cuba's NGOs: Government Puppets or Seeds of Civil Society?* (Washington, DC: Center for Latin American Studies, Georgetown University, 1995). Though written from a stance clearly adversarial to the Castro government, see also Oppenheimer's chapter "Courting the Babalao." Andres Oppenheimer, *Castro's Final Hour: The Secret Story Behind the Coming Downfall of Communist Cuba* (New York: Simon and Schuster, 1992).

22. Kenneth Routon, "The 'Letter of the Year' and the Prophetics of Revolution," in Hernández-Reguant, ed., *Cuba in the Special Period*, 132–38.

23. Hearn, *Religion, Social Capital, and Development*, 92–94.

9

The Promise of Globalization

Sustainable Tourism Development and Environmental Policy in Cuba

RICARDO PÉREZ

> In an era of globalization, it is difficult for economic
> performance that is not exceptional to lead to development.
>
> PEDRO MONREAL

With the collapse of the Soviet Union and the Eastern European socialist bloc at the start of the 1990s, Cuba suffered a major economic and political setback that forced the island government to consider alternative options for socioeconomic development and reinsertion into a globalized economy. According to estimates, in 1990 commercial trade between the Council for Mutual Economic Assistance (COMECON, the group of socialist economies formed around the former Soviet Union and Eastern Europe) and Cuba accounted for no less than 85 percent of the island's trading activities.[1] Having lost almost the entire market for its export and import products, the Cuban economy basically came to a halt. Soon after the socialist collapse the Cuban government began to look for alternatives to stay afloat in the middle of unprecedented political and economic transformations.

Since 1990 Cuba's transition to a different pattern of economic development has, as Pedro Monreal spells out, depended on three main pillars: "the intensive utilization of natural resources, the access to external rents [remittances], and the limited revenue derived from foreign loans and investment." An important aspect of the new pattern of development has been the investment by transnational corporations in various strategic economic sectors such as mining and tourism, areas that could help provide the island with rapid access to hard currency and facilitate its global reinsertion. As Monreal argues, tourism development provides the basis of a "new service economy" that relies heavily on the "intensive use of natural resources."[2]

In the Caribbean region in general, tourism has followed a well-established pattern of development since the 1950s. The postwar period ushered in deliberate efforts by the majority of the Caribbean island governments to build and modernize their economies around the "natural resources that were already in place—sand, sun, sea, and friendly people."[3] In addition, because of its multiplier effects on the economy tourism became a convenient and reliable way of earning highly sought hard currencies. As George Gmelch correctly notes, "the outward ripple of tourist dollars fosters demand for goods and services in other areas. Farmers, fisherman [sic], and merchants benefit because they must grow and supply more fish, meat, poultry, eggs, vegetables, and fruit to feed the large number of visitors. The tourists' desire for curios and souvenirs generates work for local artists and craftspeople. Early on, the large ripple effect is in the construction of hotels, guesthouses, restaurants, and other facilities needed to cater to visitors." The number of international tourists who have visited the Caribbean region since the end of the Second World War has increased steadily; for example, in 1959 1.3 million tourists arrived in the region, in 1965 the number was close to 4 million, and in 1985 the number increased to 10 million. By the year 2000, more than 17 million international tourists were traveling to the Caribbean region.[4] Therefore, it is not surprising that most Caribbean islands have come to depend heavily on revenues from international tourism to promote national economic growth.

In Cuba's case, since the start of the Special Period the country has set in place in its coastal areas an infrastructure of hotels, roads, and beach resorts catering mainly to international tourists; and tourism was particularly significant to the island's economic recovery after the late 1990s because the industry had an impact on nearly all sectors of the national economy—from telecommunications to construction—and all areas of culture and society.[5] But while revolutionary Cuba can be considered a relative newcomer to the international tourism industry, recent data show that the country is on a steady path to be among the leading destinations in the Caribbean. For example, by 2004 Cuba was receiving more than two million tourists, with revenues from the industry soaring to well over $2 billion. Moreover, during the second half of the first decade of the twenty-first century, according to Cuba's National Office of Statistics, the number of international tourists to Cuba remained steady at around 2.2–2.3 million a year, with revenues in 2008, for example, standing at $2.5 billion. Figures for the number of tourists in 2009, 2010, and 2011, respectively, were 2,429,809, 2,531,745, and 2,716,317.[6] The growth of the tourism industry was so rapid and successful that by the beginning of the new century tourism had not only transformed the island into a leading tourist destination in the region but also replaced sugar as Cuba's main source of hard currency. By 2004, moreover, Cuba had become the eighth most visited tourist destination in Latin America and the Caribbean, moving up from ninth place the previous year and, remarkably, up from twenty-third place in 1990. Cuba's tourism industry since the late 1990s has clearly shown impressive development.[7] For example, in 1989 international tourists to Cuba numbered 275,000 and in 1990 their number increased to 327,000. While in 1990 only 3 percent of the international tourists to the Caribbean region visited Cuba, by 2003 Cuba's share of international tourists to the region was 11 percent.[8]

Since the 1980s the international visitors have tended to come from roughly the same sources: the majority arrive from Canada; followed by Western European countries such as the United Kingdom, Spain, Italy, Germany, and France; and Latin American countries such as Mexico and Argentina—a pattern and distribution of tourist arrivals maintained into the present (figure 9.1).

The opening of revolutionary Cuba's doors to international tourists presents important challenges to the promotion of sustainable tourism development. Conservationists consider the island to be the "biological superpower" of the Caribbean; in other words, Cuba is the most biologically diverse island in the

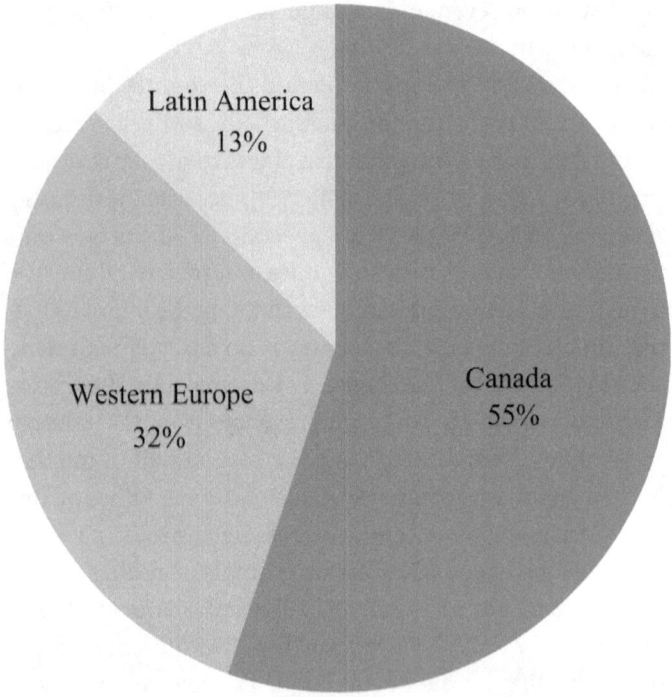

Figure 9.1. Sources of international tourism, 2011

region and, as a result of the country's centrally planned economy, uncontrolled urban and industrial growth is not widespread or as common as it is in most Caribbean islands.[9]

The burgeoning literature on Cuba's tourism development since the start of the Special Period has misrepresented Cuba's tourism industry as problematic: most authors tend to focus mainly on the prostitution of Cuban women, sex (and gay sex) tourism, and the rise of social disparities.[10] The overemphasis on sex tourism and prostitution, nonetheless, seems to be in line with cultural studies of tourism development in other Caribbean islands such as the Dominican Republic and Jamaica. The environmental impacts of tourism in the Caribbean, however, are generally unknown; the few studies that do exist on the subject lack substantial field research data. Even in Caribbean countries such as Jamaica, the Dominican Republic, and Puerto Rico, where international tourism has been a part of economic development programs for a long time, the environmental consequences of a growing tourism industry have remained unexamined. For the Cuban case, Sergio Díaz Briquets and Jorge Pérez López's historical analysis of environmental issues before and after the Cuban revolution and Stephen Wilkinson's limited study of tourism's impacts on the environment since the late 1990s open a line of inquiry with the potential to render a refreshing perspective on "Cuba's tourism boom."[11]

In particular, the Cuban approval of environmental policies during the late 1990s had a significant effect on the promotion of sustainable tourism development in the island. As Daniel Whittle, Kenyon Lindeman, and James Tripp argue, the Environmental Law of July 1997 would provide a framework for the creation of a different model of coastal tourism growth that promised not to degrade coastal and marine resources.[12] It also made a powerful statement regarding Cuba's newfound interest in promoting both tourism development and environmental conservation, with obvious implications for our understanding of tourism in the Caribbean in general. Indeed, tourism development constitutes the best and most rapid, albeit controversial, alternative for Cuba's reinsertion into global markets. Although this chapter does not focus on the social problems associated with tourism development, it should be acknowledged that tourism has played a main role in the noticeable increase in social and racial inequalities that have resulted from unequal access to hard currencies.[13] Instead, I will argue that tourism's contribution to the island's economic recovery outweighs its most negative outcomes and that Cuba is rapidly becoming a model for sustainable tourism and environmental conservation that will be of benefit to other Caribbean islands.

Phases of Tourism Development from the Late Nineteenth to the Late Twentieth Century

The history of Cuban tourism can be traced back to the nineteenth century, when the capital city of Havana had already become the center of economic, political, and cultural affairs for the island. According to historical accounts described by Rogelio Quintana and his co-authors, during the second half of the nineteenth century Havana was already the location of various impressive hotels, such as Hotel Inglaterra and Hotel Telégrafo, which accommodated diplomats, businessmen, and international tourists. As early as that historical moment, Havana constituted the most developed province in the island and had the most advanced infrastructure of roads, communications, aqueducts, and hotel accommodations.[14]

In 1919 the Cuban government approved the Comisión Nacional para el Fomento del Turismo (National Commission for Tourism Promotion), which had among its goals the expansion of leisure activities such as casino gambling and the construction of horse and dog racetracks that fostered illegal betting.[15] The creation of the National Commission coincided with the 1920 approval in the United States of the Volstead Act, which prohibited alcohol consumption and illicit gambling activities. Partly as a result of Prohibition, during the 1920s the number of U.S. visitors to Cuba increased dramatically as tourists, merchants, and businessmen found in the island a safe haven to engage in activities that were being forbidden or were considered illicit in the United States.[16] The dramatic increase in the number of U.S. tourists and the revenue from their lavish expenditures turned tourism into the third most important economic sector in Cuba, behind only the cultivation of agricultural commodities such as sugarcane and tobacco. By the end of the decade the number of U.S. tourists reached 86,270, and revenues from tourist expenses were estimated at $12.6 million.[17]

In 1934 the Cuban government acknowledged the importance of tourism for the economic stability of the country and recommended the expansion of tourist activities away from Havana, where the majority of the tourist installations were still concentrated—not just to emphasize the natural beauty of the country's beaches and mountains but also to discourage pastimes associated with casino gambling, betting, and other related "vices."[18] From this moment on it was clear that Cuba's natural beauty was being considered an important element of the country's plans for tourism, even though the main tourist development continued to be the construction of big hotels with casino facilities and other attractions. On October 16, 1934, the Cuban government approved Decree-Law 599, which created the Corporación Nacional de Turismo (National Tourism Corporation), replacing the 1919 commission. The Tourism Corporation, however, had little effect on tourism development and promotion due to the lack of financial resources and institutional support to carry out its mission.[19] Therefore, during the 1930s and 1940s Cuba's tourism industry was severely set back by three interrelated global events: the world economic depression that had begun during the late 1920s; the elimination in 1934 of Prohibition in the United States, which legalized alcohol consumption and some gambling activities in that country; and the economic and political instability resulting from the Second World War. Among many other outcomes of these global events, during this period the number of international tourists decreased dramatically and the construction of new hotels was halted. The tourist infrastructure remained heavily concentrated in the capital city, Havana.

The next major phase in the growth of Cuba's tourism industry began with the postwar period. The 1950s saw a resumption in the building of tourist infrastructure, especially hotels, with the construction of hotel rooms proceeding at the pace of 1,500 to 2,000 rooms per year.[20] The city of Havana continued to grow and increase its tourist infrastructure, with big hotels and grandiose casinos that resembled those built in the early period of illegal gambling in the 1920s. Not surprisingly, the early 1950s marked the return to power of Fulgencio Batista, who as president during the 1920s and 1930s had maintained close links with the most influential U.S. businessmen and hustlers, spurring the growth of gambling and illicit activities on the island.[21] On June 12, 1952, the Batista regime approved Decree-Law 137, which created the Instituto Cubano del Turismo (Cuban Institute of Tourism), replacing the National Tourism Corporation. Also during this decade, the Cuban government began to construct the first hotel (Hotel Intercontinental) and tourist facilities at Varadero Beach, which would soon become the premier beach resort in the island. This step signaled the decisive expansion of the tourist industry outside Havana city and province, although it remained in close proximity to them. Highway construction allowed the transportation of tourists from the city of Havana to Varadero, and the beaches and territory east of the capital city became accessible to international tourists and members of the Cuban elite and middle classes.

As Quintana and his co-authors indicate, during the last year of the prerevolutionary period more than 80 percent of the international tourists who came to Cuba arrived from the United States. In 1957 alone, for example, more than 330,000 U.S. tourists visited Cuba.[22] The disproportionate presence of U.S. tourists in Cuba in the years up to 1958 was based on a number of factors:

first, the heavy economic influence of U.S.-based transnational corporations and U.S. capital in key sectors such as telecommunications, agriculture, and finance; second, the geographical proximity of Cuba to Florida, which made it easy for U.S. tourists and businessmen to travel to Havana, Varadero, and the other resort areas being established along the north coast; third, the development in Cuba of leisure activities associated with the tourist industry, such as casino gambling, cabarets, and nightlife attractions, which made the island a preferred destination for wealthy individuals seeking this type of diversion; and fourth, the neocolonial relationship that the U.S. government still maintained with Cuba, which guaranteed a relatively stable and secure political environment for business expansion and consolidation.

With the triumph of the Cuban revolution in 1959, international tourism came to a halt and the new Cuban government rapidly began to develop modest tourist installations for its own citizens. The revolutionary government nationalized most tourist facilities, and tourist centers that had previously been earmarked for the exclusive use of the Cuban elite and middle classes became available to the entire Cuban population. For example, in February 1959 the Cuban government approved Law No. 100, which allowed the creation of the Departamento de Playas del Pueblo (Department of Popular Beaches), under the jurisdiction of the Ministry of Defense, making the beaches and coastal areas open and accessible to all. Later that year, on November 20, 1959, the Cuban government approved Law No. 636 creating the Instituto Nacional de la Industria Turística (National Institute for the Tourist Industry), which replaced the Cuban Institute of Tourism created by Batista in 1952. Between 1960 and 1969 the Cuban government promoted the development of the national tourism industry by constructing modest tourist installations in coastal and mountainous areas with the goal of making the island's natural beauties even more accessible to the Cuban population. In the early 1960s the Cuban government also built the first installations to promote ecotourism and camping—the Complejo Turístico de Guamá–Laguna del Tesoro (Guamá–Laguna del Tesoro Tourist Complex)—in the Zapata Swamp, located on the southern coast of Matanzas Province. The number of international arrivals to Cuba decreased from 272,000 in 1957 to 87,000 in 1960, mainly as a result of the travel restrictions imposed on its citizens by the U.S. government and the termination of business operations by international tour operators who were pressured by the U.S. government to stop doing business with the Cuban government.[23]

It was not until the start of the 1970s that the promotion of the international tourism industry began to be emphasized once again. This time, however, Cuban government officials were interested in developing tourist attractions and activities unrelated to gambling and the other illicit activities common during the prerevolutionary period. From then on the Cuban government encouraged visitors from the Soviet Union and the Eastern European socialist bloc; small groups of tourists from Canada, Western Europe, and Latin America began to arrive on the island as well, but their numbers did not surpass the visitors arriving from the socialist bloc. According to Quintana and his co-authors, even though the number of tourist arrivals from Canada and Western Europe increased, in 1975 64 percent of the international tourists came from the member countries of COMECON.[24] As a result of the political and administrative reorganization of the Cuban government after the First Congress of the Cuban Communist Party in 1975, the Cuban government created the Instituto Nacional de Turismo (National Institute of Tourism) in 1976. The new agency was responsible for coordinating the development and promotion of national and international tourism, whereas the newly created assemblies of popular power maintained control of the smallest tourist installations and of services associated with the preparation and distribution of food and beverages. The National Institute of Tourism effectively established a management system based on the specialization of the tourist industry and the creation of various agencies to supply the needed resources to serve international and national tourists.[25]

By the late 1980s the Cuban government began to promote the island as a viable tourist destination for international tourists from Western Europe in what Norman Medina and Jorge Santamarina refer to as a highly "planned and organized manner that considered, above all, the island's national interests."[26] Tourists from Western Europe now surpassed the number of tourists arriving from the Soviet Union and Eastern Europe, and smaller groups of tourists were also arriving from Latin American countries such as Mexico and Argentina. By 1987 the number of international tourists had reached levels comparable to those attained in 1957, except that now, not surprisingly, only a few visitors were coming directly from the United States. In contrast to a common perception that revolutionary Cuba began to promote international tourism as a result of the economic collapse that resulted from the disappearance of the socialist economies in the former Soviet Union and Eastern Europe, during the Third Congress of the Cuban Communist Party in 1986 the government was already considering tourism development as a main economic strategy. President Fidel Castro stated at that time, "We expect to receive in the next five years 1,200,000 tourists; this is twice the number of tourists that we received in the previous five years. With this goal in mind, our five-year plan foresees an ambitious investment program centered especially in the tourist areas of Havana, Varadero, and Cayo Largo and comprises the improvement of the existing infrastructure as well as the construction of new hotels and tourist infrastructure."[27]

Tourism Development since the Special Period

In the first half of the 1990s Cuba encountered a profound economic crisis that prompted the introduction of political and economic reforms to get the island back on track. Some reforms, such as the free circulation of U.S. dollars and the increased promotion of international tourism, could not even have been imagined a few years before the crisis. But when compared to the economic debacle in the former Soviet Union and Eastern Europe, the Cuban crisis was rather short-lived. By the second half of the decade the economy had begun to show signs of recovery, as indicated by reports of higher and better economic performance as a result of the economic liberalization policies implemented during the earlier part of the decade.[28]

Indeed, the growth of international tourism gave a great boost to Cuba's economic recovery during the past two decades. For example, in 1996, 1 million international tourists visited Cuba, and by 2000 that figure had nearly doubled, to 1.7 million. In the early years of the twenty-first century, for the first time Cuba reached the goal of welcoming more than 2 million tourists; this trend was maintained, with small fluctuations, until the end of the first decade of the new century.[29] According to Whittle, Lindeman, and Tripp, international tourism to Cuba during the late 1990s "dramatically outpaced tourism growth rates in the rest of the Caribbean and throughout the world." If we consider that Cuba started at a point much lower than the rest of the Caribbean islands, it is fair to describe tourism development in the island as impressive. More important, as Whittle and colleagues pointed out in 2003, "planning officials indicate that there are 558 kilometers of sandy beaches of high interest for tourism development. Currently there are fifty-eight areas (*polos*) in the country where tourism may be developed. Of these, MinTur (the Ministry of Tourism) and the Ministry of Planning have identified eight priority areas for tourism development over the next five to ten years; the majority of these eight zones are on the coast, including the four regions—Havana, Varadero, Sabana-Camagüey, and North Holguín—where the most intensive hotel developments are currently under way."[30] One of the main tourist areas identified as a target of development, due to its cultural and biological richness, is the archipelago that forms a strip of about 465 kilometers along the Cuban northern zone between the provinces of Matanzas and Camagüey—and which, according to Cuban scholars, contains about 60 percent of all keys found in Cuba.[31] This ecosystem contains archaeological sites with evidence of pre-Columbian habitation, as well as numerous species of fauna and flora endemic to the Cuban archipelago. In Cayo Coco (in the Province of Ciego de Avila), tourist facilities and installations are located in areas distant from ecologically sensitive environments such as the sand dunes. In addition, the design and construction of hotel installations have taken into consideration the landscape features of the coastal environments to discourage the building of architectural elements that do not harmonize with the natural contours of the cays. The resulting hotels are mostly two or three stories high and primarily offer all-inclusive packages to the mostly Canadian families and young couples attracted by the area's relative isolation from the more hectic tourist zones of Havana and Varadero and by the calm blue waters of the Atlantic Ocean.

Yet another "emerging tourist area" is that of Caibarién–Cayo Santa María, in the Province of Villa Clara.[32] Unlike Cayo Coco, Cayo Santa María, at least by 2007, had not yet fully developed the infrastructure needed to promote international tourism on a large scale—that is, airport facilities and tourist resorts capable of receiving high numbers of tourists. But by 2007 large-scale tourism development projects were already under way throughout the cay, with various construction projects sprouting along the irregular shores. These construction projects were in addition to three medium-sized hotels that had already been built in the most secluded beaches of the cay. In contrast to the tourism development projects of the early 1990s (and the projects undertaken before the Special Period), tourism development in the Caibarién–Cayo Santa María tourist area represents a good example of the Cuban government's new approach, both to promoting sustainable tourism development and to raising environmental awareness among the Cuban population. In the town of Caibarién, for example, the local community is now actively participating in tourism development and conservation efforts by collaborating with government authorities to minimize the potentially harmful effects of tourism development on the environment and the sociocultural well-being of the local residents.[33]

A main feature of tourism development in the Sabana-Camagüey Archipelago has been the construction of *pedraplenes* (stone embankments) that connect the larger cays such as Cayo Coco and Cayo Santa María to the Cuban mainland. Unquestionably, the pedraplenes have been essential to the expansion of the tourist industry in north Cuba, but at the same time environmentalists have expressed growing concern that these massive constructions may endanger the sensitive coastal ecosystems in the area. As Díaz Briquets and Pérez López note, for example, "The *pedraplenes* block the movement of water in the intracoastal waters, exacerbating contamination and destroying coastal and marine habitats. Many of these semi-enclosed water bodies are already subject to weak circulation regimes and high organic matter contents."[34]

It is precisely this environmental awareness that lies at the center of Cuban authorities' renewed interest in designing economic development policies that also consider the protection of the natural environment. Although in the early period construction and development in the area seem to have been relaxed and somewhat careless, the more recent developments have been prepared with careful attention to the potential for environmental damage. Such is the case, for example, of the pedraplén between Caibarién and Cayo Santa María, designed and constructed to allow the free movement of sea currents and marine fauna through forty-six arches along the almost 2,300-meter-long stone embankment. Indeed, in 2001 the San Benito de Alcántara Foundation in Spain awarded the Ibero-American Puente de Alcántara Award to this pedraplén for the "quality of its design, the preservation of the environment, and its economic contribution to the island of Cuba."[35]

Sustainable tourism development is perhaps the newest buzzword in international tourism studies. For the Cuban government, however, sustainable development is much more than an academic fad. The government is engaged in deliberate efforts to carefully design and implement tourism development plans that consider four main areas of life: culture, society, economy, and the environment.[36] Moreover, the idea of sustainable development itself responds to a major restructuring of Cuba's environmental and regulatory policies since the start of the Special Period (figure 9.2). Among many other important changes, this restructuring involved the foundation in 1994 of the Ministry of Tourism; the approval in 1996 of the Foreign Investment Law (Law No. 77), which provides the legal framework for the creation of joint ventures between

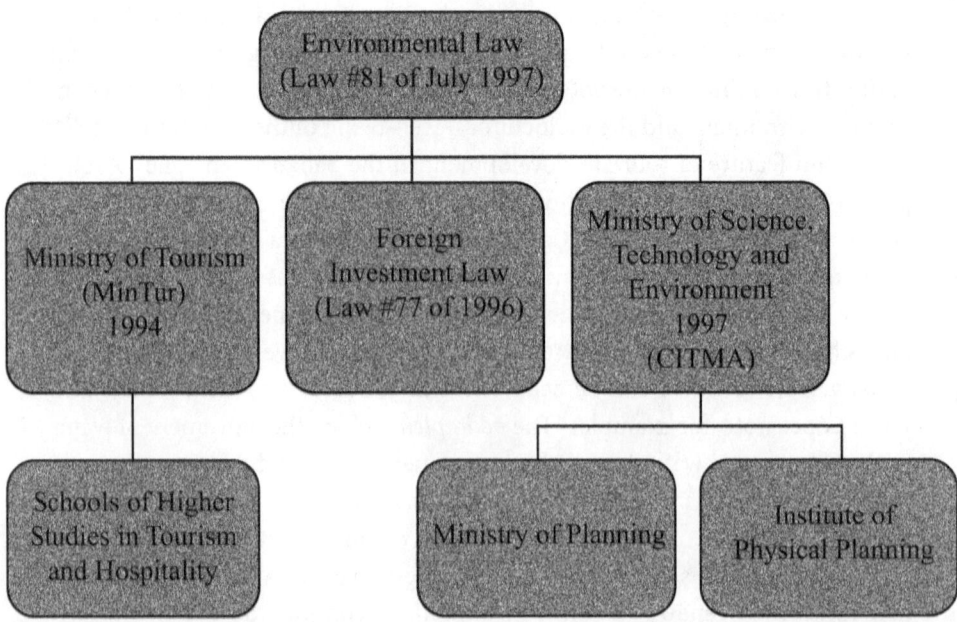

Figure 9.2. Cuban government restructuring of development and conservation policies

transnational corporations and the Cuban government; the approval in 1997 of the Environmental Law (Law No. 81), which provides the political and legal framework for the growth of the tourist industry in accordance with the government's ideal of sustainable development; and the reorganization in 1997 of the scientific and bureaucratic base of the former Academy of Sciences into a single ministry (Ministry of Science, Technology, and Environment, popularly known on the island as CITMA).

CITMA is responsible for the implementation of legislation to regulate and manage tourism in coastal areas and for the education of the Cuban population on aspects of sustainable tourism development. It works closely with the Ministry of Tourism, the Ministry of Planning, the Institute of Physical Planning, and other government agencies in all aspects of coastal tourism development, such as granting environmental licenses to international developers, designing and implementing tourism development plans, and ensuring that every tourism development project follows strict environmental assessment procedures.[37] For its part, the Ministry of Tourism is responsible for the creation and implementation of policies to promote international tourism across the national territory and for the management of the tourist industry in accordance with the highest levels of professionalism as now expected by international tourists and tour operators. With this and other goals in mind, the Ministry of Tourism is also responsible for the administration of a national system of seventeen tourism and hospitality schools that provide a comprehensive program of education to train Cuban tourism workers in the newest industry trends.

The Challenge of Sustainable Tourism

Even as a relatively new undertaking, tourism development in revolutionary Cuba has produced considerable gains, making tourism the leading economic sector on the island. The organization and planning of tourism development have been so successful that Cuba has already surpassed other Caribbean islands that have more experience as a main destination for the kind of sun-and-sand tourism that prevails in the region. Sustainable development practices in Cuba have so far been positive. For instance, in the 2006 Living Planet Report, the World Wildlife Fund identified the series of political and economic reforms of the Special Period as the main reason for Cuba's newfound interest in sustainable development, and concluded that the island is the only place in the world where sustainable development has indeed occurred.[38] Even so, no concrete evidence exists to indicate that sustainable development of the tourism industry can be easily achieved, although the award given to the pedraplén in the Caibarién–Cayo Santa María tourist area is a sign that the environmental and legal restructuring of the Cuban state is working toward environmental conservation. As a group of leading environmental scholars and policymakers noted, "If sustainable development practices were to characterize the new Cuban coastal tourism products, the potential that other Caribbean markets would competitively adopt environmentally progressive practices may be increased."[39]

Like sugar and tobacco—agricultural commodities that once provided Cuba with numerous opportunities for economic development—tourism is subject to the fluctuations of the global economy. The current global economic recession has demonstrated the vulnerability of relying on an economic development path centered on luring international tourists who might be reluctant to travel long distances for a tourist offering (mostly beaches, sun, and sand) that can be found in many other places, and often at more convenient prices.[40] The global economic recession will surely increase competition among Caribbean tourist destinations offering similar packages and attractions. The real challenge for sustainable tourism development in Cuba is how to maintain a high level of quality in service, affordability, and infrastructural development comparable with other popular Caribbean destinations, such as the Dominican Republic, Puerto Rico, and Jamaica, without compromising the lofty ideal of environmental conservation.

As a relatively new but vibrant tourist destination, Cuba will be able to maintain a healthy and prosperous tourism industry by marketing the island aggressively to international tourists unfamiliar with Cuba. For example, Cuba was able to withstand the decline in international tourist arrivals and revenues at the start of the twenty-first century by attracting tourists from countries that have not historically traveled to the island regularly—for instance, from the United Kingdom, which in 2004 showed a 34 percent increase in the number of citizens visiting the island. Cuba is also making important efforts to attract tourists from Venezuela and China—two countries with which the island has recently established important economic and political agreements.[41]

Clearly, the growth of the international tourism industry has helped Cuba reinsert itself rather quickly into global processes of capitalist development, and Cuban government authorities now recognize tourism as the motor of the island's economy. As one commentator aptly noted, it appears that "there will be no going back."[42]

Notes

This chapter is a slightly revised version of a paper presented at the international conference "The Measure of a Revolution, Cuba 1959–2009," Queen's University, Kingston, Ont., May 7–9, 2009.

Epigraph source: Pedro Monreal, "Globalization and the Dilemmas of Cuba's Economic Trajectories," in Jorge I. Domínguez, Omar E. Pérez Villanueva, and Lorena Barbería, eds., *The Cuban Economy at the Start of the Twenty-First Century* (Cambridge, MA: Harvard University Press, 2004), 95.

1. Daniel Whittle, Kenyon C. Lindeman, and James T. B. Tripp, "International Tourism and Protection of Cuba's Coastal and Marine Environments," *Tulane Environmental Law Journal* 16 (2003), 545.

2. Monreal, "Globalization," 100, 102.

3. George Gmelch, *Behind the Smile: The Working Lives of Caribbean Tourism* (Bloomington: University of Indiana Press, 2003), 7.

4. Ibid., 9, 8.

5. See, for example, Lydia Chávez, ed., *Capitalism, God, and a Good Cigar: Cuba Enters the Twenty-First Century* (Durham, NC: Duke University Press, 2005); Domínguez, Pérez Villanueva, and Barbería, *Cuban Economy*; Damián J. Fernández, ed., *Cuba Transnational* (Gainesville: University Press of Florida, 2005). "Special Period in Time of Peace" is the name that Cuban government officials use to refer to the economic and political reforms that resulted from the collapse of the socialist economies in the former Soviet Union and the Eastern European Bloc.

6. Stephen Wilkinson, "Cuba's Tourism Boom: A Curse or a Blessing?" *Third World Development Quarterly* 29, no. 5 (2008), 986. See also República de Cuba, Oficina Nacional de Estadísticas de Cuba, "Turismo. Llegada de visitantes internacionales," www.one.cu/publicaciones/06turismoycomercio/llegadadevisitantes/201012llegadadevisitantes.pdf; and Turismo internacional. Indicadores seleccionados," www.one.cu/publicaciones/06turismoycomercio/indturismointernac/publicaciondic11.pdf.

7. Domínguez, Pérez Villanueva, and Barbería, *Cuban Economy*, 8; and see *Enfoques, Turismo: En el filo del cambio* (a thematic magazine published by the International Press Service's Cuban Office), 1–11 (May 2005), 2.

8. Rogelio Quintana, Manuel Figuerola, Mariano Chirivella, Damarys Lima, Miguel A. Figueras, and Alfredo García, *Efectos y futuro del turismo en la economía cubana* (Montevideo, Uruguay: Editorial Tradinko, 2004), 100, 112–13.

9. Linden Eugene, "The Nature of Cuba," *Smithsonian Magazine*, May 2003, 96; Whittle, Lindeman, and Tripp, "International Tourism," 534–39; see also Quintana et al., *Efectos y futuro*.

10. See, for example, Chávez, *Capitalism, God, and a Good Cigar*; Domínguez, Pérez Villanueva, and Barbería, *Cuban Economy*; Fernández, *Cuba Transnational*; Gisela Fosado, "Gay Sex Tourism, Ambiguity, and Transnational Love in Havana," in ibid., 988–89.

11. Sergio Díaz Briquets and Jorge Pérez López, *Conquering Nature: The Environmental Legacy of Socialism in Cuba* (Pittsburgh, PA: University of Pittsburgh Press, 2000); Wilkinson, "Cuba's Tourism Boom," 983–85.

12. Whittle, Lindeman, and Tripp, "International Tourism."

13. See Alejandro de la Fuente, "Race and Income Inequality in Contemporary Cuba," *North American Congress on Latin America* 44, no. 4 (2011), 30–33; Katrin Hansing, "Changes from Below: New Dynamics, Spaces, and Attitudes in Cuban Society," *North American Con-*

gress on Latin America 44, no. 4 (2011), 16–19; Ricardo Pérez, "On the Cuban Road to Development: Reflections on Sustainable Tourism, Environmental Conservation, and Globalization," *Newsletter of the Society for Applied Anthropology* 21, no. 3 (2010), 47–49; and L. Kaifa Roland, *Cuban Color in Tourism and La Lucha: An Ethnography of Racial Meanings* (New York: Oxford University Press, 2011).

14. Quintana et al., *Efectos y futuro*.

15. Ibid., 73.

16. Rosalie Schwartz, *Pleasure Island: Tourism and Temptation in Cuba* (Lincoln: University of Nebraska Press, 1997).

17. Quintana et al., *Efectos y futuro*, 74, 75.

18. Ibid., 74.

19. Ibid., 77.

20. Ibid., 79.

21. Schwartz, *Pleasure Island*.

22. Quintana et al., *Efectos y futuro*, 88; Norman Medina and Jorge Santamarina, *Turismo de naturaleza en Cuba* (Havana: Ediciones Unión, 2004), 17; see also Miguel A. Figueras Pérez, "El turismo internacional y la formación de *clusters* productivos en la economía cubana," in Omar E. Pérez Villanueva, ed., *Cuba: Reflexiones sobre su economía* (Havana: University of Havana Press, 2002).

23. Quintana et al., *Efectos y futuro*, 91.

24. Ibid., 98.

25. Ibid., 100.

26. See Medina and Santamarina, *Turismo de naturaleza en Cuba*, 17–18. All quotations from Spanish-language sources are translations by the author.

27. Quoted in Quintana et al., *Efectos y futuro*, 106.

28. See Domínguez, Pérez Villanueva, and Barbería, *Cuban Economy*.

29. See Whittle, Lindeman, and Tripp, "International Tourism," 555–56; *Enfoques, Turismo*, 3; Wilkinson, "Cuba's Tourism Boom," 986.

30. Whittle, Lindeman, and Tripp, "International Tourism," 555.

31. See Pedro M. Alcolado, Elisa E. García, and Nelson Espinosa, *Protecting Biodiversity and Establishing Sustainable Development in the Sabana-Camagüey Ecosystem*, Report by the GEF/UNDP Project, Sabana-Camagüey, 1999, 15. The data presented in this section come from materials available at the José Martí National Library and the Center for the Circulation of Tourism Information (CIDTur) in Havana and from fieldwork between 2005 and 2007 in tourist areas within the Sabana-Camagüey Archipelago (known to Cuban tourism officials and international tourists as Jardines del Rey). Since 2005 I have conducted field research in the provinces of Havana, Matanzas, Villa Clara, and Ciego de Avila and have studied the effects of tourism development in two tourist areas within the Sabana-Camagüey Archipelago. Field research in Cuba was partially funded by the CSU-AAUP (Connecticut State University–American Association of University Professors) Faculty Research Grants Program.

32. Interview with Dr. Manuel González Herrera, professor of tourism studies, Universidad Central de las Villas, Santa Clara, Cuba, August 3, 2007.

33. See J. M. Spiegel, M. González, G. J. Cabrera, S. Catasus, C. Vidal, and A. Yassi, "Promot-

ing Health in Response to Global Tourism Expansion in Cuba," *Health Promotion International* 23, no. 1 (2008), 60–69.

34. Díaz Briquets and Pérez López, *Conquering Nature,* 264. See also Joseph L. Scarpaci and Armando H. Portela, *Cuban Landscapes: Heritage, Memory, and Place* (New York: Guilford Press, 2009), 129–31.

35. Quintana et al., *Efectos y futuro,* 162.

36. Linda Litkus, "Sustainable Development and Social Exclusion: Cuba's National Environmental Strategy," paper delivered at the International Conference "The Measure of a Revolution."

37. See Kenyon C. Lindeman, James T. B. Tripp, Daniel J. Whittle, Azur Moulaert-Quirós, and Emma Stewart, "Sustainable Coastal Tourism in Cuba: Roles of Environmental Assessments, Certification Programs, and Protection Fees," *Tulane Environmental Law Journal* 16, no. 3 (2003), 591–618.

38. Danielle Barav, "How Environmental Conservation Helped Save Cuba," World Security Institute, 2008, www.worldsecurityinstitue.org.

39. Lindeman et al., "Sustainable Coastal Tourism," 593.

40. See Omar E. Pérez Villanueva and Pavel Vidal Alejandro, "Situación actual del turismo en Cuba," paper delivered at the Twenty-Eighth International Congress of the Latin American Studies Association, Rio de Janeiro, Brazil, June 11–14, 2009.

41. *Enfoques, Turismo;* Pedro Monreal, "Cuban Development in the Bolivarian Matrix," *North American Congress on Latin America* 39, no. 4 (2006), 22–26; Luis Suárez Salazar, "Cuba's Foreign Policy and the Promise of ALBA," *North American Congress on Latin America* 39, no. 4 (2006), 27–32.

42. Oliver Houck, "Thinking about Tomorrow: Cuba's 'Alternative Model' for Sustainable Development," *Tulane Environmental Law Journal* 16, no. 3 (2003), 525; see also Monreal, "Globalization and the Dilemmas."

10

The Heart of the Matter

The Impact of Cuban Medical Internationalism in the Global South

ROBERT HUISH

See if you can guess who said this:

> Our nation supports a lot of different things. We develop water, we do economic development, we do education all over the world, we do joint research, we train soldiers, we provide weapons, and we even give money. But there is nothing more powerful that we do than to administer to the health of people who are in need. Why? Because, the language of health is really heard in the heart. The richest and poorest of us are bound together by the uncertainty of our mortality and the desperation of pain.

Given that this chapter is part of a collaborative publication on Cuban internationalism, you might mistake this as an excerpt from one of Fidel Castro's speeches. Or maybe you guessed that it was in a missive of Che's?

But no, not even close. Here's another hint. The speaker went on to say:

> You give a mother with HIV/AIDS the ability to live and raise her children, and she will give you a gratitude that will never wane. Heal a father's child and he'll never forget. You give a teenager with disfigured limbs the gift of mobility and the dignity of mobility and he will praise your name forever. . . . Health diplomacy is the highest octane fuel that a soft power machine has.

These are the words of Michael Leavitt, George W. Bush's onetime secretary of health and human services.[1] In this speech given at the Center for Strategic and International Studies in Washington, DC, in late 2008, after he had left his post as secretary, Leavitt defended the Bush administration's hard power interventions in Iraq and Afghanistan, but he argued that this was not the way for the country to proceed in the future. He suggested that the best way for the United States to secure its immediate and long-term interests was through strategies of medical diplomacy. In other words, he called for policies to heal bones, not for actions to break them.

At a time when many nations, including the United States, are seeking ways to embrace global health,[2] Cuba's fifty-year history of medical internationalism provides an invaluable example. The case of Cuban medical internationalism illustrates how dedicated attention to global health can serve to fulfill national policy objectives while providing much-needed humanitarian assistance.[3] Many Cuba scholars and policy critics, regardless of ideological affinity, have recognized Cuba's impressive example of cooperation aimed at strengthening the most feeble health-care systems in the global South. Cuba's medical internationalism is a working example of how ethical health strategies can assist low-income countries to build important foundations for comprehensive health-care capacity. Cuba's provision of health-care services and its strategies for building long-term human resource capacity are seen as successes in both political and public health terms.[4]

As Ken Cole notes, many economists are puzzled as to how Cuba can suffer from such enormous economic hardships and still maintain its own social institutions, let alone develop a global health workforce.[5] This impressive effort has helped to improve the quality of life for millions by building much-needed capacity in areas that have been traditionally marginalized by medical systems. Yet a great deal of work still lies ahead.

Cuba's medical internationalism serves to benefit both the country's own foreign relations and its long-term strategic objectives.[6] Indeed, no nation would willingly construct foreign policy that goes against its own interests. To pursue such policy through methods that alleviate suffering among the desperately poor is an innovative approach that may challenge the realist presumptions of foreign policy. With the economic superpowers—in particular, the United States and China—looking toward health-care provision as a means of meeting their global strategic objectives, it is important to understand the impact of medical internationalism beyond that of serving a nation's own political interests. Economic superpowers could contribute enormous amounts of wealth and social capital to overcoming suffering and disease for the world's poor. And yet without appropriate vision and foresight, health aid resources could be limited through highly symbolic interventions, such as short-term responses after natural disasters, instead of building long-term capacity within marginalized communities. The global health challenge for many economic powers will be to understand the political value and to embrace the transformative potential of working toward universal health-care access for the poor over the long term.

If wealthy nations approach medical aid simply as the act of sending personnel and resources abroad on a short-term basis, it may be represented as a highly symbolic intervention, but without long-term capacity building there may be little benefit in aiding communities to manage their own health-care challenges. Although short-term interventions and disease-specific campaigns often do bring relief of suffering to many, a focus on treating diseases alone rarely develops the long-term capacity to overcome systemic suffering. The end result of such programs is that some medicine gets to some people, some people get some care, and a certain amount of care makes some diseases less pesky in some regions. The focus might be on antiretroviral medicine for HIV, and billions of dollars may be committed to the cause. But what about the dozens of symptoms that HIV patients experience, from chronic hunger to chronic pain, paralysis, infected lesions, and the psychological consequences of succumbing to the virus? All too often hospitals in sub-Saharan Africa receive donations of antiretroviral drugs, but antibiotics can remain a rarity as a result of a lack of donations. Although HIV holds 33 million people in its grasp, severe poverty's health risks, involving the most basic preventable diseases, claim 50,000 lives on a daily basis. If wealthy nations cannot collaborate with poor nations to develop guaranteed, constant access to primary health care as part of their global health strategies, this grim picture is likely to continue.

A global health strategy, as reflected in Cuba's policy of cooperation, is designed to treat people rather than just targeting diseases. By working at the community level to address the social and environmental determinants of health, a global health policy aimed at system-level capacity building holds enormous promise for the pursuit of sustainable primary-care services in areas that currently go without. Cuba's medical internationalism exemplifies how a broad approach to global health is not about donating health-care workers and medicines a few weeks every year for specific disease interventions; it is about finding the means to build sustainable primary care from within communities—and especially communities that suffer structural violence and systematic inequity. Since 1960 Cuban medical internationalism has taken this route by applying two key methods: providing primary care to those in urgent need, and training students from vulnerable communities to take up the very same tasks and responsibilities.[7]

Powerful nations should not assume that Cuba's international political and socioeconomic gains have been purely symbolic. Rather, the strength of the Cuban model comes from the way in which its health-care workers pursue transformative care programs on the ground. It is the nature of care that matters in medical internationalism, not just the physical numbers of physicians or the amount of money spent on projects. All too often global health initiatives are announced and praised for the quantity of money dedicated to a cause, for example, the Muskoka Initiative, announced at the 2010 G-20 summit in Toronto, saw wealthy nations dedicate more than $5 billion to maternal health initiatives. The funding is meant to strengthen health-care systems and expand access to health services. While the specifics of how to train health workers remain vague, the initiative has specific plans set out for funding vaccines, medicines, and nutrition programs. If the Muskoka Initiative is to succeed in addressing maternal health, then there needs to be planning dedicated to human resources for health training, and specifically how to ensure that those resources reach the most vulnerable communities.

One of the most important lessons from Cuban medical internationalism is that it has been politically successful because it has made noticeable impacts on the ground.[8] Many global health policies boast high monetary contributions but often fail to deliver substantial transformative action on the ground in the form of long-term quality care at the local level. The methods that Cuba uses in its overseas health brigades, and the institutional ethics of its international medical education, are unique and effective in delivering appropriate long-term care to poor communities. Cuba provides its health-care workers and its medical graduates with the appropriate skills and confidence to practice in vulnerable communities and to build capacity for health care over the long term. While the political benefits of Cuba's medical internationalism have received much attention, the public health impacts of its approach deserve further recognition.

Cuba's medical internationalism works to the benefit of the marginalized of the global South for three reasons. First, it succeeds through the training of much-needed health personnel. Cuba has established nine overseas medical schools in Yemen, Guyana, Ethiopia, Uganda, Gambia, Equatorial Guinea, Haiti, Guinea-Bissau, and East Timor. Also, Cuba brings foreign students to the island to be trained in its Escuela Latinoamericana de Medicina (Latin American School of Medicine, or ELAM). Cuban programs thrive through a set of institutional ethics that extend from the medical curriculum. The program embraces the social and environmental determinants of health, instills confidence for personnel to work in underserved regions, and values medicine as a public good rather than for the pursuit of profit.[9] Cuba has an impressive ability to train health-care workers on an enormous scale, but the ethical framework in which the training takes place is also significant. It affords practitioners the clinical confidence to meet the needs of vulnerable populations. An example of this is the curriculum and development of Cuba's ELAM.

Second, medical internationalism flourishes through long-term investments in building capacity at the local level and by focusing on strengthening primary care before complex interventions. This is even reflected in emergency disaster relief efforts. Unlike much of the medical outreach from the North to the South—outreach that is brief, costly, and focuses on a specific disease or condition—the Cuban approach builds a base of primary care to address rooted diseases of poverty that often get missed by short-term humanitarian interventions.

Third, medical internationalism succeeds because it operates on the moral platform of cooperation. It is not aid. Cuba acknowledges its place as a country that is working toward overcoming underdevelopment challenges. Cooperation between Cuba and other countries is grounded on the premise that Southern nations can work together for mutual benefit.[10] Unlike classic humanitarian outreach that implies a sense of acting with moral authority in an under-resourced country, cooperation is a means of supportive solidarity that recognizes the need for partnership to achieve the mutual benefit of both countries.

Institutional Ethics

In the global South health-care worker migration to Northern countries, or to lucrative private sectors within the South, has weakened public health-care system capacity. In South Africa about a third of the country's trained physicians migrate to Europe, Canada, the United States, or Australia. In Ghana 40 percent of the nation's physicians leave home.[11] At a time when the global South, and particularly the African continent, is being ravaged by preventable and easily treatable diseases such as malaria and tuberculosis, much-needed human resources for health are fleeing the region at an alarming rate.

While the global South copes with the flight of human resources for health, Cuba has effectively countered this trend by sending its own health brigades to work in vulnerable communities in countries that have been hurt by the brain drain. Cuba has also trained foreign medical students from "donor countries" under the moral agreement that they will serve their home country.[12] By 2010 Cuba's ELAM had received more than 15,500 students from thirty-two countries, including the United States. The goal of the program is to offer a free medical education to students under a moral obligation that they will serve in the communities where they are most needed. The majority of the more than 5,500 graduates since 2005 have either returned to their home communities to provide much-needed care or they have continued pursuing community-oriented specializations in Cuba.

Countries in the global South tend to have at least a limited capacity to train human resources for health, and few have found successful means of retaining health workers. Many scholars argue that poor working conditions, pitiful wages, and a sense of near hopelessness drive medical students away from vulnerable communities.[13] Indeed, these factors are significant in understanding why health-care workers migrate, but medical education itself also plays an important role in the migration pipeline.

Many Southern medical schools admit that their programs are attuned toward training students for working conditions in Europe or North America. Many medical schools overlook community-oriented care, and encourage students to pursue specializations that require advanced technology and resources. Furthermore, as some studies have shown, the faculty members themselves are in pursuit of migration opportunities, and their attitudes transmit to the students through both official content in the classroom and unofficial medical school culture.[14] In the end students come away with a skill set that suits Northern demands rather than local needs. Morally, medical education in the South can instill a normative sense that dignity as a practitioner lies in practicing in the North rather than in the South.

The institutional ethics of Cuba's medical curriculum are unique from the typical culture of medical education in the South.[15] The institutional ethics of Cuban medical education, as reflected in ELAM's curriculum, has four crucial aspects that make the system unique.

First, ELAM sets out to recruit students from marginalized communities across the global South. The school specifically seeks out students who would not likely have the opportunity to study medicine in their home country, due to either financial or social discrimination. It has been well acknowledged that medical students from marginalized backgrounds or of humble means are far more likely than the typical student to return to serve such communities.[16] Furthermore, ELAM does not require students to have completed the Medical College Admission Test (MCAT) or any other standardized test in order to be accepted to the program. Instead, the interview process, often held at a Cuban embassy, explores themes of humanism, ethics of service, and willingness to work in marginalized and low-resource settings. Most medical schools seek applicants who are likely to excel in pure sciences, and rarely does the selection process seek candidates who demonstrate interest and compassion for service to the vulnerable.[17]

The lack of a standardized recruitment scheme allows for a greater diversity of applicants to ELAM. While Cuban embassies handle the processing of applications to Escuela Nacional de Salud Pública (ENSAP), applicants are recruited in a variety of ways. In South America many ELAM applicants learn about the program via labor unions and Cuban solidarity organizations. In the United States the religious nongovernmental organization Interreligious

Organization for Community Organization (IFCO) disseminates information on the program. Also, Cuban medical brigades working in countries like Haiti, Pakistan, and Gambia recruit local youth from within the communities that they serve. While the application process is standardized with the Cuban embassies and within ENSAP, the recruitment process is open and dynamic to suit local conditions and to ensure that the widest possible net is cast for potential recruits.

The second important feature of Cuban medical education involves the emphasis on social and environmental determinants of health within the core curriculum. Many medical schools offer electives in subjects such as environment and health, epidemiology, and the social determinants of health, but they do not position these subjects as core curriculum. Indeed, the emphasis of many medical schools is to adhere to a rigorously science-based curriculum.[18] Cuba's six-year medical curriculum adheres to scientific rigor, but it prominently positions themes of community-based care, disease prevention strategies, and health promotion programs.[19] The initial textbooks that medical students receive at ELAM emphasize these values and pay special attention to the external dynamics that shape and impact the health of individuals.[20] Moreover, students understand how primary care requires the exchange of information and broader support from multiple sectors and health workers, such as nurses, pharmacists, teachers, and social workers, in order to identify persons at risk and to maintain practices of health promotion and disease prevention.[21] This approach is incredibly important for resource-poor areas where communities have limited access to advanced reactive care. By emphasizing health promotion and disease prevention, health workers can develop low-cost community-based routines that monitor health risks at the local level. While topics like demographics, epidemiology, communication skills, and data collection methods may be offered as electives in many medical schools, for Cuban medical education these skills matter as much as biomedical science in practicing medicine.

Beyond the "soft-science" skills, the curriculum also includes attention to traditional and natural medicine (TNM—referred to as *medicina verde* in Cuba). The idea is to show genuine respect for alternative knowledge of medicine, and to study the practice so that certain local methods can be incorporated into routines of health promotion. The Cuban Ministry of Health (MINSAP) now has a research branch in TNM, and many Cuban doctors take courses in massage therapy and acupuncture.[22] Many ELAM graduates will practice medicine in marginalized communities where shamans (traditional healers) are regarded as the leading community health providers. Often medical education has a tendency to distance or discredit TNM as quackery, but the Cuban approach offers students the opportunity to engage with it, which has enormous benefits in building cross-cultural competency in the field.[23] Combining TNM with community-based primary care is an innovative step in global health outreach that allows for a demystification of medical knowledge so that communities are not passive recipients of institutional biomedical care, but rather health is addressed in an inter-sectoral and collaborative setting. As much as this approach can bring much-needed health services to marginalized communities, it also succeeds in building trust and easing social tensions within communities.

The third important dimension of the Cuban approach is that students develop clinical skills through working with doctors in groups of four or fewer in polyclinics and hospitals. Beginning in the second year, the practice is to keep bedside instruction purposefully small, which provides for excellent mentorship and affords students time to interact with both patients and instructors. Through hands-on experience in the clinic, students also gain clinical confidence from the early stages of their medical education. The expectation is that by the end of their tenure they will be confident leaders in their home community clinics.

The fourth important aspect involves the lead-by-example teaching style of the four hundred faculty members who have participated in one of Cuba's 110 international health cooperation missions since 1960. Many faculty members not only have experience working in challenging conditions, but they also bring a sense of pride and valor for service to the poor. Class sizes are kept intentionally small to promote contact and mentorship with faculty. Many students have commented that ELAM faculty routinely put in extra hours of tutoring and mentorship to assist students in passing the regular tests and examinations.[24] Aside from their willingness to provide additional tutoring, the faculty at ELAM is selected based on their proven excellence in research and teaching and also on their own field experience abroad. Structuring a faculty around these values works to promote a "hidden curriculum" of tacit lead-by-example mentorship.[25] *Hidden curricula* are the lessons, values, morals, and practices that students acquire not from the textbook but from observed behavior of mentors and professors. If the faculty collectively projects values of service, outreach, and humanism, these will reflect into the normative ethics of the training program and ultimately establish an institutional ethics of humanism and solidarity.

When all of these education aspects are combined, the result is the development of a pedagogy that fosters a willingness to serve vulnerable communities combined with an appropriate skill set that matches the challenges of working in low-resource environments in the field. The message here is that medical education is not neutral, and that simply investing in capacity building by building more medical schools that focus squarely on the biomedical model is not enough to ensure improved access to care in vulnerable communities. Rather, the approach must pay attention to who the students are, what they learn, and how they are taught. The program stands as an impressive example of how important a medical school's operations are in training a health-care workforce that meets the needs of the global South.

Long-Term Primary Care First

Training health-care workers for rural and marginalized communities is the first lesson that Cuba offers the global health community. The second message is that primary care must come first. Even in times of disaster relief, Cuba's medical internationalism embraces primary care alongside other service provision, as the story of the Henry Reeve Brigade demonstrates.

In 2005 following the devastation of Hurricane Katrina, which claimed 1,836 lives and caused billions of dollars in damages, Cuba offered to send 1,097 specialists in general medicine; 351 general practitioners; 72 specialized health professionals; and 66 specialists in cardiology, pediatrics, epidemiology, surgery, and psychiatry to the United States.[26] Even the members of ELAM's first graduating class, who finished their program two weeks before Katrina, offered their assistance. Some eighty-five graduates offered their services to Fidel Castro in a letter, stating

> We have followed the horrific events that have unfolded in New Orleans resulting from the devastation caused by hurricane *Katrina* and listened to your statement on the afternoon Round Table program and we, Hondurans and other graduates from the Latin American School of Medicine (ELAM), are moved by the situation our brothers in the United States are enduring. Thus, as victims of a natural disaster (hurricane *Mitch*) ourselves, we want to express our solidarity with the American people at this tragic hour and join the doctors you have offered to send to this sister nation in response to this critical situation. You can be confident that we are "doctors willing to go where we are most needed." With infinite love and eternal gratitude.—Signed: The first graduates from ELAM.[27]

The 1,586 health professionals were given the name Henry Reeve Brigade after a young American Civil War veteran who served Cuba in the First War of Independence (1868–78). This initial, on-the-spot collection of doctors developed into a highly organized group trained specifically for delivering emergency services and primary care in post-disaster areas. Regrettably, Washington refused to accept the offer, and while the brigade could have been on the ground in New Orleans just hours after the initial offer, the victims of New Orleans waited days before sufficient medical attention and supplies reached them from other sources.

The brigade's first campaigns came just weeks after Katrina, when Hurricane Stan devastated Guatemala on October 4, 2005, leaving 840 dead and another 600 missing. Guatemala was the first country to accept three hundred health workers from the Henry Reeve Brigade. By the end of the month their numbers had grown to six hundred.[28]

On October 8, 2005, a devastating earthquake rocked Pakistan. Despite the enormous distances involved, as well as cultural and linguistic hurdles and a historically tepid political relationship, the brigade went to Pakistan. Indeed, it was the only foreign delegation to remain on site well after the initial relief efforts had subsided. The quake killed 70,000, injured 69,000, and displaced as many as three million people.[29] Led by Dr. Luis Oliveros, 130 physicians specialized in disaster medicine, including fifteen surgical teams, went to Pakistan with the Henry Reeve Brigade. The team was on the ground within seventy-two hours of the quake, constituting one of the largest medical delegations in the region. An additional 770 physicians arrived in the following weeks, and by the end of the campaign 2,381 Cuban health workers had served in Pakistan. The brigade constructed two field hospitals, and even though these collapsed due to snowfall on one occasion, they still managed to treat 110,000 patients in the affected region. The medical team attended "773 major operations, performed 2,436 minor operations, attended 34 births with zero infant mortality, and administered 10,000 immunizations against tetanus."[30] As well, team members traveled to rural communities to deliver care despite the difficulties of coping with lack of infrastructure and transportation in mountainous terrain. Furthermore, the Cuban brigade helped to coordinate scholarships for Pakistani youth to attend medical school in Cuba. In sum, Cuba's intervention was sizable, and rather than focusing solely on the immediate needs of affected communities, it also conducted foundational work for long-term capacity building for human resources for health.

Since its inception the Henry Reeve Brigade has met with a consistent global demand for its work. Even while the Pakistan campaign continued, the brigade sent another division to Java to assist in the aftermath of a 2006 earthquake.[31] Unlike Cuba's comprehensive health programs, in which doctors remain in the country for an indefinite length of time, the Henry Reeve Brigade remains for a fixed period and does not charge the receiving country for its services. Unlike most international relief efforts that offer narrowly targeted treatment, Cuban teams provide comprehensive primary care in the affected region. General checkups go hand in hand with trauma treatment and sanitation improvement. For example, after most other relief workers left Pakistan, the Cubans remained and continued to play an important role in Pakistan's health-care provision. MINSAP has offered one thousand ELAM scholarships to train Pakistanis who would be willing to return home to practice where they are needed most. More than 350 students arrived in Cuba in 2006, and over 900 in 2008. In 2010 the team deployed to Haiti following the devastating earthquake there. Close to six hundred Cuban health workers were in Haiti before the earthquake, and the brigade arrived within a day to supplement their efforts and begin providing services in rural and outlying areas. As of 2012 there is an ongoing presence of two thousand Cuban health-care workers, on a rotating basis, providing primary care services. The long-term goal is to train the same number of Haitians as physicians by 2016.

The Moral Platform

The final lesson that Cuba offers the world is that *cooperation* rather than *aid* is the better means toward global health equity. This is hardly a purely semantic distinction because it represents a unique approach to engaging in foreign policy. Aid has and always will imply that one country is in a subordinate position to the other. It assumes that philanthropy, goodwill, and humanitarianism can be afforded only from a donor nation to a poorer nation because that donor nation is in an elevated economic position.

Cuba openly admits that it is one of many nations struggling to overcome the challenges of underdevelopment. The nation has great needs, including infrastructure improvements, natural resources, and food security. For Cuba, cooperation is a means of sharing its own domestic strengths with nations abroad, in the hope that at least some economic or social exchange can flourish. Often the programs of cooperation are in place before real trade agreements are hashed out.[32]

Cuba's cooperation with Venezuela has often been labeled "doctors for oil." Cuba's contribution of sending 19,000 health professionals to Venezuela is significant. But while the cooperation between Cuba and Venezuela has been enormous, the label overlooks how Cuba aligns its foreign policy within international and pan-regional trade agreements, and how the country manages flourishing partnerships with other nations that are eager to address human development challenges at the local level.

Cuba's and Venezuela's cooperation within the Caribbean Economic Community (CARICOM) is particularly noteworthy, as this has brought Cuba into important economic trade agreements. Cuba has extended an offer to send health-care workers to any CARICOM nation upon request.[33] The host country is expected to cover basic costs such as airfare, housing, and salaries of the Cuban doctors. In countries like Haiti or Guatemala, these costs would amount to less than $5,000 per year per physician. In countries like Brazil or South Africa, where the cost of living is higher, the annual fee would be increased. As well, Cuban health-care workers abroad receive their regular salary in pesos nacionales plus $100 CUC (pesos convertibles) per month.[34] This salary is often held in Cuban bank accounts until the end of the contract. This is a sizable financial bonus that has created tensions with the Cuban physicians who have chosen to remain in the country to practice without supplementary remuneration.

Notably, cooperation and solidarity have flourished between Cuba and Venezuela. Whereas Cuba offers health-care workers to any country in CARICOM, Venezuela offers these countries petroleum with reduced tariffs in order to help them reduce their GDP expenditure on energy imports. These policies of regional cooperation have warmed relations between the countries, and have had a noticeable regional impact. At the 2005 summit in Sandrino, Venezuela, the two countries created the Alternativa Bolivariana para las Américas (ALBA), a multilateral trade and cooperation alliance that aims to enhance actions of cooperation and solidarity through foreign policy.[35]

Haiti had benefited significantly from such pan-regional policies. Before the 2010 earthquake Haiti received more than five hundred Cuban doctors and, while still receiving exports from the United States, was able to lessen its trade deficit by purchasing oil at reduced prices and on extended credit from Caracas. In an earthquake-ravaged country with hobbled government institutions and services, and with more than 7 percent of its GDP consumed by foreign imports of which 0.5 percent is oil imports, these cooperative policies offer some relief and social benefit.

Cuba works within international law and trade pacts to promote its own interests, but it also assists other nations in coping with underdevelopment. The supposed economic and political benefits for Cuba are far less spectacular than some believe.[36] According to officials of the Cuban Ministry of Foreign Affairs (MINREX), the economic gains from medical diplomacy with low- or middle-income nations can be significant—as seen from cooperation with Venezuela, South Africa, Qatar, China, and other Latin American nations—or negligible because poor countries, like Gambia, receive Cuban doctors and pay only for their expenses, without paying the Cuban government any fees for services rendered.[37]

The remuneration received through cooperation from wealthier nations like Qatar or South Africa creates obvious financial benefit to the Cuban government. But consider Cuba's interventions in Gambia, a West African sliver of a country whose economy consists mostly of peanut exports. This small country has little in the way of economic resources or political clout to offer back to Cuba. In 1996 it had only one physician for every 50,000 people. Cuba has engaged in medical cooperation with the country since that year, and thanks to the Cuban presence, the doctor-to-patient ratio improved to one physician for every 21,000 people—still a hopeless ratio to even begin thinking about universal primary care, let alone universal access to complex procedures. By 2004, four years after Cuba established the University of the Gambia Medical School, Gambia's doctor-to-patient ratio had improved to one physician for every 9,174 persons. There is still space for enormous improvement, but within six years the doctor-to-patient ratio moved from being impossible to manageable. What has Gambia given back to Cuba? The country has lobbied the European Union to include Cuba on select trade agreements. This is not much, but it is what the country can do. Truly, it is the essence of cooperation, bringing to the table what you can and doing for your partner what you can.

The political gains that Cuba garners from medical internationalism in forums such as the United Nations are notable. Most nations support Cuba in calling for an end to the U.S. embargo, building a consensus that has condemned the embargo through multiple UN votes.[38] Only the United States and Israel perennially vote to maintain it; and despite the overwhelming international opposition to the embargo, it remains.[39] In the case of overturning this policy, it is questionable how much political weight sending physicians to the poorest countries on the planet renders. But aside from the embargo, Cuba's global cooperation may actually be working to change attitudes and build strategic partnerships throughout the South by way of a good example.[40]

Building Dialogue, Strengthening Human Resources

The global North has much to learn from Cuban medical internationalism. Engaging in internationalism through health, as Michael Leavitt has advocated, holds enormous transformative potential for the marginalized of the global South. Still, many governments, including that of the United States, continue to mirror the Cold War mindset of maintaining strained if not hostile relations with Cuba. Scaling up medical internationalism will require dialogue. Cuba's capacity-building programs, comprehensive medical brigades, and partnerships with other Southern countries have all been aimed at strengthening human resources for health through primary care at the community level. These efforts could only be strengthened through trilateral cooperation with wealthier nations in the global North who commit to global health equity.

Certainly the Bush years and the War on Terror provided evidence of hard power failing to meet the strategic objectives of the North to spread its strategic interests globally. In his 2008 statement Leavitt admitted as much. If policymakers are to produce knowledgeable strategies for the twenty-first century, students, researchers, and others who have an interest in, or whose lives have been altered by, Cuban medical internationalism will have to tell their stories to ensure that together we can move one step closer to a world that cooperates and heals rather than divides and destroys.

Notes

1. Michael Leavitt, "Increased Role of Health Diplomacy in U.S. Foreign Policy," 2008, Center for Strategic and International Studies, http://csis.org/event/michael-o-leavitt-increased-role-health-diplomacy-us-foreign-policy.

2. Sara Davies, "What Contribution Can International Relations Make to the Evolving Global Health Agenda?" *International Affairs* 86, no. 5 (2010), 1167–90; Harley Feldbaum, Kelly Lee, and Joshua Michaud, "Global Health and Foreign Policy," *Epidemiologic Reviews* 32, no. 1 (2010), 82–92.

3. Robert Huish and John M. Kirk, "Cuban Medical Internationalism and the Development of the Latin American School of Medicine," *Latin American Perspectives* 34, no. 6 (2007), 77–92; Robert Huish and Jerry Spiegel, "Integrating Health and Human Security into Foreign Policy: Cuba's Surprising Success," *International Journal of Cuban Studies* 1, no. 1 (2008), 1–13.

4. John M. Kirk and Michael H. Erisman, *Cuban Medical Internationalism: Origins, Evolution, and Goals* (New York: Palgrave Macmillan, 2009).

5. Ken Cole, *From Revolution to Development* (London: Pinter, 1998).

6. Julie Feinsilver, *Healing the Masses: Cuban Health Politics at Home and Abroad* (Berkeley: University of California Press, 1993); Kirk and Erisman, *Cuban Medical Internationalism*.

7. Robert Huish, "How Cuba's Latin American School of Medicine Challenges the Ethics of Physician Migration," *Social Science and Medicine* 69, no. 3 (2009), 301–4.

8. Robert Huish, "Going Where No Doctor Has Gone Before: The Role of Cuba's Latin American School of Medicine in Meeting the Needs of Some of the World's Most Vulnerable Populations," *Public Health* 122, no. 6 (2008), 552–57.

9. Huish, "How Cuba's Latin American School of Medicine Challenges," 301–4.

10. Ronaldo López del Amo, "Cuba y la cooperación internacional," *Embajada de Cuba en Egipto* (2010), emba.cubaminrex.cu/Default.aspx?tabid=11788.

11. Ted Schrecker and Ronald Labonte, "Taming the Brain Drain: A Challenge for Public Health Systems in South Africa," *International Journal of Occupational and Environmental Health* 10, no. 4 (2004), 409–15; Pascal Zurn, Mario R. Dal Poz, Barbara Stilwell, and Orvill Adams, "Imbalances in the Health Workforce," *Human Resources for Health* 2, no. 13 (2004).

12. Donor countries are those that train health-care workers who then seek employment in the global North or in wealthier countries of the South.

13. Paul Clark, James Stewart, and Pauline Clark, "The Globalization of the Labour Market for Health-Care Professionals," *International Labour Review* 145 (2006), 37–64.

14. Avraham Astor, Tasleem Akhtar, María Alexandra Matallana, Vasantha Muthuswamy, Folarin A. Olowu, Veronica Tallo, and Reidar K. Lie, "Physician Migration: Views from Professionals in Colombia, Nigeria, India, Pakistan and the Philippines," *Social Science and Medicine* 61, no. 12 (2005), 2492–2500; Mohamed Omer, "Can Medical Education Rise to the Challenge of the African Crisis?" *Annals of Tropical Pediatrics* 25 (2005), 227–41.

15. Conner Gorry, "Healing Globally, Empowering Locally: Cuban Medical Cooperation in Africa," *Caminos: Revista Cubana de Pensamiento Socioteológico* no. 42 (2006).

16. Elma de Vries and Steve Reid, "Do South African Medical Students of Rural Origin Return to Rural Practice?" *South African Medical Journal* 93 no. 10 (2003), 789–92.

17. Jonathan White, Keith Bronwell, Jean-Francois Lemay, and Jocelyn Lockyer, "'What Do They Want Me to Say?' The Hidden Curriculum at Work in the Medical School Selection Process: A Qualitative Study." *BMC Medical Education* 12 no. 17 (2012), DOI: 10.1186/1472-6920-1112-1117.

18. Molly Cooke, David Irby, William Sullivan, and Kenneth Ludmerer, "American Medical Education 100 Years after the Flexner Report." *New England Journal of Medicine* 355, no. 13 (2006) 1339–44.

19. Victor Neufeld, Christel Woodward, and Stuart MacLeod, "The McMaster M.D. Program: A Case of Renewal in Medical Education," *Academic Medicine* 64, no. 8 (1989), 423–32.

20. Roberto Álvarez Sintes et al., *Temas de medicina general integral*, 2 vols. (Havana: Editorial Ciencias Médicas, 2001).

21. Jerry Spiegel, "Daring to Learn from a Good Example and Break the 'Cuba Taboo,'" *International Journal of Epidemiology* 35 (2006), 825–26.

22. MINSAP, "Medicina Natural y Tradicional," *Atención primeria de salud* (Havana: MINSAP, 2007).

23. F. Bosch Valdés, "La medicina tradicional y natural en Cuba," *Resumed* 12, no. 1 (1999), 3–6.

24. Huish, "Going Where No Doctor Has Gone Before."

25. Barret Michalec, "The Pursuit of Medical Knowledge and the Potential Consequences of the Hidden Curriculum," *Health* 16 no. 3 (2012) 267–81.

26. Fidel Castro, "Speech by Fidel Castro: The Henry Reeve Brigade Is Created to Assist American Brothers and Sisters," *Cubanow.net*, 2005, www.medicc.org/publications/.

27. Ibid.

28. Conner Gorry, "Cuban Disaster Doctors in Guatemala, Pakistan," *Medicc Review* 7, no. 5 (2005).

29. Ibid.

30. Ibid.

31. Staff, "Cuban Medical Brigade Returns from Helping Indonesia," *Granma International*, 2006.

32. Ministerio de Relaciones Exteriores de Cuba, "Cooperation in The Gambia," *Cuban Embassy to Gambia Web Portal*, emba.cubaminrex.cu.

33. Anthony Maingot, "Bridging the Ideological Divide: Cuban Doctors for Caribbean

Recognition," *Focal Point* 5, no. 4 (2006), 4; Ronald Sylvia and Constantine Danopoulos, "The Chavez Phenomenon: Political Change in Venezuela," *Third World Quarterly* 24, no. 1 (2003), 63–76. CARICOM evolved from the Caribbean Community and Common Market, which came into effect in 1973. Cuba has not signed on as an official member, but has maintained cooperation and economic relations with the group since 1973.

34. Kate Macintyre and Jorge Hadad, "Cuba," in Bruce Fried and Laura M. Gaydos, eds., *World Health Systems: Challenges and Perspectives* (Chicago, IL: Health Administration Press, 2002), xii, 563. Cuba has two currencies: the national peso (CUN) and convertible peso (CUC). The CUN is valued at 26 to 1 CUC. The CUC is used for foreign exchange and can be traded for other currencies. Since 2003, when the CUC replaced the U.S. dollar as the foreign-exchangeable currency, the CUC has increased in value from being equal to the U.S. dollar to being nearly equal to the euro. Respectively, this has increased the value of the CUN and has increased the purchasing power of both currencies. The figure of $5,000 as the cost of sending doctors abroad is a rough estimate that considers the cost of return airfare as about $800 (maximum) for a flight in the Caribbean from Havana; rural area lodging at $150 per month; and the contract salary for a Cuban doctor working overseas at $150 per month. Of course, depending on the specific field site, costs can be estimated accordingly.

35. ALBA is designed as a cooperative alliance aimed at overcoming underdevelopment through the sharing of human and material resources. Unlike regional free-trade alliances, ALBA focuses on building health-care and education capacity. The agreement is meant to include nations in Latin America and the Caribbean.

36. Katryn Hansing, "Cuba's International Development Assistance: A Model for the Non-Aligned Movement?" *Focal Point* 5, no. 7 (2006), 2; Maingot, "Bridging the Ideological Divide"; Joaquín Roy, "Cuba: The Role of the International Community," *Focal Point* 5, no. 8 (2006), 5.

37. The only exception is South Africa, where a unique medical exchange program has been established. In this case South Africa does pay the Cuban state directly in addition to paying the Cuban physicians' salaries in South Africa.

38. Gustavo Roman, "Epidemic Neuropathy in Cuba: A Plea to End the United States Economic Embargo on a Humanitarian Basis," *Journal of Public Health Policy* 16, no. 1 (1995), 5–12.

39. Conner Gorry, "It's a Consensus: World Condemns U.S. Embargo against Cuba," *Medicc Review* 6, no. 2 (2004).

40. Spiegel, "Daring to Learn from a Good Example."

11

Cuba's Revolutionary Agro-Ecological Movement
Learning from the Experience of Food Sovereignty

EFE CAN GÜRCAN

The global food crisis of 2005–8—which drove an estimated 75 million people to hunger and another 125 million people to extreme poverty[1]—is but a specific instance of a far more general phenomenon: the breaking up of the existing neoliberal agro-food order, which has itself been trapped in a perpetual state of emergency. An examination of the sociocultural aspects of the food crisis and its repercussions under neoliberalism clearly reveals the true nature of the crisis. Global food prices increased by about 83 percent between 2005 and 2008, leading to violent food riots in more than twenty different countries.[2] These riots were the precursor of a "rapidly growing groundswell" of a grass-roots-level "opposing current" that came to be known as the "food sovereignty alternative."[3]

As framed by La Vía Campesina, one of the world's most influential transnational social movements, food sovereignty represents "the right of nations and peoples to control their own food systems, including their own markets, production modes, food cultures, and environments." The food sovereignty concept places a special emphasis on "how, where, and by whom food is produced." As such, it promotes the rethinking of human relationships not merely with food, agriculture, and the environment, but also societal relationships with one another relative to democracy and social justice.[4]

In Cuba the food sovereignty movement led to the world's "largest conversion from conventional agriculture to organic and semi-organic agriculture"[5]—providing a particularly relevant example for the developing world of ecologically friendly alternatives that can challenge the neoliberal agro-food order. Cuba has shown that it is possible—in the words of Steven Gorelick, Todd Merrifield, and Helena Norberg-Hodge—to "successfully shift from a focus on global food to a focus on local food" and to "implement policies that are friendly to the needs of people, communities, and the environment."[6] With policies built on a vast network of cooperation and interactions between domestic and transnational actors, the Cuban experience has become a model for the formulation of food sovereignty policies by newly emerging left-leaning governments and social movements in countries such as Venezuela.[7] In the Cuban model, food sovereignty policies are built on a four-pillar agrarian strategy: the collectivization of land through formation of cooperatives; the institutionalization in society of urban agriculture based on participatory methods; the guaranteeing of local access to food through the establishment of free agricultural markets; and the transnationalization of domestic agro-ecological movements. In Cuba this strategy was implemented through initiatives of the National Association of Small Farmers (ANAP), the basic units of cooperative production (UBPCs), and many other projects involving several transnational actors such as the Bolivarian Alliance for the Peoples of the Americas (ALBA), the Latin American Campesino a Campesino (farmer-to-farmer) Movement, and La Vía Campesina. The implementation of this strategy depends on a combination of local, national, and international efforts undertaken through decentralized decision-making processes, strong societal structures, and consensual policy networks in the countryside.

The following sections will address each of the four pillars of Cuban agriculture and extract the main lessons from Cuba's food sovereignty experience (table 11.1).

Table 11.1. The four pillars of food sovereignty policies (Cuba as a model example)

Pillar	Components of Pillar
Collectivization of land	Land distribution to peasant cooperative
	Decentralization of production
	Diversification of civil society
	Establishment of worker control
Institutionalization of urban agriculture into society	Building of a new agro-ecological societal structure in cities
	Development of a spirit of community
	Increase in citizen participation
Opening of free agricultural markets	Local access to food
	Decentralization of decision making
	Initiation of peasant cooperation and productivity
Transnationalization of the agro-ecological movement	Broadening of alliances for food sovereignty
	Sharing of knowledge and resources
	Establishment of food sovereignty as an international norm

The Collectivization of Land and Cooperative Production

In 1993, Cuba went through a radical land reform that revolutionized its entire agrarian structure to be better aligned with principles of food sovereignty. Prior to that reform the Cuban agrarian structure had been dominated by the state sector, which promoted the activities of large state farms controlling 74.3 percent of agricultural land.[8] Capital-intensive and large-scale agricultural practices had led to a litany of severe socioeconomic and ecological consequences: overspecialization; monocropping; excessive intensification and dependence on external inputs; large-scale deforestation; salinization, erosion, compaction, and fertility loss of soils; and heavy rural-urban migration due to poverty among agricultural workers. This model of agrarian development suffered from high levels of dependency and inefficiency, which in turn aggravated Cuba's dependence on massive amounts of food imports. In the pre-reform era, 57 percent of Cubans' total consumption of calories depended on imports of petroleum, equipment, agricultural inputs, and foodstuffs. More than 30 percent of arable land was dedicated to the production of sugarcane, which had both reduced Cuba's agricultural diversity and contributed to the dependency on food imports.[9] Similarly, before the collapse of the international socialist system, 69 percent of the domestic consumption of cereals, 99 percent of grains, 21 percent of meats, 94 percent of fats, and 38 percent of milk and its derivatives were originating in Cuba's economic relations with the Council for Mutual Economic Assistance (COMECON).

Following the demise of the international socialist system, Cuba experienced a decline of nearly 30 percent in its foreign trade volume, with a drop of greater than 60 percent in the import of pesticides, 77 percent in the import of fertilizers, and 50 percent in the availability of oil for agriculture. Food imports dropped by more than 50 percent.[10] In consequence, daily calorie consumption per capita declined from 2,728 in 1990 to 1,863 in 1993.[11]

The need for radical agro-ecological land reform was readily apparent. Following this restructuring, 92 to 94 percent of Cuban agricultural production depended on low-input agricultural practices that to a great extent immunized Cuban peasant communities against price drops in food, oil, and raw materials and against environmental contamination.[12] The balance of power in the Cuban countryside shifted in favor of the peasantry with the establishment of UBPCs—thus setting in place the first pillar of the agricultural restructuring.

UBPCs are in essence local agrarian micro-organizations that rely on their own profits and function according to the principles of self-administration and self-sufficiency. As Beatriz Díaz Gonzáles argued, "The creation of the UBPCs constitutes the highest form of diversifying Cuban civil society, promoting sustainable rural development by decentralizing the economy at the local level and increasing the participation of producers in the decision-making."[13] The role of the UBPCs went beyond agricultural production, as they became key actors in community development. In 1996 alone the expansion of UBPCs contributed 73 percent of the newly created jobs in the country. Some UBPCs became involved in the resolution of Cuba's chronic housing problem by creating special funds for the improvement of community housing.[14]

As Pierre Raymond acknowledges, the speed and extent of the expansion of UBPCs was astounding (table 11.2). Between September and December 1993, just before the harvest of 1993–94, 1,576 sugarcane UBPCs were created with the participation of 146,524 members on 87 percent of the land previously owned by the state, including fallow fields.[15] By August 1994, 2,643 UBPCs, with more than 257,000 members, had been established on 2,960,000 hectares (50 percent of productive land under state control). In February 1995, 1,440 non-sugarcane UBPCs were established with the participation of 126,723 members. With an average size of 1,125 hectares and about 97 members each, the UBPCs accounted for 80 percent of sugarcane production, 33 percent of meat production, 13 percent of vegetable production, 24 percent of coffee production, 8 percent of tobacco production, and 46 percent of milk production.[16]

The UBPCs were developed based on the model of Agricultural Production Cooperatives (CPAs). Established following the First Congress of the Communist Party of Cuba in 1975, CPAs brought together local small-scale farmers and their families who were seeking better access to electricity, housing, education, and medical care. UBPCs and CPAs have similar administrative structures. A general assembly made up of all cooperative members is the highest authority of the cooperative, and assembly members elect nine board members as managers for a term of five years. Normally the board consists of the general manager, the senior engineer, and the chiefs of economy, production, services, machinery and land, as well as two other members of the cooperative. Cooperative members have the right to vote on the admission of new members and

Table 11.2. Percentage of arable land in Cuba by form of landownership

Ownership	1993	2000	2008
State	56.5	33.1	23.2
UBPC	26.5	40.6	39.8
CPA + CCS + individual producer	17	26.3	37

Source: Fernando R. Funes-Monzote, "Farming Like We're Here to Stay: The Mixed Farming Alternative for Cuba" (PhD diss., Wageningen University, The Netherlands, 2008), 27.

expulsion of existing members who are not performing their duties properly. Unlike the CPA model, which relies on the principle of private ownership of land, landownership remains public in the UBPCs, although the cooperative members hold the right to cultivate their land in perpetuity as long as they make productive use of it.[17]

In terms of its financial management, some 50 percent of the cooperative surplus is shared among the UBPC members, while the other half is mainly used for the repayment of equipment loans and other production-related expenses such as the purchase of inputs. Any funds remaining after these expenses are covered is devoted to the development of infrastructure and services such as housing, recreational facilities, health care, and technical training. In addition, since the UBPCs are also considered to be a means of community development, the National Bank of Cuba (NBC) provides the cooperatives with credits for basic community needs such as housing. On housing loans the NBC offers an interest rate of 2 percent in mountainous areas, and 3 percent in other areas of the country.[18]

Cuba's agro-ecological restructuring was not limited to the creation of UBPCs. The reform also introduced New Type State Farms (GENTs), which enjoy greater administrative autonomy than traditional state farms do. Worker cooperatives run the GENTs, and workers themselves share in 50 percent of the profits, although the farms remain under state ownership. The GENTs constitute a transitional but important step in the expansion of UBPCs: the government actively supports successful GENTs in transforming themselves into UBPCs.[19]

Similarly, the agro-ecological reform also reorganized the Credit and Services Cooperatives (CCSs), groups of individual producers who want to acquire greater access to credit, machinery, fertilizers, and technical assistance.[20] Officially, the main objective of the CCSs is to enable "the sharing of irrigation and other installations, services, and productive means, as well as collective arrangements for credit, even though the land, tools, and production of each farm remain private."[21] In 1995 ANAP decided to strengthen the CCSs by improving their management and providing better-quality services.[22] Simultaneous land reform encouraged the consolidation of CCSs by merging small cooperatives into larger units to attain better efficiency. Compared to the old CCS model, the new cooperatives have a higher quality of professional services and are now capable of developing production plans on a collective basis with ACOPIO, the state food collection and distribution agency.[23]

In general the agro-ecological land reforms have been successful in enhancing agricultural diversity, increasing small farmers' contributions to agricultural production, and raising farmers' income. The production of sugarcane was reduced by one-third in the first half of the 2000s, and the land dedicated to sugarcane production had fallen to 397,000 hectares by 2006, a considerable reduction from the 1.3 million hectares devoted to this purpose during the 1980s and 1990s.[24] Small-farmer productivity increased by almost 200 percent between 1988 and 2009, with small peasants contributing nearly 60 percent of vegetables, more than 75 percent of corn, almost 95 percent of beans, about 30 percent of rice, more than 95 percent of fruit, more than 50 percent of cow's milk, and more than 60 percent of total meats, including 75 percent of pork and more than 50 percent of cattle produced.[25] Between 2001 and 2006 the income of farmers working in the non-state sector increased significantly, by 42 percent, and the average monthly agricultural wage went up by 62 percent. Farming became one of the highest-paying professions in the country.[26]

Social Participation in Urban Agriculture

Agro-ecological reform also led to the institutionalized practice of urban agriculture, which emerged in 1989 as a grassroots movement in Cuba and expanded considerably following the collapse of the Soviet Union.[27] Broadly speaking, the practice of urban agriculture in Cuba is built on three basic principles: the use of "organic methods, which do not contaminate the environment, the rational use of local resources, and the direct marketing of produce to consumers."[28] Based on these principles, the Department of Urban Agriculture organized numerous workshops and educational programs on organic gardening with the motto "produce while learning, teach while producing, and learn while teaching!"[29] In turn voluntary organizations in urban communities established informal "horticultural clubs," designed to encourage the sharing of experience and knowledge in urban gardening among urban farmers. These clubs would provide urban communities with greater access to workshops, larger farmer networks, profitable markets, and public recognition.[30]

The institutionalization of urban agriculture was also facilitated through "extension services." "Extensionists"—organizers, teachers, and experts—help farmers by facilitating communication among them, encouraging participation in workshops, and guaranteeing access to knowledge and other resources. By 1998 more than 30,000 people had participated in training sessions and seminars organized by the extension services and research institutions in the city of Havana. Another development was seed banks, which emerged from public-private partnerships. These banks specialize in the sale of gardening inputs such as seeds, tools, and bio-fertilizers.[31]

The expansion of urban agriculture through participatory methods has greatly contributed to strengthening Cuban civil society. People's Councils, one of the most important grassroots movements in the country, encouraged local urban agriculture initiatives based on citizen participation with a community spirit.[32] Likewise, the Fundación Antonio Núñez Jiménez emerged as a key actor, offering assistance to urban farmers to help them develop production techniques and increase their access to information.[33]

By the first decade of the new century, then, urban agriculture had become widespread. Between 1995 and 1999 popular participation in urban agriculture increased significantly, from 3,966 to 26,604 urban farmers. In the early 2000s urban agriculture covered 12 percent of the land of Havana city, involving more than 22,000 urban and peri-urban producers who had ceased to produce only for subsistence and shifted to commercial production. By 2003 urban agriculture had created more than 326,000 jobs. By 2006 about 90 percent of the agricultural produce consumed in Havana came from urban agriculture.[34]

The Reopening of Free Agricultural Markets

The efforts to decentralize the agricultural sector and democratize decision making also led to the reopening of agricultural free markets in 1994 with the promulgation of Decree-Law 191, which authorized the sale of farmers' surplus at prices determined according to the mechanism of supply and demand.[35] Drawing on the free-market experience of 1980–86, the reopening of free markets was intended to undermine the black market, increase peasant productivity, and reduce high levels of liquidity caused by the limited amount of currency in the economy. It was also aimed at reducing the budget deficit caused by social expenditures through collecting taxes from small farmers who participated in free markets.[36] Free agricultural markets, jointly managed by the Ministries of Agriculture and Internal Trade, were exempted from certain regulations. The UBPCs were allowed to sell 20 percent of their production goal and 20 percent of their surplus in free markets as long as they were meeting the minimum 80 percent of their overall production goals broken up into monthly allotments.[37]

By December 1994 more than two hundred markets had been established, backed by broad popular support.[38] Within the first year of their establishment, free markets reached sales of more than 20,000 tons of agricultural produce and meat, which corresponded to 25–30 percent of the total production sold to the public. This volume amounted to somewhere between nearly a quarter to a third of total calories consumed by the Cuban population. By 1999 the sales volume had tripled, and the annual fees collected by the government reached more than $5 million pesos. In the long run free markets would prove to be preferable to the black market in terms of offering lower prices and increasing access to food, although they are still subject to serious criticism related to their focus on relatively high-income earners.[39]

The Campesino a Campesino Program and Transnationalization of the Agro-ecological Movement

The fourth pillar of Cuba's food sovereignty policies rests on the development of the Campesino a Campesino program and the transnationalization of the Cuban agro-ecological movement under the initiative of ANAP and the Cuban government. Following the introduction of land reforms, ANAP officially declared its support for the agro-ecological transformation of the country from the bottom up. Taking on as a primary task the encouragement of agro-ecological methods among farmers, the organization redefined its goals around three basic agro-ecological principles: "To restore and promote the practices of small farmers through direct farmer-to-farmer exchanges of sustainable agricultural techniques; to support horizontal technology transfers through participatory methods that encourage the use of appropriate sustainable technologies; to conduct the research necessary to carry out successful agroecological extension, public education, and appropriate technology transfers."[40]

Building on its crucial role in deepening the agro-ecological agrarian reform, ANAP expanded its scope through disseminating the Campesino a Campesino program nationwide. As defined by ANAP, Campesino a Campesino is "a way of promoting and improving the production systems so as to obtain higher levels of sustainability based on the principle that the participation and empowerment of their own players [peasants] are intrinsic components of sustainable development, a principle that focuses on the initiative and the role of farmers."[41] At the grassroots level the initiative, participation, and empowerment of peasants are ensured thanks to the mobilization of agro-ecologically conscious and well-educated political cadres known as "promoters," "facilitators," and "coordinators."

Promoters constitute the lowest-level actors of Campesino a Campesino. They are chosen from among volunteer farmers dedicated to community development and environmental protection. Facilitators are cooperative members or workers contracted by the cooperative to promote and spread agro-ecological methods by planning and organizing training workshops. They are selected based on their vocation, communication skills, and availability, but unlike promoters some of them are paid by their cooperative. The coordinators are likewise a core group of qualified executives who are directly linked to the ANAP leadership and are responsible for forming agro-ecological working groups in municipalities and provinces. Unlike facilitators, who work within the boundaries of their cooperatives, the coordinators work beyond the confines of their communities; they also contribute to the establishment of links among various allied agencies on a national scale.[42]

The Cuban Campesino a Campesino program relies upon a large number of activities, such as workshops, visits, meetings, and several forms of cultural communication. Most ANAP activities take place in the organization's regional and provincial offices, and this decentralized structure has been effective in maintaining strong relationships with members and achieving the equitable distribution of agricultural information, thereby increasing the scope of the program.[43] Among other reasons, workshops are organized for the aim of "socializing the agro-ecological experience and collectively building new knowledge." Visits and exchanges are also common among those program members who value agro-ecological exchanges between communities. Likewise, agro-ecological meetings, organized at regional, municipal, provincial, and national levels, host agro-ecological promoters, facilitators, coordinators, and other relevant actors. Finally, the dissemination of agro-ecology is not confined to purely technical meetings, but also makes use of didactic and cultural means such as testimonies, demonstrations, songs, poems, dramatic performances, poster art, exhibitions, and photography.[44]

ANAP's Campesino a Campesino program was recognized as a "mass movement" following the first national meeting, which took place in February 2001 with the participation of about 5,800 peasant families and 200 promoters, facilitators, and other leaders of ANAP. By 2008 the program was active in 155 municipalities (in 85 percent of the country), involving 3,052 facilitators and 9,211 promoters. By 2011, the number of facilitators had decreased only slightly, to 3,031, but the number of promoters had reached 11,935. Similarly, the number of coordinators had reached 170, and the participation of peasant families had climbed to 110,000.[45]

Broadly speaking, the success of the Cuban Campesino a Campesino movement is even greater than that of the Mesoamerican movement as a whole. Whereas the Mesoamerican movement gained only 30,000 members in thirty years, the movement in Cuba gathered more than 100,000 members in only a decade.[46] Even so, the success of the movement is not solely measurable by the size of its membership and activities, but by the transnationalism it engages in through the regional initiatives of ANAP and the Cuban government.

The transnationalism dates back to 1993, when some member cooperatives of ANAP established contacts and exchanges with the Mexican and Nicaraguan branches of the Campesino a Campesino Movement. In the summer of 1995 ANAP hosted Bairon Corrales and Marcial López, two leaders of the Nicaraguan National Farmers and Ranchers Association (UNAG), to discuss the improvement of agro-ecological methods and how to increase the effectiveness of sustainable agriculture. During this visit ANAP was invited to the Sixth Regional Meeting of the Campesino a Campesino Movement, which took place in Honduras in November 1995. In November 1996 Cuba was the host country for the Seventh Regional Meeting of the movement, attended by about ninety delegates from Central America, Mexico, and the Caribbean. At the meeting ANAP was elected to the Committee of Liaison and Monitoring of the movement. The Cuban Campesino a Campesino program itself was established following this meeting. After 1996 the program was supported by a long list of transnational actors.[47]

As a member of La Vía Campesina, ANAP occupies a key position in the transnationalization of food sovereignty policies: it coordinates the International Commission of Work in Sustainable Agriculture, a commission responsible for developing strategies of resistance and defense for peasant and family agriculture, and constructing practical options for the expansion of food sovereignty. The committee strives to create a lively synergy among the members of La Vía Campesina to establish a basic agro-ecological knowledge structure that recognizes the importance of traditional farmers and indigenous knowledge. To this end, the committee documents and systematizes agro-ecological experiences among Vía Campesina members as a means of facilitating horizontal learning between countries.[48] As the policy documents of La Vía Campesina, adopted at its Fifth Conference, held in Mozambique in October 2008, state: "The experiences of many Vía Campesina member organizations, most notably that of ANAP in Cuba, have demonstrated that the 'campesino a campesino' methodology is the best way for peasants and family farmers to develop and share their own agro-ecological farming technologies and systems."[49]

In its international relations, ANAP pays special attention to the development of peasant movements in Venezuela. Within the context of the "project of integral training for peasants and indigenous peoples with an agro-ecological approach," 34 ANAP staff members work permanently in 22 states and 205 municipalities of Venezuela. They have thus far opened 565 agro-ecological classrooms and seven regional schools of agro-ecology that have served 10,744 people. ANAP has also educated 641 Venezuelan peasant leaders at its Niceto Pérez Learning Center in Cuba.[50]

The transnationalization of Cuban food sovereignty policies is not confined to the activities of ANAP. The close collaboration between Cuba and Venezuela in the field of agro-ecology has been a determining factor in the increased role of the Cuban agro-ecological movement within the context of ALBA, which represents one of the most powerful tools for the transnationalization of food sovereignty in Latin America. As Ximena de la Barra and Richard A. Dello

Buono note, the fundamental goals of ALBA (which has Cuba and Venezuela among its founding members) include land distribution and food security.[51]

Following the global food crisis of the mid-2000s, food sovereignty became a ruling principle among the nations of ALBA. In 2008 ALBA announced the construction of a regional alliance to tackle the food crisis through a food security fund of $100 million, and ALBA members signed the Agreement for Cooperative Programs in the Area of Food Security and Food Sovereignty in order to improve the food industry in Latin America. In addition, ALBA's Food Program has initiated a $9 million agricultural project in Haiti and has developed ten projects costing about $13 million in various Caribbean countries.[52] In February 2009 ALBA members signed the Agreement for Food Security and Sovereignty and decided to create a supranational food company, ALBA Alimentos, aiming to "ensure food sovereignty" in Latin America, with an initial investment of $49 million. In 2010 ALBA invested more than $831,000 in Cuba to carry out Project Endogeno, which is installing irrigation systems and pig-farming units, constructing repair shops, and distributing tools and parts for trucks and tractors.[53]

Learning from the Cuban Experience

Its close relationship with the Soviet Union had helped Cuba to experience the highest economic growth rate in Latin America and to acquire a high degree of social equity and welfare, but at the expense of becoming a mono-exporter and multi-importer country that was extremely dependent on commercial privileges provided by the international socialist system.[54] When the collapse of the Soviet Union revealed the vulnerability of Cuba's agrarian structure, Cuba—through the introduction of a radical agro-ecological agrarian reform in 1993—went on to undertake the largest transition from conventional, industrial farming to organic and semi-organic farming in the history of humankind. Indeed, as Sinan Koont would argue, the Cuban experience of revolutionary agro-ecology can point the way for other developing countries that are striving to establish food sovereignty based on their own resources.[55]

Thanks to the successful implementation of food sovereignty policies built on a four-pillared agrarian strategy, the contribution of Cuban small farmers to domestic food production has increased rapidly. Meanwhile, farmers' income has also risen considerably to the point that farming has become one of the highest-paying professions in the country. The collectivization of land led to the establishment of workers' control over production and cooperative democracy by also diversifying and consolidating Cuba's social structure, thanks to both expansion of UBPCs and GENTs and consolidation of CCSs.

Paralleling the rise of the cooperative movement, participatory urban agriculture became a popular agro-ecological practice based on the principles of organic production, rational use of local resources, and direct marketing. The growth of this grassroots movement was nurtured with the establishment of horticultural clubs, extension services, seed banks, and People's Councils seeking to find long-term solutions to community problems and to facilitate access to information, training, and other resources. Similarly, the reopening of free agricultural markets was another instance of agricultural decentralization and democratization of decision making in the context of agro-ecological reform. Finally, the agro-ecological reform process led to the development and transnationalization of the Cuban food sovereignty movement through the initiative of ANAP and participation in ALBA.

Cuba has emerged as a leading actor in the transnationalization of food sovereignty and agro-ecology in the developing world, occupying key positions in major transnational peasant organizations such as La Vía Campesina and the international Campesino a Campesino Movement. Thanks to its bilateral support for the development of agro-ecology in Venezuela, Cuba has established food sovereignty as a "ruling norm" in that country, as well as in ALBA, which eventually adopted several multilateral measures such as establishing a food security fund, a food bank, a multinational food company, and numerous food programs.

As previously discussed, the transnationalization of Cuba's agro-ecological movement has important implications for Latin America and the Caribbean. These are particularly apparent in ANAP's active contribution to the development of the Latin American Campesino a Campesino movement, Cuba's close cooperation with Venezuela in areas of sustainable agriculture and food sovereignty, and its leadership role among the ALBA members in setting the institution's agenda toward food sovereignty. Having experienced the highest dietary energy supply level by 2007 and the best food production performance between 1996 and 2005 in the region—alongside an annual growth rate of 4.2 percent in per-capita food production, compared to a 0 percent regional average growth rate[56]—Cuba provides a shining example for other countries in Latin America and the Caribbean of what can be achieved with a "knowledge-intensive model"[57] of agrarian development prioritizing small-scale agriculture and agro-ecological techniques. Furthermore, one could also argue that Cuba's food sovereignty policies have contributed considerably to the diversification of its international relations through the channels of ALBA and thanks to its cooperation with Venezuela, helping to reverse its isolation from the rest of the continent.

The theory and practice of the revolutionary Cuban agro-ecological movement indicate that food sovereignty is not solely a local issue, nor is it limited to the sphere of civil society. In contrast, the genuinely emancipatory potential of food sovereignty policies is realized only if local struggles can be tied to both national and transnational solutions that rely upon a progressive alliance among numerous social movements and left-leaning governments. Achieving solutions on such a broad scale requires decentralized decision-making processes that succeed in balancing individual initiatives and institutional control. It also depends on the existence of a strong societal structure ensuring the diversification of civil society, alongside a network of consensual policies based on an agro-ecological political culture of agrarian development.

Notes

A longer version of this article appeared in *Latin American Perspectives* in late 2013.

1. Walden Bello, *The Food Wars* (London: Verso, 2009), 1.

2. Anuradha Mittal, "The 2008 Food Price Crisis: Rethinking Food Security Policies," United Nations Conference on Trade and Development, www.unctad.org/en/docs/gdsmdpg2420093_en.pdf; *Nourrir les hommes: Un dictionnaire* (Paris: Atlande, 2009), 269–70.

3. Steven Gorelick, Todd Merrifield, and Helena Norberg-Hodge, *Bringing the Food Economy Home: Local Alternatives to Global Agribusiness* (London: Zed Books, 2002), 1–2.

4. Annette Aurélie Desmarais, Nettie Wiebe, and Hannah Wittman, "Origins and Potential of Food Sovereignty," in Desmarais, Wiebe, and Wittman, eds., *Food Sovereignty. Reconnecting Food, Nature, and Community* (Halifax, N.S.: Fernwood, 2010), 2–4. See also Desmarais, *La Vía Campesina: Globalization and the Power of Peasants* (Halifax: Fernwood, 2007), 34.

5. Medea Benjamin and Peter Rosset, *The Greening of the Revolution: Cuba's Experiment with Organic Agriculture* (Melbourne, Australia: Ocean Press, 1994), 5.

6. Gorelick, Merrifield, and Norberg-Hodge, *Bringing the Food Economy Home*, 112.

7. Sinan Koont, "Food Security in Cuba, " *Monthly Review* 55, no. 8 (2004).

8. José Alvarez, *Cuba's Agricultural Sector* (Miami: University Press of Florida, 2004), 44.

9. Benjamin and Rosset, *Greening of the Revolution*, 3; Bharat Mansata, *Organic Revolution!* (Kolkata, India: Earthcare Books, 2009), 10; María Caridad Cruz and Roberto Sánchez Medina, *Agriculture in the City: A Key to Sustainability in Havana* (Kingston, Jamaica: Ian Randle, 2003), 3.

10. Delia Luisa López García, "Economic Crisis, Adjustments and Democracy in Cuba," in José Bell Lara, ed., *Cuba in the 1990s* (Havana: Editorial José Martí, 1999), 23; Benjamin and Rosset, *Greening of the Revolution*, 3–4, 20.

11. Cruz and Sánchez Medina, *Agriculture in the City*, 4.

12. Elisa Botella-Rodríguez, "Cuba's Alternative/Inward-Looking Development Policies— Changing Production Patterns and Land Decentralisation: Towards Sustainable Small Farming (1990–2008)," *DT-SEHA* 10–11 (Sociedad Española de Historia Agraria, 2010), 28.

13. Beatriz Díaz Gonzáles, "Collectivization of Cuban State Farms: A Case Study," in Lara,

Cuba in the 1990s, 111; Evelio Vilarino Ruiz, *Cuba: Socialist Reform and Modernization* (Havana: Editorial José Martí, 1998), 121.

14. Eugenio Espinosa Martinez, "The Cuban Economy in the 1990s: From Crisis to Recovery," in Lara, *Cuba in the 1990s*, 97; Vilarino, *Cuba*, 121.

15. Pierre Raymond, "¿Hacia una nueva orientación para la agricultura cubana?" *Análisis Político* 47 (2002), 15.

16. Alvarez, *Cuba's Agricultural Sector*, 76; Raymond, "¿Hacia una nueva orientación para la agricultura cubana?" 15.

17. Alvarez, *Cuba's Agricultural Sector*, 80; Laura J. Enríquez, *Reactions to the Market: Small Farmers in the Economic Reshaping of Nicaragua, Cuba, Russia, and China* (University Park: Penn State University Press, 2010), 129; Frederick S. Royce, "Agricultural Production Cooperatives: The Future of Cuban Agriculture?" *Transnational Law and Contemporary Problems* 14, no. 1 (2004), 23–24, 30–31.

18. Alvarez, *Cuba's Agricultural Sector*, 80, 77–78.

19. Mavis Alvarez, Martin Bourque, Fernando Funes, Lucy Martin, Armando Nova, and Peter Rosset, "Surviving Crisis in Cuba: The Second Agrarian Reform and Sustainable Agriculture," in Michael Courville, Raj Patel, and Peter Rosset, eds., *Promised Land* (Oakland, CA: Food First Books, 2006), 235; Julia Wright, *Sustainable Agriculture and Food Security in an Era of Oil Scarcity* (London: Earthscan, 2009), 139–40.

20. Nancy Forster and Howard Handelman, "Food Production and Distribution in Cuba: The Impact of the Revolution," in John C. Super and Thomas C. Wright, eds., *Food, Politics, and Society in Latin America* (Lincoln: University of Nebraska Press, 1985), 184; Orlando Valdés, *La socialización de la tierra en Cuba* (Havana: Editorial de Ciencias Sociales, 1990), 84.

21. Royce, "Agricultural Production Cooperatives," 23.

22. Adilén María Roque Jaime, Dana Rocío Ávila Lozano, Peter Michael Rosset, and Braulio Machín Sosa, *Revolución agroecológica: El movimiento de campesino a campesino de la ANAP en Cuba* (Havana: ANAP and La Vía Campesina, 2011), 58.

23. Wright, *Sustainable Agriculture and Food Security*, 140.

24. Ibid., 232.

25. Roque et al., *Revolución agroecológica*, 93–94.

26. Wright, *Sustainable Agriculture and Food Security*, 233.

27. Cruz and Sánchez Medina, *Agriculture in the City*, 3–4; Mansata, *Organic Revolution!* 45.

28. Nelso Companioni, Yanet Ojeda Hernández, Egidio Páez, and Catherine Murphy, "The Growth of Urban Agriculture," in Fernando Funes, Martín Bourque, Luis García, Nilda Pérez, and Peter Rosset, eds., *Sustainable Agriculture and Resistance: Transforming Food Production in Cuba* (Oakland, CA: Food First Books, 2002), 220.

29. Mansata, *Organic Revolution!* 47; Sinan Koont, "The Urban Agriculture of Havana," *Monthly Review* 60, no. 10 (2009).

30. Mansata, *Organic Revolution!* 47–48; Catherine Murphy, "Cultivating Havana: Urban Agriculture and Food Security in the Years of Crisis," in Mansata, *Organic Revolution!*, 116.

31. Murphy, "Cultivating Havana, " 117–20.

32. Cruz and Sánchez Medina, *Agriculture in the City*, 24, 6–7.

33. Adriana Premat, "State Power, Private Plots and the Greening of Havana's Urban Agriculture Movement," *City and Society* 21, no. 1 (2009), 34.

34. Pamela Stricker, *Toward a Culture of Nature: Environmental Policy and Sustainable Development in Cuba* (Plymouth, MA: Lexington Books, 2007), 42; Cruz and Sánchez Medina, *Agriculture in the City*, 4–5.

35. Botella-Rodríguez, "Cuba's Alternative/Inward-Looking Development Policies," 11.

36. Alvarez, *Cuba's Agricultural Sector*, 134; Japji Anna Bas, "Reorientation in Agriculture," in Mauricio A. Font, ed., *Adjusting to New Rules for the Old Game. Cuba in Transition? Pathways to Renewal, Long-Term Development and Re-integration* (New York: City University of New York, 2006), 58.

37. Alvarez, *Cuba's Agricultural Sector*, 98, 78–79.

38. Jennifer Abbassi, "The Role of the 1990s Food Markets in the Decentralization of Cuban Agriculture," in Jorge Pérez-López, ed., *Cuban Studies* (Pittsburgh, PA: University of Pittsburgh Press, 1998), 32.

39. Bas, "Reorientation in Agriculture," 58–59.

40. Funes et al., *Sustainable Agriculture and Resistance*, 85.

41. Roque et al., *Revolución agroecológica*, 66.

42. Ibid., 85–86, 88–89.

43. Alvarez et al., "Surviving Crisis in Cuba," 243.

44. Roque et al., *Revolución agroecológica*, 70–74.

45. Ibid., 17, 75–76; Fernando R. Funes-Monzote, "Farming Like We're Here to Stay: The Mixed Farming Alternative for Cuba" (PhD diss., Wageningen University, the Netherlands, 2008), 31; Roque et al., *Revolución agroecológica*, 92.

46. Roque et al., *Revolución agroecológica*, 61.

47. Ibid., 62–63; Mavis D. Alvarez Licea, "Estructuras de producción y sostenibilidad en la agricultura campesina cubana," in Fernando Funes, Martín Bourque, Luis García, Nilda Pérez, and Peter Rosset, eds., *Transformando el campo cubano: avances de la agricultura sostenible* (Havana: Asociación Cubana de Técnicos Agrícolas y Forestales, 2001), 86–88. The members after 1996 included Bread for the World, La Vía Campesina, Institute for Food and Development Policy/Food First, Latin American Consortium for Agroecology and Development, Trade Union Institute for Cooperation and Development, International Center for Rural and Agricultural Studies, Oxford Committee for Famine Relief (OXFAM), Group of Civilian Volunteers of Italy, International Network for Agriculture and Democracy, Norway Popular Assistance, Land of Men (Terre des hommes), National Center for Development, Uruguayan Cooperative Center, and Association for Cooperation with the South.

48. Roque et al., *Revolución agroecológica*, 27.

49. La Vía Campesina, "Policy Documents," International Operational Secretariat, Indonesia, 2008, 186.

50. Roque et al., *Revolución agroecológica*, 115.

51. Ximena de la Barra and Richard A. Dello Buono, *Latin America after the Neoliberal Debacle* (Lanham, MD: Rowman and Littlefield, 2009), 255.

52. ALBA-TCP, "Acuerdo para la implementación de programas de cooperación en materia de soberanía y seguridad alimentaria," http://www.fao.org/fileadmin/templates/cfs/Docs1112/CFS39Docs/SpecialSession/CFS_39_Special_Session_Alba_Food_Sp.pdf; Sistema Económico Latinoamericano y del Caribe, "The Increase in Food Prices: SELA's Response," www.sela.org/

DB/ricsela/EDOCS/SRed/2008/06/T023600002822-0-The_increase_in_food_prices-SELAs_response.pdf; Humberto Marquez, "Latin America: Stemming Food Crisis Must Be Regional Priority," Inter Press Service http://www.highbeam.com/doc/1P1-171058873.html.

53. ALBA-TCP, "Acuerdo de seguridad y soberanía alimentaria de los países miembros de Petrocaribe y el ALBA. Alba Alimentos," http://www.alba-tcp.org/public/documents/pdf/Presentacionalbaalimentos.pdf; James Suggett, "ALBA Trade Bloc Forms Joint Food Company at Summit in Venezuela," Venezuelan Analysis, venezuelanalysis.com/news/4165; Radio Rebelde, "Cuban Farmers Benefit From ALBA Project," www.radiorebelde.cu/english/news/cuban-farmers-benefit-from-alba-project-20100507/.

54. Peter M. Rosset, "Cuba: A Successful Case Study of Sustainable Agriculture," in Fred Magdoff, John Bellamy Foster, and Frederick H. Buttel, eds., *Hungry for Profit: The Agribusiness Threat to Farmers, Food and the Environment* (New York: Monthly Review, 2000); Forster and Handelman, "Food Production and Distribution in Cuba"; Benjamin and Rosset, *Greening of the Revolution*, 3.

55. Koont, "Food Security in Cuba."

56. Miguel A. Altieri and Fernando R. Funes-Monzote, "The Paradox of Cuban Agriculture," *Monthly Review* 63, no. 8 (2012).

57. Peter Rosset, "Organic Farming in Cuba" *Multinational Monitor* 16, no. 11 (November 1994).

12

Postcards from Abroad

The Cuban Special Period through Spanish Eyes

ANA SERRA

Since the time of the Special Period (roughly 1990–2005), Cuba has attracted international attention as the last bastion of socialism in the Western world. Spain is arguably among the countries that have evidenced the greatest interest in Cuba. A 1993 Cuban government decree allowing Cuban writers and artists to publish and exhibit their work abroad opened the Spanish market to Cubans living on the island, causing a veritable publishing boom. In addition, the active promotion of tourism by the newly created Cuban Ministry of Tourism (April 1994) invigorated the already steady flow of visitors from Spain to Cuba; and Cuban laws facilitating foreign capital investment brought a large number of Spanish companies to the island. Changes in Cuba triggered a response in Spain whereby the number of Spanish publications on Cuba increased considerably, especially in the fiction genre, and public debate over the state of the Cuban revolution was revived.

The intensity of Spanish-Cuban relations is not new: the strong bond between the two countries dates back to an exceptionally long period of Spanish domination of Cuba relative to other countries in the region, with the exception of Puerto Rico. Since the so-called disaster, as the loss of the Cuban colony was termed in Spain, the Spanish people have proven that Cuba occupies a very strong position in the country's imagination. Likewise, the Spanish influence on Cuba remained prevalent in the postcolonial period, when the Spanish population in the island continued to thrive and extend its influence, to the point that Fernando Ortiz spoke of "Cuba's second reconquest by Spain"; after successive waves of Spanish migration, during the Spanish Civil War as well as during the decades of Francisco Franco's dictatorship, Spaniards collectively perceived Cuba as a familiar place, despite the divergent trajectories of the two countries. With the transition to democracy in Spain, Cuba embodied the achievement of the leftist utopia that many viewed as having been thwarted with the demise of the Second Republic and the Civil War. On the other hand,

Spain has also been the recipient of numerous Cuban immigrants, particularly since the 1990s. The "Grandchildren Law" (Ley de nietos) has made it possible for close to 200,000 Cubans to apply for Spanish citizenship, as descendants of Spanish immigrants who immigrated to the island between 1936 and 1955. Most of the new Spanish citizens from Cuba will immigrate to Spain in the foreseeable future. Thus the circle of exchanges of population and ideas between the two countries continues.

This essay addresses an important aspect of Cuba's internationalism and transnationalism, namely how the island nation is perceived by other countries, particularly Spain. As a cultural critic, my role is not to analyze international relations policies, but to examine representations and opinions that at times reflect, inform, and shape those policies. I have chosen two novels about Cuba by Spanish authors who are widely popular, not only as fiction writers and essayists, but as bloggers and outspoken editorialists. One of them is Belén Gopegui's *El lado frío de la almohada* (2004, The cold side of the pillow); and the other is Rafael Argullol's *Davalú o el dolor* (2001, Davalú, or Pain, first published in Catalan as *Davalú o el dolor: crònica d'un duel*). As I show, their perceptions are echoed and commented on by other fiction writers and numerous readers on the Internet and in print sources in Spain, and in the case of Gopegui, in Cuba as well. The latter writer was invited to the 2010 International Book Fair in Havana. In other words, both novels are paradigmatic examples of influential representations of Cuba as it is perceived in Spain.

My title—"Postcards from Abroad"—attempts to evoke the often peculiar relationship between visitors to Cuba and the island nation itself. For the tourist who selects a postcard, the image on the front captures an important aspect of the country being visited. On the back of the postcard, the brief self-narrative reconstructs the tourist's experience of the place. Similarly, *El lado frío de la almohada* and *Davalú o el dolor*, both by authors who visited Cuba during the Special Period, are like postcards, showcasing how Spanish progressive intellectuals have engaged with, or imagined, that transitional period in Cuba. The two writers selected images they found emblematic of the country, but in describing their experiences they turned what they saw into a projection of their *selves* and reinforced Spaniards' preconceived notions of the island. In recent years, indeed, the radical left in Spain, the publishing industry in Cuba and Spain, and the political circumstances of the Cuban Special Period have all contributed to reviving iconic functions of Cuba among seemingly progressive Spanish writers. The uses of Cuba in Spanish public discourse reveal strong desires among many Spaniards to have Cuba either embody their political aspirations or illustrate their disappointment in promises unfulfilled. Significantly, in the process of these explorations intellectuals relegate Cuban voices to a subordinate role in the cultural dialogue between the two countries. But Cuba as a whole receives the fallout of the widespread transmission of ideas concerning the state of the revolution post–Special Period, and both negative and positive portrayals contribute to strengthening the thriving market for Cuban books in Spain, as well as the influx of Spanish tourists to the island. Gopegui, in particular, has assumed iconic status in the island as a Spanish writer who firmly believes in the Cuban revolution after 1959. Though Gopegui's understanding of the revolution is only partial, as the next section shows, her unwavering support becomes highly representative of the status of revolutionary ideology in both countries.

Belén Gopegui and the Resurgence of Radicalism

The publication of Belén Gopegui's *El lado frío de la almohada* is associated with the reappearance of the Spanish left in the last thirty years, after having been driven underground by the harsh repression that accompanied the Spanish Civil War decades earlier.[1] The Frente Popular (Popular Front)—a coalition of anarchists, unionists, communists, and Marxist-Leninists that won the 1936 democratic election in Spain—was prevented from taking power when the Civil War broke out, and thereafter was driven underground through the almost forty-year dictatorship of Francisco Franco (1939–75). After the death of the Generalísimo the transition to democracy was too delicate to permit inclusion of the radical left that had sparked the coup d'état prior to the Civil War and that threatened a certain idea of national unity. The radical left was further pushed aside by two governments led by the much more moderate PSOE (Partido Socialista Obrero Español, or Socialist Worker's Party, in 1982 and 1986 respectively); Spain's entrance into the European Union and the NATO alliance (both in 1986); and the heavy political and financial toll imposed by celebrations of the quincentennial of the discovery of the Americas and the 1992 Olympic Games.[2]

The year 2000, coinciding with the second term of a conservative government under José María Aznar, fostered a public attitude of conformism and watered-down liberalism that persists in Spain to this day. After the fall of the Berlin Wall most Western European regimes allied themselves with neoliberalism. While most leftist intellectuals still act to agitate the social conscience, few clamor for changes that would shatter the foundation of the neoliberal economic system. Despite the inauguration of President Rodríguez Zapatero's government in 2004—which introduced progressive measures such as same-sex marriage and a massive amnesty for illegal immigrants—Spain continued to endorse the policies of the largest European economies and remained at arm's length from the radical leftist regimes elected in Latin America.

Nevertheless, the leftist opposition in Spain became highly mobilized at the beginning of the new millennium, starting when President Aznar endorsed the U.S. invasion of Iraq in 2003 and, a month later, when seventy-five dissidents were jailed in Cuba, which triggered the imposition of Spanish sanctions until 2007.[3] For Belén Gopegui these two events are situated at opposite ends of the ethical spectrum: the war in Iraq represents an expression of U.S. imperialism and the global hegemony of profit-driven regimes; whereas the jailing of the Cuban dissidents embodies a strong will to contain opposition to the regime's radical project.[4]

Born in 1964, Gopegui belongs to a generation of Spaniards who have only a vague memory of the transition to democracy. According to the Spanish writer herself, her cohort falls in between the generation that took an active part in that transition and the generation already disenchanted by it. Her generation grew up at a time when people spoke about politics rather than playing a role in it. As a result, they tend to be passive, leaning toward conservatism and allegiance with the bourgeoisie. In Gopegui's opinion, when progressive people in the Spanish political climate use the word *left*, it really means watered-down liberalism and a kind of "aesthetic ritual," with a superficial aversion to certain things such as conspicuous consumption.[5] For Gopegui, the dominant political parties in Spain do not attack the capitalist system at its roots, as a communist party would, and Cuba represents the only true challenge to the norm of Western neoliberalism.

The Book as Commodity: Figurations of Cuba in Spain

El lado frío de la almohada was published in the midst of a clash between two forces: on the one side, the conformism and lethargy in Spanish leftist circles during the new millennium, together with a globalized economy and widespread technological literacy; and on the other side, the Cuba that emerged toward the end of the Special Period, a time of severe economic scarcity and far-reaching social changes unleashed by the fall of the Soviet Bloc and the subsequent withdrawal of aid to Cuba.

Among these significant changes came the November 1993 decree granting Cuban authors permission to publish abroad, which started a notable boom of Cuban books being published in Spain. The favorable conditions of the Spanish market caused the frontiers of Cuban culture to be redrawn and complicated beyond the diaspora. Writers such as Pedro Juan Gutiérrez became as widely read as others who had occupied center stage long before, such as Zoé

Valdés, who resides in Paris. To various degrees Cuban writers publishing in Spain—among them Abilio Estévez, Ena Lucía Portela, and Rolando Menéndez—exploited the allure of an arguably anachronistic socialist society, with exotic images of hyper-racialized women, enticing ruins, and virtuous poverty, and managed to expose the European source of these myths.

The popularity of Cuban books in Spain produced in turn a fresh crop of books by Spanish writers who focused on the island. Those books included not only Belén Gopegui's *El lado frío de la almohada* but also *Así en La Habana como en el cielo* (1998) and *El niño de luto y el cocinero del papa* (2001) by J. J. de Armas Marcelo; *Amanecer con hormigas en la boca* (1999) by Miguel Barroso; *Habanera* (1999) by Ángeles Dalmau; *La noche de la jinetera* (1997) and *Regreso a La Habana* (2001) by Jordi Sierra i Fabra; *Davalú o el dolor* (2001) by Rafael Argullol Murgadas; and *Por el cielo y más allá* (2001) by Carme Riera, among others.

In addition, a considerable expansion of the book market in Spain further complicated Gopegui's complex relationship with Cuba. In 2005, right after *El lado frío de la almohada* was published, some 500 publishing houses varying in size and scope were reportedly producing more than 50,000 books a year, of which 500 were first-time novels.[6] At this time newspapers were receiving 12,000 books a year to review, with the reviews being widely read and leading to the purchase of more books. The prestige of *having a book* increased in Spain, although the number of actual readers remained low: only 8 percent of Spaniards have regular reading habits, and four out of ten Spaniards do not read books. According to José Luis Velázquez and Javier Memba, literature has become one more item in the flourishing entertainment and leisure industry. As a result it is no longer used as a platform for social criticism.[7]

In this booming book market, certain publishing houses tried to target specific readers. Some of the still small but growing presses, such as Caballo de Troya or El Viejo Topo, brought out books related to radical political issues in which Cuba features in protagonist or ancillary roles.[8] Other publishing houses, such as Colibrí, focused on writers of the Cuban diaspora, many of whom are critical of the Cuban regime. Established publishers such as Alfaguara, Tusquets, or Planeta absorbed the vast numbers of Cuban books published abroad since the 1990s. To date, all of Gopegui's novels have been published by the well-established Anagrama, which made significant Cuban authors such as Pedro Juan Gutiérrez world renowned.

The politics of literary prizes and book promotion events increased the status of the book as a commodity to a degree unprecedented in Spain. Authors' writings on the Internet and appearances in public forums fostered the culture of "author brand" and "book spectacle"; that is, the construction of a public, coherent persona for a writer beginning with the celebratory book launch.⁹ In this regard, *El lado frío de la almohada* generated a great deal of attention, resulting in four editions in Spain and one in Cuba (Arte y Literatura, 2005), discussion forums in the popular Spanish dailies *El Mundo* and *El País*, and numerous interviews and publications in the Cuban journals *La jiribilla* and *La gaceta de Cuba* and in radical Spanish journals and websites such as Youkali: Revista crítica de las artes y el pensamiento or www.rebelion.org. In addition, Gopegui received lavish praise from Francisco Umbral, an influential figure among Spanish leftist intellectuals. Zoé Valdés, on the other hand, criticized Gopegui for her very personal view of the dissident crisis.[10] Regardless of whether Gopegui deserves criticism or praise, Cuba has aided in solidifying Gopegui's own "author's brand," as she moved from being a critic of an apathetic left in Spain to a proponent of an existing model, perhaps the product of her own vision, on the island of Cuba.

Toward the Cold Side of the Pillow: Dreams of a Different Reality

Given Gopegui's support of the Cuban regime, it is surprising that the narrative of *El lado frío de la almohada* takes place not in Cuba, but in Madrid. The plot itself is rather uncomplicated and uneventful: though a spy novel, it does not entirely follow the conventions of the genre. The main conflict stems from a fake operation by Cuban agents aimed at framing an American agent in Madrid—the agent is a rather hard-line supporter of sanctions against Cuba, and the Cubans want her to lose her position. Following a theme echoed in other spy novels, the "good" characters are Cuban state security agents who conspire against U.S. agents, but overall the recounting of all the characters' actions is rather dispassionate. The heart of the book is the relationship between the two protagonists, a female Cuban spy named Laura and Phillip Hull, a fifty-seven-year-old U.S. diplomat/agent stationed in Madrid at the end of a lackluster career. As their relationship matures, irreconcilable differences emerge. Indeed, Laura's love affair with Hull is destined to fail from the beginning of the novel due to their diverging political beliefs and her unswerving commitment to the revolution.

Eventually, Laura "chooses Cuba over Hull,"[11] and behaves like a true revolutionary, at least according to Che Guevara's definition: "The true revolutionary is guided by great feelings of love.... Our vanguard revolutionaries must make an ideal of this love of the people.... They cannot descend, with small doses of daily affection, to the level where ordinary men put their love into practice."[12] At the conclusion of the devastating Special Period, when revolutionary fervor in Cuba is withering away, Laura emerges as the epitome of a conscientious official, one who cannot make choices for her own life because ideology always comes first.

And yet what really is Gopegui's proposal for social change? The characters in the novel are unable to overcome their isolation and find love: Hull betrays Laura, not with ulterior motives, but out of an inability to act. Characters in this novel do not have self-will, but act in response to forces that seem larger than they are, such as ambition, the power of money, or ideology. Indeed, the author has repeatedly stated that she did not intend to discuss the problems of Cuba itself in this novel, but rather to explore the place of Cuba in the Spanish imagination.[13] For Gopegui, writers should attempt to raise consciousness about how it should still be possible to undermine the alliance between democracy and capitalism from a Marxist point of view. Citing Santiago Alba, a Spanish writer who contributes to the website rebelion.org, for which Gopegui also writes, she states that one has not only to support revolutions, but also "rely on them" ("apoyar la revolución y apoyarse en la revolución"), by which she refers to the belief that Cuba offers tangible evidence that it is possible to challenge the ethics of material gain.[14]

This belief is rather paradoxical considering the historical period in which this novel is set (around 2003), when dire need pushed Cubans into hot pursuit of the dollar—now convertible pesos—in numerous business ventures, both legal and illegal.[15] The disconnect between Gopegui's ideal of Cuba and the experience of Cubans on the island can be explained by the fact that, by her own admission, Gopegui made only two twenty-day trips to Havana and Matanzas, and the scope of her research for this novel was rather limited. The author clearly fulfills the four characteristics of what Iván de la Nuez, a Cuban writer residing in Madrid, calls "the red rhapsody of the revolution"—referring to the praise that ideological tourists give to the revolution as the embodiment of freedom. These characteristics are (1) providing reassurance to Western democracies of Cuba's record as a triumphant revolution against all those that failed; (2) brief exposure to life in Cuba in short trips, which leads to the elaboration of untested theories; (3) a physical and critical distance, making it easy to defend the revolution from the standpoint of unequal, if permissive, social freedoms in Western democracies; and (4) a reliance on a double standard, given that Cuban voices are silenced in foreigners' accounts of the ideal revolution.[16] In her unswerving support for the revolution, despite her lack of experience in the island, Gopegui conforms to the profile of the ideological tourist.

For Gopegui, the unresolved absence of utopia in contemporary Spanish politics nurtures the dream that becomes a metaphor in "the cold side of the pillow." A person turning to the cold side of the pillow in bed comes into contact with what inspires fear and hope, perhaps one's desire for an alternative reality. For Gopegui, Cuba acts as a symbolic space that moves one to action and shatters one's accommodation to the pleasures of bourgeois life. And yet there is no poetic justice at the end of the novel. Laura lets herself be killed so that Hull can continue to live his elusive dream of a better future, which he never gets to realize anyway. The book concludes with an inquiry into why we have stopped thinking about Cuba, and the cold side of the pillow brings us to other dreams. Gopegui prefers to keep Cuba as a space of possibility, as something that surpasses us and therefore becomes a sort of benchmark.

El lado frío de la almohada illustrates how a thinly built narrative with superficial characters, an unsupported ideological stance, and substantial lack of documentation can still become a success given the appropriate political climate in Spain. Since Hull, the character who tries to lead the Cuban heroine astray, is a U.S. agent, the narrative exonerates Spain from any symbolic guilt. Hull's allies are Spanish businessmen, double agents, and neutral bystanders, but they play minor roles in the story and do not seem to have an opinion on Cuba. Laura's ideas are tested only from Hull's standpoint, which represents U.S. neoliberal views. By making Madrid a mere background stage for the story, the author does not examine the active role that Spanish citizens themselves have played in stifling the radical left. Cuba itself does not appear as a civil society, where people might have opinions about the complex issue of the seventy-five jailed dissidents. The Spanish government sanctions against Cuba are also left out of a narrative in which the Cuban revolution continues to be a buzzword for the unrealized potential of the Spanish radical left.

The success of *El lado frío de la almohada* attests to the continuing strength in Spain of the dream of Cuba as utopia, and the positive response to the book in Cuba demonstrates that Cuban cultural institutions relish that Spanish dream. Still, for some people the enthusiastic reception of the novel is a wake-up call to a new awareness that Cuba has to be approached on its own terms, and not as a projection of the collective dreams of others.

Painful Metaphors: *Davalú o el dolor*, A Writer's Journey in Havana

Although some critics characterize Rafael Argullol as a philosopher, his work does not follow the mode of inquiry of any one discipline. He has written numerous poetry collections, novels, and books of essays on topics as varied as painting, European thought, and contemporary politics. The novel *Davalú o el dolor* epitomizes the hybrid nature of Argullol's writing. It is on the one hand a highly poetic and profound meditation on pain and a narrative of a professor's visit to Havana and, on the other, perhaps to the author's surprise, a showcase of dominant motifs in foreigners' imagination of Cuba. It is a novel that once again takes Cuba as an extension of the Spanish self, the embodiment of its fears, vulnerability, and disillusionment.

Rafael Argullol maintains a strong presence in public forums as a professor of aesthetics at Universidad Pompeu Fabra in Barcelona, a speaker, and a blogger in the popular Spanish paper *El País*.[17] He is extremely knowledgeable and curious about a variety of subjects, yet accessible and thoughtful to his many readers. Although Cuba is very much present in Spanish public discussion, Argullol has not taken an explicit position regarding the contemporary situation on the island. Nevertheless, in *Davalú o el dolor* his opposition to totalitarianism is at the core of his vision of Cuba. In this perspective, Argullol aligns with other Spanish philosophers of his generation, writers who were influenced by post-Franco-era radical politics and student activism but who have now become more persuaded by a "nondogmatic" concept of utopia. For these writers, an individual's responsibility as a citizen entails understanding the "pain, irrationality, or evil" inflicted during the world wars, which were in turn reproduced in our own Civil War and in forty years of totalitarian rule under Franco.[18]

The concept of an elusive utopia is dominant in Argullol's work. As Isabel Soler points out, although Argullol admits to having been attracted to Eastern Europe as a result of his "utopian education," he was disappointed to see that the socialist utopia was "mediocre" and "pedestrian." For Argullol, Western ideals oscillate between the two poles of Prometheus and Mephistopheles, or action and transformation: the failed attempts to bring about social and political utopias ended in destruction, just as the roles of Prometheus and Mephistopheles entail heroic deeds, but also enormous risks.[19] This dichotomy no doubt characterizes the narrator of *Davalú* in his visit to Havana, a city that epitomizes both the resilience and the cost of socialism in the Western world.

Although the novel makes no specific reference to the time in which it takes place, the mention of "pesetas" as Spanish currency situates it prior to 2002, the year when the euro was introduced in Spain and the Special Period in Cuba was drawing to a close.[20] The unnamed protagonist is a scholar who decides to go to a conference he was scheduled to attend in Havana, despite the pain he is suffering from a spinal lesion. While in Cuba, intense pain makes the professor numb and distant, and the city becomes transformed into a witness and mirror to his suffering. As the pain increases, the narrator gives it a name, Davalú, and refers to it as a monster he intends to defeat. Soon after returning to Barcelona from his trip he undergoes a procedure that improves his condition. At the core of the novel is an investigation into the experience of pain, its meanings and implications in human relationships with others, and how it conditions perceptions.

The writer's intention may not have been to write a political story in the literal sense, but it is hard to avoid reading the novel against a political context. In the words of the Cuban writer Iván de la Nuez, since the 1960s Cuba has become for numerous writers "the embodiment of a redeeming dream, or the ideal therapy to locate in a picturesque and faraway place their discomfort with Western culture's discontents."[21] The idea that Havana can become the repository of a personal fantasy is realized to an extreme degree in this novel, in which a very intimate, incommunicable feeling such as pain becomes articulated through the sufferer's observations of the city. In an interview Argullol stated that the novel is somewhat autobiographical because he himself traveled to a conference in Havana under the strain of severe pain. And yet, as he put it, "It is only by chance that Havana turns into the setting that accommodates my representation of pain. However, since nothing is arbitrary when we contemplate it after the fact, *it is* possible that Davalú, in addition to expressing a battle of the senses, illustrates a spiritual tension reflected in our contemporary era, beyond the Cuban horizon that constitutes its immediate reference."[22] In the context of Argullol's work, the "spiritual tension" of "our contemporary era" refers to the backlash from "the fall of imperialism, colonialism, and Utopias," after which Europe became aware that the world is "multicentered and multicultural" but yet it failed to embody these two values. In Argullol's view, "Europeans are in the desert.... Latin America, Africa and Asia today constitute the true laboratories of ideas."[23] Pain in Argullol's novel constitutes a symptom of his uneasiness toward a country that he recognizes as trying to fashion its own future while it also inevitably reminds him of the failure of past utopias.

Although pain limits what the character can see and hear in the city, Havana at the end of the Special Period is in such a state of crisis that this drama cannot be completely left out of the narrator's account. Davalú, as the narrator explains, is the name of an Armenian demon whose blood turned solid and became petrified. This monster of hardened blood evokes the enormity of the battle that the protagonist must wage against his own suffering. But more importantly Davalú evokes the sinister monument that presides over and mediates the writer's observation of Havana—a stone of solidified blood that silently attests to the suffering and repression of Cubans on the island, a state of affairs that often goes unnoticed by foreigners who are absorbed in their own musings.

The style of *Davalú o el dolor* resonates with that of a classic Cuban novel written at the dawn of the revolution, *Memorias del subdesarrollo* (1963; *Memories of Underdevelopment*, 2004), by Edmundo Desnoes. Both works are fictional diaries written as first-person narratives in the present tense, and they thus lend a sense of immediacy to events. Both protagonists are self-centered individuals, but unlike the Catalan intellectual who brings his own baggage to his visit to Cuba, the narrator of *Memorias del subdesarrollo* cannot remain detached from current events: at the end of the novel the Missile Crisis renders the character bedridden and unable to speak or write. The two texts offer a contrast in that Desnoes is steeped in the Cuban experience and his character cannot escape the historical changes that are taking place, whereas Argullol's writing deterritorializes and dehistoricizes Havana and begs the question of why it is relevant to write about pain in this city.

The professor's view of Havana resembles photographic accounts of the city, in which the capital appears, in Ana María Dopico's words, as "the theater of the uncanny . . . on the threshold of imagination or nightmare."[24] The professor's effort to rein in his pain is so intense that everything existing outside the boundary of his skin seems fictional. The people he observes become reduced to their intense gazes, which he needs to feel on himself in witness to the pain he suffers. After many references to these looks, the professor states, "The best architecture in Havana is those fiery glares."[25] Yet he fails to understand the demand for recognition that the eyes of the *habaneros* shoot at him, as they have become invisible and mute in his representations.

The character in *Davalú o el dolor* is forced to interact with others, and it is possible to perceive the voices and attitudes of those others coming through the veil of his misperception, even if only through ironic reversals. The metaphor of performance usefully illustrates both the illness the character suffers and the behavior of the people he encounters. During his meditations on pain the professor realizes that social situations become forced, almost overacted, as he attempts to disguise the struggle he is waging inside himself. In his words, "My shield is continuous movement, metamorphosis, disguise, a masquerade, a farce, even a performance of resistance that may seem heroic to me. The great abstractions are, for now, shields with holes."[26]

The metaphor of performance as a means of controlling pain is a strikingly ironic mirroring of the environment of the Cuban Special Period, where self-censorship was the norm and repression and survival instincts impelled the use of a *doble moral*, or different behaviors and levels of expression according to with whom one is speaking.[27] Notable Cuban writers have exploited the idea of performance in their fiction, including Abilio Estévez in the novel *Los palacios distantes* (2002), in which the protagonist, a clown, states: "We cannot help but conclude that the city has been erected on a theater . . . reproducing it in corners, walls, streets, parks, and buildings."[28] Nevertheless, the narrator of *Davalú*, who visits Havana at the time that Estévez is describing it, fails to note the performance taking place around him. He turns a blind eye to people who have been immersed in an unparalleled situation of scarcity, deprivation, and uncertainty since the onset of the revolution in Cuba.

Another instance in which what happens in Havana serves as an objective correlative of the character's feelings, with reference not to the city but to himself, is his observations on how pain stalls the progression of time. After he is told that he can go back to Barcelona, the narrator reflects that his life in Havana is unfolding as "permanently provisional," in "the kind of present that pain demands, without a future or a past." He adds, "This present time is lonely, death-like, an inhabitant of postponed decisions."[29] Similarly, the Cuban writer Antonio José Ponte described the experience of time in the Special Period as "an overwhelming appearance of eternity" and "a spatial orbit that is made up of one point" (the beginning point of the revolution).[30] José Quiroga elaborates on this idea when he states that, due in large part to the break with the Soviet bloc, the Special Period inaugurated a time of memorialization; that is, of reification of the memory of previous revolutionary times. Memorialization results in a contemplative state in the present. At the same time the apparent failure of Soviet socialism to deliver on its promises caused Cubans to project themselves into a future in which the fulfillment of those promises is indefinitely deferred.[31]

In light of the character's imminent departure, Havana becomes for him a place of transition, a waiting room, before he can receive relief. That state of heightened awareness also inadvertently corresponds to the experience of passage that the decade of the 1990s signified in Cuba. Described as a "special" period because of the unprecedented situation of a Cuban revolutionary economy without Soviet subsidies, the decade was dominated by a sense of expectation, which came from different fronts. As Rafael Rojas put it, referring to the state of Cuba after the fall of the Soviet bloc, "political statism in Cuba has to do with the intricate web of passivity favored by the art of waiting. The Cuban people live waiting that somebody . . . does something. Fidel Castro and the hard line of the communist party are vigilant for an international miracle that will bring the Soviet Union back to life. The reformists in the government wait for Fidel Castro to share a small portion of his immense power. . . . Citizens live in waiting."[32] In an interview Argullol described Western culture as permeated by *waiting*, epitomized in the senseless attitude of the characters in Samuel Beckett's *Waiting for Godot*. But for Argullol, the situation in Beckett's play may become more fruitful when one considers that an antidote for passive waiting is *memory*. The act of remembering makes waiting more powerful and active because it is only by resorting to memory that one can "recognize the signs" of what is to come.[33] Just as the memory of the habaneros is obscured by a sense of rupture with the past and a loss of trust in revolutionary ideals, the protagonist's memory is also impaired by his inability to engage with the situation in Cuba and his lack of awareness of how this period relates to the past.

Toward the end of the novel the character realizes that in his visit to Havana he has condensed the city in the experience of his pain. At the same time he fails to note that the city is experiencing the same feeling of critical momentousness that he is finding in himself. As he himself admits, "Havana has been a ghostly city for me, though it is a visually concrete city, with such neat contours, with an existence that is contrasted without limits. Life comes out through the holes in all houses, through the pores on the ground. Despite these, Havana for me is a city covered by a veil. I see the city through a thick fog . . . its image is completely blurred."[34] His highly sensorial and electrifying experience of Havana might very well have led to a dialogue with people living at the edge of survival. Nevertheless, because he was possessed by his pain, the character became numb to the experience of others.

In both *El lado frío de la almohada* and *Davalú o el dolor* the intimate experiences of one's own sleep and one's pain become vehicles to express two extreme attitudes seen among intellectuals in Spain: a suspension of all criticism against the island, or a profound disillusionment and uneasiness toward Cuba for not living up to expectations. In both novels the narrators behave like tourists and provide impressionistic accounts of the situation in Cuba with little regard to the opinion or experience of Cubans living on the island. In these and other recent Spanish novels Havana acts as a metonymic space for the whole country, becoming an object through which the visitor can look at other issues and reflect on other landscapes. In that respect, Cuba appears as a colonized space—a place on which others continue to project their own visions of the present and future of the island nation.

The fact that Gopegui (1963–) and Argullol (1949–) belong to two different generations straddling the Spanish transition to democracy undoubtedly explains their positions. Gopegui in a sense takes democracy for granted, at least when it comes to the freedom of expression of which she avails herself. For instance, her latest novel, *Access Denied* (*Acceso no autorizado*, Mondadori, 2011) is scathingly critical of the last PSOE legislature for its inability to live up to the social commitment of a leftist party. Just as she had projected on Cuba her dream of a socialist utopia in *El lado frío de la almohada*, in *Access Denied* the World Wide Web becomes an unbound democratic space in which hackers are able to unlock documents that incriminate the socialist government in Spain. Gopegui perhaps is unaware that the degree of Internet access and freedom of expression she enjoys are considerably restricted in

Cuba, despite the great strides made since the Special Period. In the case of Rafael Argullol, who lived his formative years in Barcelona under Franco, it is not surprising that he values the free expression of cultural identities over and above the political objectives of a radical regime. For Gopegui, for whom the Spanish Second Republic remains an idealized past, the idea of revolution is still attractive; whereas for Argullol, who witnessed part of the rise and decline of the Soviet Union and its sphere of influence, it is an experiment that did not live up to expectations. Both antagonistic positions are very much present in contemporary Spain and create the conditions of possibility for Cuba's relations with Spain and the rest of the world.

Notes

1. A more extensive study of Belén Gopegui, which includes an analysis of *El lado frío de la almohada* in a literary context, appears in Ana Serra, "Desde *El lado frío de la almohada*: la izquierda española imagina la revolución cubana," *Hispanic Research Journal* 12 no. 3 (June 2011), 244–59.

2. For different accounts of how these events influenced the development of the left and public discourse, see Jo Labanyi, "Introduction: Engaging with Ghosts; or, Theorizing Culture in Modern Spain," in Jo Labanyi, ed., *Constructing Identity in Contemporary Spain: Theoretical Debates and Cultural Practice* (Oxford: Oxford University Press, 2002); Eduardo Subirats, *América o la memoria histórica* (Caracas: Monteávila, 1994); Teresa M. Vilarós, *El mono del desencanto: Una crítica cultural de la transición española (1973–1993)* (Madrid: Siglo XXI, 1998).

3. Thanks to an agreement brokered between the Cuban government and the Catholic Church in July 2010, the last of the Cuban dissidents jailed during the 2003 crackdown was released on March 17, 2011.

4. Gopegui agrees with the claim that the crackdown on the Cuban dissidents was legitimate, as by some accounts they were being supported by the United States to undermine Castro's regime. On this issue she sets herself against other celebrated intellectuals such as Günter Grass, José Saramago, Susan Sontag, Pedro Almodóvar, Manuel Vázquez Montalbán, Josep Ramoneda, and Antonio Tabucchi, who had supported the revolution for years but signed a letter protesting what they deemed a violation of human rights. See Iván de la Nuez, *Fantasía roja: Los intelectuales de izquierda y la revolución cubana* (Barcelona: Debate, 2006), 65.

5. Gopegui, in an interview with Marta Rivera de la Cruz, "Belén Gopegui: cada vez hay menos gente que quiere asumir la responsabilidad de saber más que otro. Entrevista," *Espéculo: Revista de estudios literarios* 7 (November 1997), www. ucm.es/info/especulo/ numero7/gopegui.htm; Gopegui in an interview with Eva Legido-Quigley, "Conversación con Belén Gopegui: la necesidad de una vía política," *Ojáncano: Revista de literatura española* 16 (1999), 90–104, 99; and Belén Gopegui, *La conquista del aire* (Barcelona: Anagrama, 1998), 60.

6. Salvador Montesa, ed., *Novelistas en el siglo XXI: Creación, mercado, editores* (Málaga: Congreso de literatura española contemporánea, 2005), 17.

7. José Luis Velázquez and Javier Memba, *La generación de la democracia: historia de un desencanto* (Madrid: Ediciones Temas de Hoy, 1995), 122.

8. Of note are Santiago Alba Rico (writing on behalf of Colectivo Todoazen), *Leer con niños, El año que tampoco hicimos la revolución* (2005), or *Una puta recorre Europa*, by Alberto Lema (2008). El Viejo Topo, affiliated with the website rebelion.org, published *Cuba: construyendo futuro* (2000), by several authors; also see Salim Lamrani, ed., *Estados Unidos contra Cuba: la guerra contra el terrorismo y el caso de los cinco* (Barcelona: Ediciones de Intervención Cultural, 2005).

9. Germán Gullón, *Los mercaderes en el templo de la literatura* (Barcelona: Caballo de Troya, 2004), 73.

10. Francisco Umbral, "Los placeres y los días: Belén Gopegui," *El Mundo*, September 10, 2004, November 3, 2008, www.elmundo.es/papel/2004/09/10/ultima; Zoé Valdés, "A la loma de Belén," *El Mundo*, October 2, 2004, 30, www.elmundo.es/diario/opinion/.

11. Belén Gopegui, *El lado frío de la almohada* (Barcelona: Anagrama, 2004), 208. All translations from the original text are mine.

12. Ernesto Che Guevara, "Socialism and Man in Cuba," in *Socialism and Man in Cuba* (New York: Pathfinder, 1989), 15.

13. Rosa Miriam Elizalde and M. H. Lagarde, "Belén Gopegui: 'Tengo una posición rara en la literatura española,'" www.rebelion.org/, October 19, 2004.

14. Javier Burgos Tejero, "Entrevista a la escritora Belén Gopegui," www.dprogresivo.com/nuevoclaridad/, November 12, 2007.

15. See Juliana Barbassa, "The New Cuban Capitalist," in Lydia Chávez, ed., *Capitalism, God, and a Good Cigar: Cuba Enters the Twenty-First Century* (Durham, NC: Duke University Press, 2005), for a journalistic account of this process. For an insider's account of the changes of the Special Period, see Antonio José Ponte, "La fiesta vigilada" (The supervised party), in Iván de la Nuez, ed., *Cuba y el día después: Doce ensayistas nacidos con la revolución imaginan el futuro* (Barcelona: Mondadori, 2001), 23–33. Both accounts mention the emphasis on money in this period.

16. De la Nuez, *Fantasía*, 12.

17. Rafael Argullol, *El Boomeran(g): Blog literario en español*, www.elboomeran.com/blog/2/blog-de-rafael-argullol/.

18. Alberto Ruiz de Samaniego and Miguel A. Ramos Sánchez, *La generación de la democracia: Nuevo pensamiento filosófico* (Madrid: Tecnos, 2002), 53, 52.

19. Isabel Soler, "Entrevista con Rafael Argullol," *Cuadernos hispanoamericanos* 586 (1999), 91–101, 95.

20. Rafael Argullol, *Davalú o el dolor* (Barcelona: RBA Libros, 2001), 103.

21. De la Nuez, *Fantasía*, 10.

22. Argullol, interview with the author, January 29, 2009.

23. Eduardo Portella, ed., *Thinking at Crossroads: In Search of New Languages* (Paris: UNESCO, 2002), 149.

24. Ana María Dopico, "Picturing Havana: History, Vision and the Scramble for Cuba," *Nepantla: Views from the South* 3, no. 3 (2002), 451–93, 11.

25. Argullol, *Davalú*, 82.

26. Ibid., 78.

27. As defined by Damián Fernández, *doble moral* refers to the distance between socialism in theory and in practice, which results in "ritualistic participation" in politics and "a dual set

of behaviors, attitudes, and opinions, one set for the public sphere and one for the private." Fernández, "The Good, the Bad and the Ugly: The Normalization of Cuba's Society in Post-Transition," in Marifeli Pérez-Stable, ed., *Looking Forward: Comparative Perspectives on Cuba's Transition* (Notre Dame, IN: University of Notre Dame Press, 2007), 96–119.

28. Abilio Estévez, *Los palacios distantes* (Barcelona: Tusquets, 2002), 96.

29. Argullol, *Davalú*, 96.

30. See Ponte, "La fiesta vigilada," 27.

31. See José Quiroga, *Cuban Palimpsests* (Minneapolis: University of Minnesota Press, 2005), 27.

32. Rafael Rojas, *El arte de la espera: Notas al margen de la política cubana* (Madrid: Colibrí, 1998), 147–48.

33. Soler, "Entrevista," 101.

34. Argullol, *Davalú*, 97.

III

Transnationalism

13

Transnationalism and the Havana Cigar

Commodity Chains, Networks, and Knowledge Circulation

JEAN STUBBS

After the 1959 Cuban revolution, when the United States declared its trade embargo on Cuba, the race was on to produce a quality "Havana cigar" and leaf elsewhere in the Caribbean. This was a new twist to a long history. By the mid-nineteenth century the handmade "Havana" had become world famous as *the* luxury cigar, and while by the mid-twentieth century, in Cuba and the world over, cigarettes far out-shadowed cigars in terms of production and sales, the Havana still held its own niche luxury market. It also lay at the heart of transnational processes linked to commodity chains, networks, and knowledge circulation. Seed, agricultural and industrial know-how, and human capital were all transplanted for its replication, a process accentuated by major migratory waves linked to such landmark political upheavals as Cuba's late nineteenth-century struggles for independence from Spain, early twentieth-century U.S. occupation, and the mid-century revolution. This led to often-disputed identical brands, produced in Cuba and abroad, by island and émigré Cubans; distributed through parallel chains, networks, and circuits; and promoted through high-profile cigar conferences and events, both in Cuba and abroad. In turn, this phenomenon created a complex multi-tiered licit and illicit system that aimed to capitalize on the prestige of the "authentic" product. A similar phenomenon is to be observed in brand disputes and international court cases regarding other products of Cuba, most notably rum—Bacardi and Havana Club being a case in point. The Havana cigar, however, has been elevated to almost iconic status, which makes it of particular interest as a prism to explore broader issues. Here I have chosen three Caribbean island territories—Jamaica, Puerto Rico, and the Dominican Republic—to illustrate this. Each played a major part in Havana cigar history, and the fortunes of all three have waxed and waned in tandem with not only Cuba but also their own transnational commodity and migration histories.

A Framework for Understanding the Global Havana Cigar

Global commodity chain analysis[1] tends to focus on the substitution of a product or parts of a product by other such products that are cheaper to produce, different in quality, or new on the market; and on opportunities for traders to reorganize supply and create consumer alternatives, unbound by former dependencies and monopolies of suppliers. The appearance of new products or varieties does not necessarily entail the collapse of the older chain because parallel structures frequently develop. The emergence of informal or illicit economies and their impact on a chain are more difficult to trace, yet these hidden parts of a global commodity chain may be essential to an understanding of its entire functioning. Historians have frequently presented chains as linear connections among producers, traders, and consumers. Extending the analysis to encompass networks and circuits of knowledge challenges us to understand the fragilities and disconnections of their political, social, and cultural dimensions.[2]

The Havana cigar as a global commodity cannot be understood as an element in a primarily economic chain but, rather, as an article shaped by markers whose political, social, cultural, and migratory ramifications not only create parallel, substitute, informal, and illicit commodity networks but also whole competing social and cultural worlds and imaginaries. In this process neighboring Caribbean islands and surrounding mainland territories—the Dominican Republic, Jamaica, Honduras, Mexico, Nicaragua, and Puerto Rico—feature prominently. They are, however, part of a far wider network of territories, ranging from the Americas—Brazil (Bahía), Colombia (El Carmen), Ecuador (close to Quito), and the United States (Connecticut, Florida-Georgia, New York)—to Europe (the Canary Islands), Africa (Cameroon), and Asia (the Philippines and Indonesia).[3]

Agricultural science and technology (that is, management, land tenure, labor, migration, and consumption patterns) and forms of communication all play a part in this complex. Thus the publication *Cigar Aficionado*, from its founding in the early 1990s, was highly successful in engineering—socially and culturally as well as commercially—an anti-antismoking campaign to promote the consumption of cigars, nurturing a cult of "cigar cool" whose epitome was the Havana.[4] Written for the connoisseur and punctuated by aggressive marketing, its articles signal where Havana seed leaf is being grown outside of Cuba, and by whom, and also who is manufacturing and marketing off-island Havanas, and where. This, then, is the world of the "offshore Havana cigar," or what those in the trade in Cuba refer to as *dobles marcas*—the term replacing the older *imitaciones* and *falsificaciones* long lamented by the Cuban industry. Today, as in the past, these competing brands raise issues of ownership and sovereignty, economic pragmatism, and political nationalism.

In twenty years of research on the "global Havana cigar," my own conceptual questions initially centered around such issues, with the Havana as my prism. My approach was threefold. First, I traced the formation, growth, and decline of post-1868 and post-1959 Cuban cigar émigré communities, exploring economic, social, and political processes in receiver territories as well as in Cuba. Second, I charted the response to those communities from political and corporate tobacco and political interests abroad, especially the extent to which they were co-opted and the ways in which they subsequently had an impact on the broader tobacco and political history. Third, I delved into the politics of historical myth and memory in émigré culture, associated in the United States with post-1868 political idealism and post-1959 political conservatism.

A more sweeping global history began to emerge, however. By the mid-nineteenth century the Havana cigar had become the yardstick by which other cigar economies were measured: if the Cuban cigar economy was depressed, other cigar economies tended to ride high, and vice versa.[5] Several of the histories of these other economies are today all but forgotten, while others have been reinvented, but a fourfold typology linked to Cuba can be posited.

Thus, there are firstly the closely interlocking cigar-manufacturing histories of territories with significant migratory flows out of and into Cuba. This would apply to the Florida-Cuban cigar history, whose product was boosted and eventually destroyed by two U.S. trade embargoes on Cuba: 1890, in the buildup to Cuba's final war of independence from Spain; and 1960, after the revolution. Over and beyond the better-known Cuban émigré South Florida cigar histories of Key West, Tampa, and Ybor City, the history encompasses the lesser-known histories of the Florida-Georgia shade-tobacco belt, and links the aptly named cigar centers of Amsterdam and Havana, as well as Jacksonville, Quincy, Thomasville, and others.[6] There are also the little-known nineteenth- and early twentieth-century histories of the tobacco workers, manufacturers, and growers who left Cuba to work in New York cigar manufacturing and the Jamaican tobacco economy. Across the Atlantic the traveling cigar is integral to Canary Islands history, from the late nineteenth- and early twentieth-century mass migratory waves of Canary Islanders into Cuban tobacco, in the context of the Canaries' geostrategic position on the route between Spain, Europe, Africa, and the Americas. Subsequent return migration was to fuel the Canaries' own tobacco-growing and production, using a blend of tobaccos from different parts of the world.

The closely intertwined histories of Puerto Rican and Cuban tobacco show no significant tobacco migration, but do reveal closely monitored trade networks and circuits of knowledge. Puerto Rico's turbulent tobacco history in the late nineteenth and early twentieth centuries, fostered by U.S. capital with the U.S. occupation of 1898 after the end of Spanish colonial rule, in turn was undercut in the mid-twentieth century in the U.S.-blessed, Puerto Rican strategy of Operation Bootstrap. The early twentieth century saw considerable numbers of Puerto Rican cigar workers heading north to U.S. centers of cigar manufacturing, especially New York, where they joined Cuban émigré cigar workers. State-engineered migrant farm labor programs of the third quarter of the twentieth century then transported displaced farmers and agricultural laborers from what were once Puerto Rican tobacco areas to Connecticut, whose shade tobacco can be traced back to Cuban leaf and cigars.

Still other cigar histories have seen small yet significant catalysts of Cuban cigar migration—including those of late nineteenth-century Mexico and late twentieth-century Nicaragua and Honduras, and also Ecuador and Brazil. Most notably these also include the Dominican Republic, which was hitherto far behind in the Havana cigar stakes but during the 1990s was reinvented as home to the born-again Havana cigar for the U.S. market, where the real Havana was forbidden fruit.

Finally, the history shows Asian and African interconnections, linked to global and imperial cigar expansion involving the United Kingdom, the Netherlands, Germany, and France. The shade tobacco of Cuba, Florida-Georgia, and Connecticut was derived from, and in competition with, that of Sumatra (and Java), itself derived from Cuban and U.S. seed (tobacco being indigenous to the Americas). Developed initially by the Dutch and marketed primarily in the Netherlands and Germany, the cheaper Indonesian leaf and ultimately cigar were destined to flood the global market. Likewise, the French moved into territories such as Cameroon, whose leaf also became part of the global cigar blend; while the tobacco history of the Philippines—the third-last colony of Spain, along with Cuba and Puerto Rico, and a U.S. colony until 1946—mirrored that of its erstwhile colonial counterparts.

What follows traces the commodity and migration histories linked to the cigar of one Caribbean territory drawn from each of the first three groupings. First is Jamaica, which witnessed foundational Cuban cigar migration, followed by Puerto Rico, with insignificant migration but significant trade and knowledge transfer. Both islands' flourishing late nineteenth-century and early twentieth-century tobacco economies have today all but disappeared. Finally is the Dominican Republic, where post-1959 Cuban migration catalyzed its contemporary positioning as an offshore cigar production epicenter.

Jamaica: From Cuban Émigrés to "Soldiers of War"

Tobacco was grown and manufactured in Jamaica by Cubans fleeing from Cuba's First War of Independence from Spain. A half century later, what initially developed as an economic mainstay of the émigré community and became a springboard for support of Cuba's independence effort had evolved into a Jamaican sector, employing British and U.S. capital.[7]

Strategically close to Cuba, Jamaica was an important route for late nineteenth-century gunrunning and expeditions to the island, and provided refuge for some of Cuba's leading independence leaders, activists, and their families. Among them were tobacco growers and cigar workers, dealers, and manufacturers, notably Benito and Juan Machado, whose factory heralded Kingston's early industrialization. Predating this, in 1873, a treatise on the growth, culture, and manufacture of tobacco was published in Kingston by Guillermo González, "in grateful idea towards a country in which his compatriots have found congenial shelter." This was a time when it was declared "a scandal that with the East and West Indies in our possession we [the British] had not a good cigar from either."[8]

Efforts were made to support Cuban refugees by combining Cuban seed with technical knowledge, and by 1883–84 the Blue Book Departmental Report could cite former Cuban General Villegas as "an extensive cultivator of Havana tobacco at Colbeck's plantation."[9] The quality of the leaf was upgraded using the best Cuban Vuelta Abajo seed brought in through the offices of the British consul in Havana and Hope Gardens in Kingston, and with improved methods of cultivation. By 1891–92 the Governor's Report claimed that an increase in cigar exports indicated a taste for quality Jamaican-made cigars, and the Machado Company took a London Chamber of Commerce prize for its product.[10]

After the introduction of the cigar machine in the late 1920s and 1930s, handmade cigar operations wound down. They ended in 1954, when the then B. & J. B. Machado Tobacco Company became the Cigarette Company of Jamaica Ltd., later to be bought by British-owned Carreras, subsequently part of Imperial Tobacco. A new chapter opened in Cuban-Jamaican cigar manufacturing in 1965, when exiled Havana cigar manufacturer Ramón Cifuentes established the General Cigar Company of Jamaica, renamed Cifuentes y Cía in 1976, and produced brands such as Partagás. There was a renewed spurt in Jamaican growing and manufacturing in the 1990s, but both sectors have since relocated to the Dominican Republic.

What is of interest here, however, is a little-known offshore interlude to Jamaica's cigar history during the Second World War, linked to another Havana cigar story in what was once known as Connecticut Tobacco Valley. At its height in the early 1920s, the famous shade wrapper was grown from a leaf that agronomists perfected from Cuban seed.[11] A 1960s revival was not on a scale to stem the steady tide of long-term decline that had started with competition from the Sumatra leaf and was compounded with the 1950s introduction of a homogenized binder and wrapper and the 1964 U.S. Surgeon General's report on the hazards of smoking; the failure was sealed with offshore relocation, again primarily to the Dominican Republic.

Often recounted as a proud New England story of family dynasties, shade tobacco growing was, according to writer James O'Gorman, "a high risk, labor intensive, controversial but potentially rewarding occupation for owners if not for laborers. Cultivation demands constant attention, backbreaking hard work in the fields and under the tents, and knowledgeable adherence to detail in the curing sheds and stripping and sorting rooms."[12] Laced with cutthroat business and labor practices, the Connecticut tobacco story was narrated in snapshot detail by local writer Mildred Savage, whose best-selling 1958 novel *Parrish*, made into a 1961 Hollywood movie of the same name, was described at the time as a scenic, tobacco-road soap opera.[13]

Growers met seasonal labor requirements with immigrant and migrant workers—Irish in the nineteenth century, followed by eastern and southern Europeans of peasant stock—often met off the boats by middlemen and sold to farmers, a practice described in 1911 as "a little nearer the slave trade than anything I had experienced."[14] The growers employed child labor until legislation prevented that; they then turned to local high school students and southern black college students from Florida, Georgia, and Virginia, disparagingly referred to locally as "plantation darkies or plantation negroes."[15]

During the Second World War, with tobacco having been declared essential to the Allied war effort, growers recruited men from the British West Indies. Invariably referred to as "Jamaicans," these laborers came primarily from Jamaica but also from the Bahamas, Barbados, Grenada, Antigua, and British Honduras. Fay Clarke Johnson, a Jamaican who in the early 1970s relocated with her family from Montreal to Hartford, worked with the West Indian Social Club in Connecticut to document testimonies of their all but lost history in her 1995 book *Soldiers of the Soil*.[16] They told her of their U.S. points of entry in Florida, of Louisiana holding barracks, and of then being sent to Michigan, Ohio, New York, and Connecticut; of sailing on the SS *Shank*, with 4,000 to 5,000 of them packed together in a ship made to hold only 1,900; and subhuman conditions with little food and water. The camps they lived in were basic, and men kept to camp or moved in groups, because they met with hostility even while being praised for conducting themselves "as gentlemen and as good British subjects." There were nonetheless those who demanded their rights, as expressed, for example, in a telegram sent to President Franklin Roosevelt from George Christie, of Manchester, Jamaica: "Jamaicans dissatisfied of conditions on General Cigar Farm, driven as dumb cattle, work under intimidation. United Nations fight for freedom, justice and fair play. We should have same. Please investigate."[17]

The war's end in 1945 signaled the end of the "Jamaican" program, and more than thirty thousand Jamaicans, Bahamians, other West Indians, and Hondurans working on farms were to be sent home at the end of the season. Few who had been there for six years had plans to return home—those who worked for seven were entitled to stay permanently—and Hartford's West Indian Social Club was instrumental in helping them settle and find work. Hence, in Savage's novel, Parrish and his mother are greeted when they arrive on the tobacco farm by Gladstone, "one of the Colored boys," who speaks in what Parrish describes as "a strange Calypso rhythm."[18] The "boy" is from Jamaica, Parrish is told—one of those who stayed.

Puerto Rico: From Factories and Fields to New York and New England

By the 1940s more than half of the grading of Connecticut shade tobacco was done in Puerto Rico, with some of the tobacco going into cigars made on the island, but most returning for machine manufacture on the U.S. mainland. After the war, in 1948, the Puerto Rican Department of Labor Migration Division (Departamento de Trabajo División de Migración, DTDM) was set up, and one-quarter of the Puerto Rican migrants sent to the mainland United States went to work in tobacco. Many of them were recruited from what were once tobacco areas: San Lorenzo, Barranquitas, Caguas, Comerío, Cayey.

Ruth Glasser charted the link between island and mainland in *Aquí me quedo* [Here I stay]: *Puerto Ricans in Connecticut* (1997). She documented the agricultural and industrial upheavals behind migration, from U.S. occupation in 1898 to the decline of small farming and displaced rural families pouring into San Juan. Most significantly, the post–Second World War Operation Bootstrap was designed to attract manufacturing, but companies failed to provide sufficient jobs to compensate for the loss of agricultural land to industrialization, which displaced more rural families and workers, and resulted in an estimated 78 percent decline in the agricultural labor force in the years 1940–79. Island officials concluded that at least sixty thousand workers a year would have to leave in order for unemployment not to rise. Years earlier, Connecticut tobacco concerns had gone to Puerto Rico and there employed many who later became migrants from Puerto Rico's own tobacco valley to Connecticut. "Ironically," Glasser commented, "they came to the mainland to try to get a living wage from the very same employers."[19]

Puerto Rican historians have documented the late nineteenth- and early twentieth-century heyday of Puerto Rican tobacco, and its paradigmatic relationship with the United States and Cuba; and the life stories of feminist writer and cigar factory "lector" (reader) Luisa Capetillo and of New York–based cigar maker Bernardo Vega provide glimpses into the Cuban–Puerto Rican–U.S. cigar connection.[20] By the mid-1960s, the story was very different: 20 percent of the Puerto Rican migration to the United States was to Connecticut, second only to New Jersey. The records of the Connecticut Shade Tobacco Growers Agricultural Association, the DTDM Hartford Office, and Connecticut local press and other holdings from the mid-1950s to the mid-1970s all extensively detail the use, and abuse, of Puerto Rican migrant labor.[21]

Signed annual contracts stipulated that laborers had to be strong in physique, in good health, free from communicable diseases, and accustomed to hard work; they must have no police records or reputation as troublemakers, and be willing to work and live in the same boardinghouses with domestic workers and British West Indian workers. At least one in ten must have a working knowledge of English.

Most telling was how the battle to improve wages and conditions contributed to the suspension of the program. By the late 1960s, the churches, the Young Lords activists, the Hartford branch of the Puerto Rican Socialist Party, and lawyers from Legal Services offices all worked in support of the farmworkers, as did the Industrial Mission of the Episcopal Church in Puerto Rico, which hired a staff of organizers for the Puerto Rican Migrant Support Committee, replaced in 1972 by the Ecumenical Ministry of Agricultural Workers. Incoming workers in 1973 might have been met with jostling and insults: "cerdos que se venden por unos centavos" (pigs bought for a few cents), "negros sucios" (dirty niggers), "esclavos de la colonia" (slaves from the colony),[22] but the more that growers tried to curb access to farms and camps, the greater the protests.

In summer 1974, United Farm Workers' leader César Chávez lent support to the struggle, but the attempt to have a farmworkers bill passed in the Connecticut General Assembly was frustrated. Growers, it was reported, "insisted that an anti-strike clause must be included in the bill, or else their livelihoods would be in danger. The tobacco growers also threatened to move their operations to Latin America, where they hoped to find both good growing conditions and a docile labor force."[23] Newspaper articles, protests, and court cases had focused a great deal of attention on the Puerto Rican migrant farmworker program, which shrank from some twelve thousand workers in 1974 to less than two thousand in 1984 as farms mechanized and operations relocated abroad; Puerto Ricans still in the state sought to settle in nearby cities and find other work.[24]

The Dominican Republic: From Connecticut to Cibao to New York

The late twentieth-century Cuban-Dominican connection directly follows from this Puerto Rican history, as companies headed south.[25] In the accepted twentieth-century periodization of Dominican tobacco history, 1903–29 saw the rise of manufacturing in cigars and then cigarettes, in tandem with the growth of the central Cibao region's agriculture and industry and of its capital, Santiago de los Caballeros, home to León Jimenes's La Aurora cigar factory.[26] From 1930 to 1961 the Cibao stagnated under General Rafael Leónidas Trujillo's state monopoly Compañía Anónima del Tabaco (CAT). The post-Trujillo years, 1962–82, saw renewed expansion, with León Jimenes undercutting CAT, and post-1982 witnessed the rise of the Cibao's global cigar positioning.

After the 1959 Cuban revolution, the seeds were (literally) sown for the Cuban-type Dominican leaf to replace the embargoed Cuban leaf on the U.S. market, and Dominican overtook Cuban production and export levels by the late 1980s. In 1962 Washington sent the exiled Cuban tobacco agronomist Napoleón Padilla to help set up the Dominican Tobacco Institute (INTABACO).[27] In 1963 Cuban cigar leaf seed was introduced; 1964–65 saw the first experiments in producing the San Vicente wrapper, also from Cuba, although it was not planted commercially until 1974. By now administrators and other employees of tobacco estates and processing and packing plants were exiled Cubans. Thus, Fernando Ferrán refers to "the help of Cuban farmers and producers who transposed a technology that was relatively complex ... after Castro took power in Cuba. It was in the interest of the Dominican government ... to take over the market that the Cuban government had lost in the United States."[28]

Tobacco exports doubled in value from 1962 to 1971, with the Cibao region producing 70 percent of the country's tobacco.

Cuban émigré tobacco interests operated in Nicaragua after 1963, with land grants and concessions from President Anastasio Somoza, but the 1979 Nicaraguan revolution ushered in a shift to Honduras and the Dominican Republic, where free trade zones (FTZs) offered cheap labor and tax concessions for foreign investors.[29] In 1978, in the three main FTZs of La Romana, San Pedro de Macorís, and Santiago, some forty FTZ tobacco plants employed more than four thousand workers.[30] By 1984 the country had sixty such plants, and by 1988 it was the largest supplier of leaf to the United States and the leading world cigar exporter (more than 50 million units), followed by Cuba (49 million) and Honduras (32 million). By the early 1990s a small group of companies dominated the sector—León Asensio in Tamboril was one of the largest agro-industrial complexes—and trade was controlled by six U.S., Dutch, and Spanish exporting companies and their Dominican subsidiaries.

The time was ripe for the engineered comeback of *Cigar Aficionado*, whose 1992 inaugural issue carried three features: two on Cuba, in crisis following the breakup of the Eastern European socialist bloc, and one on the burgeoning Dominican Republic.[31] Dominican exports grew from 73 million in 1994 to 320 million in 1998, predominantly to the United States, and tobacco was third in exports (after ferro-nickel and sugar). The *Miami Herald* delightedly reported that Cuban cigar experts would be spending several weeks in the Dominican Republic in the winter of 1998, observing production and marketing techniques.[32] There were by then 130 registered cigar manufacturers in the Dominican Republic, 18 in FTZs, employing 125,000, with some 55,000 in agriculture. Santiago's Victor Espaillat Mera FTZ (established 1975) produced 80 percent of the country's cigars, and Santiago's population had doubled from the early 1980s to the mid-1990s, as had other cigar centers (Villa González, Licey, San José de las Matas, Licey, Janico, Villa Bosono, and Tamboril).

Yet all was not well. While traditional companies strengthened, a multitude of smaller companies formed. Some of these were operated by Cubans long in the business, but many others had little or no knowledge, which led to poor-quality leaf and cigars. According to Cuban American Carlos Fuente, who relocated from Tampa in 1980, Tamboril was a Vietnam, a war zone—they were shooting machine guns in the streets. A Santiago FTZ was attractive by comparison, and export factories clustered there, busing in workers from Tamboril. This changed with the boom, when newcomers in Tamboril began poaching in earnest. "We woke up one January," Cuban American Manuel Quesada declared, "and between Fuente, Davidoff, ourselves and León Jimenes, we were missing 300 to 400 cigar-makers."[33] La Romana, in the east, was sheltered from the "roller wars," whereby Tabacalera de García fared better than most. Tamboril, however, which went from two to eighty factories, saw sixty of these "mavericks" go out of business in 1997–99. Such was the tobacco glut that, pressured by growers, the state intervened to buy tobacco at above-market prices and restrict planting; and President Leonel Fernández was urged to find a solution to the worst tobacco crisis in memory.

It was the major companies that subsequently picked up the business, such that in 2002 five main manufacturers were in place: Tabacalera Arturo Fuente; Tabacalera de García (subsidiary of Altadis U.S.A, whose brands included H. Upmann, La Corona, Montecristo, and Romeo y Julieta); General Cigar (including Cohiba, Macanudo—for which Jamaica was once famous—and Partagás); MATASA; and Tabacos Dominicanos (including Davidoff). Tabacalera de García's La Romana factory was declared the largest factory under one roof in the world.

Nothing, however, could stem a rural-urban-overseas drift. In the 1980s Fernando Ferrán and Patricia Pessar studied seven communities linked with major export commodities, including, for tobacco, Licey and Tamboril, and Max Castro also studied Licey.[34] These researchers documented small farmers driven into the ranks of the landless searching for agricultural work, for whom emigration became a strategy. From 1980 to 1990 the "Dominican York" population doubled, becoming the fastest-growing ethnic group in a city that by 2000 was home to more than half the million-plus Dominicans in the United States. A dynamic enclave small-business economy emerged, including small storefront *tabaquerías* that hand-rolled cigars, some bought from Cubans, others started up by Dominicans but playing on Cuba's name—as in Rosa Cubana. Typically these entrepreneurs came from Tamboril, Licey, and Santiago.[35]

At What Cost and Whither the Future?

In the peak year of 1997, the Santiago de Caballeros daily *Listín Diario* brought out a new supplement, *Cigarro,* whose second issue featured a congratulatory letter to the editor from José León: "In this day and age of real globalization and world integration, in which the comparative advantages of each nation need to be strongly promoted, the Dominican Republic must show the world that it is we who offer the best beaches, the best sun, the best *merengue,* and above all, the best cigar in the world."[36]

David Savona, writing in 2004 in *Cigar Aficionado,* was more circumspect: "It's hard to imagine a cigar world without the Dominican Republic, but the country hasn't been a market leader for long. Although its oldest cigar maker, La Aurora S.A., has been in business for a century, most of the cigars it made in the past were for local consumption. In the 1970s the first free trade zones opened in the country, welcoming companies that would make cigars strictly for export. It took nearly a decade for the Dominican Republic to overtake the Canary Islands and Jamaica to become the leading cigar producer for the United States."[37]

At the start of the Dominican boom, Guillermo León was named executive vice-president of La Aurora. Charged with developing the U.S. market, he became a stalwart of ProCigar, the Dominican cigar association. Questioned by *Cigar Aficionado*, he doubted that they would establish a factory in Cuba—not only were their roots not Cuban, but they were also very traditional and very Dominican, defending their national pride to the end. "We have good relationships with people from Havana. They have visited us at La Aurora. But that's it.[38]

Dominican cigar "success" is undeniable. Yet at what cost, with the loss of Jamaican and Puerto Rican tobacco, and with a Dominican model whereby the dispossessed have poured out of the countryside and into the cities of Santiago, Santo Domingo, and New York? And what might happen when the U.S. embargo on Cuba does finally end? Will the Dominican-produced cigar hold its own or will the inevitable delight of the forbidden fruit of Cuba oust it from favor, notwithstanding the higher price of the "authentic" Havana? The intrepid U.S. cigar smoker already acquires Cuban cigars through various channels—buying them when traveling abroad in third countries or over the Internet or through distant friends. More importantly perhaps, in the fast-changing global economy in which China has already emerged as Cuba's principal cigar market, the real question to be asked is whether the U.S. market might be destined to remain marginal, with or without the embargo.

Notes

For the ideas expressed in this article I am indebted to my colleagues in the Commodities of Empire British Academy Research Project, jointly hosted by the University of London's Institute for the Study of the Americas and the Open University's Ferguson Centre for African and Asian Studies; and in our sister collaborative projects Plants, People and Work (International Institute of Social History, Amsterdam) and Global Commodity Chains (University of Konstanz). The research underpinning this article was facilitated through semesters spent as a Rockefeller Scholar at the University of Florida (1993) and at Florida International University and the University of Puerto Rico (1998), and by funding from the British Academy and London Metropolitan University's Caribbean Studies Centre. I owe a special debt of gratitude to the Center for Latin American Studies, University of Florida, for having me as their 2011 Spring Semester Bacardi Scholar, enabling me to further my Florida research and to benefit not only from their excellent Latin American and Caribbean Library Special Collections but also from the knowledge and ideas of colleagues who have helped inform my thinking.

1. A classic on this subject is Gary Gereffi and Miguel Korzeniewicz, eds., *Commodity Chains and Global Capitalism* (Westport, CT: Praeger, 1994), which includes Terence Hopkins and Immanuel Wallerstein, "Commodity Chains: Construct and Research."

2. I am thinking here of Appadurai's regimes of values and concepts of commodification. See Arjun Appadurai, ed., *The Social Life of Things: Commodities in Cultural Perspective* (Cambridge: Cambridge University Press, 1986); and *Modernity at Large: Cultural Dimensions of Globalization* (Minneapolis: University of Minnesota Press, 1996). See also James Ferguson, "Cultural Exchange: New Developments in the Anthropology of Commodities," *Cultural Anthropology* 3 (1988), 488–513; Philip Raikes, Michael Friis Jensen, and Stefano Ponte, "Global Commodity Chain Analysis and the French *Filière* Approach: Comparison and Critique," *Economy and Society* 29, no. 3 (August 2000), 390–417; Peter Dicken, Philip F. Kelly, Kris Olds, and Henry Wai-Chung Yeung, "Chains and Networks, Territories and Scales: Towards a Relational Framework for Analysing the Global Economy," *Global Networks* 1, no. 2 (2001), 89–112; Alex Hughes and Suzanne Reimer, eds., *Geographies of Commodity Chains* (London and New York: Routledge, 2004).

3. This is detailed in my "*El Habano* and the World It Has Shaped: Cuba, Connecticut and Indonesia," *Cuban Studies* 41, no. 1 (2010), 39–67.

4. I discuss this in "Havana Cigars and the West's Imagination," in Sander L. Gilman and Zhou Xun, eds., *Smoke: A Global History of Smoking* (London: Reaktion Press, 2004).

5. I concur with Juan José Baldrich's analysis of "the Cuba paradigm," derived from his work on Puerto Rican tobacco. See, for instance, Juan José Baldrich, *Sembraron la no siembra: los cosecheros de tabaco puertorriqueños frente a las corporaciones tabacaleras, 1920-1934* (Río Piedras, P.R., Ediciones Huracán, 1988).

6. I am indebted to Paul Losch, assistant head of the Latin American and Caribbean Library at the University of Florida, for initially dropping the comment that there had been Cuban cigar factories in Gainesville and pointing out the footnote in Gerardo Castellanos, *Motivos de Cayo Hueso* (Havana: Ucar, García y Cía, 1935), 300. Both he and head librarian Richard Phillips have since plied me with references and articles, and Kyle Doherty has been conducting research with me that suggests a more significant North Florida history than previously thought, spanning Gainesville, Fernandina, Lake City, Live Oak, St. Augustine, and Waldo.

7. I documented the earlier Cuban-Jamaican history in "Political Idealism and Commodity Production: Cuban Tobacco in Jamaica, 1870–1930," *Cuban Studies* 25 (1995), 51–81.

8. Guillermo P. González, *Tobacco Culture: As Practiced in Cuba* (Port Royal, Jamaica: De Cordova, McDougal, 1873). For the British declaration, see Hon. W. Fawcett, "Tobacco in Jamaica," *West Indian Bulletin* 8, no. 2 (1907), 209. See also *The Machado Story: A Pioneer Industry in Jamaica, 1874–1962* (Kingston, Jamaica: B. & J. B. Machado Co. Ltd., n.d.). They began importing the leaf from Cuba and employing some twenty-five Cuban cigar makers in 1874. Within a few years they had three hundred workers, and they registered their first trademarks: Fantasía Habanera Cigarros Superiores and La Tropical.

9. "Governor's Report on Blue Book of 1881," *Jamaica Departmental Reports* (Kingston,

Jamaica: Government Printing Establishment), xxv. In the report the general's name was given as "Vijegas."

10. "Governor's Report on Blue Book of 1891–92" and "Director of Public Gardens and Plantations," *Jamaica Departmental Reports* (Kingston, Jamaica: Government Printing Establishment), xvii.

11. See P. J. Anderson, "Growing Tobacco in Connecticut," *Connecticut Agricultural Experiment Station Bulletin* 564 (January 1953); and Randall R. Kincaid, "Shade Tobacco Growing in Florida," *Quincy North Florida Experimental Station Bulletin* 136 (May 1960 [1956]). Anadel Schnip and Katya Williamson, eds., *Changing Landscape through People: Connecticut Valley Tobacco, a Documentary of Photographs and Writing for the 1980s* (n.p., n.d.), is one of several nostalgic photographic books capturing Connecticut's shade past.

12. James F. O'Gorman, *Connecticut Valley Vernacular: The Vanishing Landscape and Architecture of the New England Tobacco Fields*, with photographs by Jack Delano (Philadelphia: University of Pennsylvania Press, 2002), 5.

13. Mildred Savage, *Parrish* (New York: Simon and Shuster, 1958).

14. Quoted in O'Gorman, *Connecticut Valley Vernacular*, 37.

15. S. K. Close, "The Ties That Bind: Southwest Georgians, Black College Students, and Migration to Hartford," *Journal of South Georgia History* 15 (2000), 19. For employment of high school students, see *Windsor Storytellers: A Chronicle of 20th Century Life in Windsor*, vols. 1 and 2 (Windsor, CT: Windsor Historical Society, 1999).

16. Fay Clarke Johnson, *Soldiers of the Soil* (New York: Vantage Press, 1995). She recalls, "Fifty years ago, around the World War II years, there was no talk about the hazards of tobacco. Rather, tobacco was considered to be the savior of the day . . . almost as important as bullets" (p. 3). Smoking promised contentment, satisfaction, consolation. The rallying cry was "Keep the Boys in Smokes." Thousands of Jamaican men signed up to contribute to the war effort while also seeking adventure and economic betterment.

17. Clarke Johnson, *Soldiers of the Soil*, 70, 80; quotations are from Jamaica's *Daily Gleaner*, October 11, 1943, and *Hartford Courant*, July 29, 1944.

18. Savage, *Parrish*, 12.

19. Ruth Glasser, *Aquí me quedo: Puerto Ricans in Connecticut* (Middletown: Connecticut Humanities Council, 1997), 54–55.

20. See Juan José Baldrich, "From the Origins of Industrial Capitalism in Puerto Rico to Its Subordination to the U.S. Tobacco Trust: Rucabado and Company, 1865–1901," *Revista Mexicana del Caribe* 3, no. 5 (1998), 80–106; M. Burgos Malave, "El conflicto tabacalero entre Cuba y Puerto Rico," *Revista de Estudios Generale*s 4, no. 4 (1989–90), 181–91; Teresita A. Levy, "The History of Tobacco Cultivation in Puerto Rico, 1899–1940," PhD diss., City University of New York, 2007. See also Norma Valle Ferrer, *Luisa Capetillo: Historia de una mujer proscrita* (Río Piedras, P.R.: Editorial Cultural, 1990 [1975]); Julio Ramos, ed., *Amor y anarquía: Los escritos de Luisa Capetillo* (Río Piedras, P.R.: Ediciones Huracán, 1992); and César Andreu Iglesias, ed., *Memoirs of Bernardo Vega*, trans. Juan Flores (New York: Monthly Review Press, 1984 [1977]).

21. Records housed in the Library of CENTRO, the Center for Puerto Rican Studies, Hunter College, City University of New York, were catalogued and made available for public consultation in late 2004. They include the archives of the Farm Labor Program (1848–1993), Connecti-

cut Shade Tobacco Growers Agricultural Association Files (STGAA) (1955–76), Regional and Field Offices (1948–93), Hartford Regional Office (1961–84), and Regional Field Office Farm Laborer Files (1958–83). Rich collections are also housed at Hartford State Library; the Hartford Project, Trinity College, Hartford; University of Connecticut, Storrs; Windsor Tobacco Museum; and the Windsor Historical Society.

22. STGAA, CEPR, Windsor, File 30, Box 2526.

23. Ibid.

24. The Trinity College Hartford Project holds video copies of two excellent documentaries on the Connecticut Puerto Rican and tobacco history: *Puerto Rican Passages* (1995) and *Connecticut's Tobacco Valley* (2001).

25. I draw here on my more detailed discussion in "Reinventing Mecca: Tobacco in the Dominican Republic, 1763–2007," Commodities of Empire Working Paper no. 3, October 2007, www.open.ac.uk/Arts/ferguson-centre/commodities-of-empire/working-papers/index.htm.

26. Grupo León Jimenes celebrated the centenary of La Aurora by opening the state-of-the-art Eduardo León Jimenes Centro Cultural and publishing José Alcántara Almánzar and Ida Hernández Caamaño, *Huella y memoria: E. León Jimenes: un siglo en el camino nacional, 1903–2003* (Santo Domingo: Grupo León, 2003). For the most recent of a spate of tobacco studies since the 1970s, see José Chez Checo and Mu-Kien Adriana Sang, *El tabaco: historia general en República Dominicana* (Santo Domingo: Grupo León Jimenes, 2007).

27. Napoleón S. Padilla, *Memorias de un cubano sin importancia* (Hialeah, FL: A. C. Graphics, 1998).

28. Fernando I. Ferrán, *Tabaco y sociedad: la organización del poder en el ecomercado de tabaco dominicano* (Santo Domingo: Fondo para el Avance de las Ciencias Sociales, 1976), 58.

29. The FTZ explosion had its early beginnings in 1967, when the U.S. conglomerate Gulf & Western took over the U.S.-owned South Puerto Rico Sugar Company, and with it almost 300,000 acres of land around La Romana refinery, and then rapidly diversified. In 1985, when the sugar industry was in crisis, and having profited greatly by speculating on Dominican sugar on the futures market, Gulf & Western sold its Dominican holdings to a Palm Beach–based consortium headed by the Fanjul family—émigrés from Cuba with major sugar holdings, which is a whole other story.

30. Economist Intelligence Unit, *Dominican Republic: Annual Supplement, 1978* (London: EIU, 1978).

31. Gordon Mott, "CigarLand: The Dominican Republic Has Become One of the World's Largest Producers of Premium Cigars," *Cigar Aficionado*, Autumn 1992.

32. Juan O. Tamayo, "Castro to Firm up Ties with Dominicans," *Miami Herald*, August 17, 1998.

33. Marvin R. Shanken, "An Interview with Manuel Quesada: Owner, MATASA, Makers of Fonseca, Licenciados, Romeo y Julieta, Jose Benito, Cubita, Royal Dominicana, Credo and Casa Blanca Cigars," *Cigar Aficionado*, February 1998.

34. Fernando Ferrán and Patricia Pessar, "Dominican Agriculture and the Effects of International Migration," in *Small Country Development and International Labor Flows*, ed. Anthony Maingot (Boulder, CO: Westview Press, 1991); Max Castro, "Dominican Journey: Pat-

terns, Context, and Consequences of Migration from the Dominican Republic to the United States," PhD diss., University of North Carolina, 1985. The creation of the Dominican Studies Institute at City College, City University of New York, provided an impulse to Dominican migration studies; an early entry was Sherri Grasmuck, "International Stair-Step Migration: Dominican Labor in the United States and Haitian Labor in the Dominican Republic," in *Research in the Sociology of Work: Peripheral Workers*, vol. 2, ed. Richard L. Simpson and Ida Harper Simpson (Greenwich, CT, and London: JAI Press, 1983).

35. This I gleaned from an informal survey I conducted in 2006, using a snowball approach, to visit the shops and talk with the rollers.

36. *Cigarro,* magazine of *Listín Diario*, 2 (October 24, 1997), 4.

37. David Savona, "Dominican Dominance," *Cigar Aficionado*, May–June 2004.

38. Gordon Mott, "An Interview with Guillermo León: President, León Jimenes Cigars," *Cigar Aficionado*, July–August 1998.

14

Through the Eyes of Foreign Filmmakers

Contradictions and Paradigms of Cuban Cinema after the Revolution

MARÍA CARIDAD CUMANÁ

The global impact of the Cuban revolution emerged on the sociopolitical map of the 1960s in several different ways. Artists, politicians, sociologists, philosophers, athletes, and celebrities from many countries were curious to visit the island to see for themselves the feat of a group of bearded youngsters under the leadership of a lawyer-turned-leader of the independence movement and later commander-in-chief: Fidel Castro. In the midst of dramatic changes in the economic, social, political, and cultural structures of the country, the government started enforcing new legislation aimed at building a nation not only free from illiteracy, police abuse, and administrative corruption but also, above all, free and independent from U.S. rule. But with the collapse of the Soviet Union and the onset of the Special Period in Cuba, Cuba underwent further change. Thus, in the context of this analysis of Cuban cinema, there exist two separate periods of filmmaking. The 1960s was the beginning of a new historical moment for Cuba with the triumph of the revolution in achieving complete independence from the United States. In addition, there was the advent of faith in new values through complete social, economic, and political changes on the island. Moreover, Cuba became one of the best allies for the socialist bloc in the Caribbean zone. This situation changed by the 1990s with the fall of the Berlin Wall and the disappearance of the socialist bloc as the utopian dream of a better country and the theory of the "new man" died. Cuba lost all of the support that it had received from its socialist allies from the 1960s to the 1980s. The subsequent deep economic crisis affected the whole structure of society in the so-called Special Period and Cubans began a new phase of their survival. Many foreigners attempted to film these changes but with a different perspective: it was not a romantic approach but, rather, a more realistic way to document what was happening on the island after the support that Cuba had received disappeared.

From the very beginning of the revolution, Cuban leaders were aware of the need to educate the people in the ideological principles of the governing system that was chosen to rule the island: the socialist system.[1] The whole educational, political, and cultural structure was immediately geared to that objective, resulting in the creation of several cultural institutions for the preservation and promotion of national culture based on the principles of socialism. In January 1959 the newly established Division of Culture of the Rebel Army undertook the production of two documentaries: *Esta tierra nuestra*, by Tomás Gutiérrez Alea, and *La vivienda*, by Julio García Espinosa. Both films were produced by the Instituto Cubano del Arte y la Industria Cinematográficas (ICAIC, Cuban Institute of the Film Arts and Industry), created on March 24, 1959. Another organization, Casa de las Américas, was founded shortly thereafter, in April 1959, to develop and extend sociocultural relations with the other countries of Latin America; and it was followed in January 1961 by the establishment of the National Council for Culture.

In subsequent years, in the context of these new cultural institutions, the changes and transformations that took place within the Cuban revolution would be captured by the cameras of foreign filmmakers who visited the country. The particularities of the films these visitors made, and what their work shows as documentaries of a given time, are highly revealing—shaping the image of the revolution abroad, mostly in Europe, in the 1960s and 1970s.

In July 1959 French actor Gérard Philipe arrived in Cuba with the intention of making a film about the armed struggle in the Sierra Maestra. Although this project never materialized (Philipe died in November of that year), it was notable as the first attempt by a foreigner to make a film about the country's very recent history after the triumph of the revolution. At the end of that year, Italians Otello Martelli (cinematographer) and Cesare Zavattini (writer) arrived in the country. Martelli would collaborate on what would become the first film made by ICAIC, *Historias de la revolución*, directed by Tomás Gutiérrez Alea. Zavattini collaborated on the script of *El joven rebelde*, made by Julio García Espinosa in 1961. The Italians provided technical support for the then-young Alea and García Espinosa and brought with them the influence of Italian neorealism, but otherwise did not particularly mark the aesthetics of these films.[2]

In September 1960, also at the invitation of ICAIC, Dutch filmmaker Joris Ivens came to Cuba to teach several workshops. As a final exercise, he made the documentaries *Carnet de viaje* and *Pueblo en armas*. Cuban technicians Jorge Herrera, Gustavo Maynulet, Ramón Suárez, Jorge Fraga, José Massip, and Saúl Yelinn participated. As the head of ICAIC's Information Center, Dr. Mario Rodríguez Alemán, noted at the time, "*Carnet de viaje* is a film message to Charles Chaplin, in which Ivens reveals all the truth about Cuba and its Revolution. . . . *Pueblo en armas* shows the creation of the national militia and the operation against the 'worms' in the Escambray Mountains. The exhibition of these documentaries was banned in France by the Ministry of Information, fearful perhaps of the great revolutionary teachings they present."[3] Both documentaries are proof of the filmmaker's enormous interest in showing the new Cuba and its novel social system to the rest of the world. *Carnet de viaje* presents footage of scenes shot in Havana, the Zapata peninsula, Manzanillo, Trinidad, Santiago de Cuba, and the Sierra Maestra, among other places; *Pueblo en armas* presents the war against the bandits in El Escambray.[4]

At the end of 1960, Roman Karmen, the well-known Soviet documentary filmmaker, visited Cuba. Karmen made two documentaries, *Alba de Cuba* and *La lámpara azul*, the latter about the literacy campaign. Then, at the beginning of 1961, the French documentary filmmaker Chris Marker visited Cuba. Marker made two notable documentaries, *¡Cuba Sí!* and *Libertad*. The epic nature of these documentaries and Marker's eagerness to publicize internationally the transformations implemented in Cuba, as well as the close bond existing between Fidel and the people, caused them to be banned in France. The Cuban newspaper *El Mundo* commented on this censorship:

> News has come through *Les Lettres Françaises,* the great Parisian literary weekly newspaper: the Ministry of Information of General de Gaulle's government has banned the screening of *¡Cuba Sí!* and *Libertad*, two documentaries on the Cuban revolution made by Chris Marker. The argument behind the measure is that the two films "constitute an apologia to Castro's regime," and even though it admits that "what the films say or inform about the previous regime is in agreement with the historic truth," it notes that "passing from a right-wing totalitarian regime to another extreme left-wing totalitarian regime has not prevented the occurrence in Cuba of new excesses and multiple violations of freedoms, of which the films in question do not provide any testimony."[5]

Unquestionably, the images captured by Marker revealed his admiration for Fidel Castro as a leader. In an interview Marker stated, "Well, the answers to Castro's questions are chorused by the people, who become increasingly aware of a given problem. But Castro takes these questions from one level to another, gradually enabling everyone to fully understand the issue. And you know, it is extraordinary to see how a million people understand the agricultural program, U.S. imperialism, and socialism."[6]

As closer ties were being established with the countries of the socialist bloc, more filmmakers from these countries visited Cuba. In 1962 Czech filmmaker Vladimir Cech arrived to make the film *Para quién baila La Habana*. The year before, as part of a Czech delegation visiting Cuba, Cech stated, "just like everyone who had a chance to see for the first time the revolutionary enthusiasm of the Cuban people, I was captivated. And I wanted to preserve and convey that impression to everybody else. So I had this idea that it would be interesting to make a film about Havana, about the transformation of old Havana into a new Havana."[7] His good intentions, however, were not enough to produce a good film, as he was not able to capture the spirit of the Cuban people either through the actors or with the script, nor was he careful with certain obvious details, such as showing in the film an edition of *El Quixote* published after the time in which the story takes place. When the film premiered, it received bad reviews. The well-known Cuban critic Guillermo Cabrera Infante, in his article "¿Para quién bailamos?" stated: "The coproduction lacks knowledge of Cuban reality, it fails to understand the psychology of the average Cuban, and the actors' performance is falsely emotional."[8]

ICAIC did not assimilate the lesson it should have learned from this film's false representation of Cuban reality; on the contrary, it allowed four more films to be made by foreign filmmakers, all of whom also failed to capture the Cuban essence. These films were *Crónica cubana* (1963, by Ugo Ulive of Uruguay), *El otro Cristóbal* (1963, by Armand Gatti of France), *Preludio 11* (1963, by Kurt Maetzig of East Germany), and *Soy Cuba* (1964, by Mikhail Kalatozov of the Soviet Union).

Crónica cubana presents the revolutionaries' actions at the beginning of the revolution. The story starts on January 1, 1959, and ends with the victory of the Cuban troops at Playa Girón (Bay of Pigs). The idea of covering in a single film several events in the political scenario of the country's recent history (sabotage to stores—specifically the El Encanto department store—the ideological struggle in universities, the creation of the revolutionary militias, and the Bay of Pigs invasion) turns the actors into caricatures. Once again the reviews criticized the placing in foreign hands of the responsibility for presenting the key events of Cuban history: "the other very serious problem that plagues the film is the inability of Argentine Osvaldo Dragún—scriptwriter—and Uruguayan Ugo Ulive—director—to construct a Cuban atmosphere and to make the characters Cubans. . . . In *Crónica cubana* no one or almost no one seems to be Cuban. The actors move slowly, with great composure; there are long periods of silence and intense looks, in the best tradition of the Argentine or Mexican melodrama."[9] The lack of authenticity weighed down the product of this film project, which apart from being a bad propaganda piece, could not meet the expectations of the audience and much less of the critics.

Gatti's *El otro Cristóbal* is a curious case because, in spite of its artificial and terrible adaptation to cinema, the film was entered and accepted for competition in the 1963 Cannes Film Festival. The synopsis says the film is a satirical parable that presents the destruction of political and moral slavery through the struggle of the people in an imaginary Latin American country. The reviews in France describe the film as "deranged," "completely crazy," "poetic," "naive," and even "wonderful." The French left tried to justify its tangled, complicated plot, while the right described it as "Castro's propaganda" and "demagogic." As the prestigious critic José Manuel Valdés Rodríguez stated,

> "it was a mistake, perhaps a major mistake, of Armand Gatti in this film to use elements of Afro-Cuban mythology, which requires not only a quantitative, but a qualitative and in-depth understanding. . . . One of our Cuban filmmakers, fully mastering the mythology and the rituals, could have used the Afro-Cuban component. But even then, it would have been too risky."[10]

Gatti should never have attempted to capture a theme as complicated as Afro-Cuban mythology, something that calls for years of research and systematic practice.

Maetzig's *Preludio 11* was another film that showed an ignorance of Cuban culture, and of rural and urban life. Very similar in plot to *Crónica cubana*, it presents the clash between revolutionaries and counterrevolutionaries in a simple, schematic manner, with no nuances and above all in a very unnatural manner disconnected from Cuban idiosyncrasies. In this regard, after the premiere, Cuban critic Alejo Beltrán wrote: "Kurt Maetzig does not know the Cuban countryside or the revolution (except in theory). Therefore, if we strike out the word 'revolution,' and eliminate the name of 'Cuba,' the film would be (and actually is) a story of adventures in the Philippines, Nicaragua or Madagascar seen by a person from the moon."[11] Although other critics at least praised the cinematography, the performance of the German actors, and the action scenes, the film did not manage to portray the depth of the conflicts it depicted.

Kalatozov's *Soy Cuba* is a rare case of the rediscovery of a 1964 film that had fallen into oblivion until 1992, when it was screened at the Telluride Film Festival in the United States. It was later shown in San Francisco in 1994, where Francis Ford Coppola and Martin Scorsese saw the film and were struck by Sergei Urusevsky's powerful photography. Both Coppola and Scorsese promoted the release of the film on laser disc. Later, in 1996, it was transferred to VHS in the United States and received favorable reviews and comments. The interest in the film has since continued, with essays, articles, and other texts attempting to deconstruct Kalatozov's objectives in this epic film about the Cuban revolution.

After the premiere, however, several unfavorable reviews were published in the Cuban press. In one of them, critic Luis M. López stated that the camera movements made him suffer from vertigo. Because Urusevski was intent on making each shot a unique photograph, instead of conditioning his camerawork to the actions, the filmmaker did the exact opposite, constantly conditioning the actions to the camera. The result is a feeling of an external folkloric and superficial look at Cuban reality treated in a light and schematic way.

Moreover, foreign critics did not give the film particularly favorable reviews. For example, *Positif* magazine published a particularly harsh comment:

> the photography is constantly deformed, continuously tortured; the characters adopt extremely unnatural sculpture-like positions, against a cloudy background hardly ever seen in Cuba; the peasants look like *mujiks*; the episodes are a "déjà vu" by an overflowing "poetic" mind, and this "transposition," which deprives the film of verisimilitude and of all the interest in a documentary work, is made in an ineluctably pompous sense.[12]

Even outside Cuba, then, the story, the acting, and the ambience were perceived as lacking in legitimacy.

These four nearly simultaneous feature films—the first three produced at the same time and the last one a year later—were not the "fresco" of the most recent struggles for independence in Cuba that the creators had intended them to be. On the contrary, they served only as temporary propaganda for the Cuban revolution abroad, and none of them illustrated the real dimension of building a socialist society that was taking place on the island. Nor did they manage to reveal the essence of Cuban revolutionary culture or of its most elementary social practices. All four of the films reiterate the clashes between revolutionaries and counterrevolutionaries and the attacks and acts of sabotage against Cuba by Yankee imperialism—and all this subject matter is treated naively and unsubtly.

Necessary Nuances in the Imaginary of the Sixties

Critics have said that the foreigners who made documentaries in 1960s Cuba did capture the changes that were taking place and that they also encouraged the young filmmakers who had studied in the workshops to ponder several issues, such as the role of women in the new society, marginality, education, class equality, race, the search for national roots, the need to have an identity as a people, and above all popular participation in the building of socialism.

Although the documentary *¡Cuba Sí!* made by Marker in 1961—described by British researcher and critic Michael Chanan as a film devoted to extolling the revolution—is the best example of this kind of documentary, it is not the only one found in the film production of those years.

In 1963 French filmmaker Agnès Varda visited Cuba, filmed several sequences in Havana, and took many photographs for a documentary she would eventually make, *Saludos cubanos*. In a very skillful and enjoyable manner, the documentary presents a synthesis of Cuban history with its traditions, its cultural background, its heritage values, its religious practices, its struggle for independence, its dances, its music. It even gives a special tribute to Benny Moré, one of the greatest musicians in popular music, who had died while she was editing the film.

The subtlety with which Varda describes how Cuban men protectively embrace their girlfriends or their wives, with a certain sense of possession and domination, constitutes a shrewd touch that shows the sense of masculine authority prevailing on the island, a sort of patriarchal hegemony in a country in the midst of changes, a country that had just undergone a social revolution. This is even more evident in her portrayals of the cowhands, with the influence of the genre of U.S. westerns notable in how Cuban cowboys dress and in their attitudes. The documentary lists all the laws passed to better the people, highlighting the benefits that the revolution brought to the majority of the people. The audiences identified with the romantic, brave, and daring rebels, who were at the same time heroes in flesh and blood: Fidel Castro, Raúl Castro, Juan Almeida, Camilo Cienfuegos, and Che Guevara.

The film also informed audiences in a positive and genuine manner about Cuba and its revolution and contributed to reaffirm in the international community the collective enthusiasm of the Cuban people and their participation in the building of a socialist society. Each event or occasion is shown as a battle of a brave people who decided to fight for a country free from bourgeois atavisms, of people seeking better living conditions.

In 1962 Danish filmmaker Theodoro Christensen visited the country for a showcase exhibition of Danish films. He returned to Cuba in 1963 to work as adviser to ICAIC's Department of Artistic Productions, where he guided and taught young Cuban filmmakers. In 1964, during his time in Cuba, he made the documentary *Ellas*, structured as a series of questions. Do Cuban women have the same rights as men? Are women taking part in the work of the revolution? To what extent? He interviewed a wide variety of women from all sectors of society: housewives, students, shop assistants, peasants, schoolteachers, secretaries, political cadres.

Critics responded warmly to the validity of this filmmaker's project. His selection of what was a sensitive problem at the time, the integration of women into the workforce and into the work of the revolution, was highly controversial and appreciated even in the context of strong male domination. Mario Rodríguez Alemán stated in a review: "The thirty-minute film is attractive and natural. The women interviewed talk to the camera naturally, as if they were at home, not at all shy. This gives the film a special charm and a special character. Each work of art should have a form to match its contents. Christensen proves this axiom."[13] Christensen's extensive contact with young Cuban filmmakers probably contributed to the making of a film in which his status as a foreign filmmaker was not evident. He was an artist who knew how to capture the essence of his chosen topic and was able to put it on the screen, mastering in a remarkable way the Cuban scenario.

In reference to the global documentary cinema movement and to the interest in such outstanding figures as Ivens, Marker, Christensen, and others, Chanan points out in his book on Cuban cinema, "Cuba became a subject of great interest to practitioners of the new documentary because the whole circumstance of the Revolution made a great deal much more directly available to the camera than was normal elsewhere. And because it was a symbol of the throwing off of shackles, which was part of the spirit of the new documentary too."[14] The timely coincidence of all those factors provided the documentary genre with ideal conditions to film any story in the period of unrest during the 1960s. The surrounding reality could truly provide the camera with all it needed to register the transformations that were becoming the face of the Cuban revolution for the rest of the world.

The Cuban Film That Never Was: History of a Film That Was Never Screened

Between 1967 and 1969 Cuban directors created the four films that are today considered "the classics of Cuban cinema of the sixties": *Las aventuras de Juan Quin Quin* (1967, Julio García Espinosa); *Lucía* (1968, Humberto Solás); *Memorias del subdesarrollo* (1968, Tomás Gutiérrez Alea), and *La primera carga al machete* (1969, Manuel Octavio Gómez).[15] Each of these films marks a turning point in the emerging aesthetics of the national cinema and shaped a visual map revealing a characteristic common to all four: the influence of the documentary in fictional films.

Meanwhile, in 1968 Japanese filmmaker Kazuo Kuroki came to Cuba at the invitation of ICAIC officials who had previously visited Japan to buy some films. Kuroki planned to explore the possibility of making a film in Cuba. Once he had made his inquiries, he returned to Japan to find funding, then came back to the island to make the feature film *La novia de Cuba*, also known as *Más cerca de ti . . .* (the title in Spanish as it appears on the commercial DVD and in some international databases).[16] For unknown reasons, the film was never screened in Cuba, though it was shown in Japan and other countries.

The protagonist is Akira, a Japanese sailor who lives on the island and falls in love with Marcia, a young and beautiful Cuban woman determined to join the guerrilla movement in Latin America. Akira decides to accompany Marcia as she travels to Santiago de Cuba to visit the graves of her relatives. Eventually they develop a physical relationship, but Marcia's guerrilla calling is much stronger and she decides to leave for her mission. The plot, however, is not much more than a pretext to make a road movie, telling a story that travels across the island to well-known Cuban locations and cities that had been sites of the Revolutionary Army's armed struggle against Batista—the cities of Santiago de Cuba, Trinidad, Santa Clara, and Havana.

The woman who played Marcia was not a professional actress, and many of the scenes in the film show the marked influence of the free cinema. Akira's actions as he talks to people in the streets—people who clearly were not recruited to participate in the film as actors—demonstrate the director's fascination with something undoubtedly exotic for him: an unknown society that he never quite unravels and never manages to represent with authenticity.

Although the film did not capture the essence of the Cuban spirit, audiences and critics at the time were unfairly prevented from seeing and evaluating it. Today, with the passage of many years, the reception of the movie, with new standards in place for assessment, is very different. But its earlier screening in Japan is especially notable. Obdulia Plasencia, the actress who played the role of Marcia, was able to travel to Japan for the premiere, thanks to the financial contribution of her co-protagonist, Masahiko Tsugawa, who played the role of Akira. In an interview Tsugawa said, "The audience was a 'minority' and for obvious reasons, most of the attendees had a strong political motivation, which explains the interest created by a film coming from distant and admired Cuba."[17]

From the 1990s On: New Times, New Subjects, and Transnationalization

Cuban film production started changing in the 1990s. The fall of the Berlin Wall and the disappearance of the socialist bloc meant the collapse of the national economy. The impact of this collapse on the industrial sector extended to the modest Cuban filmmaking sector, practically wiping out any possibility of producing films with national resources.

Cuban filmmakers were forced to find funding for their films abroad, and coproductions became a necessity rather than an option. Several authors have suggested ways to classify the films made under such an arrangement. For example, British film critic Mike Wayne, in *The Politics of Contemporary European Cinema*, presents a classification of "national cinema produced to operate in an international environment."[18] He suggests that the prevailing types are (1) *embedded films*: typically national projects produced essentially for the domestic market either because of budget constraints or because of their excessive localism; (2) *disembedded films*: those with the cultural potential and budget to succeed in the U.S. market; (3) *cross-border films*: those that make it to the international market outside the United States, particularly the European market, and offer a sort of porosity of national identities within the framework of a more generic European identity; and (4) *antinational-national films*: those defined by their criticism of the collective myth sustaining the national identity.

In his *Elogio posmoderno de las coproducciones*, Spaniard Manuel Palacio offers three different categories of coproductions. The first group consists of "strictly economic coproductions in which two or more companies pool their financial resources together for a better position in international markets, and in which even though there could be some degree of exchange of artists or crews, the national look is still predominant." The second is made up of coproductions with an international flavor that "try to wipe out all vestiges of the national viewpoint in a search for an international style." And the third is that of multicultural or hybrid coproductions—in his opinion the only true coproductions—that cannot be "limited to an economic agreement between partners," but "reflect the ambivalence in the construction of a collective identity" and "break with 'official stereotypes.'"[19]

Based on these different classifications, three coproductions provide particularly good examples of the representation of new aspects of Cuban society—aspects highlighted because of the international interest in them. They are *Maité* (1994, Spain-Cuba, by Eneko Olasagasti and Carlos Zabala); *¿Quién diablos es Juliette?* (1997, Mexico-Cuba, by Carlos Marcovich), and *Habana Blues* (2005, Spain-Cuba, by Benito Zambrano).

The topics treated are the search for marriage with a foreigner to enable emigration; prostitution; Cuban music; the deterioration of values; the destruction of the city; the black market as the only possible means of survival; the revival of the old glories of Cuban music; the desperation over not having opportunities for individual development and prosperity; and the obstinate persistence in using certain forms of representation associated with "the Cuban," which in fact only reaffirm stereotypes of what is globally understood as Cuban.

Maité is the story of two Basque entrepreneurs who establish businesses in Cuba. One of them meets a five-year-old girl, through whom he meets the mother and falls in love with her. This romantic comedy could be classified as a multicultural or hybrid coproduction given its interest in breaking with traditional stereotypes about unions between Cubans and foreigners, because the girl's mother is the manager of a hotel—a woman who earns her living in gainful employment rather than as a prostitute, which counters what many people would assume when hearing of this type of marriage. The respect with which the directors presented the topic was welcomed by Cuban audiences in the International Film Festival of the New Latin American Cinema of Havana, where it won the Popularity Award.

¿Quién diablos es Juliette?, by Carlos Marcovich, was made between 1995 and 1997 and filmed in Havana, New York, Los Angeles, Morelia (in central Mexico), and Mexico City. It is the story of two orphaned young women, a Cuban prostitute, Yuliet Ortega, and a Mexican fashion model, Fabiola Quiroz. In various ways, Marcovich explores Yuliet's desire to become a model, though he does not stop there, further exploring the origins of this young girl marked by negative experiences that have pushed her to prostitution as the only way out of her economic hardships. The style of this false documentary, or "mockumentary," allows the director to articulate a discourse aimed at showing the differences, similarities, and aspirations of women in completely different places.

According to Mike Wayne's classification, this is a cross-border film because it reveals a sense of national identity in crisis and features porosity according to his definition. Regarding the character of Yuliet, Deborah Martin says, "Yuliet appears to internalize such exoticizing discourses concerning Cuban woman as sexual and colonial other and which serve the interests of those who would emphasize the 'sensual' rather than the 'intellectual' capacities of the colonial subaltern. Interestingly, Yuliet's father tells us he chose her name because it is Italian. Yuliet herself learns to speak Italian through the Italian tourists she meets on the beaches of Havana, and whose money she accepts for sex. So Yuliet's father has inscribed her in a system of both mimicking Europe and of prostituting herself to it."[20] Martin goes on to point out that

> reflecting the new constellation in which Cuba finds itself at the beginning of the 1990s, the film resists the centre/margin binary by using four locations (Cuba, Mexico, New York and New Jersey). It privileges Cuba, making it the centre of the film and thus turning any notion of Cuba as periphery on its head. Yuliet's choice of Cuba over a career abroad reinforces this, and can be read as Cuban resilience at a time when political

and economic independence was suddenly imperative. The implication throughout the film (and generally in the international media) is that of a generalized desire in Cuba to 'get out.'"[21]

This Mexican filmmaker pries open the personal history of Yuliet Ortega, recreating aspects of life in a Havana suburb where the quality of life is extremely low and all the conditions are present for the development of illicit criminal activities, which the community nonetheless considers natural. The character of the country has changed radically since the romanticism of the early sixties, when the will for change rose above all other things, to the deterioration and abandonment of all desire for transformation and improvement.

The musical *Habana Blues*, by Benito Zambrano, shows no signs of a foreigner's hand, perhaps because this Andalusian director studied at the International Film and Television School (EICTV) in San Antonio de los Baños for two years and was able to immerse himself in the Cuban reality. He eventually turned his experiences into a script, and later into a film, providing a very contemporary and up-to-date story of the underground world of musical production in the Cuban capital.

Applying Manuel Palacio's classification scheme to this film, we can include it as a type of multicultural or hybrid coproduction. It tends to distance itself from the official discourse to delve deeply into aspects such as the Havana black market, the makeshift recording studios, the promotion of the individual, the prostitution of men, the predatory nature of foreign talent scouts, and particularly the absence of economic advancement for young musicians in their search for professional success—artists who are blocked by the lack of spaces where they can promote themselves and who also face severe restrictions on traveling abroad and exhibiting their work internationally.

Undeniably, Cuban culture has been transnationalized by these and other films. The original efforts made to present the advantages of building a new world, free from bourgeois vice and lack of opportunities to study and rid economic, political, and social injustice, have shifted to a recognition of a country in which social blights such as prostitution, marginalization, housing shortages, and family overcrowding, as well as lack of resources for repairing houses, have inevitably proliferated.

Cuban ruling authorities and power circles face the enormous challenge of working to recover those underprivileged and disadvantaged social strata and to reconfigure the aspirations for social justice and humanism that for so many years were the symbol of the Cuban revolution. Film, then, has been a transnational medium—publicizing that challenge and assessing the evolution of the Cuban reality with increasing realism.

Notes

1. The socialist character of the revolution was officially declared in 1961 at the funeral of the victims of the bombings of Ciudad Libertad and San Antonio de los Baños airports.

2. Italian neorealism was a cinematic movement that developed in Europe shortly after the Second World War. It was characterized by presenting the bare facts of the everyday lives of ordinary people. Some of its most notable representatives were Roberto Rossellini, Vittorio De Sica, Luchino Visconti, and Cesare Zavattini. Cuban filmmakers Tomás Gutiérrez Alea and Julio García Espinosa studied in Rome in the 1950s and had firsthand experience of this genre; it was evident in their early films, although it was assimilated and integrated into the personal poetry of their respective works.

3. Dr. Mario Rodríguez Alemán, letter, May 25, 1961, in *Carnet de Viaje* film dossier, Cuban Cinematheque, Havana.

4. The war against the bandits was the struggle fought for six years (1960–66) by the militias of Fidel Castro's government against counterrevolutionary bands that had emerged in the Escambray Mountains shortly after the establishment of the revolutionary government.

5. *El Mundo* (Havana), March 2, 1962, in *¡Cuba Sí!* film dossier, Cuban Cinematheque.

6. Chris Marker, interview by journalist Francis Gendron for *Miroir du Cinéma*, in film dossier, Cuban Cinematheque.

7. Interview with Jirima Klimentová, Prensa Latina news service, published in the "Cinema" section of *Girón* (Matanzas), July 18, 1962, in film dossier, Cuban Cinematheque.

8. *Revista Mella*, "¿Para quién bailamos?" October 5, 1964, in film dossier, Cuban Cinematheque.

9. José de la Colina, "Crónica de una crónica," review article, *Revolución* (La Habana), July 20, 1964, in film dossier, Cuban Cinematheque.

10. *El Mundo*, review, January 2, 1964, in film dossier, Cuban Cinematheque.

11. *Hoy* (Havana), February 6, 1964, in film dossier, Cuban Cinematheque.

12. P. L. Thirard, "Semana de cine cubano," review, *Positif* 67–68 (February–March 1965), in film dossier, Cuban Cinematheque.

13. Mario Rodríguez Alemán, review, *Revista Mujeres*, December 1, 1964, in film dossier, Cuban Cinematheque.

14. Michael Chanan, *Cuban Cinema* (Minneapolis: University of Minnesota Press, 2004), 193–94.

15. Ibid.; see also Juan Antonio García Borrero, *Otras maneras de pensar el cine cubano* (Santiago de Cuba: Editorial Oriente, 2009); Rufo Caballero, introductions by Francisco López Sacha and Enrique Álvarez, *Lágrimas en la lluvia: crítica de cine, 1987–2007* (La Habana: Ediciones ICAIC: Editorial Letras Cubanas, 2008); Joel del Río, *Contextos, conflictos y consumaciones: análisis crítico del cine cubano entre 2000 y 2006* (Camagüey: Editorial Ácana, 2008).

16. Mario Piedra, "La novia (desconocida) de Cuba," unpublished essay, 2011. The year 1969 is the most widely accepted date for the film's premiere. This film was rediscovered thanks to painstaking research carried out by Piedra, a researcher and university professor who teaches Cuban cinema to students of art history at the School of Arts and Letters, University of Havana. His research has enabled critics and researchers of Cuban cinema to watch the film on

DVD, first because he obtained a copy of the film from Japan, and second because he has written a comprehensive essay in which he explains in detail the steps in the production and postproduction of the film, which undoubtedly should be reclaimed at least as a document.

17. Ibid.

18. Alejandro Pardo, "Coproducciones internacionales españolas: ¿estrategia financiera o expresión multicultural?" www.unav.es/fcom/comunicacionysociedad/es/articulo.php?art_id=47.

19. Ibid.

20. Deborah Martin, "Spectatorship, Performance, Resistance: Carlos Marcovich's *¿Quién diablos es Juliette?*" *Journal of Latin American Cultural Studies* 15, no. 3 (2006), 341–53, quotation on 347.

21. Ibid., 349.

15

Cubans in Spain

Transnational Connections and Memories

METTE LOUISE BERG

The relationship between Cuba and its post-1959 diaspora has been characterized by antagonism and mutual recrimination—and that is especially the case in relations between the Cuban government and the Miami-based exile community in the United States. Indeed, a wealthy and politically powerful sector of Cubans living in the United States has been so successful in monopolizing the representations and narratives of the Cuban diaspora that its internal complexity has been all but eclipsed. Dissenting voices; experiences and trajectories; and discussions of gender, class, race, and generations within the diaspora have accordingly tended to be restricted to a relatively small network of scholars and intellectuals.[1]

Yet the Cuban diaspora is more complex than allowed for by the dominant exile narrative, the official Cuban government narrative, or media representations. It is characterized by diversity in migration trajectory, legal status, and class position, as well as in "race," religion, and political identification and orientation. Furthermore, for Cubans as for other diasporic groups, young and old, men and women tend to position themselves differently vis-à-vis home, homeland, country of residence, and each other. In recent years new studies have contributed toward a historically embedded and geographically and socially more representative understanding of contemporary Cuba and its diaspora.[2] I am writing here—with my focus on the memories and transnational connections of Cubans living in Spain—in the spirit of adding to an emergent and more nuanced picture of Cuban diasporic experiences over the past half century.[3] Elsewhere, I have argued for a historically embedded generational approach to understanding diasporic diversity.[4] Here my concern is twofold: first, resonating with the aims of this volume as a whole, to place the Cuban diaspora in a wider set of relations than the Cuba-U.S. binary; and second, to apply a wider historical lens to the understanding of Cuban mobility and migration.[5]

Ever since the colonial period and for many different reasons, Cubans have settled in Spain, whether permanently or temporarily. Cuba's national hero and leader of the independence struggle, José Martí, spent many years in Spain, and active associations of Cubans have existed in Spain since the nineteenth century.[6] Today a heterogeneous group of approximately sixty thousand Cubans lives in Spain.[7]

In a case as pervasively politicized as the Cuban diaspora, memories of the past and the homeland are intensely contested, and both the Cuban government and diasporic groups claim moral authority through memories. Cubans are not alone in using memory to draw boundaries and to define who belongs and who does not. As Paul Antze and Michael Lambek have observed about the late twentieth century, "memory has found a prominent place in politics, both as a source of authority and as a means of attack."[8] Yet memories are never simply records of the past. Rather, they are "interpretive reconstructions that bear the imprint of local narrative conventions, cultural assumptions, discursive formations and practices, and social contexts of recall and commemoration."[9] To understand the intensity of passions and the stakes involved in diasporic memory politics, we therefore need to situate memory claims and narratives in their historic context. For example, differences between Spain and the United States in the reception of Cubans and in the national political contexts have been important for shaping the relations that diasporic Cubans have been able to maintain with their homeland. Spanish cultural proximity, historical connections, and shared language with Cuba have created a different context for Cubans living there as compared to those living in the United States, which has a different history of relationships and an English-language majority. The immigration histories of the two countries also make for palpable differences in how Cubans and other migrant groups are perceived and represented. Notwithstanding these differences, both Spain and the United States have been more welcoming of Cubans than of other migrant groups, and both countries have made special concessions to Cuban migrants not made to other groups.[10]

The political context of the Cold War and the international relations that socialist Cuba became enmeshed in are clearly important for understanding its contemporary diaspora. Yet even if the current diaspora is primarily a postrevolutionary phenomenon, it needs to be understood in the light of Cuba's longer colonial and postcolonial history. The Caribbean constitutes Europe's oldest colonial sphere; as a region, argues Jean Besson, it "reflects extreme experiences of disjuncture through time and space: early globalisation, intense colonisation, trans-Atlantic indenture and enslavement, and transnational migration."[11] We need to situate and understand Cuba's contemporary diaspora against this quincentennial history of incorporation into the global system.

Since the colonial period, through Cuba's republic, and in the half century after the revolution, Cuba and Spain have been closely linked through flows of people and trade between the two countries. From the perspective of the colonial power (Spain), Cuba occupied a special place: not only was it in Spanish possession for four centuries, but it was also the richest and most treasured colony. The loss of Cuba to the United States in 1898 therefore constituted a severe blow to Spanish self-conceptions, and connections between the ex-colony and its former colonial master were never severed. Instead, the period after Cuban independence saw large-scale Spanish migration to Cuba.[12] After the 1959 revolution, migration in turn flowed from Cuba to Spain, giving rise to the contemporary diaspora.

Cubans in Spain embody a diversity of trajectories and subject positions. Like Cubans in the United States, they are not representative of the island population.[13] Those who most benefited from the revolution (nonwhites and the working class) have neither wanted to leave nor been able to marshal the resources, including transnational kinship and other connections, necessary to leave. Meanwhile, historical connections, including citizenship laws, have made it easier for Cubans of Spanish descent to settle in Spain. Notwithstanding, since the 1990s more nonwhite and working-class Cubans have settled in Spain.

Since there is no residential clustering of Cubans in either Madrid or Barcelona, where the majority of Cubans in Spain have settled, and there are only a few shared organizations, diasporic Cubans have few means of meeting other Cubans beyond their personal social networks. Furthermore, many Cubans actively avoid activities organized on the basis of shared nationality; they simply do not want to get too close to other Cubans or prefer not to identify themselves through being Cuban. In short, there is not an identifiable diasporic "community." This context is very different from that of the United States. The relative and absolute size of the diasporic groups in the two countries, as well as political traditions, culture, economic context, and history, are all important for understanding the differences. Cubans living in the United States account for an estimated 89 percent of the Cuban diaspora globally, and they far outnumber Cubans in Spain.[14] Furthermore, the U.S.-based diaspora quickly established a critical mass in Miami and were supported economically and politically by the U.S. government. Many were able to re-establish themselves economically in their new country, supported by the emerging ethnic enclave in Miami, and they then mobilized their social and political capital to form a strong organizational base, united by anticommunism.[15] In Spain, Cuban émigrés received no comparable government aid or political support. Additionally, ideological differences between socialist Cuba and the United States were clear-cut and Cold War–defined, but in the relationship between Castro's Cuba and Franco's Spain, colonial ties, shared language and culture, and the recent history of mass-migration from Spain to Cuba complicated any simple ideological divide.[16] These differences, which were established soon after the Cuban revolution, have continued beyond the end of the Cold War and Spain's transition to democracy.

For some Cubans, settling in Spain did not mark the beginning of life in diaspora; this had for them begun much earlier, for some even while they still lived in Cuba. They felt displaced by the comprehensive economic, social, and political transformations of their homeland in the wake of the revolution, effectively making them feel "homeless" at home.[17] Equally, for many, leaving Cuba was not the beginning of life as migrant, nor was settling in Spain the endpoint. Many have complex family histories of mobility across the Atlantic and within and beyond the Cold War–defined East-West divide. Against this background, it is not helpful to assume that living away from the island means the same to all Cubans, or that they all remember and identify with their homeland in the same way. A better approach is to ask how Cubans themselves identify their belonging. In this context I was drawn to collecting life-story interviews, which yielded rich insights into individual and family experiences.

In the context of the Cuban diaspora, telling such individual and family stories decenters the monolithic narrative of a unified and politicized exile community based in the United States, and situates the diaspora within an ongoing story of mobility that started in the colonial period. In the wider Latin American context, life stories have been used to give voice to subaltern subjects, including women, the poor, blacks, and former slaves.[18] I found that the diasporic Cubans I knew in Spain were familiar and comfortable with the format of life stories. Some, especially elderly and retired white, middle-class men, were already engaged in writing down their own and their families' life stories for posterity. As examples here I draw first on the stories of two Cuban families, self-defined exiles, as narrated to me in Madrid. I then turn to the story of a more recent migrant to Spain. I begin with Mario's story, which has more detail than many others, exactly because he had the inclination and resources—time and wealth—to devote to researching and pondering his family history. As *narratives* the stories presented here are not typical, but the experiences narrated, and the patterns of multigenerational mobility, were shared by many within the diaspora.

Mario's Story: Multigenerational Mobility in the Iberian Atlantic

Mario was a retired civil servant who was writing his family history.[19] His paternal grandparents married in Valencia, Spain, in 1890. After the birth of a son, Mario's grandfather was drafted into the army and sent to fight the nationalist rebels in Cuba in 1895. In Cuba, after falling ill and becoming disenchanted with the colonial project, he deserted the army and settled in Mexico. Later his wife traveled to Mexico in a vain attempt to find her husband. She eventually settled in Veracruz on Mexico's Caribbean coast with her son, Eusebio, who would eventually become Mario's father. As a young man, Eusebio worked as an accountant for Shell in Veracruz.

Meanwhile, Mario's maternal grandparents were struggling in Madrid. Of their fourteen children, only four survived beyond infancy; Mario's mother, Marta, was the youngest. Searching for a better future, the family left Madrid for Argentina and then Uruguay, where they set up a restaurant in Montevideo. After losing the restaurant they returned to Spain, but then left again, bound for Cuba, in 1907. In Cuba Mario's grandfather became the accountant on a sugar plantation. In the 1920s Marta, as a young woman, returned to Spain, where she met a man whom she later married in Cuba. The newlyweds moved to New York, but Marta did not get on with her husband and returned to Cuba with her young daughter. Back in Cuba she petitioned for divorce and later met Eusebio, who had been transferred from Veracruz to work for Shell in Havana. With the outbreak of the economic crisis in 1929, Eusebio lost his job, and in 1933 the couple, now married, decided to return to Spain, where the new republic seemed more promising than the dictatorship in Cuba. They spent a couple of years in Madrid, where Mario's brother was born. Eusebio set up a small cosmetics factory in Valencia, but in 1936 the Spanish Civil War broke out. With luck they managed to escape the fighting and made their way back to Cuba.

In 1938 Mario was born in Havana. His parents enrolled him in a private Catholic school, where he learned English and French, which later ensured him translation work. Mario went on to become a revolutionary and socialist and studied in Prague. It was here that he met and married a Czech woman, Ivana. Mario and Ivana were called back to Cuba in 1967, but Mario was disappointed with the direction the revolution had taken and they soon returned to Prague. In 1970 they were again required to return to Cuba, but they deserted when the boat that was to take them back stopped in the Netherlands. Even though Spain was under the rule of Franco, Mario believed that this country would be the only place he could feel at home. They settled there and both became civil servants. Their two children were born in Madrid.

Don Orlando's and Isabel's Story

When I first met don Orlando he was ninety-nine years old, and I had the privilege of being among the guests at his hundredth birthday party. He lived then with his only daughter, Isabel, in a modest flat in a Madrid suburb. Orlando was born in Asturias in northern Spain. He was the youngest of ten siblings, four of whom were to emigrate to Argentina and two to Cuba. After his father's death the family fell on hard times and his mother feared that he would be drafted to fight in the Spanish-Moroccan War (1909–27). In 1915, when he was about fourteen years old, Orlando's mother therefore decided to send him to Cuba, where he could stay with his sister, who was already married and living in Havana. It was the first time that Orlando had left the immediate surroundings of his native village.

Orlando's first job was as a janitor in a hospital. Through luck, dedication, and hard work he made it to the University of Havana to study medicine, but due to political upheavals in the 1930s, which led to the closure of the University of Havana for several years, Orlando did not finish his medical degree. Instead, he was licensed to practice as a "laboratory doctor." Although Isabel often urged him to talk about later events in his life, Orlando preferred to talk about the 1950s, when he owned a medical clinic and was an active board member of the hometown association for immigrants to Cuba from his village in Asturias. Through the hometown association, Orlando remitted money to his village to build a school and restore the church. He proudly showed me the framed diplomas from the Spanish societies in Havana acknowledging his work for and support of them.

Soon after the Cuban revolution in 1959, Isabel and don Orlando started to feel alienated from the new political order. Don Orlando thought the United States would intervene to topple Castro, as it had intervened so many times before in Cuba in the twentieth century, but when it became clear that was not going to happen they decided to leave. Isabel married in 1961 on the understanding that she and her husband, Jorge, would emigrate as soon as possible. After the wedding Isabel's husband moved in with Isabel and her parents in the family home, built by don Orlando. Jorge Jr., their only child, was born in 1963. After their son was born, Jorge Sr. "became a revolutionary," as Isabel put it, and decided he did not want to leave the country. Marital tensions increased as Jorge Sr. and his mother threatened to denounce Isabel and her parents as counterrevolutionaries, and his mother secretly taped Isabel's mother criticizing the government as evidence.

Since Jorge Sr. would not permit Isabel to leave with their son, she had to decide between staying in Cuba or leaving her son behind, and so for seven years Isabel continued living with her estranged husband and her mother-in-law, who had also moved in. By 1970, according to Isabel, Jorge Sr. had fallen in love with another woman, Lucy, and agreed to let Isabel leave with their son. Don Orlando and Isabel's mother left with them. Jorge Sr. stayed in the house and later married Lucy. Jorge Sr. and Isabel maintained only rudimentary contact in the following decades.

However, the return to Spain was not as don Orlando had anticipated and, disappointed, he decided to move to New York with his wife. They hoped that he might find work there more easily than in Spain, where his age and qualifications from abroad prevented him from practicing. Not long after, Isabel and Jorge joined them. Isabel enjoyed her time in New York and later New Jersey. In contrast to her experiences in Spain, she felt she was respected professionally and felt no stigma as a divorced mother. However, Jorge had problems in school and the family decided to move back to Spain. Then, during the transition to democracy in Spain, they, like other Cuban exiles, feared a socialist takeover in Spain and decided to move back to the United States, this time to Miami. Once there Isabel changed her mind and they all returned yet again to Madrid, where Isabel's mother died. In the 1990s Jorge Sr. suddenly turned up in Madrid and re-established contact with Isabel and Jorge Jr. Jorge Jr. has since visited his father in Cuba, and Isabel maintains some contact with him as well. She still considers herself the rightful owner of the house in Havana. Don Orlando died in Madrid in 2003.

Making Sense of Diaspora Stories

How should we make sense of stories such as these? Clearly there is a family dynamic that led individuals in both families to migrate; there were also family goals of social mobility.[20] In parallel with this, there are the vagaries of colonialism, international labor demands, and economic crises and booms. Mario, don Orlando and Isabel, and their families migrated variously because of colonial projects, war, poverty, political repression, instability, a search for opportunities, or a belief that they would feel more at home somewhere else. The multigenerational mobility across the Atlantic, up and down the Americas, and within and beyond the Cold War–defined East-West divide certainly complicates the ideas of the Cuban diaspora as uniquely and solely a post-1959 story. Mario's years in Prague and marriage to Ivana speak of the new transnational world in which Cuba became enmeshed after the revolution, suggesting the need to look beyond the U.S.-Cuba relationship to appreciate mobility in and out of Cuba in the second half of the twentieth century.

That don Orlando, Isabel, and Mario came to think of themselves as Cuban exiles in Spain, when they could instead have identified as Spanish return-migrants, speaks both of processes of exclusion in Spain and of the tense and politicized context of their departure from revolutionary Cuba. In other words, their stories are about the importance of both homeland and host-society contexts in diaspora formation, and of the role of the state in structuring, channeling, and defining migration and its effects on the migrants themselves. As Mario commented, the notion that you need a passport, now taken for granted, is actually a relatively recent phenomenon: "In that epoch [early twentieth century] people didn't have passports, you didn't need citizenship or work permits; you just went and said "look, I'd like work." . . . It wasn't like today when you need seventy-five permits from the authorities to do anything, only to be told that the problem is that there are no jobs."

The stories speak eloquently for themselves of mobility and the historical embeddedness of Cuban-Spanish ties, yet within them are also issues that remain unspoken, notably "race." Cuba's troubled and violent twentieth-century history of race relations has been amply documented, but the issue of race within the diaspora still needs further research.[21] In the early twentieth century Cuba received large numbers of both white Spanish and black West Indian immigrants, yet for the black newcomers possibilities for social mobility and integration in the new republic were severely curtailed by discriminatory practices and legislation that favored white European immigrants.[22] Conversely Don Orlando's trajectory from impoverished child migrant to medical doctor and owner of a private practice in Havana is testament to the racialized privilege of white immigrants to Cuba in the century. Yet memories of racial inequalities and structural discrimination have been erased in his narrative and those of many other exiles.

Another unspoken issue is the privileging of ideology and politics as primary reasons for leaving Cuba in these exile narratives. Unlike more recent Cuban migrants, these exiles define themselves as politically motivated émigrés, but politics was entwined with economics—nationalizations, confiscations of private businesses, and so on—and the fact that their lifestyle and class-based privileges had become untenable in revolutionary Cuba. The separation of economic from political motivations for migrating was a cornerstone in Cold War politics, and remains important for diasporic Cubans, but in most cases the two are linked.

The New Cuban Diaspora

So far I have focused on the first generation of diasporic Cubans in Madrid; namely, those who left Cuba in the first decade after the revolution, many of whom by some measures could be seen as return-migrants to Spain.[23] In Cuba they tended to cultivate a sense of Spanishness, which conferred racialized privilege. Upon "return" to their mother country, stripped of their wealth and class privileges, and uncertain about the future, they became Cuban exiles. Despite narratives of rootedness in Cuba, their family histories reveal a great deal of transatlantic mobility, which opens questions about home, belonging, and identity across time and space.

Yet the story of the Cuban diaspora in Spain involves other subjects too, with different stories, memories, and sets of transnational connections. Those who arrived in the 1960s, who were mainly white, middle class, and from Havana, found that Spain was a poorer and less-developed country than the Cuba they had lived in. They also tended to be conservative and Catholic. Meanwhile, Cubans arriving in the 1970s, after Spain's transition to democracy, found that they could identify relatively easily with the socialist government of Felipe González, with whom they, unlike the earlier generation of "exiles," shared democratic socialist ideals and a critical stance toward the United States. For the Cubans who arrived from the 1990s onwards, conditions had changed yet again. They left austerity-marked Cuba, and were in turn overwhelmed, dazzled, and disgusted in about equal measures by the abundance of commodity capitalism. From being a country of emigration, Spain was now receiving labor migrants from throughout the global South, of which Cubans made up only a small fraction.

These Cubans have often left close family behind on the island and, if possible, would prefer to travel back and forth between Spain and Cuba. For many of them, this is nearly or completely impossible; they are stuck for protracted periods as undocumented migrants and therefore cannot leave Spain since they may not gain access again. Those who do have residence permits, and who are able to save up for the trip, still face considerable bureaucratic hurdles to overcome on the Cuban side, as well as the anxiety of not being allowed to leave the island again.

The story of Lucy, who worked as a waitress in a café in central Madrid, was not unusual. Lucy was white and in her twenties or early thirties. She had been in Spain with her husband for a year and eight months when I met her. She had left an eleven-year-old daughter by a previous husband in Cuba with her own mother. Lucy and her husband had been recruited in Cuba to work on foreign-owned cruise liners and made the decision to defect together while they were still in Cuba. Lucy informed her family about their plans, as she had to make sure her daughter would be looked after. Her husband's family did not know of their plans. On their final trip, the cruise ship stopped in Egypt and Italy before reaching Seville in Spain. Lucy and her husband were uncertain about where to get off, but when another Cuban crew member deserted in Seville, the remaining crew were told that they would not be allowed to go ashore. Lucy and her husband therefore made a quick decision to leave during the night. They later learned that all the Cuban crew members had defected, one by one. When they set foot in Spain, Lucy and her husband had only US$80 in cash, as their wages were normally retained until they had completed their period of employment and returned to Cuba. From Seville, they made their way to Madrid, where they had friends. Both Lucy and her husband quickly found jobs, Lucy in a Cuban restaurant. They stayed with their friends until they found their own flat more than a year after arriving, and obtained residence permits through a general amnesty to undocumented migrants. Lucy was hoping to bring her daughter to Spain soon, and told me she phoned Cuba every other Sunday. Of course she missed Cuba a lot, she said, but at the same time there were compensations. In Madrid she felt she could save up to buy a flat, buy new clothes and other things she liked, and had the possibility of going out with friends. Like other recent migrants, Lucy was emphatically not interested in political activities, and stated with pride that she had not been "in trouble"—that is, she had not been involved in politics before leaving.

Recent Cuban immigrants like Lucy are characterized by a pragmatic orientation toward supporting family at home and a desire to make it in *el capitalismo*, the capitalist world; they have minimal or no interest in exile politics. Unlike the earlier exiles they define themselves as economic migrants and aspire to visit Cuba as often as they can afford to do so, provided there are no legal obstacles from either Spain or Cuba. Many have benefited from revolutionary Cuba's investment in education and have experienced upward social mobility. Their primary loyalty however is not to the revolution. They identify with their kin, and with the home, street, and neighborhood in which they grew up, not with any lofty revolutionary or counterrevolutionary ideas of nation or homeland.

Conclusion: Toward a New Politics of Memory?

The Cuban diaspora in Spain has been molded by particular historical connections between Spain and Cuba, by global Cold War politics, and by Spain's political culture, which in important respects is different from that of the United States. Importantly, even the narratives of Cuban exiles that superficially cement the notion of nationally rooted identities, when looked at in detail, suggest a historically more fluid landscape of belonging, ossified through Cold War politics and binaries.

Given the history of antagonism between the Cuban government and its diaspora, is it possible to imagine a future deterritorialized Cuban nation-state, with the Cuban government reaching out to its diasporic citizens in the manner of neighboring Haiti? That consideration would require a reassessment of the basis for belonging in Cuba. It would require a new politics of memory concerned with reconciliation and tolerance, rather than recrimination and exclusion.[24] Seen from the bottom up, contours of shared spaces of memory and belonging are emerging from the transnational practices of recent, pragmatic Cuban migrants settled in Spain, the United States and elsewhere. These include return visits and remittances, the cross-border circulation of video and audio tapes, the practices of religious groups, and the use of online social networking sites.[25] Yet diaspora-homeland relations remain a fraught issue and a fault line within the diaspora. This chapter has argued that to understand mobility and transnational practices we need to ground the diaspora socially, culturally, and politically and be cognizant of diasporic diversity. A historically informed approach helps in understanding the dynamic relations between the Cuban homeland, the diaspora, and countries of significant Cuban settlement. It also calls for a wider context than that of a narrowly defined U.S.-Cuba nexus.

A recent development underscores the importance of a wider perspective. The Spanish law referred to as the Ley de Memoria Histórica, or Law of Historical Memory, has opened a window for new sectors of Cubans to obtain Spanish nationality and thereby to emigrate to and settle in Spain. In recognition of the injustice inflicted upon those Spaniards who were forced into exile during the Spanish Civil War (1936–39) and the ensuing dictatorship (1939–75), the law opened the possibility for grandchildren of Spanish exiles, and by extension émigrés, to obtain Spanish citizenship even if their parents did not hold it, provided they applied by the end of 2011.[26] Initially, Spanish consular officials in Havana estimated that up to 400,000 Cubans were eligible for Spanish citizenship on the basis of the new law, but that figure was later adjusted to 150,000.[27] In February 2009, Norberto Díaz, a thirty-eight-year-old cardiologist from Havana, became the first Cuban to obtain a Spanish passport in accordance with the law; his three siblings were equally granted Spanish nationality. Díaz was planning to migrate to Spain immediately, and in a press interview explained that he had always wanted to "return to my country" (*mi tierra*).[28]

Ironically, a legal gesture to heal the memories and wounds of exile and diaspora created by the Spanish Civil War and Spain's dictatorship may thus give rise to a new diasporic generation of Cubans in Spain—people with the full privilege of Spanish citizenship—and new configurations of transnational connections and memories; a twenty-first-century twist in the legacy of mobility between Spain and Cuba.

Notes

1. Introduction to Andrea O'Reilly Herrera, ed., *Cuba: Idea of a Nation Displaced* (Albany: State University of New York Press, 2007), 3.

2. Mette Louise Berg, *Diasporic Generations: Memory, Politics, and Nation among Cubans in Spain* (Oxford: Berghahn Books, 2011); Ruth Behar, ed., *Bridges to Cuba/Puentes a Cuba* (Ann Arbor: University of Michigan Press, 1995); Ruth Behar and Lucía M. Suárez, eds., *The Portable Island: Cubans at Home in the World* (New York and Basingstoke, UK: Palgrave Macmillan, 2008); Susan Eckstein, *The Immigrant Divide: How Cuban Americans Changed the U.S. and Their Homeland* (New York: Routledge, 2009); O'Reilly Herrera, *Cuba*; Yolanda Prieto, *The Cubans of Union City: Immigrants and Exiles in a New Jersey Community* (Philadelphia, PA: Temple University Press, 2009); Ruth Behar and Humberto Chávez Mayol, *An Island Called Home: Returning to Jewish Cuba* (New Brunswick, NJ, and London: Rutgers University Press, 2007). See also Eckstein, this volume.

3. The material presented in this chapter is based on seventeen months of ethnographic fieldwork carried out in 2001–2 in Cuba, Spain, and the United States, with return visits to Spain in 2009 and 2012. The main part of the fieldwork took place in Madrid, but I also spent time in Barcelona and Cádiz. Research involved participant observation and unstructured and semi-structured interviews with a range of diasporic Cubans, and a collection of written material, including fiction, poetry, and essays, some in public circulation and others not. I was fluent in Spanish from the outset of the research, and all my interaction and interviews with research subjects were in Spanish. I established contact with Cubans through NGOs, trade unions, and other organizations, and used the snowball method. For more details, see Berg, *Diasporic Generations* and "Between Cosmopolitanism and the National Slot: Cuba's Diasporic Children of the Revolution," *Identities: Global Studies in Culture and Power* 16, no. 2 (2009), 129–56.

4. Berg, *Diasporic Generations*.

5. In this chapter, I focus primarily on Cubans who settled in Spain during the 1960s or 1970s, although I do allude to the development since the 1970s of a more diverse diaspora. For a fuller story, see Berg, *Diasporic Generations*.

6. Berg, *Diasporic Generations*.

7. The diaspora in Spain is a small group compared with the approximately 1.6 million Cubans and Cuban Americans living in the United States, but in the 1960s possibly as many as 200,000 Cubans lived in Spain, making up nearly half of all immigrants in the country at the time. Many Cubans in Spain in this period were in transit and eventually settled in the United States. On Cubans in the United States, see Pew Hispanic Center, "Hispanics of Cuban Origin in the U.S., 2007" (Washington, DC: Author, 2009). On Cubans in Spain, see Vicente Romano, *Cuba en el corazón: testimonios de un desarraigo* (Barcelona: Anthropos, 1989), 17. Some Cubans settled in Spain in the years just before the revolution, but most arrived later. Berg, *Diasporic Generations*.

8. Preface to Paul Antze and Michael Lambek, eds., *Tense Past: Cultural Essays in Trauma and Memory* (New York: Routledge, 1996), vii.

9. Ibid.

10. Maryellen Fullerton, "Cuban Exceptionalism: Migration and Asylum in Spain and the United States," *University of Miami Inter-American Law Review* 35, no. 3 (2004), 527–75.

11. Jean Besson, "Sacred Sites, Shifting Histories: Narratives of Belonging, Land and Globalisation in the Cockpit Country, Jamaica," in Jean Besson and Karen Fog Olwig, eds., *Caribbean Narratives of Belonging: Fields of Relations, Sites of Identity* (Oxford: Macmillan Education, 2005), 17.

12. Hugh Thomas, *Cuba* (London: Pan Books, 2001), 236; Consuelo Naranjo Orovio and Carlos Serrano, eds., *Imágenes e imaginarios nacionales en el ultramar Español* (Madrid: Consejo Superior de Investigaciones Científicas, 1999); Jordi Maluquer de Motes, *Nación e inmigración: los españoles en Cuba (ss. XIX y XX)* (Colombres, Spain: Ediciones Jucar, 1992).

13. On Cubans in the United States, see Max J. Castro, "The Trouble with Collusion: Paradoxes of the Cuban-American Way," in Damián J. Fernández and Madeline Cámara Betancourt, eds., *Cuba, the Elusive Nation: Interpretations of National Identity* (Gainesville: University Press of Florida, 2000), 303; Eckstein *Immigrant Divide*.

14. Eckstein, *Immigrant Divide*, 11.

15. On Cubans in Miami as an ethnic enclave, see Kenneth L. Wilson and Alejandro Portes, "Immigrant Enclaves: An Analysis of the Labor Market Experiences of Cubans in Miami," *American Journal of Sociology* 86, no. 2 (1980), 295–319. See also Eckstein *Immigrant Divide*.

16. See Alistair Hennessy, "Cuba, Western Europe and the U.S.: An Historical Overview," in Alistair Hennessy and George Lambie, eds., *The Fractured Blockade: West European–Cuban Relations During the Revolution* (London: Macmillan Caribbean, 1993), 11–63; George Lambie, "Franco's Spain and the Cuban Revolution," in ibid., 234–75.

17. See also Ruth Behar, *The Vulnerable Observer: Anthropology That Breaks Your Heart* (Boston, MA: Beacon Press, 1996), 144; Iván de la Nuez, *El mapa de sal. Un poscomunista en el paisaje global* (Barcelona: Mondadori, 2001), 14; Gustavo Pérez Firmat, *Next Year in Cuba. A Cubano's Coming-of-Age in America* (Houston, TX: Scrivenery Press, 2000), 30.

18. For examples in the Cuban context, see María de los Reyes Castillo Bueno and Daisy Rubiera Castillo, *Reyita: The Life of a Black Cuban Woman in the Twentieth Century* (London: Latin American Bureau, 2000); Esteban Montejo and Miguel Barnet, *The Autobiography of a Runaway Slave* (London: Bodley Head, 1968).

19. I have changed all names to preserve anonymity. Mario's story is an abbreviated version of the story he told me over the course of several interviews conducted in his family home, a flat in a 1960s apartment block in Madrid.

20. See also Mary Chamberlain, "Family Narratives and Migration Dynamics," *Nieuwe West-Indische Gids* 69, no. 3–4 (1995), 256.

21. For discussions of "race" in twentieth-century Cuba, see, for example, Aline Helg, *Our Rightful Share: The Afro-Cuban Struggle for Equality, 1886–1912* (Chapel Hill: University of North Carolina Press, 1995); Alejandro de la Fuente, *A Nation for All: Race, Inequality, and Politics in Twentieth-Century Cuba* (Chapel Hill and London: University of North Carolina Press, 2001); Aviva Chomsky, "'Barbados or Canada?' Race, Immigration, and Nation in Early-Twentieth-Century Cuba," *Hispanic American Historical Review* 80 no. 3 (2000): 415–62; Na-

dine T. Fernandez, *Revolutionizing Romance: Interracial Couples in Contemporary Cuba* (New Brunswick, NJ: Rutgers University Press, 2010).

22. Alejandro de la Fuente, "'With All and for All' Race, Inequality and Politics in Cuba, 1900–1930," PhD diss., University of Pittsburgh, 1996, 363.

23. For a discussion of diasporic generations, see Berg, *Diasporic Generations*.

24. On Haiti, see Linda Basch, Nina Glick Schiller, and Cristina Szanton Blanc, *Nations Unbound: Transnational Projects, Postcolonial Predicaments and Deterritorialized Nation-States* (Langhorne, PA: Gordon and Breach, 1994), 267; on Cuba, see Rafael Rojas, "The Knots of Memory: Culture, Reconciliation, and Democracy in Cuba," in Bert Hoffmann and Laurence Whitehead, eds., *Debating Cuban Exceptionalism* (Basingstoke, UK: Palgrave Macmillan, 2007), 167.

25. Eckstein, *Immigrant Divide*; Lisa Maya Knauer, "Audiovisual Remittances and Transnational Subjectivities," in Ariana Hernández-Reguant, ed., *Cuba in the Special Period: Culture and Ideology in the 1990s* (New York: Palgrave Macmillan, 2009); Sarah J. Mahler and Katrin Hansing, "Toward a Transnationalism of the Middle: How Transnational Religious Practices Help Bridge the Divides between Cuba and Miami," *Latin American Perspectives* 32, no. 1 (2005); Berg, "Between Cosmopolitanism and the National Slot."

26. Gobierno de España, Ministerio de Justicia, "Concesión de la nacionalidad española a descendientes de españoles (hasta el 27 de diciembre de 2011)," 2007, leymemoria.mjusticia.es/paginas/es/descendientes.html.

27. Mauricio Vicent, "Las abuelas olvidadas de la memoria histórica se rebelan en Cuba," *El País,* 2010, http://elpais.com/diario/2010/01/03/espana/1262473207_850215.html, "El primer cubano con pasaporte español por "ley de nietos" emigrará enseguida," *Público.es,* 2009, www.publico.es/agencias/efe/197995/primer/cubano/pasaporte/espanol/ley/nietos/emigrara/enseguida?nr=1.

28. EFE, "El primer cubano con pasaporte español."

16

Oral History and Constructions of Racial Memory

YVETTE LOUIS

In 1891 José Martí, Cuba's most prominent and popular intellectual, wrote, "There is no racial hatred because there are no races." The Cuban revolution would later take up Martí's call and revive his status as icon in its own campaign to eradicate racial inequality. The Preamble of the Cuban Constitution ends with a quotation from Martí: "I want the first law of our Republic to be the Cuban devotion to the total dignity of man." In 1959 Fidel Castro affirmed this goal by declaring, "Let whites and blacks all get together to end hateful racial discrimination."[1]

Racial constructions are remarkably resistant, however, and rhetoric extolling a nation free of racial prejudice often does little to change racist paradigms, social practices, or the material conditions of blacks. Oral history provides a window into precisely how individuals are affected by and experience race in their daily lives within these larger political systems. Clearly, institutional racial practices have changed since the revolution. How do Cubans perceive and experience postrevolutionary racial constructions compared to pre-revolution racism? The oral histories of Cubans of African descent living on the island or abroad not only highlight how national racial constructions are enacted upon the lives of individuals, but also reveal how racial constructions persist or change across historical and national boundaries.

Despite social policies set in place to do away with institutionalized racism, race discrimination remained alive and well in Cuban society. In a 2006 interview, after nearly half a century of antiracist policies, Castro admitted "the Revolution, over and above the rights and guarantees achieved for all its citizens of whatever ethnic background or origin, has not had the same success in its fight to eradicate the difference in social and financial status for the black population of the country. Blacks don't live in the best houses; you find that they still have the hardest, most physically wearing and often worst-paid jobs and that they receive much less help from their family members no longer in Cuba, in dollars, than their white compatriots."[2] This statement merely articulated within the public sphere what had long been the experience of Cubans of African descent. In 2002 Nancy Morejón, the first black woman to be awarded Cuba's most prestigious literary prize, El Premio Nacional de Literatura, explained, "Racial prejudices still exist, which these forty years of efforts have not been able to eradicate completely. This is a reality. I can tell you that, in this sense, racial prejudice is defeated but not dead."[3] Racist attitudes cannot be legislated away. Racial constructions are transmitted culturally, socially, and discursively, and they tend to resist legislation. The assumption that without an institutional base, racism would gradually disappear over time has been proven wrong.

The Persistence and Signifiers of Racism

Refusing to discuss race will not make it cease to exist. Alejandro de la Fuente writes about how "race became a taboo in public discourse, its open discussion tantamount to an act of divisionism" and how, paradoxically, Cuba's "official silence contributed to the survival ... of racist ideologies and stereotypes." According to de la Fuente, "What disappeared from public discourse found fertile breeding ground in private spaces, where race continued to influence social relations among friends, neighbors, co-workers, and family members." Nadine Fernandez proposes that "racist ideologies were reproduced in part *despite* and in part *because* of the revolution's color-blind stance on the racial question."[4] Because racial constructions are transmitted discursively and analysis occurs through discourse, both public and private conversations are essential to unraveling the problems of racial discrimination—resistance notwithstanding.

Analyses of racial discrimination often focus on the differences in social and financial status between blacks and whites, but the modus operandi of race is much more complex. There is a logical tendency to view race as a social construction that results from political or economic ideology, but racial constructions play an important role in social mythologies. In 2010 a Cuban report to the United Nations not only connected racial constructions to the private sphere, but also correctly historicized race: "some personal prejudices have survived for historical and socio-cultural reasons. Fifty years of non-discriminatory Revolution have been unable totally to eradicate stereotypes from a society which had been racist for more than 500 years. The ways in which the family is structured and functions do not change as quickly as legislation and State policies may change."[5] Social mythologies that transmit negative stereotypes are learned through language and become reinforced in daily use. According to Ferdinand de Saussure's theory of signs, "A linguistic sign is not a link between a thing and a name, but between a concept and a sound pattern," both of which exist in the mind. The sound pattern of the word is the signifier, and its accompanying concept is the signified. Together they form a "two-sided psychological entity."[6] For each word we learn the concept (signified) by learning its corresponding sound pattern (signifier). Through conventional usage, the racialized linguistic images that constitute stereotypes and all their phobic and fetishistic qualities are inherited through community, and mostly in life's most intimate spaces, where language is learned and discourse is largely unfettered.

Saussure's theories further suggest a framework for reexamining how racial constructions have been transmitted for centuries: "but to say that a language is an inheritance from the past explains nothing unless we take the question further. Is it not possible from time to time to change established laws which have been handed down from the past? This question leads us to consider a language in its social context and to pursue our enquiry in the same terms as for any other social institution. How are social institutions handed down from generation to generation?"[7] Since race is a social construct and language is the means by which racial constructions are "handed down from generation to generation," it would make sense to analyze how discourse operates and influences social forces and institutions and, hence, the material realities of those who live within this "social context." Perhaps one approach to resolving the persistence of racism is to address its linguistic heritage and thereby to consider whether it is possible to "change established" social practices.

Racial constructions and social mythologies vary by nation, region, history, language, and other local particularities. Esteban Morales Domínguez explains, "As opposed to what takes place in the United States, where discrimination is practiced based on the percentage of black blood, in Cuba, this doesn't make the least difference. What determines whether to discriminate or not is skin color."[8] Arguably, skin color defines the limits of racial identification throughout the African diaspora. Passing for white in the United States, for example, depended mostly upon skin color and appearance. In Cuba, "someone can be considered white if they have one drop of white blood," yet this does not apply if that person has "black skin."[9] Both one-drop rules and even notions of hybridity form part of essentialist racial constructions—albeit by enacting differing mythologies—because they depend upon biological constructions of race. The interpretations of signs of blackness—whether those be skin color or other features—hinge not on biology but on the value attributed to difference by social and cultural mythologies disseminated by signs, through language.

The tools of the social sciences are indispensable in scrutinizing the outcome of racist practices, but racial constructions themselves do not function to provide accurate information about demographics; otherwise, Cuba's primary racial constructions—blackness, whiteness, and mestizaje—would so often "forget" Asians. These racial fictions serve not to reflect the realities of identification or classification, but to maintain access to power along lines of stratification. Like stereotypes, race is a mental image that does not serve to reflect reality at all, but rather imagines identity by projecting anxieties onto a racialized Other in an attempt to gain access to social and cultural domination.

Racialized images are part of a global vocabulary, easily accessible to individuals when an image of the Other is conjured up during times of anxiety. Sander Gilman describes the objectification of the Other and suggests how images of the Other can serve so many sometimes apparently conflicting purposes in different historical moments:

> Every social group has a set vocabulary of images for this externalized Other. These images are the product of history and of a culture that perpetuates them. None is random; none is isolated from the historical context. While all of these images exist simultaneously, the ones that are invested with relatively greater force vary over time. An image can gain in potency partly as a result of actions by the corresponding real entities. When, for example, a group makes demands on a society, the status anxiety produced by those demands characteristically translates into a sense of loss of control. Thus a group that has been marginally visible can suddenly become the definition of the Other. Categories of difference are protean, but they appear as absolutes. They categorize the sense of the self, but establish an order—the illusion of order in the world. This constant admixture of myth and unconscious deformation of reality is the basis for stereotyping.[10]

The revolution was unable to abolish racial stereotypes that had five hundred years of history because the racialized Other continued to serve as the currency of power in social relationships.

Even into the twenty-first century the discourse inherited from slavery continues to generate meaning. In a 2007 interview reported in the *Miami Herald*, a young Cuban man recited what he called "seven different types of blacks in Cuba. From darkest to lightest, they are: negro azul, prieto, moreno, mulato, trigueño, jabao and blanconaso."[11] Anthropologist L. Kaifa Roland maps an even more complex stratification of what she calls the "race-color continuum," emphasizing that her "field research found that the general populace seems to accept the position that 'el color no importa'—color doesn't matter—despite realities of racial discrimination and prejudice in day-to-day practice."[12]

Does the term *negrita* persist as a pejorative term and as a term of endearment? Is there an awareness that the popular word *mulato/a* has its origins in slavery? The Real Academia Española defines the word *mulato/a* as "de mulo, en el sentido de híbrido" (from the mule, in the sense of hybrid) and downplays its historical discursive role in the animalization of people of color.[13] The mule served as an effective symbol in the invention of race because it referred to the offspring of two animals of different species, emphasizing the profoundly racist notion that blacks and whites are separate species. The infertility of the mule symbolically underscores the futility of racial mixing to the project of whiteness and European civilization. The image of the mule represents the utility of people of color redefined as beasts of burden and as part of the means of production. *Mulato/a* simultaneously serves as a referent that reifies the psychosexual dynamic that drove the project of *blanqueamiento*. As Morales Domínguez explains, "From the end of the nineteenth to the beginning of the twentieth centuries, under the auspices of Spain, the Cuban government, and the United States, there was a program to support white European immigration to the island, mainly from Spain. At the same time attempts were made to halt immigration from the Antilles."[14] The idea was that racial mixing would eventually whitewash blackness from the body politic. Given this history, what effect does the repetition of mulata—an exoticized, often gendered, animalized symbol—have on identity? Who benefits from the existing racial constructions? Does whiteness still depend upon discursive superiority and empowerment for its existence?

Slavery, the Construction of Superiority, and Moral Panics

The discursive history of blackness as inferior and whiteness as superior originates with the African slave trade.[15] Although the expansion of that localized slave trade from minor regional practices to a transatlantic enterprise that altered the course of world history is most often attributed to economic factors, the exercise of these motivations on such a large scale was necessarily accompanied by conceptual and discursive transformations in the consciousness of the enactors who stood to profit. Economic factors certainly provided the incentive for the immense growth of an African slave trade that became an international operation and carried out the displacement and genocide of millions of Africans. The consequent wealth financed the great powers of the European empires and the imperialistic development of the Americas, and it laid the foundations for the development of the first global economy.[16] The African slave trade was clearly driven by the considerable economic benefits that it offered, but the enslavement of persons on a global scale must have required a conceptual transformation in the minds of Europeans and, later, in the minds of Euro-Americans.

That conceptual transformation was carried out through discursive means. The linguistic road from different, African, human to nonhuman, object, and ultimately commodity paved the way for the international slave trade and the subsequent amassing of vast fortunes by the colonizers. To justify the project of objectifying Africans as slaves, the discourse regarding their human status needed to be altered so that the African was no longer seen as a full human being but as a subhuman species. To think of someone as a human slave is a very different construction than to think that someone deserves to be enslaved because she or he is nonhuman. During the rise of the Atlantic slave trade, the African was denigrated in status from human and reconceived as subhuman, beast, and ultimately object and commodity. Africans stopped being merely geographically different human beings with observably different physical features and cultural practices. Instead, their differences were reconceived to justify the discursive demotion to subhuman status and their ultimate objectification. Coupled with an unfortunate preexisting Manichean dualism in the European imagination, these differences became the implements in the construction of white supremacy and black inferiority. Language changed to accommodate the shift in the conceptualization of Africans from human to subhuman status in order to justify enslavement. In this way, the negative image of the African was created discursively.

Slavery bears close examination, not only because it provides an elucidating example of extreme disparities of power, but also because it is the source from which modern societies have inherited notions of purity, racial superiority, and negative images of blackness. Orlando Patterson defines slavery as a "relation of domination" with "three sets of constitutive features corresponding to the three facets of power":

> the first is social and involves the use or threat of violence in the control of one person by another. The second is the psychological facet of influence, the capacity to persuade another person to change the way he perceived his interests and his circumstances. And third is the cultural facet of authority, "the means of transforming force into right, and obedience into duty" which, according to Jean Jacques Rousseau, the powerful find necessary "to ensure their continual mastership."[17]

The power trajectory of enslavement necessarily begins with violence upon the body and is maintained with the persisting threat of violence followed by another level of domination in which psychological and emotional deprivations and limitations impinge on the formation of identity. Patterson's third and final category is one in which the patterns of domination are integrated into the fabric of society and become assumptions. At this level, the master's abuse becomes redefined as his right, and the slave's obedience becomes his or her duty through the "sociopsychological aspect of this unusual power relationship."[18] Although it is true that whenever there is domination, there is resistance, it is also true that when domination is pervasive and persistent, power relations are internalized by both master and slave, colonizer and colonized, perpetrator and victim.

This history of slavery and domination gave rise to current racial categories. Racial constructions exist as the means of exercising relations of power. Relations of domination are expressed through the perpetuation of cultural, social, and linguistic signs. Within the context of historical violence against Africans, blackness became a symbol of slavery, of violence, of fragmentation, of subhuman status. The black body became equal to the black body in pain. The discourse accompanying slavery constructed the black body as an object of violence and served to dehumanize Africans and their descendants. The internalization of racialized images that enact disparities of power was transmitted discursively down through the centuries. Well into the twentieth century, Frantz Fanon listed the Manichean significations of black skin:

> In Europe, the Black man is the symbol of Evil. . . . The torturer is the Black man, Satan is Black, one talks of shadows, when one is dirty one is black—whether one is thinking of physical dirtiness or moral dirtiness . . . that make[s] the Black man the equivalent of sin. In Europe, whether concretely or symbolically, the Black man stands for the bad side of the character. As long as one cannot understand this fact, one is doomed to talk in circles about the "black problem." Blackness, darkness, shadow, shades, night, the labyrinths of the earth, abysmal depths, blacken someone's reputation; and on the other side, the bright look of innocence, the white dove of peace, magical, heavenly light.[19]

Blackness became the backdrop against which whiteness asserted its normative humanity, its superiority, and its power. Daniel Segal proposes that the "rendering of 'Africans' as a singular race-class meant that settlers from Europe . . . became a singular race . . . 'the white man.'"[20] Toni Morrison examines the vital role that Africanist characters play in the white imagination: "Black or colored people and symbolic figurations of blackness are markers for the benevolent and the wicked; the spiritual . . . and the voluptuous; of 'sinful' but delicious sensuality coupled with demands for purity and restraint. These figures take shape, form patterns, and play about in the pages."[21] According to David Roediger, race, then, is not a "black problem." Rather, it is "a problem among whites."[22] By the power of signs, whiteness was defined as a racialized image that Europeans internalized as their right to superiority. Negative significations and stereotypical images of blackness became embedded in discourse and thus became mutually enabling and self-justifying.

The racialized images of the African diaspora and their social dynamics were promulgated by the slave trade in the Americas. Slavery's and colonialism's legacies of racial constructions and mythologies of superiority are buoyed by their discursive power. Images of whiteness as superior and non-whiteness as the exoticized and inferior Other have become part of a global vocabulary. The racial stereotypes associated with these constructions constitute the currency of domination in social relationships and are perpetuated by discursive means. Stereotyped images are signs that are learned through words as signifying symbols. They are evoked to dominate, gain preference, privilege one person or group over another, and in many ways serve as a discursive arsenal for relations of power. These discursive signs provide a readily available repertoire that forms part of the fabric of social structures. Dominating discourse, as a form of discursive violence, perpetuates the effects of language that was born of slavery's violence.

The profound internalization of racial hierarchies that serve to privilege whiteness and denigrate blackness may be difficult to track because they operate within the private sphere and are embedded in language. During periods of what Stanley Cohen termed "moral panics," however, those internalized racial mythologies spill into the public sphere, often giving rise to racial violence. Cohen explains that "societies appear to be subject, every now and then, to periods of moral panic." Heathcott defines a moral panic as "an upwelling of intense emotion and feeling over conditions that challenge people's deep-seated values and threatens the established social order."[23] The most common ways of coping with moral panics amount to containing and controlling the Other who is perceived as a threat to the social order using methods that often result in violence. For example, Hazel Carby points out that the great migration of African Americans to the north in the United States during the turn of the twentieth century resulted in a series of moral panics that led to social policies and cultural imperatives designed to police and contain blacks—black women in particular.[24] In Cuba, even though slavery had been abolished, as Tomás Fernández Robaina explains, "Blacks and people of mixed race were free, but were not able to enjoy the same rights as whites. For centuries, colonial society had considered them simply as animals and had created legal traps, mores, and customs that would impede their full development. It was impossible that this same society would change from morning to night based on a simple decree."[25] The abolition of slavery and the continuing demand for equality in the face of independence led to waves of moral panics.

The formation of a national black political party once again raised anxieties among the white Cuban elite. The increasing insistence on equal rights on the part of Afro-Cubans and the resistance of the Cuban white elite to granting those privileges culminated in the massacre of 1912, which effectively obliterated the Independent Party of Color. Thousands of black Cubans were killed in a violent expression of moral panic that was fueled by racist discourse in newspapers. Aline Helg argues that "The 'race war' of 1912 was, in reality, an outburst of white racism against Afro-Cubans."[26] What Helg calls "black-bashing" confirms the accessibility of discursive signs denigrating blackness and their expedient use at times of increased anxiety in the body politic. Discourse included "cartoons printed by mainstream newspapers in 1912 [that] were particularly explicit... [u]sing in a comic way the traditional stereotypes that helped to mobilize whites against blacks." These expressions of racial superiority in the media were not counterbalanced by protests against the racist violence of the massacre as "very few Cubans protested the indiscriminate killing of blacks." The massacre of 1912 is a tragic instance of how violence against black persons served to alleviate moral panic. Because domination along racial lines is so internalized and continuously reinforced through discourse, the "underlying racism against blacks that was unmasked by the 'race war' remained long after 1912.... Moreover, it signified the end of black Cuban radicalism even up to the present."[27]

A more recent, albeit less violent, example of moral panic in Cuba occurred during the Special Period of the 1990s. The economic pressures of Cuba's Special Period raised anxieties, allowing the underlying racial constructions to be seen publicly as they broke through into a moral panic. As de la Fuente points out, a "revival of racism and racially discriminatory practices happened during the Special Period" and "led to growing resentment and resistance in the black population, which suddenly finds itself in a hostile environment without the political and organizational resources needed to fight against it."[28] The readily available racial constructions that had been repressed and had gone underground into the world of the familiar now bubbled over. The Special Period provides a remarkable example of how racialized dominating discourse persists even within the context of a revolution that was to provide Cuban citizens with "an alternative non-racist discourse, an inclusive ideology of national identity, and real structural changes that fostered racial equality and integration."[29]

Gilman's theories make clear, however, that during times of distress stereotypes serve a psychological function. Fears and anxieties are projected onto the perceived Other when "the line between 'good' and 'bad' responds to stresses occurring within the psyche.... Although this activity seems to take place outside the self, in the world of the object, of the Other, it is in fact only a reflection of an internal process, which draws upon repressed mental representations for its structure."[30] Given the history of slavery in the Americas, these "mental representations" are inflected by constructions of race that identify blackness as Other. Racism is based on social constructs that stereotype the Other and operate by means of discursive signs that conceive of blackness as threatening. Within a social context that historically reifies white supremacy as a deep-seated value, the negative signification of blackness serves as the justification for objectifying and denigrating black persons, and controlling the black Other can be seen as an attempt to relieve the anxieties of moral panics.

The question to ask when analyzing dominating discourse or moral panics is "qui bono"—who benefits? What are the racial (or gender or class) constructions that are operating, and what are their dynamics? After abolishing slavery and even after banning institutional racism, how does one undo the language rich with meaningful images that perpetuate the dishonor attached to blackness? How are assumptions of white superiority to be dismantled?

The Evidence of Oral Testimonies

The gathering of oral histories of Cubans on the island and abroad may provide anecdotal evidence about how racism is experienced, how racial constructions have changed over time, and what racial images operate in the discourse. For the purpose of comparison, this project covers the twentieth and twenty-first centuries and Cubans living both on the island and off. Whereas the temporal and geographic breadth of the project is wide, its focus is narrow. The survey addresses issues of self-identification in terms of race, skin color, and ethnicity. Questions focus on racial constructions, personal anecdotes about race, and how racial experiences influence life decisions. The interviews provide anecdotal evidence of how Cubans change (or do not change) their self-identification in racial or ethnic terms over time and across geographical locations. In particular, the interviews provide raw material for discursive analysis.

Oral testimony confirms that racial segregation made life difficult for those of African descent in the 1940s. Pilar, who was born in Santiago de Cuba in 1913, explains why she moved to Havana:

> I wanted to be a kindergarten teacher but it was too difficult there. There was a very big problem in Santiago. There was too much racial bias. If you were white, you had no problem, but if you were mulatto or black, you were not welcome. There was no opportunity for you in the bank or in any good job. The only jobs you could get were in manufacturing,

construction, jobs like that. But . . . that's why I left. I didn't want to have anything more to do with those people. There were many, many, many things. I had some really tough times. For example, if there was a party at school, you were not allowed to participate. Santiago was the most racist province. So much racism! They did not want blacks. Blacks were worth less than a dog. Blacks could be bricklayers, carpenters, like that, but to become a teacher, go to university, forget about that![31]

Pilar found greater opportunities in Havana, where she became a music teacher and gave lessons in a school in El Cerro neighborhood. But she also experienced a different sort of discrimination there: "There were places that I could not go with my husband, who was white. That made my life difficult and I got tired of that."

There is a sharp contrast between the discrimination of the 1940s and the racism that was impressed upon Ramón, a forty-five-year-old man who grew up in the Vedado section of Havana in the 1970s. After the revolution, Ramón's parents moved to El Vedado, a wealthy, traditionally white neighborhood in Havana. Ramón describes overt instances of racism: "When my father moved to El Vedado, they used to put notes under the door that said, 'When this is over, we are going to drag you through the streets.'"

When asked if he himself had experienced racism as a child, Ramón responded:

Blacks were in the minority in my neighborhood, El Vedado. Yes, the preference shown to white students, the preference shown to white students who had parents holding certain positions, the idea of good hair, of bad hair. As children we all played together. There wasn't that type of racism. That existed, but the racism against someone who looked really black was very strong. Obviously, when you are a child, you don't recognize this; you think that it's for other reasons—they don't like me or I don't know what their problem is. But the whites would close ranks. The saying, "had to be a black guy," the sayings that try to classify you: "no, he's a Moor, a little Moor; no, he is a mulatto. That is, constantly trying to put you in your place, to define you, not by your name, not by who you are. That is racism. It wasn't legal, but it existed, that secret division, at the level of the familiar.

The differences in institutionalized racist practices in these two testimonies are dramatic. In the 1940s higher education and job possibilities were denied and racial segregation permeated social institutions. By the 1970s the black child had access to these opportunities, but racial prejudices "at the level of the familiar" persisted. Despite being of different generations, both these Cubans expressed resentment over the preferential treatment given to whites in both public and private spheres. Childhood experiences of racial bias seemed to have had a particularly deep effect. Their awareness of these disparities determined the choices that they made as individuals and continued to influence their self-perception.

Ramón recalled an incident that exemplifies how adolescent psychosexual dynamics are expressed along a racial divide:

> "I remember I had a friend, between twelve and thirteen years old, who had a girlfriend. For example, we would go visit his girlfriend, his friend, and I noticed that I was relegated to a secondary sphere, as if I am the servant, I am the companion. But in reality, I had no hope of having that girl as my girlfriend. There was no basis for competition. That much was clear. And this happened as well sometimes at parties when the white boys would dance with a black girl, with a white girl, and when I danced with a white girl, they would cut in."

This testimony paints a vivid, quotidian enactment of the construction of superior white masculinity against the assumed inferiority of black masculinity. Within the highly charged atmosphere of adolescent romance and burgeoning desire, the black friend becomes the Other, relegated to a secondary, inferior, and even emasculated position in the service of defending whiteness. The society's racial mythologies were clearly readily available to these young people, who understood the signs and their valuation. Their behavior makes clear how children learn the dynamics of racial exclusion and superiority and act upon them. Decades later, the resulting anger and confusion remained fresh in Ramón's mind.

Ramón's testimony raises at least this question: How do repeated threats to safety and the internalization of racial terror affect the formation of self-esteem, of trust, and of a belief in a successful future? It is easy to see how these accumulated experiences could culminate in post-traumatic stress disorder, especially when they occur in childhood. Racial constructions that were inherited from slavery, passed down from generation to generation, and internalized in every new generation make it difficult to eradicate social problems. Joy DeGruy Leary, a social worker, explains that "debilitating beliefs and assumptions . . . are also part of the legacy of trauma. Most of us raise our children based upon how we ourselves were raised. We know that if a child comes from a home in which one or both parents went to college, there is a greater likelihood that child will go to college. We know that our children receive most of their attitudes, life skills and approaches to life from their parents. We also know that most of these are learned by the time they are five or six years old. In addition to the family, the legacy of trauma is also passed down through the community."[32] Leary acknowledges that "the direct relationship between the slave experience . . . and current major social problems . . . is difficult to empirically substantiate."[33] But an acknowledgment that racial constructions are spread discursively and disseminated through cultural mythologies that are acted out in daily life makes the route of transmission become clearer. Every generation that learns the discourse of racial inferiority and experiences the psychological dissociation of being objectified and alienated by their white peers is traumatized by the legacy of slavery. Every generation that learns to feel the pleasure of superiority and learns to use race to dominate their peers reinscribes the pathological power dynamics passed down from enslaving empires.

In a 2009 interview, Caridad, a forty-eight-year-old housewife from La Habana Vieja who is president of her local people's committee, emphasized how racism had changed since the revolution: "that does not exist. Sometimes you find someone who thinks like that, yes, but very few; not racism, but more about class. The example about the person who experienced racism in El Vedado, it's because he grew up in an area that was historically for whites. But not in my neighborhood. What does exist now is that there are some who have more opportunities, fewer opportunities, or no opportunity at all." Putting aside the question of how her loyalty to the revolution colors how she represents racism in contemporary Cuba, the reality is that this black housewife lives in a building that is in such poor condition that the floor caved in. Both she and her husband work at low-paying jobs and have not taken full advantage of the free higher education made available by the revolution.

Her testimony raises interesting questions. Does being clustered among a predominantly black population offer protection against prejudice? Why are so few blacks in this circle taking advantage of educational opportunities? Despite the pride about racial progress expressed by the statement "not in my neighborhood," is there an internalized reluctance to venture into higher education and more challenging work? Are there symptoms among black Cubans of what Leary has termed "post-traumatic slave syndrome"? Do more white Cubans assume that they will succeed, and do fewer black Cubans make that assumption? Does the perception that whites close ranks against blacks persist? How pervasive are racist images and language? How do these influence how people feel about themselves and each other?

Meeting the Perpetual Challenge

The examination of how racial constructions are expressed discursively is important to understanding racism because, as the linguist Saussure postulated, both signifier and signified are mental entities, and it is in the discursive and discoursing mind that signification is altered. If the construction of white superiority depends upon the construction of blackness as a signifier for animalization and inferiority, then discourse is the place, the nexus, at which signification must be altered if the material conditions of African descendants are to improve.

While specific racial constructions reflect their specific national, cultural, and linguistic contexts, slavery and colonialism created—and now technology and globalization disseminate—common images and discourses that reconstruct blackness as inferior and whiteness as superior. That process makes race an international issue. Applying discourse analysis to oral histories suggests certain possibilities for critically dismantling violent discourse. Critical discourse analysis employs a variety of disciplines to explore the connection between language as a social practice and relations of power.[34] Can critical discourse analysis diffuse discursive violence and provide a practical methodology for disarming the signifying arsenal that maintains dominating relations of power? History cannot be altered, but signification can. As James Baldwin wrote, "The time has come to realize that the interracial drama acted out ... has not only created a new black man, it has created a new white man, too. ... For even when the worst has been said, it must also be added that the perpetual challenge posed by this problem was always, somehow, perpetually met."[35]

Notes

1. José Martí, *Tres documentos de nuestra América* (Havana: Casa de las Américas, 1979), 32; Constitución Política de la República de Cuba de 1976, Preámbulo, 617, Political Database of the Americas, 2008, pdba.georgetown.edu/Constitutions/Cuba/cuba2002.html#mozTocId333; and Fidel Castro, Castro Speech Database, Latin American Network Information Center (LANIC), University of Texas at Austin 2009, wwwl.lanic.utexas.edu/project/castro/db/1959/19590323.html. The original statement of Martí, in Spanish, is, "No hay odio de razas, porque no hay razas." Unless otherwise noted, all translations are my own.

2. Ignacio Ramonet and Fidel Castro, *Fidel Castro: My Life: A Spoken Autobiography* (New York: Scribner, 2009), 230.

3. Nancy Morejón, interview by Sapphire, *Bomb* 78 (Winter 2001–2), 72–75.

4. Alejandro de la Fuente, "Recreating Racism: Race and Discrimination in Cuba's Special Period," in Philip Brenner, Marguerite Rose Jiménez, John M. Kirk, and William M. Leo-

Grande, eds., *Reinventing the Revolution: A Contemporary Cuba Reader* (Lanham, MD: Rowman and Littlefield, 2008), 321; Nadine T. Fernandez, *Revolutionizing Romance: Interracial Couples in Contemporary Cuba* (New Brunswick, NJ: Rutgers University Press, 2010), 110.

5. United Nations, International Convention on the Elimination of All Forms of Racial Discrimination, *Reports Submitted by States Parties under Article 9 of the Convention*, January 30, 2010, www2.ohchr.org/english/bodies/cerd/cerds78.htm.

6. Ferdinand de Saussure, *Course in General Linguistics*, trans. Roy Harris (Chicago, IL: Open Court, 1986), 66.

7. Ibid., 72.

8. Esteban Morales Domínguez, *Desafíos de la problemática racial en Cuba* (Havana: Fundación Fernando Ortiz, 2007), 104.

9. Ibid., 104, fn. 101.

10. Sander Gilman, *Difference and Pathology: Stereotypes of Sexuality, Race, and Madness* (Ithaca, NY: Cornell University Press, 1985), 13, 20, 25.

11. "A Rising Voice: Afro–Latin Americans, a Barrier for Cuba's Blacks," *Miami Herald*, June 20, 2007, www.miamiherald.com/multimedia/news/afrolatin/part4/index.html.

12. L. Kaifa Roland, "Tourism and the Negrificación of Cuban Identity," *Transforming Anthropology* 14 (2006), 152.

13. Real Academia Española, *Diccionario de la lengua española*, 22nd ed., s.v. "mulato, ta," http://buscon.rae.es/draeI/SrvltConsulta?TIPO_BUS=3&LEMA=mulato.

14. Morales Domínguez, *Desafíos de la problemática racial*, 127.

15. Some of these theories were first argued in my dissertation. See Yvette Louis, "Body Language: The Slave Body and the Word in African Diasporic Literature," PhD diss., Princeton University, 2004.

16. Thomas C. Holt, *Race in the Twenty-First Century* (Cambridge, MA: Harvard University Press, 2000); Eric Williams, *Capitalism and Slavery* (Chapel Hill: University of North Carolina Press, 1994); Orlando Patterson, *Slavery and Social Death: A Comparative Study* (Cambridge, MA: Harvard University Press, 1982).

17. Patterson, *Slavery and Social Death*, 1–2.

18. Joy DeGruy Leary, *Post Traumatic Slave Syndrome: America's Legacy of Enduring Injury and Healing* (Milwaukee, WI: Uptone Press, 2005), 121.

19. Frantz Fanon, *Black Skin, White Masks*, trans. Charles Lan Markmann (New York: Grove, 1967), 189.

20. Daniel A. Segal, "'The European': Allegories of Racial Purity," *Anthropology Today* 7, no. 5 (1991), 7, www.jstor.org/stable/3032780.

21. Toni Morrison, *Playing in the Dark: Whiteness and the Literary Imagination* (Cambridge, MA: Harvard University Press, 1992), ix.

22. David R. Roediger, *The Wages of Whiteness: Race and the Making of the American Working Class* (New York: Verso, 1999), 6.

23. Stanley Cohen, *Folk Devils and Moral Panics* (New York: Routledge, 2003), 1; Joseph Heathcott, "Moral Panic in a Plural Culture," *Cross Currents* 61, no. 1 (2011), 39–44.

24. Hazel V. Carby, "Policing the Black Woman's Body in an Urban Context," *Critical Inquiry* 18 (Summer 1992), 738–55.

25. Tomás Fernández Robaina, *El negro en Cuba: 1902–1958* (Havana: Editorial de Ciencias Sociales en Cuba, 1994), 21.

26. Aline Helg, *Our Rightful Share: The Afro-Cuban Struggle for Equality, 1886–1912* (Chapel Hill: University of North Carolina Press, 1995), 232.

27. Ibid., 228, 234.

28. De la Fuente, "Recreating Racism," 323.

29. Fernandez, *Revolutionizing Romance*, 110.

30. Gilman, *Difference and Pathology*, 18.

31. All interviews were conducted in confidentiality and the names of the interviewees are withheld by mutual agreement.

32. Leary, *Post Traumatic Slave Syndrome*, 122–23.

33. Ibid., 124.

34. Norman Fairclough, *Language and Power* (New York: Longman, 1989); Martin Reisigl and Ruth Wodak, *Discourse and Discrimination: Rhetorics of Racism and Antisemitism* (New York: Routledge, 2001).

35. James Baldwin, *Notes of a Native Son* (Boston, MA: Beacon Press, 1955), 175.

17

Cubans without Borders

From the Buildup to the Breakdown of a Socially Constructed Wall across the Florida Straits

SUSAN ECKSTEIN

In recent decades Latin Americans have accounted for about half of all immigrants to the United States, and once in the States these newcomers tend to remain deeply enmeshed in ties with their homeland. In particular, they often generously share earnings in their new country with friends, and especially family, back home, even when they struggle to make do in their new land.

Between 1959 and 1989 Cuban immigrants were an exception to this tendency. In 1990, when Latin American immigrants as a whole remitted $5.7 billion to their home countries, members of the Cuban diaspora sent a mere $50 million—even though Cubans at the time constituted the second-largest foreign-born group in the United States. Moreover, few Cuban immigrants made trips home to visit the friends and family they left behind. According to a study of immigrants from eleven Latin American countries, only Guatemalans made fewer trips.[1]

Only since 1990 have Cubans followed the example of other Latin American immigrants. By 2003 remittances to Cuba were estimated to have reached more than a billion dollars, 80 to 90 percent of which came from the United States, where nearly 90 percent of Cuban émigrés settled. After 1990 the number of émigrés who visited Cuba also increased. Between 1990 and 2003 the number of trip-takers rose from an estimated 5,000 to 7,000 to more than 120,000.[2]

What accounts for this sudden, dramatic rise in Cuban American cross-border bonding and generosity?[3] The Cuban experience demonstrates that immigrants do not necessarily enmesh their lives across borders. Studies typically point to certain characteristics of immigrants to explain variability in homeland ties, such as motivation for migration (economic versus political), time elapsed since uprooting, family remaining in the home country, country-of-origin language retention, and income.[4] Yet Cuban immigrants remitted little even though they were, on average, the wealthiest Latin American immigrants. They sent little even though they continued to have close family in Cuba, and even though they continued to speak Spanish after resettling in the United States.[5] The Cuban experience points to the import of institutional and cultural forces to transnational engagement, at both the macro level and the informal level at which people's lives transpire.[6] For three decades formal and informal barriers stood in the way of Cuban immigrant transnational engagement. It took the crisis that ensued in Cuba when Soviet aid and trade ended with the dissolution of the Soviet Union to break down, first, people-to-people, then state-to-state, barriers to such ties. The impetus for the breakdown in barriers came initially from Cuba.

Institutional and Informal Barriers to Transnational Ties, 1959–1989

People-to-people ties, including visits and income sharing, might be assumed to be a personal matter, of personal choosing. But during Castro's first three decades of rule—years during which 7 percent of the Cuban population had immigrated to the United States—both institutional and informal barriers constrained such ties.[7]

Institutional Barriers

Both the U.S. and Cuban governments imposed barriers. Washington, opposed to the revolution, instituted an embargo in 1962 that constricted visits to, plus investment and spending in and trade with, Cuba. The embargo was intended to strangulate the Castro-led regime to the point of collapse. President Jimmy Carter (in office 1977–81) lifted the travel ban and permitted Cuban immigrants to remit up to $500 quarterly to their island families. President Ronald Reagan (1981–89), however, reinstituted bans on homeland visits and remittance sending. Both U.S. and Cuban authorities also made mail and telephone communications difficult.

In his concern to consolidate the revolution, Castro, in turn, instituted means to keep Cubans on the island from associating with those who, opposed to the country's radical makeover, had fled the country. Along with restricting émigré visits, except in the period under Carter, he discouraged cross-border ties by stigmatizing those who left. He portrayed émigrés as worms, scum, and traitors. His government also penalized Cubans with (known) diasporic ties. They were denied access to the Communist Party— and membership in the Party was a prerequisite for attaining prestigious high-level jobs. Through simultaneously outlawing the possession of U.S. dollars, the government discouraged Cubans from securing remittances from family who had emigrated.

Informal Barriers

When laws are unpopular, people are likely to evade them informally, illegally, and covertly. Compliance with rules and regulations is most likely when the strictures are consonant with people's wants. Indeed, between 1959 and 1989 most Cuban émigrés and island Cubans reinforced the socially constructed wall across the Straits that their respective governments had put in place. They did so because they ascribed to the values on which the wall was premised: namely, disassociation with compatriots who opposed their stance on the revolution. Informal social dynamics in both Cuban American and Cuban neighborhoods further discouraged cross-border ties.

The Cubans who settled in Miami and Union City, initially the two most important émigré enclaves, built strong social and economic ties "among their own."[8] Perceiving themselves as exiles, the hundreds of thousands who emigrated during the first two decades of Castro's rule adamantly opposed ties with their fellow Cubans who had stayed behind and sided with the revolution. They ostracized, stigmatized, penalized economically, and sometimes violently attacked fellow Cuban Americans who defied their taboo of dealings with Cuba under Castro. The emergent Cuban American leadership—who almost without exception had emigrated in the first years of the revolution or were progeny of parents who had—in turn used their influence to enforce and reinforce the wall.[9]

On the island, Cubans had their own psychological, principled, and pragmatic reasons for shunning ties with those who had left. The psychological wounds were deep and stood in the way of cross-border bonding. Cubans resented close family members who had abandoned them. They also saw diasporic ties as a liability, in that job advancement and Party membership were reserved for those without such ties. Under the circumstances, Cubans had their own reasons to either sever ties with family members who emigrated or maintain ties covertly. They never publicly challenged state-sanctioned norms.

Cubans even rejected gifts from family members who emigrated. Imported goods defied the non-materialistic norms of the revolutionary society-in-formation that Che Guevara personified. They also symbolized ties with Cubans who had been uprooted in opposition to the revolution. A cinematographer in Cuba noted in an interview for my study that those who fled "sent packages with the most basic items, such as Colgate toothpaste and brand-name shampoo. . . . We didn't fight a revolution for Colgate toothpaste! We fought for more important rights." In this manner, transnational gift giving soured transnational ties.

Informal social pressures even led Cubans who had not been won over by the revolution to conceal received gifts. An émigré who visited Cuba in 1983, for example, remembered his island cousin showing him a closet filled with packages that the cousin's mother had sent from the United States. The cousin dared not wear the clothes sent for fear that doing so would cause problems at work. Imported clothes were markers of shunned-upon diasporic ties.

Because Cubans remained deeply committed to family values, emigration often strained, but did not entirely rupture, kinship ties among Cubans who did and did not emigrate. However, the ties that persisted were intermittent, rarely face-to-face, and often covert.

The Breakdown of Informal Cross-Border Barriers: The Post-Soviet Era and Diasporic Kin to the Rescue

Cuba under Castro was heavily dependent on the Soviet bloc.[10] Consequently, with the superpower's demise the cutoff in Soviet aid and trade caused the Cuban economy to contract by more than 30 percent between 1989 and 1994.

While the government sought amidst the crisis to sustain the cradle-to-grave welfare benefits intricately associated with the revolution, rationing came to meet no more than one-third to one-half of family monthly needs. Meanwhile, scarcities fueled a dollar-based black market in which non-rationed foods sold at prices unaffordable with formerly adequate peso paychecks. In desperation, Cubans reached out to family members in the diaspora for help. Remittances became ordinary Cubans' main source of dollars.[11]

For remittances to be forthcoming, both Cuban Americans and Cubans had to defy the informal and formal barriers that had kept cross-border social and economic ties at bay for three decades. They needed to form relations based on trust and commitment, which were rare during the Soviet era. Although ordinary Cubans led the impetus for the change, new Cuban government policies and then, more hesitantly and inconsistently, new U.S. policies created the bedrock for Cubans on the two sides of the Straits to bond.

Changes in Cuba

As the island economy dipped into deep recession, Cubans re-envisioned overseas family members as a potential economic asset, no longer as a liability. The Cuban government contributed, directly and indirectly, to the positive revaluation of the diaspora, and accordingly to cross-border bridge building. To deal with the crisis the government abandoned revolutionary precepts. It decriminalized possession of U.S. dollars and permitted Cubans for the first time to use dollars for everyday purchases (and after 2004 to use Cuban convertible pesos, known as CUCs, with dollar value in Cuba). The government, in addition, removed restrictions on émigré visits and on emigration.

Cubans, in turn, became pragmatic. Their commitment to the utopian revolutionary project fizzled. When survival became their primary concern, they perceived their family abroad as a potential source of dollars to address their subsistence needs.[12] Cubans who attained U.S. dollars, unlike Cubans who were peso-dependent, could afford goods sold on the black market and at the new dollar-only stores that the government established.

Not all Cubans, however, had overseas relatives to turn to, either because no family had previously emigrated or because relations with those who had left had been damaged beyond repair by their opposing views toward the revolution. Afro-Cubans without family in the diaspora found themselves at a particular disadvantage. Because they had benefited from the revolution, few of them had emigrated.[13]

Cubans without overseas networks tried to create them, typically by attempting to have their most employable family members emigrate. Less frequently Cubans married foreigners, for money if not love, to improve their family's lot along with their own. Upon moving abroad they could send remittances to relatives who remained on the island. For this reason an informal foreign marriage market emerged in Havana around embassies. In 2002 the "going rate" on the marriage market for a Spaniard was $4,000 to $5,000, for a Costa Rican $1,000, and for a Panamanian $500. The different rates reflected the perceived economic worth of marriage to someone from the respective countries. Cubans also advertised their marriageability on Internet websites or, more frequently, turned to tourist-based prostitution to earn hard currency (sometimes resulting in marriage, a ticket to move abroad).[14]

In my interviews some Cubans spoke about how quickly the crisis broke down informal barriers between kin who had been divided politically over the revolution. Reflecting on the crisis-based change, a child psychiatrist who had been a dedicated Communist Party member noted, "During the moments of most extreme hardship . . . [when] people couldn't eat . . . it was remarkable. There was a feeling of . . . being rescued by those abroad. . . . This is when there was a sudden change in perceptions of, and relations with, family abroad."

Ceasing to stigmatize those who left, the government increased the number of Cubans in the diaspora who might send remittances. It even publicly reimagined the diaspora. Following a growing trend among third world governments to reclaim their diasporas, it began to speak of the Cuban community abroad, the equivalent of long-distance nationalists.[15] Its changed stance was rooted in its own desperate need for hard currency in the post-Soviet era, to finance imports, foreign debt payments, and investment. The government's new permissiveness of small-scale private economic activity since Raúl Castro assumed power is likely to further induce Cubans in the United States to send remittances and to strengthen the ties on which transnational income sharing rests.

Changes in the United States

In turn, for transnational ties to take hold Cuban émigrés needed to be both willing and able to associate with family members who remained in Cuba. The Cuban American leadership continued to oppose such ties, and they leveraged their wealth and mounting political influence to obstruct cross-border ties. They became sufficiently influential in the post–Cold War era to convince Congress and the White House to restrict travel and remittance sending to Cuba, even after Washington had reestablished diplomatic and economic relations with other remaining communist countries, most notably with China and Vietnam.[16] Cuban American leaders' influence varied somewhat by year, however. In most years they convinced the U.S. government to limit visitation rights to once a year. However, in 1996 and again in 2004, the Clinton and George W. Bush administrations, respectively, officially tightened the so-called personal embargo. Clinton required political reform in Cuba before restrictions on travel would be removed, and Bush restricted visits to once every three years, and only to see immediate kin. Influential Cuban Americans also convinced U.S. officials to cap permissible income transfers, in most years at $300 quarterly. During these years, 11 percent of Latin American immigrants made more than one annual trip to their homeland and, on average, remitted more than the cap imposed on Cuban immigrants.[17]

To pursue cross-border ties ordinary Cuban Americans had to defy the leadership pressures, and sometimes also official regulations. Indeed, despite the constraints, while island Cubans shifted their stance toward transnational engagement an increasing number of Cubans in the United States did the same. As previously noted, Cuban American visits to Cuba and remittance sending rose dramatically after 1990.[18] Via travel through third countries, émigré visits increased even during the years in the 1990s when Washington prohibited direct travel. Only in 2004, when President George W. Bush dramatically restricted rights to homeland visits and remittance sending, did the number of Cuban American travelers and the amount of money remitted drop off. Transnational ties picked up anew in 2009, when President Barak Obama ended the so-called personal embargo on rights to travel and send remittances. Reportedly, in 2010 some 300,000 Cuban Americans visited Cuba, triple the number who went the previous year; and estimated remittances to Cuba (from all countries) exceeded $1 billion—the same level as before Bush tightened the personal embargo.[19]

The surge in Cuban American transnational engagement, sometimes in conformity with, while at other times in defiance of, U.S. regulations, built on changes in the Cuban American community. At the same time that some Soviet-era émigrés reluctantly extended a helping hand to desperate family members in Cuba, the Cubans who emigrated in the post-Soviet era were the main cross-border bridge-builders. With approximately twenty thousand Cubans emigrating annually since the mid-1990s, recent émigrés have come to account for an ever greater percentage of the Cuban American community.[20] The new émigrés had very different, Cuba-formed perspectives on life than did the Soviet-era arrivals and, accordingly, very different views toward cross-country engagement. The crisis-formed generation tended to perceive of themselves as immigrants, in contrast to the earlier émigrés (especially those who had emigrated between 1959 and 1979, who see themselves as exiles),[21] and in their move abroad they remained morally committed to maintaining ties with, and helping economically, family members they left behind. Miami survey data show, for example, that in 2007 nearly 2.5 times as many post–Soviet-era as 1959–64 émigrés sent remittances. Moreover, the post–Soviet-era émigrés sent more money even though, on average, they were far poorer.[22] The more recent arrivals were also twice as likely to have made a return trip to Cuba, even though they had far fewer years in the United States in which to travel, and they were about three times as likely to feel there should be no restrictions on travel.[23]

Thus, in the United States the buildup of transnational ties, and of normative underpinnings for such ties, rested first and foremost on the emigration of Cubans with very different views toward transnational ties than was characteristic among Soviet-era émigrés, especially those who fled in the first years of Castro's rule. Most self-defined exiles remained committed to their pre- and anti-revolution Cuba-formed mindset.

Materialist Norms in Post–Soviet-Era Cuba

The buildup of transnational ties has also rested on normative changes in Cuba. As cross-border ties built up, Cubans began to embrace, and openly so, the materialistic lifestyle that the United States epitomized and overseas relatives personified. Cubans began to covet U.S. goods that in the heyday of revolutionary fervor they had shunned as counterrevolutionary. Consequently, Cubans came to yearn for dollars not merely for basic subsistence, but also to purchase electric fans, televisions, VCRs, iPods, prestige-label clothing and shoes, and the like. By the early 2000s Cubans tended to know far more U.S. brand names than did people in many other non-English-speaking countries.[24] Lifestyle differences between families on the two sides of the Straits began to hinge more on differences in their pocketbooks than on differences in values.

The taboo on American-style consumerism broke down to the point that Cubans proudly flaunted materialism in their everyday lives. Pointing to the change, a man who worked for a state enterprise noted to me how "the Miami Cuban culture promotes Lycra, puffy hair, lots of makeup, and gold." He himself embraced the materialistic lifestyle that remittances from his siblings who had emigrated made possible. With money from one sister who left in 1980 and from another who left in 1998, he was able to live in a freshly painted house, which he fenced in and furnished with a TV, VCR, CD player, stereo, computer, wireless phone, and beautiful artwork.

His home renovations revealed a new Cuban desire to be conspicuously materialist. In this vein, a city planner noted, "Whereas it used to be taboo to show that you were living better than others, now people want to show that they live better.... They put up fences and paint the outsides of their houses."

The Cuban government tacitly contributed to the new norms. It expanded the range of goods that Cubans could purchase at the new state hard-currency-based stores. The availability of more goods, in turn, made Cubans covet all the more remittance-generating ties with the diaspora (unless they accessed hard currency through tourism, which the government also encouraged in the post-Soviet era).

The Transnationalization of the Cuban American Economy and the New Cuban Materialism

Economic changes on the U.S. side of the Straits further fueled the buildup of transnational ties and Cubans' new materialistic yearnings. Entrepreneurial Cuban Americans capitalized on the changed milieu. Regardless of how entrepreneurs privately felt about the revolution, they took advantage of, and promoted, bridge-building businesses. Some became what Alejandro Portes, William Haller, and Luis Guarnizo call transnational entrepreneurs, while others transnationalized the reach of their formerly Cuban American–oriented enclave businesses.[25]

For one, a new occupation evolved entirely grounded in transnational ties and trust. So-called *mulas* make a business of carrying money and goods from the United States to the island. Numbering possibly in the thousands around the turn of the millennium, they were known by word-of-mouth. Their economic success rested on their reputations and on their networks of contacts, extending from Cuban American neighborhoods to customs officials and distributors in Cuba.[26] In Cuba they sometimes offered home delivery services through a network of Cuba-based mulas that they built up. Many of the U.S.-based mulas are self-employed, but some work for travel agencies that have taken advantage of the new remittance-transfer market.

My interviews uncovered other small-scale informal, covert businesses built on transnational ties and trust. These included "mini-banks." The "bankers" take deposits from fellow Cuban Americans that island kin can withdraw almost immediately from island "bank" partners. Both the mulas and "bankers" created niches for their services by underpricing formal remittance-transmitting services,[27] by imposing no bureaucratic procedures, such as compliance with U.S. and Cuban regulations, and by building on and deepening a cross-border trust that had been nearly nonexistent during the first three decades of Castro's rule.

In turn, a late-1990s émigré who could not make use of his island medical training in the United States established an informal "1-800-Flowers for Cuba" venture. Cuban Americans in Miami pay him for funeral arrangements for island family. The doctor-turned-businessman arranges through a Cuba-based network for the delivery of flowers and food to grieving island families.

Another post–Soviet-era émigré offers a Cuban home-delivery grocery business, in coordination with island relatives. The island partners purchase fruits and vegetables from small farmers and deliver the produce, paid for by Miami kin.

In the 1990s Miami stores also contributed to the buildup of the new island materialism and to the transnational ties that fueled it. Neighborhood pharmacies and shipping companies offered island delivery services, while large discount stores began to appeal to nascent Cuban consumer yearnings, to the point of advertising that they had "everything for Cuba." Such advertising encourages Cuban Americans to purchase goods for island families. An owner of one of Miami's main low-ticket-item stores acknowledged in 2000 that most of his $1.2-million worth of annual sales was ending up on the island.[28] So common are purchases for Cuba now that stores provide scales on which customers can weigh merchandise, to determine how much they can buy to take in their suitcases on trips home. (The poundage that travelers can take on planes is tightly controlled.)

Even businesses that are not owned by Cuban Americans have fueled the buildup of economically consequential transnational ties. Multinational wire service companies, such as Western Union, have been permitted to operate with Cuban partners since the late 1990s. Although the companies charge higher fees than the informal "bankers" and mulas do, and more for transfers to Cuba than to other countries in the Caribbean and Central America,[29] they appeal to Cuban Americans who want to comply with U.S. law and who believe that the regulated businesses are more trustworthy than informal transfer agents.

The Informal Transnationalization of Cuba's Base of Social Stratification

Economic transfers flow almost entirely in one direction, from the United States to Cuba. With little to offer materially in exchange, remittance recipients symbolically reciprocate in kind. They bestow status on those abroad who share, and are likely to share, earnings. As a result, diaspora material sacrifices involved in remittance sending generate their own reward. The reward is entirely embedded in transnational ties, and rests on a transformation and transnationalization of Cuba's bases of social stratification. Humble new immigrants are the most appreciative of the symbolic rewards that nonimmigrants offer.

This phenomenon—what might be called transnational-embedded symbolic capital—has diverse dimensions. For one, remittance giving raises émigré social status within the homeland context, in a manner that has turned the 1959 to 1989 cross-border status schema on its head. Cubans have re-envisioned the people of the diaspora—the people whom the government had previously pejoratively portrayed as scum—as heroes.[30] The shift came during the crisis. The new stature is a reward for cross-border income sharing.

Cuban émigrés who share earnings, in turn, gain respect. For example, an anesthesiologist from Havana had been the victim, in her words, of "almost a civil war" at work and in her neighborhood when her family fled in the 1960s, and then again when she tried to flee in 1980. But after she successfully emigrated in the late 1980s she was treated "like a *señora*" when she returned to visit in the 1990s. Arriving with thousands of dollars and gifts for island family, she found herself treated as a guest of honor.

Moreover, some income-sharing émigrés acquired new authority vis-à-vis their families in Cuba. An unemployed woman, formerly estranged from her mother who had abandoned her in order to emigrate in 1980, re-envisioned her mother in the 1990s as, in her words, "the matriarch." The change came when her mother became the primary income provider for the island family. New transnationally embedded authority also extends to marital relations that ended in divorce. As a Cuba-trained doctor who works in a Miami factory told me, his former wife's family had come to appreciate him more since he moved to the United States, even though his professional status had taken a nosedive. As he noted, he now had "decision-making power in his former wife's household" because of the money he was sending.

Emigration has become so status enhancing in the new transnationalized context that it matters not how those who left earn a living.[31] Cubans now see those living abroad as superior regardless of their source of income. In the words of the city planner, "They could be trash collectors! It doesn't matter. Cubans feel they are part of the elite."

Comparable status, respect, deference, and prestige are not bestowed on Cubans engaged in low-skilled work either in Cuba or in the communities in which they resettle in the United States. Instead, the values are embedded in the cross-border context, associated with remittance sending and the prospects of it.

The new symbolic rewards that come with the new transnational moral commitment to share money and goods with non-migrants are not entirely voluntarily sustained. Cross-border income sharing echoes Marcel Mauss's claims about nonvoluntary aspects of gift giving. Income sharing has come to be seen as a duty, as an imperative.[32] A man who had worked in Europe noted, "The pressure on you is tremendous. . . . There is a strong implicit social contract between a migrant and his family." He talked about how in going abroad Cubans were pressured to solve all their family's problems.

The emergent informal transnationalized status schema is eroding the previous Cuba-based relationship between skills and status. The most educated Cubans who formerly had the most prestigious and best-paying state jobs cannot afford the same lifestyles on their official salaries that remittance-receiving Cubans with less prestigious and lower-paying peso jobs enjoy. Status on the island has come to rest less on work, human capital, and political loyalty than on who Cubans know abroad. Those who stayed in Cuba and worked their way up the skill-based socialist hierarchy have experienced downward mobility in lifestyle relative to many remittance recipients.

Conclusion

Immigrants from Latin American and other developing countries have become increasingly enmeshed in relations with their homelands, even as they assimilate in their new land. Cuban immigrants were long an exception to this tendency, but in the post-Soviet era they too have become transnationally engaged, when the conditions became conducive to that transformation.

The Cuban experience demonstrates that transnational engagement is only partially explicable at the individual level, in terms of immigrant wants and ability to afford homeland visits and income sharing. Structural and cultural conditions must also be conducive, both in immigrant homelands and in receiving countries where immigrants resettle. For Cubans, conditions only became conducive in the post-Soviet era.

Notes

1. Deborah Aller Meyers, "Migrant Remittances to Latin America: Reviewing the Literature," 1998, www.thedialogue.org/Publications Files/meyers.pdf; Susan Eckstein, *The Immigrant Divide: How Cuban Americans Changed the U.S. and Their Homeland* (New York: Routledge, 2009), 203, table 6.3; Manuel Orozco, B. Lindsay Lowell, Micah Bump, and Rachel Fedewa, *Transnational Engagement, Remittances and Their Relationship to Development in Latin America and the Caribbean* (Washington, DC: Institute for the Study of International Migration, 2005), 16. The survey targeted immigrants in five U.S. cities (including Miami) in 2003–4. Orozco and colleagues found that Guatemalans were the only Latin Americans to make fewer homeland trips than Cubans, largely because many of them were illegal immigrants who risked problems reentering the United States if they made homeland trips. In contrast, the Cuban Adjustment Act entitles all Cubans who set foot in the United States a path to legal residency and citizenship, even if they emigrated illegally.

2. Eckstein, *Immigrant Divide*, 179, 133; José Alejandro Aguilar Trujillo, "Las remesas desde exterior," in *Cuba: investigación económica* (Havana: Instituto Nacional de Investigaciones Económicas, 2001), 71–104, 84; Paolo Spadoni, "The Role of the United States in the Cuban Economy," Papers and Proceedings of the Thirteenth Annual Meeting of the Association for the Study of the Cuban Economy (ACSE), 2003, http://www.ascecuba.org/publications/proceedings/volume13/pdfs/spadoni.pdf

3. In this study I draw on statistical, census, and survey research data, plus news and relevant secondary source materials. I also draw on semi-structured interviews that I conducted with Cubans in Havana and with Cuban Americans in the two most important Cuban American settlements, Greater Miami–Dade County (Florida) and Greater Union City, Hudson County (New Jersey), between 2000 and 2006, with assistance from Lorena Barbería. The quotations in the text come from these interviews. Over the years New Jersey became ever less and Florida ever more the home to Cuban immigrants. The U.S. census reported that 45 percent of all Cuban Americans in the United States lived in Miami and 13 percent lived in New Jersey in 1970. As of 2000 the respective percentages were 52 and 7. See Eckstein, *Immigrant Divide*, 46, as well as the introduction and appendix of that book, for more details about the field research.

4. Compare Sergio Díaz-Briquets and Jorge Pérez-López, "Refugee Remittances: Conceptual Issues and the Cuban and Nicaraguan Experiences," *International Migration Review* 31, no. 2 (Spring 1997), 423; Rubén Rumbaut, "Severed or Sustained Attachments? Language, Identity, and Imagined Communities in the Post-Immigrant Generation," in Peggy Levitt and Mary Waters, eds., *The Changing Face of Home: The Transnational Lives of the Second Generation* (New York: Russell Sage Foundation, 2002), 43–95.

5. Eckstein, *Immigrant Divide*, 52.

6. Roger Waldinger and David Fitzgerald, "Transnationalism in Question," *American Journal of Sociology* 109, no. 5 (March 2004), 1177–95, also highlight the role of the state, but they demonstrate that other institutions, as well as norms and values, may have an impact on people-to-people ties across borders, and that this impact may change when circumstances change.

7. Eckstein, *Immigrant Divide*, 203, table 6.3.

8. See Alejandro Portes and Alex Stepick, *City on the Edge: The Transformation of Miami* (Berkeley: University of California Press, 1993), 132–37.

9. Eckstein, *Immigrant Divide*, chapter 3.

10. Compare Carmelo Mesa-Lago, *Market, Socialist, and Mixed Economies* (Baltimore, MD: Johns Hopkins University Press, 2000); Economic Commission on Latin America and the Caribbean (ECLAC, Comisión Económica para América Latina y el Caribe) of the United Nations, *La Economía Cubana* (Mexico, DF: Fondo de Cultura Económico, 2000); William LeoGrande and Julie Thomas, "Cuba's Quests for Economic Independence," *Journal of Latin American Studies* 34, pt. 2 (May 2002), 325–64.

11. U.S.-Cuba Trade and Economic Council (UCTEC), "Economic Eye on Cuba," March 17, 2002, 11, 12, www.cubatrade.org; Spadoni, "Role of the United States."

12. On changes in Cuban life-views, see Susan Eckstein and Catherine Krull, "From Building Barriers to Bridges: Cuban Ties across the Straits," *Diplomacy and Statecraft* 20 (Spring 2009), 341–59.

13. This issue of Afro-Cuban emigration is complex. In this context, see chapter 16 in this volume, especially the introduction and the section "The Persistence and Signifiers of Racism."

14. Cubans who took on international assignments, for example as doctors and teachers in Venezuela, were also partially paid in hard currency. However, their work abroad did not provide the bedrock for sustained transnational social and economic ties. Information on the "going rate" for marriage comes from an interview I did with a Cuban economist in 2001.

15. See Nina Glick Schiller and Georges Fouron, *Georges Woke Up Laughing: Long Distance Nationalism and the Search for Home* (Durham, NC: Duke University Press, 2001); and Robert Smith, "Contradictions of Diasporic Institutionalization in Mexican Politics: The 2006 Migrant Vote and Other Forms of Inclusion and Control," *Ethnic and Racial Studies* 31, no. 4 (May 2008), 708–41.

16. For a discussion of U.S. government travel and remittance policies in the post–Cold War period, see Susan Eckstein, "The Personal Is Political: The Cuban Electoral Policy Cycle," *Latin American Politics and Society* 51, no. 1 (2009), 119–48; and Eckstein, *Immigrant Divide*, chapters 3, 4, 6.

17. Eckstein, "The Personal Is Political," and *Immigrant Divide*, chapter 6; Orozco et al., *Transnational Engagement*, 16, 24; Manuel Orozco, "Transnationalism and Development: Trends and Opportunities in Latin America," 2005, http://w.thedialogue.org/PublicationFiles/Part%206-Orozco.pdf, table 15.2. Orozco ("Transnationalism and Development," table 15.4) reported that immigrants from all Latin American countries besides Cuba remitted, on average, no less than $161 and as much as $394 monthly (in 2003).

18. Eckstein, *Immigrant Divide*, figure 4.1, 133; Susan Eckstein and Lorena Barbería, "Grounding Immigrant Generations in History: Cuban Americans and Their Transnational Ties," *International Migration Review* 36, no. 3 (Fall 2002), 814.

19. Arturo Lopez-Levy, "Cuban Americans Vote with Their Feet against the Travel Prohi-

bition," *Havana Note*, November 23, 2010, www.thehavananote.com/node/822; "U.S. Policy for Cash Remittances Is Holiday Gift for Cubans: An Editorial," *Times-Picayune*, January 2, 2011, www.nola.com/opinions/index.ssf/2011/01/new_US-policy_for_cash_remittance.html. Although during the Great Recession in the United States remittances to other Latin American countries declined, they increased to Cuba because U.S. restrictions between 2004 and 2009 had limited the rights and capacity of Cuban Americans to send remittances.

20. On changes in Cuba and Cuban lived experiences, and views on life so formed, see Eckstein, *Immigrant Divide*. By 2000 Cuban émigrés who arrived before 1959 and during the periods 1959–64, 1965–79, 1980–89, and 1990–2000 accounted for, respectively, 3, 9, 17, 11, and 15 percent of Cuban Americans in the United States. The U.S.-born accounted for the remaining 46 percent (Eckstein, *Immigrant Divide*, 33).

21. Cubans who emigrated in 1980 from the port of Mariel tend to interpret life through the same anti-revolution lens as earlier émigrés, but having experienced more of Cuba under Castro, they tend to be more nuanced in their understanding of Cubans who did not uproot, and they are more willing to maintain ties with them. On differences between émigré waves in the pre-migration lived experiences that have shaped their transnational engagement (and lack thereof), see Eckstein, *Immigrant Divide*.

22. See Florida International University (FIU), Institute for Public Opinion Research (IPOR), *FIU/Cuba Poll*, 2000, 2004, 2007, 2008, http://cri.fiu.edu/research/cuba-poll/. National survey data also point to similar émigré cohort differences. See Bendixen & Amandi International, "Remittances to Cuba from the United States," Washington, DC, May 25, 2005, http://bendixenandamandi.com/wp-content/uploads/2010/08/IAD-Orozco-Cuban-Remittances-Presentation-2005.pdf. In contrast, Sarah Blue reports that Cubans relied heavily on early émigrés and not merely the most recent; Blue, "State Policy, Economic Crisis, Gender, and Family Ties: Determinants of Family Remittances to Cuba," *Economic Geography* 80, no. 1 (2004), 63–82.

23. Eckstein, *Immigrant Divide*, 134. Although fewer earlier than more recent émigrés had close family in Cuba to visit as of the early 2000s, earlier émigrés rarely made homeland visits in the years when they did have more close kin in Cuba.

24. *New York Times*, sec. 3, May 26, 2002, 4.

25. Alejandro Portes, William Haller, and Luis Guarnizo, "Transnational Entrepreneurs: An Alternative Form of Immigrant Economic Adaptation," *American Sociological Review* 67 (April 2002), 278–98. On the Cuban American enclave economy, see Portes and Stepick, *City on the Edge*. Cuban Americans are not unique in transnationalizing an immigrant neighborhood economy. For example, stores in New York City's Little India specialize in offerings, for homeland gifts, of electrical goods requiring 220-volt current; see Johanna Lessinger, *From the Ganges to the Hudson: Indian Immigrants in New York City* (Boston, MA: Allyn and Bacon, 1995).

26. See Manuel Orozco, *The Remittance Marketplace: Prices, Policy and Financial Institutions* (Washington, DC: Pew Hispanic Center, 2004), www.pewhispanic.org/2004/06/07/the-remittance-marketplace-prices-policy-and-financial-institutions/.

27. On immigrant economic niche activity, see Roger Waldinger, "The Making of an Immigrant Niche," *International Migration Review* 28, no. 1 (1994), 3–30.

28. *Miami Herald*, August 10, 2003, 3, www.miamiherald.com.

29. Compare Orozco, *Remittance Marketplace*, 17; and Orozco, *Remittances and Social Development: The Latin American Experience* (Washington, DC: Inter-American Dialogue, 2007), 5.

30. Other governments in Latin America have also ascribed hero status to immigrants whose remittances they seek to attract. For example, the Ecuadorian government instituted the Day of the Absent Ones to honor émigrés, and Mexico's President Vicente Fox (2000–6) publicly spoke of the migrant hero. Such recognition induces immigrants to live up to societal, and not merely family, expectations.

31. Michael Piore, *Birds of Passage: Migrant Labor and Industrial Societies* (Cambridge: Cambridge University Press, 1979), similarly noted that migrants view income earned even at menial jobs abroad as a way of enhancing their status at home.

32. Marcel Mauss, *The Gift: Forms and Functions of Exchange in Archaic Societies* (New York: Norton, 1967). Georges Fouron and Nina Glick Schiller, "The Generation of Identity: Redefining the Second Generation within a Transnational Social Field," in Levitt and Waters, *Changing Face of Home*, 187, similarly report a belief in Haiti that kin abroad have an obligation to help.

18

Ernesto Che Guevara, Dispositions, and Education for Transnational Social Justice

JOHN D. HOLST

As part of its accreditation process, the National Council for Accreditation of Teacher Education (NCATE)—the largest and most important accrediting body for U.S. teacher education programs—requires the identification of a set of dispositions, along with knowledge and skills, as core standards of evaluation in the preparation of teachers. NCATE, now with more than six hundred teacher education programs under its wing across the country, originally defined dispositions as the "values, commitments, and professional ethics that influence behaviors toward students, families, colleagues, and communities and affect student learning, motivation, and development as well as the educator's own professional growth."[1] In its 2008 professional standards NCATE purposefully placed knowledge, skills, and dispositions in the first standard to highlight the importance of these factors.[2]

In 2006 NCATE listed social justice as a sample disposition for future teachers—a move that, when it became widely publicized, created considerable debate in governmental, educational, and political talk-show circles. Facing right-wing and governmental pressure NCATE quickly dropped any reference to social justice in its online glossary listing for dispositions and framed its commitment to social justice in terms of leaving no child behind.[3] This debate really centers on broader issues. To what end do we educate? Should teachers be expected to adhere to certain principles and be oriented by specific dispositions? Moreover, in any consideration of the central role of learning and educating in social movements,[4] the link between dispositions and education includes but extends well beyond the formal training of teachers or the formal education they provide in schools.

The theory and practice of Ernesto Che Guevara—as revealed in his writings, speeches, and interviews—exemplifies this nexus of dispositions and a broadly conceived notion of education within and beyond formal schooling.[5]

Guevara, generally seen as a revolutionary, but also as a pedagogue, was very much interested in promoting specific dispositions in youth and in the Cuban population as a whole.[6] Dispositions are at the heart of his idea of creating the new man and woman (*el hombre nuevo*). The new man and woman would be of a qualitatively new nature because of the "values, commitments, and professional ethic"[7] that would guide their actions in society. Guevara as a social pedagogue understood that dispositions (subjective conditions) were in dialectical relationship with the objective conditions (sociopolitical economic relations) of society.[8] Both the subjective and the objective conditions of society had to be transformed for there to be a lasting transformation of society. As Guevara often stated, in different ways, "The aim of socialism . . . is not simply to create shiny factories. These factories are being built for human beings in their totality. Man must be transformed in conjunction with advances in production. We would not be doing our job if we were solely producers of commodities, of raw material, and were not at the same time producers of men."[9]

While Guevara developed these dispositions in the context of revolutionary Cuba, he had what we could call today a transnational approach because he also worked to instill these dispositions among the people with whom he worked in the Congo and Bolivia.[10] We can even say that it was his transnationalist outlook that took him to the Congo and Bolivia in the first place. We do, however, need to be careful in applying the term *transnationalist* to Guevara because he himself never used the term. As a Marxist, he used the term *internationalist* to speak of his efforts at building solidarity among all poor and working-class people across the planet and particularly in the tricontinental nations of Africa, Asia, and America. Still, through the idea of the tricontinental, postcolonial literature shows precedents for extending the term *transnationalist* to Guevara. Robert Young cites the Tricontinental Conference of Solidarity with the People of Asia, Africa, and Latin America, held in Havana in January 1966, as the watershed moment in which postcolonialism became a truly coherent theory and practice of transnational social justice. Moreover, he argues, it was in Guevara's message to the Tricontinental Conference that "the epistemology of the postcolonial subject" was born. For Young this apex of postcolonialism as tricontinental or transnational social justice in Guevara's message is "the first moment where a general internationalist counter-hegemonic position was elaborated by a disposed subject of imperialism."[11]

The act of identifying and outlining the dispositions implicit in the theory and practice of Guevara in the context of transnational social justice also provides historical antecedents to and new ways of considering the concept of transnationalism. In the social sciences transnationalism is used to conceptualize a particular line of analysis of globalization, new patterns and consequences of human migration, newer forms of globally oriented social movement activism, and, in particular, a new wave of globally oriented feminist theory and practice.[12] It is in the area of transnational social movement activism and education that I believe Guevara's dispositions are of greatest import. Ariet García argues that Guevara was in many ways ahead of his time because his theory and practice "strike a chord" in the contemporary transnational or global justice movement.[13] But the dispositions in Guevara's praxis also have great educational relevancy, especially in the global context of increased polarization of wealth and poverty, and this is true whether that work is formal education in educational institutions or nonformal education in social movements.

A number of dispositions are prominent in Guevara's theory and practice: internationalism and Bolivarianism, anti-imperialism, intrinsic motivation of love and empathy, discipline, honesty, self-criticism, flexibility in thinking, audacity, willingness to sacrifice, rejection of privilege, and orientation toward service. Transnationalism is firmly embedded in all these dispositions documented in the theory or practice of Ernesto Che Guevara—and all of this contains important lessons for approaches to be taken up by educators.

Internationalism and Bolivarianism

From as early as his first trip through Latin America in 1952, Guevara advocated the goal of Latin American unity originated by the nineteenth-century independence leader Simón Bolívar. His diary recounts the toast he made at the going-away party that he and Alberto Granado attended at the leper colony in Peru, where they had spent time working: "We believe, and after this journey more firmly than ever, that the division of [Latin] America into unstable and illusory nations is completely fictional. We constitute a single mestizo race.... I propose a toast to Peru and to a United Latin America."[14] This disposition to fight for Latin American unity and liberation would stay with Guevara until his assassination in Bolivia in October 1967. The decision to lead the guerrilla training mission in Bolivia was a culmination of the agreement he had made with Fidel Castro in Mexico upon joining the 26th of July Movement. He agreed to fight in Cuba but wanted to be free after a period to carry on the struggle in other areas of the Americas. He confirmed this in a letter to his mother in July 1956, when he said, "After I have set wrongs [right] in Cuba, I'll go somewhere else."[15] Moreover, the Bolivia training mission had a continental scope; the plan was to train guerrilla soldiers to fight in Bolivia and also in the surrounding countries.

In subsequent years, Guevara's Bolivarianism would become internationalist or transnationalist in scope.[16] In his last widely circulated public address, first published in April 1967 but intended as a message to the Tricontinental Conference of January 1966, that outlook is clearly evident:

> Let us develop genuine proletarian internationalism, with international proletarian armies. Let the flag under which we fight be the sacred cause of the liberation of humanity, so that to die under the colors of Vietnam, Venezuela, Guatemala, Laos, Guinea, Colombia, Bolivia, Brazil—to mention only the current scenes of armed struggle—will be equally glorious and desirable for a Latin American, an Asian, an African, and even a European. Every drop of blood spilled in a land under whose flag one was not born is experience gathered by the survivor to be applied later in the struggle for the liberation of one's own country. And every people that liberates itself is a step forward in the battle for the liberation of one's own people.[17]

Anti-Imperialism

The continental scope of the Bolivia mission also indicates how Guevara's Bolivarianism and transnationalism were anti-imperialist. Guevara saw the opening of a Bolivian and later continent-wide guerrilla front—beyond being a mission to train and start guerrilla movements for Bolivia and its five border countries—as a vital part of an international fight against imperialism and most particularly U.S. imperialism. In his message to the Tricontinental Conference Guevara argued that a historic moment had arrived when in conjunction with the deepening U.S. involvement in Vietnam, anti-imperialist guerrilla fronts in Latin America and Africa could very likely defeat imperialism for good, ushering in a period of worldwide people's liberation. This is the logic behind his famous slogan, taken from this message, of creating one, two, three, many Vietnams.

The larger pedagogical point that we can derive from Guevara's transnationalism and anti-imperialism is the idea that the liberation struggles of peoples around the world are intimately linked. Eduardo Galeano makes the companion point by specifically referring to how "Latin America's underdevelopment is ... an integral part of the history of world capitalism's development."[18] If some people (classes) and some nations are rich *because* others are poor, then solidarity among the poor of the world is an essential factor for the fight against poverty and oppression. Globally, not with today's connotations of globalization and anti-globalization, but with the connotations of imperialism and anti-imperialism, Guevara understood and taught through his words and actions that people struggling against poverty and national oppression must understand the struggle as being against imperialism and being transnational in scope. "We must definitely keep in mind that imperialism is a world system, the final stage of capitalism, and that it must be beaten in a great worldwide confrontation.... The contribution that falls to us, the exploited and backward of the world, is to eliminate the foundations sustaining imperialism: our oppressed nations."[19]

Intrinsic Motivation of Love and Empathy

Guevara believed that revolutionaries must be deeply internally motivated. A revolutionary must feel "naturally that what is a sacrifice for ordinary people" is "simply a daily occurrence." They "must have an ideal that sustains them."[20] Alongside a deep-seated desire to oppose imperialism through transnational unity, Guevara highlighted a love of humanity and empathy toward the suffering of others as necessary dispositions for revolutionaries. In an oft-cited quotation and, as he said, "at the risk of seeming ridiculous," Guevara made this point: "the true revolutionary is guided by great feelings of love. It is impossible to think of a genuine revolutionary lacking this quality.... One must have a large dose of humanity, a large dose of a sense of justice and truth in order to avoid dogmatic extremes, cold scholasticism, or an isolation from the masses. We must strive every day so that this love of living humanity is transformed into actual deeds, into acts that serve as examples, as a moving force."[21] Guevara believed that, combined with love, empathy and intolerance for injustices committed against others were essential dispositions for revolutionaries. Once, when a woman with the last name of Guevara wrote to him asking if they might be related, in a short reply Che said that he doubted they were blood relatives, but commented, "If you are capable of trembling with indignation each time that an injustice is committed in the world, we are comrades, and that is more important."[22] Similarly, in a letter he left for his children in case of his death, he asked them to act with a transnational empathy: "Above all, always be capable of feeling deeply any injustice committed against anyone, anywhere in the world. This is the most beautiful quality in a revolutionary." In the Cuban context Guevara was following in the footsteps of José Martí, who, as Che was fond of quoting, said, "Every true man must feel on his own cheek every blow dealt against the cheek of another."[23]

Motivation is a topic of great interest to educators. It is at the heart of many teacher-lounge laments of student disinterest and of the agenda for education theory and research. For Guevara, motivation for transnational social justice must come from within. This particular motivation is not, however, for Guevara an innate characteristic. People must learn a disposition for transnational social justice that intrinsically motivates them to act.

Discipline

Along with internal motivation stemming from ideals, Guevara also believed that an internal discipline springing "from a carefully reasoned internal conviction" was an essential disposition of revolutionaries.[24] This facet was of particular importance for guerrilla soldiers, for whom discipline could literally be a question of life or death. Guevara argued that the internal nature of a revolutionary's discipline, stemming from convictions of love, empathy, transnationalism, and anti-imperialism, was one of the elements that made the guerrilla army qualitatively distinct from regular armies, in which discipline was externally imposed upon soldiers and represented in pointless rituals and symbols. Just because guerrilla armies did not engage in highly visible and ritualistic displays of discipline and obedience to hierarchy did not make them less orderly and disciplined. Guevara believed that an internal discipline that at times was less visible made the guerrilla soldier and army more consistently disciplined.

For Guevara, when a person learns to be internally driven by humanistic love and empathy, that person will also gain an orienting framework to guide and propel her or his actions. External motivators and orienting mechanisms are decreasingly necessary if one is given the personal and social space and institutional support to pursue actions and further learning as guided by deeply held ideals.

Honesty, Truth, and Self-Criticism

Guevara believed that every revolutionary expression must be based in the truth. In his more generalized manual on guerrilla warfare, his text on the Cuban revolutionary war, and his diary of the Bolivian campaign, Guevara emphasized over and over again the necessity of telling the truth in revolutionary propaganda; in newspapers, radio, and reports the truth was "the fundamental principle of . . . propaganda."[25] The truth was essential so that people could come to believe in the guerrillas and the revolutionary movement as a whole and begin to trust in the revolutionaries' words and actions. With the triumph of the revolution, this principle held firm, and the importance of the truth became even more essential due to the tricontinental or transnational stature of the Cuban revolution. "When the Cuban Revolution speaks," Guevara wrote, "it may make mistakes, but it will never tell a lie. In every place where it speaks, the Cuban Revolution expresses the truths that its sons and daughters have learned, and it does so openly to its friends and its enemies alike."[26]

It was also a revolutionary principle for Guevara that one must be honest with oneself in assessing one's actions. An honest, self-critical assessment was essential for people to learn from their practice. "We must analyze our work with cold objectivity and criticize it whenever it is poor."[27] As was characteristic of Guevara, he first applied to himself what he thought should apply to others as well. A good example of his self-criticism was his speech as the newly appointed minister of industry—a talk broadcast on national Cuban television—in which he criticized the failure of the revolutionary government to fully include the people in the development of the initial economic plans.[28] As with the question of truth, the importance of self-criticism had transnational dimensions due to the role of the Cuban revolution in the international arena: "we are a showcase, a mirror into which all the peoples of America can look, and we must work to make our abilities greater every day, and our disabilities fewer. We must not return to the practice of hiding our defects so they may not be seen. That would be neither honest nor revolutionary.... We must be open."[29] Self-criticism is a pedagogical tool for learning and teaching. To be effective, however, criticism requires not just honesty but an environment in which people can express their assessments of their strengths and weaknesses in a collective spirit of improvement. To engage in honest and open self-criticism is to teach others through example the ability for self-assessment, self-awareness, and the desire for self-improvement. While self-criticism is essential for the individual, to avoid bureaucratic stagnation it is also essential at the level of groups, communities, and institutions.

Audacity and Creative, Flexible, Non-Dogmatic Thinking

Because of the importance that Guevara placed on the individual, he opposed excessive centralization, bureaucratization, and dogmatic thinking. All of these tendencies were based upon stilted thinking that ultimately did not place confidence in ordinary people to learn and grow through full participation in the institutions of society. Moreover, because Guevara emphasized the development of practice based on theory, he saw the major bodies of theoretical thought such as Marxism as "only guide[s] to action." One must be as absolutely versed as possible in theory, and for his part he never stopped studying theory; but one must never try to apply theory mechanically to a given situation. He instructed party militants to use dialectical materialism as a weapon to guide practice, but also "to be creative," for "mechanical thinking leads only to stereotyped methods."[30]

Stereotyped methods were anathema to Guevara's insistence that revolutionaries must not only be careful, skillful, and principled in their actions but also audacious. This was a hallmark of the legend that grew up around Guevara due to the boldness of his actions as a guerrilla fighter and his willingness to volunteer for the most dangerous and difficult tasks. This was not just a trait of his soldiering, for it takes audacity to be trained as a doctor and soldier and agree to become president of the National Bank of Cuba. This, however, was a disposition that Guevara believed to be essential for revolutionaries. Fundamentally, this is a pedagogical stance: to show through your own audacious example that people are capable of things well beyond their oftentimes limited self-image. In ways, we see the disposition of audacity underlying the popular slogan "Sí, se puede" (Yes, we can) of the immigrant rights movement in the United States. This slogan from the 1960s and 1970s farmworkers' movement reemerged in the struggles of mainly Latino immigrant janitors in their successful unionization campaign against major U.S. corporations in Los Angeles. It was only through the audacity of these "marginalized" workers that they were victorious. Without daring to struggle, they never would have won.

Service, Sacrifice, and Opposing Privileges

Che Guevara is often described as a martyr—one who made, and maybe even sought out, the ultimate sacrifice of giving his life. This is a narrow characterization of his disposition toward service and sacrifice and his continuous rejection of privilege as essential for revolutionaries and particularly for leaders. Guevara believed that a disposition for sacrifice should be a central element in the social education of the Cuban revolution. This was a lesson he drew from the importance and examples of sacrifice in the armed struggle. "Combatants competed for the heaviest responsibilities, for the greatest dangers, with no other satisfaction than fulfilling a duty. In our work of revolutionary education we frequently return to this instructive theme. In the attitude of our fighters could be glimpsed the man and woman of the future.... Finding the method to perpetuate this heroic attitude in daily life is, from the ideological standpoint, one of our fundamental tasks."[31] There are countless stories of Guevara himself making sacrifices and going without. He refused all but one of the salaries corresponding to his various positions. He would leave on international diplomatic missions without any accompanying family members and with the most minimal allotment of clothing beyond his military fatigues—on his trip to the United Nations he left without socks because he had worn through the pair he had obtained from his monthly allotment. If in meetings there was not enough coffee for everyone, Guevara insisted that no one have any. He refused honorariums for speaking and royalties for published books.[32]

Beyond his personal example, Guevara insisted that a rejection of privilege and a disposition for sacrifice should characterize everyone, and particularly leaders. "Whoever aspires to be a leader has to be able to face or, rather, expose himself to the verdict of the masses.... We must banish totally everything that means thinking that being elected a member of some organization of the masses or of the ruling party of the Revolution... permits a comrade to enjoy the slightest opportunity to get something more than the rest of the people."[33]

Sacrifice imbued with love and empathy transformed into service was a central element of the revolutionary hegemony that Guevara believed ought to permeate the new society. The permeation of hegemony throughout a society, as Gramsci teaches us, is not a natural process, but an educational process: "Every relationship of 'hegemony' is necessarily an educational relationship."[34] Guevara understood this very well and argued forcefully for the power of what he called direct and indirect education in the formation of the new man and woman as guided by the various dispositions outlined here. This is the context for his comment that the whole of society should be converted into a gigantic school in which direct education (formal or nonformal) and indirect education (informal) would play a central role in the development of a new hegemony.[35]

In the new society sacrifices would not seem to be sacrifices, but would be the "natural" way of being and acting in a society oriented toward social justice. In a speech to youth, Guevara described the orientation of people in the new society as never having to "wonder what you should be doing. You will simply do what at the time seems to make the most sense."[36] Serving society and fellow humans through a disciplined, 110 percent, socially constructive application of one's knowledge and skills would not be a sacrifice but merely what makes the most sense. "The revolution today demands," he said, that people "learn," and "demands that they understand well that the pride of serving our fellow man is much more important than a good income; that the people's gratitude is much more permanent, much more lasting than all the gold one can accumulate."[37]

The disposition toward service was of particular importance for the professionals with whom Guevara frequently spoke during his time in Cuba. Professionals were products of the hard work and advances of the society to which they should be committed. Echoing the ideas of Freire that the educational professional cannot be neutral,[38] Guevara extended this argument to all professionals. "Whoever pretends that a technician, an architect, a physician, an engineer, or any type of scientist should merely work with his instruments in a specific field while his people die of starvation, or die fighting in battle, has already chosen sides with the enemy," Guevara said. "He is not apolitical, he is political but opposed to liberation movements."[39]

Education and Transnational Social Justice

I began this chapter by describing NCATE's insistence on dispositions as central to successful teacher education programs. Unfortunately, if we look to NCATE for suggestions on dispositions, we will be disappointed to find that the only "two professional dispositions that NCATE expects institutions to assess are *fairness* and the belief that all students can learn."[40] Therefore, we must look elsewhere for dispositions for our educational work. Moreover, if we take Guevara seriously on the political nature of a profession such as teaching and determine that our practice will inevitably endorse a certain politics, we will want to consider the politics of the dispositions we advocate for our programs. This is particularly the case given the growing polarization of wealth and poverty and the environmental destruction in the United States and globally which no longer appear to be conjectural, but rather are increasingly of a long-term nature.

I have argued in this chapter that we can look to Guevara not only for an analysis of the political nature of professions, but more specifically for a set of dispositions that can be foundational for an education oriented toward transnational social justice. With these dispositions at the center of our educational work, we should be educating for the development of service-oriented people willing to make sacrifices for others. Cuba's internationalist or transnational efforts in health care and literacy are exemplary of the social justice dispositions I have outlined. There are numerous reports of the bravery of Cuban medical missions in countries undergoing dramatic social upheaval or national disasters.[41] With the recently developed literacy program, Yo, Sí Puedo, Cuban literacy specialists are working in numerous countries around the world on large- and small-scale literacy campaigns. In an analysis of the Cuban work in the literacy campaign in Timor-Leste (East Timor), Bob Boughton highlights the fact that unlike most international literacy advisers, the Cuban advisers live alongside the people with whom they are working in the small towns and villages on a stipend that is approximately one-tenth of the norm for international advisers. The Cubans' approach in Yo, Sí Puedo is both a principled stance based on their disposition for service and sacrifice and, as Boughton argues, a pedagogical feature of the program that allows them to come to better understand local realities, which they incorporate into their constant and ongoing evaluation and modification of their literacy work.[42]

In formal educational settings, service-learning can become a form of critical social justice education when it is organized to move beyond acts of charity. Susan Benigni Cipolle provides the following distinctions within service-learning. Cleaning up a riverbank is service. Classroom-based testing of water for contaminants is learning. Students sampling local water supplies and reporting the results to local officials is service-learning. Cipolle adds to this typology the idea of "critical service-learning," which is when students test water as a part of a community's struggle for access to clean drinking water.[43]

We should transform our education work so that those with whom we work learn to be intrinsically motivated by love and empathy for others. In the case of Cuba's internationalist missions, perhaps the most poignant example of these dispositions is the Cuban Operación Milagro medical team that in 2006 successfully performed free cataract surgery on Mario Terán. In 1967, Mario Terán was the Bolivian Army sergeant chosen to assassinate Guevara while he was being held captive by the Bolivian Army in a schoolhouse in La Higuera, Bolivia. In the Timor-Leste literacy work, Boughton identifies the underlying "deep egalitarian humanism" of Cuban pedagogy. Stemming, as Boughton argues, from Martí and continued by Castro and Guevara, the pedagogical practice of Yo, Sí Puedo is based on the idea of creating the conditions in which every individual can realize his or her full human potential.[44]

In the United States, there are many lessons to be drawn from the African American civil rights movement as well in terms of educational practices that are based in and promote love and empathy. As Charles Payne argues, "The self-conscious use of education as an instrument of liberation among African Americans is exactly as old as education among African Americans."[45] Payne goes on to cite Septima Clark and Ella Baker as exemplary pedagogues driven in their social movement activism and education by a deep love of the humanity of their people; Payne calls this a "deep capacity for identifying with others,"[46] a capacity evident in Clark's[47] and Baker's[48] work in the Citizenship Schools and later Freedom Schools of the civil rights movement.

To put the dispositions of honesty and discipline at the center of our educational work, we can follow the example of another major figure of the African American civil rights movement, W.E.B. DuBois. In his famous critique of Booker T. Washington's vocationally oriented Hampton Idea, DuBois began by stating that "in the world this alone is necessary—that if a man speak and act, he speak and act the truth and not a lie."[49] For DuBois, the greatest gift he as a scholar could bestow upon learning was "Reverence of Truth, a Hatred of Hypocrisy and Sham."[50] In terms of institutions of higher education, DuBois argued that the three most important elements were "*Freedom of Spirit, Self-Knowledge*, and a recognition of the *Truth*."[51] DuBois tied freedom of spirit directly to discipline: "Through this very freedom comes discipline, and through discipline comes freedom."[52]

We should develop in people a disposition toward a critical, non-dogmatic understanding of the political economy of exploitation. We should also develop our work with an analytical flexibility to understand how a learning of this type plays out in different ways and in different areas in a global society. The popular education tradition has numerous examples of nonformal educational initiatives designed to help people come to an understanding of their location within the prevailing political economic relations in which they find themselves. Project South, based in Atlanta, Georgia, has developed a curriculum, or what they call a "toolkit," with multiple activities designed to help individuals and their organizations place themselves in the historical trajectory of capitalist development.[53] As a part of the Coalition of Immokalee Workers' efforts to improve the working conditions of farmworkers through boycotts of major fast-food chains they, in conjunction with the Mexican Solidarity Network and the Student Farmworker Alliance, developed a workshop curriculum designed to help current and potential boycott participants and activists understand the political economy of food and how it affects workers and consumers.[54] In formal educational settings, the Rethinking Schools organization has produced a book-length collection of K–16 materials for classroom use in critical teaching of globalization. As the editors make clear in the introduction, the book arose from their own teaching experience on issues of exploitation. In their teaching they found that the more they taught about a specific issue of exploitation, the more they realized they needed to see the interconnectedness of issues of exploitation while also holding in their minds the global picture.[55]

As Bolivian president Evo Morales stated in reference to the fortieth anniversary of Che's assassination in the rural Bolivian schoolroom turned temporary prison cell, "It's amazing to see that all over the world Che Guevara is still there, forty years later. But now, we're living in [different] . . . times. But to value and recognize that thinking, that struggle, and if we recognize and we value it, that doesn't mean . . . to mechanically follow the steps that he took."[56]

Indeed, we live in different times than Che Guevara did, but the injustices he struggled against are still with us, and his goal of a human being with the dispositions to create and take advantage of a democratic, participatory, and cooperative society are still before us. As we look out on a world in which about half of the total population lives on less than two dollars per day, transnational social justice seems less like a politically charged phrase and more like a burning necessity.

Notes

1. NCATE, "Glossary," www.ncate.org/public/glossary.asp?ch=143.
2. NCATE, *Professional Standards for the Accreditation of Teacher Preparation Institutions*, Washington, DC, 2008, 10, www.ncate.org/documents/standards/NCATEStandards2008.pdf.

3. Ibid., 6–7.

4. John Holst, *Social Movements, Civil Society, and Radical Adult Education* (Westport, CT: Bergin and Garvey, 2002).

5. See John Holst, "The Pedagogy of Ernesto Che Guevara," *International Journal of Lifelong Education* 28, no. 2 (2009), 149–73. The present chapter on dispositions, education, and transnational social justice is a part of a larger research project on the pedagogy of Ernesto Che Guevara. In what follows I present dispositions in the praxis of Guevara based on a thematic analysis of the writings, speeches, and interviews available in English translation. I also consulted what I consider to be important biographies and secondary sources on the educational and political thought and practice of Guevara in English and Spanish.

The biographies consulted are Hilda Gadea, *Ernesto: A Memoir of Che Guevara*, trans. Carmen Molina and William I. Bradbury (Garden City, NY: Doubleday, 1972); Iosif Lavretsky, *Ernesto Che Guevara*, trans. A. B. Eklof (Moscow: Progress Publishers, 1976); Ricardo Rojo, *My friend Che*, trans. Julian Casart (New York: Grove Press, 1968); Paco Ignacio Taibo II, *Guevara, Also Known as Che*, trans. Martin Michael Roberts (New York: St. Martin's Press, 1997). The secondary sources in English are Fidel Castro, *Che: A Memoir by Fidel Castro*, ed. David Deutschmann (Melbourne: Ocean Press, 1994); Víctor Dreke, *From the Escambray to the Congo*, ed. Mary-Alice Waters (New York: Pathfinder Press, 2002); Arthur Gillette, *Cuba's Educational Revolution* (London: Fabian Society, 1972); Fred Judson, *Cuba and the Revolutionary Myth: The Political Education of the Cuban Rebel Army, 1953–1963* (Boulder, CO: Westview Press, 1984); Michael Löwy, "Che's Revolutionary Humanism," *Monthly Review* 49, no. 5 (1997), 1–7; Michael Löwy, *The Marxism of Che Guevara: Philosophy, Economics, and Revolutionary Warfare*, trans. Brian Pearce (New York: Monthly Review Press, 1973); Peter McLaren, *Che Guevara, Paulo Freire, and the Pedagogy of Revolution* (Lanham, MD: Rowman and Littlefield, 2000); Manuel Piñeiro, *Che Guevara and the Latin American Revolutionary Movements*, ed. Luis Suárez Salazar, trans. Mary Todd (Melbourne: Ocean Press, 2001); Harry Villegas, *At the Side of Che Guevara: Interviews with Harry Villegas (Pombo)* (New York: Pathfinder, 1997); Harry Villegas, *Pombo: A Man of Che's Guerrilla* (New York: Pathfinder, 1997).

The secondary sources in Spanish are Alberto Bayo, *Mi aporte a la revolución cubana* (Havana: Ejército Rebelde, 1960); Orlando Borrego, *Che, Recuerdos en Ráfaga* (Havana: Editorial de Ciencias Sociales, 2004); Cátedra "Ernesto Che Guevara," Universidad de la Habana, *Che: El hombre del siglo XXI* (Havana: Editorial Félix Varela, 2001); Armando Hart Dávalos, *Mi visión del Che desde los [ap]90* (Turin: Ediciones Mec Graphic, 1994); Fernando Martínez Heredia, *Ché, el socialismo y el comunismo* (Havana: Casa de las Américas, 1989); Lidia Turner Martí, *Ernesto Che Guevara y las universidades* (Havana: Editorial Félix Varela, 2002); Lidia Turner Martí, *Del pensamiento pedagógico de Ernesto Che Guevara* (Havana: Editorial Capitán San Luis, 1999).

6. Paulo Freire, *Pedagogy of the Oppressed*, trans. Myra Bergman Ramos (New York: Continuum, 2001); Gillette, *Cuba's Educational Revolution*; McLaren, *Che Guevara, Paulo Freire*; Ali Sendaro and Irene Brown, "Che and Continuous Education," *Africa Review* 1, no. 1 (1973), 1–17; Martí, *Ernesto Che Guevara* and *Del pensamiento pedagógico*.

7. NCATE, "Glossary."

8. Martí, *Del pensamiento pedagógico*. For an analysis of ethics along these lines, see François Houtart, "La ética, el Che y la revolución cubana," *Contexto Latinoamericano* 5 (October 2007), 248–51.

9. Ernesto Guevara, *Che Guevara Talks to Young People*, ed. Mary-Alice Waters (New York: Pathfinder Press, 2000), 130.

10. Ernesto Guevara, *The African Dream: The Diaries of the Revolutionary War in the Congo*, trans. Patrick Camiller (New York: Grove Press, 2000); Ernesto Guevara, *Bolivian Diary*, ed. Mary-Alice Waters (New York: Pathfinder Press, 1994).

11. Robert Young, *Postcolonialism: An Historical Introduction* (Oxford: Blackwell, 2001), 212, 213; Ernesto Guevara, *Global Justice, Liberation, and Socialism*, ed. María del Carmen Ariet García (Melbourne: Ocean Press, 2002), 49–62.

12. See, for example, Jerry Harris, *The Dialectics of Globalization: Economic and Political Conflict in a Transnational World* (Newcastle upon Tyne, UK: Cambridge Scholars, 2008); William Robinson, *A Theory of Global Capitalism: Production, Class and State in a Transnational World* (Baltimore, MD: John Hopkins University Press, 2004); Leslie Sklair, *The Transnational Capitalist Class* (Oxford: Blackwell, 2001). See also, for example, Victor Roudometof, "Transnationalism and Cosmopolitanism: Errors of Globalism," in Richard Appelbaum and William Robinson, eds., *Critical Globalization Studies* (New York: Routledge, 2005), 65–74; Donatella della Porta and Sidney Tarrow, eds., *Transnational Protest and Global Activism* (Lanham, MD: Rowman and Littlefield, 2005); Vandana Shiva, *Earth Democracy: Justice, Sustainability, and Peace* (Boston, MA: South End Press, 2005); Chandra Talpade Mohanty, *Feminism without Borders: Decolonizing Theory, Practicing Solidarity* (Durham, NC: Duke University Press, 2003).

13. Ariet García, introduction to Guevara, *Global Justice*, 2.

14. Ernesto Guevara, *The Motorcycle Diaries: Notes on a Latin American Journey*, trans. Alexandra Keeble (Melbourne: Ocean Press, 2003), 149.

15. Ernesto Guevara, *Back on the Road: A Journey through Latin America*, trans. Patrick Camiller (New York: Grove Press, 2001), 110–11.

16. For an analysis of the three integrated phases of Guevara's praxis, the third being "change on a global scale," see María del Carmen Ariet García, "Che Guevara: fases integradas de su proyecto de cambio social," *Contexto Latinoamericano* 5 (October 2007), 145–63.

17. Guevara, *Global Justice*, 60.

18. Eduardo Galeano, *Open Veins of Latin America*, trans. Cedric Belfrage (New York: Monthly Review Press, 1997), 2.

19. Guevara, *Global Justice*, 58.

20. Ernesto Guevara, *Venceremos! The Speeches and Writings of Che Guevara*, ed. John Gerassi (New York: Macmillan, 1968), 344; Ernesto Guevara, *Guerrilla Warfare* (Lincoln: University of Nebraska Press, 1985), 86.

21. Guevara, *Global Justice*, 44.

22. Ernesto Guevara, *Che Guevara Reader: Writings on Politics and Revolution*, 2nd ed. (Melbourne: Ocean Press, 2003), 376.

23. Ibid., 383, 177.

24. Guevara, *Guerrilla Warfare*, 153.

25. Ibid., 146.

26. Guevara, *Che Guevara Reader*, 238.

27. Guevara, *Venceremos*, 351.

28. Ibid., 221.

29. Ernesto Guevara, *Che Guevara Speaks: Selected Speeches and Writings* (New York: Pathfinder Press, 1995), 72.

30. Guevara, *Venceremos*, 346.

31. Guevara, *Global Justice*, 30.

32. Taibo, *Guevara*.

33. Guevara, *Venceremos*, 343.

34. Antonio Gramsci, *The Antonio Gramsci Reader*, ed. David Forgacs (New York: New York University Press, 2000), 348.

35. Guevara, *Global Justice*, 35.

36. Guevara, *Che Guevara Talks*, 129.

37. Guevara, *Che Guevara Reader*, 117.

38. Ira Shor and Paulo Freire, *A Pedagogy of Liberation* (Westport, CT: Bergin and Garvey, 1987).

39. Ernesto Guevara, *Che: Selected Works of Ernesto Guevara*, ed. Rolando Bonachea and Nelson Valdes (Cambridge, MA: MIT Press, 1969), 301.

40. NCATE, *Professional Standards*, 90.

41. Steve Brouwer, *Revolutionary Doctors* (New York: Monthly Review Press, 2011).

42. Bob Boughton, "Back to the Future?: Timor-Leste, Cuba and the Return of the Mass Literacy Campaign," *Literacy and Numeracy Studies* 18, no. 2 (2010), 58–74.

43. Susan Benigni Cipolle, *Service-Learning and Social Justice* (Lanham, MD: Rowman and Littlefield, 2010).

44. Ibid., 63.

45. Charles M. Payne, introduction to *Teaching Freedom*, ed. Charles M. Payne and Carol Sills Strickland (New York: Teachers College Press, 2008), 1.

46. Ibid., 4.

47. See, for example, Katherine Mellen Charron, *Freedom's Teacher: The Life of Septima Clark* (Chapel Hill: University of North Carolina Press, 2009); Septima Clark, *Echo in my Soul* (New York: E. P. Dutton, 1962); Septima Clark, *Ready from Within: A First Person Narrative* (Trenton, NJ: Africa World Press, 1996).

48. Barbara Ransby, *Ella Baker and the Black Freedom Movement* (Chapel Hill: University of North Carolina Press, 2003).

49. W.E.B. DuBois, *The Education of Black People* (New York: Monthly Review Press, 2001), 23.

50. Ibid., 46.

51. Ibid., 65.

52. Ibid., 66.

53. Project South, *Today's Globalization* (Atlanta, GA: Project South, 2002).

54. Coalition of Immokalee Workers, the Mexican Solidarity Network, and the Student

Farmworker Alliance, "The Everyday Face of Globalization and the Taco Bell Boycott," http://cjtc.ucsc.edu/globallocalpoped/downloadable/CIW/msn_ciw_workshop.pdf

55. Bill Begelow and Bob Peterson, eds., *Rethinking Globalization: Teaching for Justice in an Unjust World* (Milwaukee, WI: Rethinking Schools Press, 2002).

56. Evo Morales, quoted in "The Life and Legacy of Latin American Revolutionary Ernesto 'Che' Guevara: Forty Years after His Death," *Democracy Now*, October 9, 2007, www.democracynow.org/article.pl?sid=07/10/09/1349235#transcript.

Contributors

Carlos Alzugaray Treto is professor at the University of Havana, where he teaches political science and international relations. From 1961 to 1996, he was a member of the Cuban Foreign Service, serving abroad in a number of postings, including ambassador to the European Union. He has been a visiting professor at universities in the United States, Canada, Mexico, Italy, and Spain and, from 1996 to 2007, a professor at the Higher Institute of International Relations in Havana. He has written three books and more than sixty articles.

Max Azicri (1934–2011) was professor of political science at Edinboro University in Pennsylvania. He specialized in Latin American politics and comparative politics; he was the author of two books and the co-editor of a third. In numerous scholarly articles, book chapters, and monographs, published in twelve countries over almost half a century, he examined the Cuban American community and Cuban issues—politics, the legal system, society, the women's movement, economics, culture, international relations. At the moment of his untimely death, he was working on a book-length study of the Cuba-Venezuela alliance and its continental impact.

Mette Louise Berg is lecturer at the University of Oxford. An anthropologist, she has studied Cuba and its diaspora since the late 1990s and is the author of *Generating Diaspora: Memory, Politics, and Nation among Cubans in Spain*. She is currently conducting new research on education, social mobility, elite reproduction, and transnational networks in socialist Cuba and its diaspora.

María Caridad Cumaná, until recently adjunct professor in art history at Havana University, is a film critic, programmer, and jury member at national and international film festivals. Now living in Florida, she writes on Cuban and Latin American cinema and has collaborated on two encyclopedias: one on cinema in Spain and the other on Cuba in the United States. In 2008 she won the AVINA Foundation prize for research journalism for a multimedia project on Latin American and Caribbean cinema. She participated as well in the National Film Board of Canada project *Out My Window*.

Kevin M. Delgado is an ethnomusicologist and associate professor of music at San Diego State University. His research focuses on the music, history, and cultural representation of the Afro-Cuban Santeria religion. His essays have appeared in *Black Music Research Journal*, *Cuba in the Special Period: Culture and Ideology in the 1990s*, *Selected Reports in Ethnomusicology*, and *A Contracorriente*.

Karen Dubinsky teaches in the departments of Global Development Studies and History at Queen's University, Kingston, Ont. She is the author of *Babies without Borders: Adoption and Migration in the Americas*, which addresses child migration and adoption conflicts in Cuba, Guatemala, and Canada. She is currently working on two projects: an anthology entitled *Habaname: The Musical City of Carlos Varela* and a book titled *How Babies Rule the World: The Iconography and Ideology of the Poster Child*.

Susan Eckstein is professor of international relations and sociology at Boston University. Her publications include *How Immigrants Impact Their Homelands* (ed.); *The Immigrant Divide: How Cuban Americans Changed the U.S. and Their Homeland*; *Back from the Future: Cuba under Castro*; *The Poverty of Revolution: The State and Urban Poor in Mexico*; *Power and Popular Protest: Latin American Social Movements* (ed.); *What Justice? Whose Justice: Fighting for Fairness in Latin America* (co-ed.); and *Struggles for Social Rights in Latin America* (co-ed.). She is a former president of the Latin American Studies Association.

Efe Can Gürcan is a PhD student in sociology at Simon Fraser University and holds a SSHRC–Joseph–Armand Bombardier CGS Doctoral Scholarship. His research interests lie in the areas of political sociology, Latin American politics and society, food studies, development theories, and Turkish politics and society. His recent and upcoming publications include a review essay on food sovereignty in the journal *Kasarinlan*, an article on Cuban agrarian movements in *Latin American Perspectives*, an article on regionalism in *Journal of Social Research and Policy*, and several book chapters on, respectively, regionalism, and Cuba, Turkey, and Gramsci.

John D. Holst is associate professor in the Department of Leadership, Policy, and Administration at the University of St. Thomas in Minnesota, where he teaches graduate courses in critical pedagogy, social theory, and educational research. He is the author of the book *Social Movements, Civil Society, and Radical Adult Education*. Along with Stephen Brookfield, he is the co-author of the book *Radicalizing Learning: Adult Education for a Just World*, which won the 2011 Cyril O. Houle World Award for Outstanding Literature in Adult Education. He is currently working on a forthcoming book tentatively titled *Gramsci, Globalization, and Pedagogy*.

Robert Huish is assistant professor of international development studies at Dalhousie University, Halifax, N.S. He is the author of *Going Where No Doctor Has Gone Before: Cuba's Place in the Global Health Landscape*. He has also published several articles on Cuba's foreign policy strategy as well as writing on issues of health-care access in lower- and middle-income countries, soft power, human security, sports and development, and Cuban medical internationalism. He is working on a three-year collaborative research project on the dynamics of Cuban internationalism through sports in Central America and sub-Saharan Africa. He teaches courses related to poverty and human rights, global health, and activism in social movements.

Marguerite Rose Jiménez is a doctoral candidate in global public health and comparative politics at the School of Public Affairs, American University, Washington, D.C. Her research focuses on public health history and comparative social policy in Latin America and the Caribbean. She is the co-editor (with Philip Brenner, John M. Kirk, and William M. LeoGrande) of *A Contemporary Cuba Reader: Reinventing the Revolution*, and is the author of the report "Cuba's Pharmaceutical Advantage" (the North American Congress on Latin America, July–August 2011).

Hal Klepak is professor emeritus of history and strategy at the Royal Military College of Canada, Kingston, Ont. He was an officer with the Black Watch of Canada and has worked at Canada's Department of National Defence and at NATO as a strategic analyst. He has served on several missions with the United Nations and the Organization of American States and has published eight books on Latin American defense issues, the latest being *Raúl Castro: estratega de la defensa revolucionaria cubana*.

Catherine Krull is professor in sociology and dean of the Faculty of Social Sciences at the University of Victoria and professor of cultural studies at Queen's University in Canada. She has been working in Cuba for many years and has published research focused on a number of issues including gender, generations, migration, women's daily life/resistance, and knowledge circuits. She is past editor of *Cuban Studies* and just completed a five year term as editor-in-chief of the *Canadian Journal of Latin American and Caribbean Studies*.

William M. LeoGrande is dean of the School of Public Affairs, American University, Washington, D.C. He has written widely in the field of Latin American politics and U.S. foreign policy, with a particular emphasis on Cuba and Central America. He is the author of *Our Own Backyard: The United States in Central America, 1977–1992* and *Cuba's Policy in Africa*; and the co-editor of *The Cuba Reader: The Making of a Revolutionary Society*; *Political Parties and Democracy in Central America*; and *A Contemporary Cuba Reader: Reinventing the Revolution*.

Yvette Louis is assistant professor of English at New Jersey City University. Her field of specialization is the African diaspora in the Americas, with particular focus on literature written in the United States and the Caribbean in English, Spanish, French, and Dutch. Her theoretical approach incorporates gender and race theory, cultural studies, and semiotics. She is currently revising for publication a book project entitled "Body Language: The Linguistics of Doubleness in the Literature of the African Americas." She has taught at New York University, Vassar College, Princeton University, Hunter College, and Sarah Lawrence College. She was born in Cuba.

Asa McKercher is a postdoctoral fellow at the Department of History, Queen's University, Kingston, and a former archival assistant at Library and Archives Canada. His publications on Canada-Cuba relations have appeared in the *International History Review*, *Cold War History*, *Diplomatic History*, and the *Canadian Historical Review*, while his book on Canada-U.S. relations in the early 1960s is under contract with Oxford University Press. His next project explores comparative reactions to the Cuban revolution across the English-speaking world.

Stanley J. Murphy is a practicing attorney in Tuscaloosa, Alabama, and is adjunct professor at the University of Alabama School of Law. He is admitted to practice law in Alabama, Florida, the District of Columbia, and before the Supreme Court of the United States. Formerly senior counsel and academic coordinator for the Cooper Cuba Initiative at the University of Alabama, he now serves as chair of the Cuba and International Relations Task Force of the Alabama State Bar.

Louis A. Pérez Jr. is the J. Carlyle Sitterson Professor in the Department of History at the University of North Carolina. His principal research interests center on the nineteenth- and twentieth-century Caribbean, with emphasis on the Spanish-speaking Caribbean, especially Cuba. His most recent publication is *Cuba: Between Reform and Revolution*.

Ricardo Pérez is associate professor of anthropology at Eastern Connecticut State University. His teaching and research interests include sustainable development and the environment, Caribbean transnational migration, and globalization. He is the author of *The State and Small-Scale Fisheries in Puerto Rico* and "On the Cuban Road to Development: Reflections on Sustainable Tourism, Environmental Conservation, and Globalization."

Ana Serra is associate professor of Spanish and Latin American studies at American University, Washington, D.C. Relevant publications include *The "New Man" in Cuba: Culture and Identity in the Revolution*; "La imagen distorsionada desde el espejo. España y Cuba en 1959" in Juan Carlos Quintero, ed., *El caribe abierto. Ensayos críticos*; and an essay on Che Guevara appearing in Victor Fowler and Alan West Duran, eds., *Cuba: People, Culture, History*. Her next book project examines the relationship between the Spanish left and revolutionary Cuba from the 1940s to the present.

Jean Stubbs is associate fellow of the Institute of the Americas, University of London; co-director of the Commodities of Empire British Academy Research Project; and professor emerita of London Metropolitan University. The recipient of Bacardi, Rockefeller, Ford, and MacArthur funding as a visiting scholar at the University of Florida, Florida International University, University of Puerto Rico, and City University of New York, and 2012 scholar-in-residence at Queen's University (Canada) Bader International Study Centre in the U.K., she was 2002–3 president of the Caribbean Studies Association and 1993–95 chair of the U.K. Society for Caribbean Studies. Awarded the 2009 UNESCO Toussaint L'Ouverture Medal, she has published on tobacco, gender, and race in Cuba and, with Catherine Krull, is currently researching the Cuban diaspora.

Index

ABC Charters v. Bronson (2009), 87
Ablonczy, Diane, 114, 116
Acceso no autorizado (book), 220
ACLU v. Miami-Dade Cnty. Sch. Bd. (2009), 88
ACOPIO, 196
Africa, 2, 217, 228, 229, 303, 305; Cuban medical involvement in, 128, 178, 180, 187, 188; Cuban military involvement in, 5, 40, 49, 51, 93, 94, 95, 114
Africa, Horn of, 49
Afro-Cuban drumming, 10, 157
Afro-Cuban religions, 10–11, 146, 148–50, 151, 153, 155, 247
Agricultural Production Cooperatives (CPAs), 195, 196
Aguirre, Eduardo, 68
Alarcón, Ricardo, 101
Alba, Santiago, 214
ALBA. *See* Bolivarian Alliance for the Peoples of the Americas
Alba de Cuba (film), 245
Alea, Tomás Gutiérrez, 244, 250
Alemán, Mario Rodríguez, 244, 249
Alén, Olavo, 156
Almeida, Juan, 249
Altadis U.S.A, 237
Alvarez, Bernardo, 139
Alverez, Lysette, 68
American Association of University Professors (AAUP), 78
American Civil Liberties Union (ACLU), 81
American Red Cross, 29
Amsterdam, 229
Angola, 1, 49, 113, 114; Cuban-Chinese differences over, 7, 94; and FNLA, 94; and MPLA, 94; and UNITA, 94
Antigua and Barbuda, 135, 232
Anti-hijacking Treaty (1973), 28
Anti-imperialism, 303, 305–6
Antonio Maceo Brigade, 68
Aragonés, Emilio, 93
Argentina, 127, 129, 131, 132; and Venezuela, 132
Argullol, Rafael, 13, 209, 212, 215; view of Cuba, 215–20, 221
Asia, 228

Asociación Cultural Yoruba (ACY), 154, 155
Australia, 180
Axworthy, Lloyd, 116, 118
Aznar, José María, 211

Babalaos, 154
Babalocha, 149
Bacallao, Esteban Vega (Cha-Chá), 144, 145, 150, 152
Bahamas, 232
Baker, Ella, 312
Balance of Terror, 48, 49
Balsero Crisis (mid-1990s), 34, 53
Bank of the South, 133, 135
Bank of Venezuela, 130
Barcelona, 259
Barroso, Miguel, 212
Basic units of cooperative production (UBPCs), 193, 194–95, 198, 202
Batalla por un idea (film), 63
Batista, Fulgencio, 5, 93, 110, 165, 166, 251; Batista government, 17, 81, 90, 115, 165
Bay of Pigs (Playa Girón) invasion, 47, 112, 113
Beckett, Samuel, 219
Belgium, 47
Board of Education v. Pico (1982), 82–83
Boehner, John, 137
Bolaños, Jorge, 33
Bolívar, Natalia, 158
Bolívar, Simón, 138, 304
Bolivarian Alliance for the Peoples of the Americas (ALBA), 9, 54, 114, 127–40, 187, 193; Agreement for Cooperative Programs in the Area of Food Security and Food Sovereignty, 135; ALBA Alimentos, 202; ALBA Bank, 135; and Cuban-Venezuelan relations, 9, 127–31, 133, 134, 187; 2005 summit, 128; 2009 summit, 135; and the United States, 133, 135, 136–38
Bolivarian Alternative for the Peoples of the Americas. *See* Bolivarian Alliance for the Peoples of the Americas
Bolivarianism, 127; and Che Guevara, 304–5
Bolivia, 54, 127, 134; and ALBA, 131–32; and 1967 guerrilla training mission, 303, 304, 305, 312, 313; and Venezuela, 131–32

Bose Corp. v. Consumers Union of the United States (1984), 88
Boughton, Bob, 311, 312
Brazil, 130, 135, 187, 228, 230
Brennan, Peter, 38
Brocklehurst, Helen, 58
Bromwich, Michael, 38, 39
Bush, George H. W., 34, 40
Bush, George W., 4, 30, 40, 54, 68, 132, 136, 176, 292, 293

Cabildo, 148
Cabrisas, Ricardo, 100
Caibarién–Cayo Santa María, 169
Camarioca exodus (1965), 28
Cameroon, 228
Campa, Roman de la, 64
Campesino a Campesino Movement, 183, 199–202, 203; Committee of Liaison and Monitoring, 201; International Commission of Work in Sustainable Agriculture, 201
Canada, 180; and "constructive engagement," 115–17, 119–20; and tourism in Cuba, 162, 167; and U.S. embargo of Cuba, 8, 109, 117–20
Canary Islands, 229
Capetillo, Luisa, 234
Carby, Hazel, 278
Caribbean, 258, 296
CARICOM (the organization of Caribbean countries), 128, 187
Carnet de viaje (film), 244, 245
Carter, Jimmy, 27, 288
Casa de las Américas (Havana), 244
Castro, Fidel, 16, 219, 243, 245, 249, 288; and ALBA, 127–31; and Angola, 94; and Canada, 8, 110, 113, 116; and Hugo Chávez, 127, 128, 129, 134, 138; and China, 7–8, 90, 92–93, 95, 96, 103; and Che Guevara, 304, 312; and Operation Peter Pan, 61; and racial discrimination, 271; and transfer of power, 4; and Union of Soviet Socialist Republics, 51, 92; and United States, 4, 29, 31, 47, 136, 137; and Venezuela, 127, 128, 129, 134, 138
Castro, Raúl, 104, 249; and Hugo Chávez, 129; and China, 101, 102, 103, 104; and Cuban military, 45, 46, 50; and reforms, 111, 130–31; and United States, 40, 136, 137, 139
Catholic Welfare Bureau (Miami), 62
Cayo Coco, Cuba, 168, 169
Cayo Largo, Cuba, 167
Cech, Vladimir, 245

Center for Chinese Language Training (Havana), 100
Center for Economic and Policy Research (CEPR), 130
Center for International Policy, 29, 35
Central Intelligence Agency, 6
Cha-Chá. *See* Bacallao, Esteban Vega
Chanan, Michael, 248, 250
Chávez, César, 235
Chávez, Hugo, 54, 136, 138; and ALBA, 127, 134, 135; and Bolivia, 132; and Fidel Castro, 127, 128, 129, 134, 138; and Raúl Castro, 129; and Cuba, 9, 127; and Nicaragua, 133; and petroleum, 128
Cheng Yinghong, 91, 93
Chen Kuiyuan, 99
Chen Muhua, 95
Chernobyl disaster (1986), 11, 34
Chiang Kai-shek (Jiang Jieshi), 90
Chile, 130, 134
China, Peoples' Republic of, 89–106, 187; and Cuba before 1989, 91–95; and Cuba, 1989–2001, 95–96; and Cuba since 2001, 96–106; Cultural Revolution, 94; Sino-Soviet schism, 49, 91; trade with Cuba, 94, 97, 98, 105
China, Republic of (Taiwan), 90, 91
China Scholarships Council, 99
Chinese Academy of Social Sciences (CASS), 99
Chinese Communist Party, 93, 105
Chirino, Willy, 68
Chovel, Elly, 70
Chrétien, Jean, 115, 116
Christensen, Theodoro, 14, 249, 250
Christie, George, 233
CIA. *See* Central Intelligence Agency (CIA)
Cienfuegos, Camilo, 249
Cienfuegos, Osmani, 93
Cifuentes, Ramón, 231
Cifuentes y Cía, 231
Cigar Aficionado (magazine), 228, 236, 237
Cigarette Company of Jamaica Ltd., 231
Cigarro (supplement of *Listín Diario*), 237
Cigars, 227–38; Connecticut, 235–37; Dominican Republic, 227, 230, 232, 235–37; Florida, 79, 232; Jamaica, 227, 231–33, 237; Puerto Rico, 227, 230, 233–35; *tabaquerías*, 237
—brands: Cohiba, 14, 237; Davidoff, 236, 237; H. Upmann, 237; La Corona, 237; Macanudo, 237; Montecristo, 237; Partagás, 232, 237; Romeo y Julieta, 237; Rosa Cubana, 237
Cipolle, Susan Benigni, 311
Clark, Joe, 119
Clark, Septima, 312

Claver-Carone, Mauricio, 33
Clean Caribbean & Americas, 37
Clinton, Hillary, 32
Clinton, William (Bill), 28, 35, 292
Coalition of Immokalee Workers, 313
Codina, Armando, 66, 68
Cold War, 61, 68, 70, 90; and Berlin Wall, 210, 243, 251; Ken Cole, 177; and Cuba, 112, 251, 258, 260, 263, 266
Colombia, 134, 228
Colonialism, 258; and anticolonialism, 303, 305–6; and postcolonialism, 258
COMECON. *See* Council for Mutual Economic Assistance
Comisión Nacional para el Fomento del Turismo, 164
Commodities of Empire British Academy Research Project, 238
Common Market of the South. *See* Mercosur
Compañía Anónima del Tabaco (CAT), 235
Complejo Turístico de Guamá-Laguna del Tesoro, 166
Conde, Yvonne, 66
Congo, 303
Connecticut: and cigars, 230, 232, 233, 235–37; Connecticut Tobacco Valley, 232; and shade tobacco, 230, 233, 235; West Indian Social Club (Connecticut), 232, 233
Connecticut Shade Tobacco Growers Agricultural Association, 234
Contra viento y marea, 67
Convertible peso. *See* Cuba: currency
Coppola, Francis Ford, 247
Corporación Nacional de Turismo, 165
Corrales, Bairon, 200
Correa, Rafael, 132, 133
Costa Rica, 134
Council for Mutual Economic Assistance (COMECON), 51, 160, 167, 194
Council on Foreign Relations, 136
Credit and Services Cooperatives (CCS), 196, 202
Crónica cubana (film), 246
Cuba: and ALBA, 114, 127, 130, 133–34, 138; and Canada, 109–20; and Canadian-Cuban special relationship, 110, 120; cinema, 14–15, 244–54; and Cold War, 1, 47, 92, 93, 112, 251, 258, 260, 263, 266; Credit and Services Cooperatives (CCSs), 196, 202; and culture, 156, 244, 248, 251, 254; diaspora, 15, 209, 211, 257–68; and drug interdiction, 53, 57; economic reforms, 2, 111, 130–31; environmentalism, 12, 163, 169, 170, 171, 172, 196, 203; foreign policy, 4–9, 177, 188; and gender, 15, 16, 257, 275, 280; and generation, 15, 16, 17, 67, 257, 260–67, 273, 282, 283, 293; and Haiti, 31–33, 186, 187; and Havana cigars, 14, 227, 228; informal transnationalism, 15–18, 296–97; and internationalism, 9–13; and Latin America, 46, 244; and marriage market, 156, 252, 253, 291; and materialist norms, 289–90, 293–96; medical research, 101; migration, 3, 6, 14, 28, 34, 40, 59, 70, 71, 149, 231, 257, 259, 260, 287, 290, 291, 297; military policy, 45–55; 1959 revolution, 1, 45, 227, 243, 262; and Operation Peter Pan, 67; and petroleum, 98, 128; and public health, 11; Puerto Rico, 230; and Russia (post-1991), 34–35, 36, 38, 39; and slavery, 147, 148, 275–78, 280; social policy, 11; and Spain, 162, 208, 215, 227, 259, 266, 275; and Special Period, 51–53, 145, 160, 168–70, 194, 208, 209, 211, 218, 219, 243, 257, 279, 290; and transnationalism, 2–3; and travel restrictions, 3, 292–93; and Union of Soviet Socialist Republics, 33, 48, 50, 160, 168, 243, 290; and Venezuela, 9, 127–31, 136, 138, 186, 187, 203
—agriculture: 12, 193; Agricultural Production Cooperatives (CPAs), 195, 196; and agro-ecology, 12, 196, 203; collectivization of land, 194–97; and food crisis (2005–2008), 192; food sovereignty, 193; free agricultural markets, 198–99; New Type State Farms (GENTs), 196, 202; urban agriculture, 197–98
—currency: CUCs, 10, 146, 147, 187, 191n34; dollars, 62, 291; SUCRE, 135
—émigrés: 3, 4, 259, 267, 287–98; economic, 293; and institutional barriers, 288–93; political, 264, 289, 292, 293, 300; and remittances, 16–17, 31, 240–43, 293–96; transnationalism, 16
—medical internationalism: 11, 177–88; and foreign policy, 177, 188; institutional ethics, 181–84; long-term primary care, 180, 184–86; moral platform, 180, 186–88; strengthening human resources, 180–84; success of, 179, 188–89; traditional and natural medicine (TNM), 182–83
—and race: 13, 15, 16, 17, 248, 257, 264, 271–84, 304; institutionalized practices, 272, 284; oral testimonies, 280–83; racial memory, 274, 284; and Special Period, 279; and Whiteness, 273–74, 276, 278
—and tourism: 12, 98, 99, 101, 145, 323; before 1950, 164–65; 1950–1959, 161, 165–66; 1950–1990, 166–67; after 1990, 10–11, 12, 53, 101, 145, 147, 151, 152, 154, 160, 161, 167–72

—and United States, 27-40, 184-85; and Bay of Pigs, 47; embargo, 2, 14, 28, 109, 117-20, 188, 288; and legal strictures, 75-86; and missile crisis, 7, 8, 29, 48, 76, 77, 112, 218; and normalization of relations, 27-40, 136-7, 139
—wars of independence: 1868–1878, 45, 184, 227, 231; 1895–1898, 16, 45, 47, 227, 229
Cuban American National Foundation, 31, 36
Cuban Communist Party, 288, 291; First Congress (1975), 167, 195; Third Congress (1986), 167; Sixth Congress (2011), 102, 104
Cuban Constitution, 271
Cuban Democracy Act (1992), 6, 118
Cuban Department of Urban Agriculture, 197i
Cuban Diaspora, 15, 209, 211, 257–68, 287–98
Cuban Interests Section (Washington), 33
Cuban Liberty and Democratic Solidarity Act (1996), 6, 39, 118
Cuban Ministry of Agriculture, 198
Cuban Ministry of Foreign Relations (MINREX), 30, 187
Cuban Ministry of Health (MINSAP), 182, 186
Cuban Ministry of Internal Trade, 198
Cuban Ministry of Planning, 168, 171
Cuban Ministry of Science, Technology, and the Environment (CITMA), 99, 171
Cuban Ministry of Tourism (MINTUR), 168, 170, 171, 208
Cuban missile crisis, 7, 8, 29, 48, 76, 77, 112, 218
Cuban National Assembly of People's Power (NAPP), 95
Cuban National Council for Culture, 244
Cuban National Office of Statistics, 161
Cuban Revolutionary Armed Forces. *See* Fuerzas Armadas Revolucionarias
¡Cuba Sí! (film), 245, 248
CUCs. *See* Cuba: currency
Czechoslovakia, 48, 61

Dalmau, Ángeles, 212
Danger in the Andes Conference, 137
Davalú o el dolor (book), 209, 215–20
Decree-Law 137, 165
Decree-Law 191, 198
Decree-Law 599, 165
Deepwater Horizon oil rig explosion (2010), 36–37
de Gaulle, Charles, 64
Del Pino, Brigadier General Rafael, 49
Deng Xiaoping, 93, 94
Denton, Harold, 35
Departamento de Playas del Pueblo, 166

de Saussure, Ferdinand, 272–73, 284
De Sica, Vittorio, 255n2
Desnoes, Edmundo, 217
Díaz, Norberto, 267
Díaz Gonzáles, Beatrice, 194
Diefenbaker, John, 8, 109, 110, 112, 115, 117, 119
Domínguez, Jorge, 28, 90
Domínguez, Lina, 99
Dominican Republic, 128, 163, 172, 228; and cigars, 14, 227, 230, 232, 235–37, 238
Dominican Tobacco Institute (INTABACO), 235
Dopico, Ana María, 218
Dorticós, Osvaldo, 91
Douglas, Justice William O., 76, 77, 78
Dragún, Osvaldo, 246
Drug interdiction, 28, 40, 52, 53, 57
DuBois, W.E.B., 312

East Timor, 179, 312
Economic Crisis (2008), 102, 127, 134–36, 146, 156
Economist Intelligence Unit, 97
Ecuador, 54, 127, 228; and Venezuela, 132–33
Eisenhower, Dwight, 62, 64
Ejército Juvenil de Trabajo, 52
Ejército Rebelde, 5, 45
EJT. *See* Ejército Juvenil de Trabajo
Eleventh Circuit, Atlanta. *See* United States Court of Appeals, Atlanta
Elián González crisis, 58, 69–71, 84. *See also* González, Elián
El joven rebellede (film), 244
El lado frío de la almohada (book), 209, 210, 211, 212, 213–15, 220
Ellas (film), 249
El Mundo (newspaper), 245
El otro Cristóbal (film), 246
El Premio Nacional de Literatura, 272
El Salvador, 113, 134
Embargo, U.S., of Cuba, 2, 14, 109, 117–20, 188, 288
Émigrés, Cuban. *See* Cuba: émigrés
Enloe, Cynthia, 59, 71
Equatorial Guinea, 179, 305
Erisman, Michael, 94
Escuela Latinoamericana de Medicina (ELAM), 12, 179, 180, 181, 182, 183, 186
Escuela Nacional de Salud Pública (ENSAP), 181, 182
Espinosa, Julio García, 244, 250
Esta tierra nuestra (film), 244
Estévez, Abilio, 212, 218
Europe, Western, 180

European Union, 4, 188, 210
Exiles, Cuban. *See* Cuba: émigrés

Faculty Senate of Fla. Int'l Univ. v. Florida (2011), 87
Faculty Senate of Fla. Int'l Univ. v. Roberts (2008), 87
Faculty Senate of Fla. Int'l Univ. v. Winn (2010), 87
Fanon, Frantz, 277
FAR. *See* Fuerzas Armadas Revolucionarias
Farabundo Martí National Liberation Front (FMLN), 134
Fernández, Cristina, 37
Fernández, Leonel, 237
Fernandez, Nadine, 272
55 hermanos (film), 67
Florida, 29, 34, 35, 36, 39, 62, 66, 67, 68, 75, 79, 80, 84, 166; and cigars, 229, 230, 232, 233
Florida *Sellers of Travel* Act, 86
Florida Statute, "Prohibition Against Contracting with Scrutinized Companies," 87
Florida Travel Act, 80
Food crisis (2005–2008), La Vía Campesina, 192, 193, 201, 203
Foreign Extraterritorial Measures Act (Canada), 118
Fox, Vicente, 301
France, 81, 162, 230; and cinema, 245, 246–47
Franco, Francisco, 13, 208, 210, 216, 221, 260, 261
Free Trade Area of the Americas (FTTA), 114, 133, 138
Free Trade Zones (FTZ), 236, 238
Fuente, Alejandro de la, 272, 279
Fuente, Carlos, 236
Fuentes, Ileana, 64
Fuerzas Armadas Revolucionarias, 5, 94; creation of, 45–46; Division of Culture, 244; drug interdiction, 52, 53, 57; Guerra de Todo el Pueblo, 50; Milicias de Tropas Territoriales, 50; Sovietization of, 48, 51; and "Special Period," 51–53; and support for foreign guerrillas, 46, 56; and U.S. military threat, 44, 47, 50, 52, 53
Fundación Antonio Núñez Jiménez (Havana), 87n19, 198
Funes, Mauricio, 134

G-20, 135, 179; Muskoka Initiative, 179
Gambia, 179, 182, 187, 188; University of the Gambia Medical School, 188
García, Ariet, 304
Gatti, Armand, 246, 247
General Cigar Company of Jamaica, 231, 237
Geographia de Cuba (book), 80
Germany (post-1990), 162, 230

Gerrish, Hal, 29
Ghana, 180
Gilman, Sander, 274, 279
Gleijeses, Piero, 94
Globalization, 9, 12, 13, 114, 133, 135, 160, 237, 303, 305, 313
Gmelch, George, 161
Gómez, Manuel Octavio, 250
González, Elián, 6, 58, 70, 84
González, Felipe, 265
González, Flora, 70
González, Guillermo, 231
González, Juan Miguel, 71
Good Neighbor Policy, 65
Gopegui, Belén, 13, 209, 210, 211, 212; and view of ideal Cuba, 213–15, 220–21
Gorbachev, Mikhail, 50
Gott, Richard, 63
Graduated and reciprocated initiatives in tension reduction (GRIT), 27, 39
Graham, Robert (Bob), 37
Gramsci, Antonio, 310
Granado, Alberto, 304
Grandchildren Law (Ley de nietos), 204
Grau, Ramón, 69
Great Britain, 2, 47, 57, 162, 180, 230
Green, Howard, 109, 117, 119
Grenada, 51, 232
GRIT. *See* Graduated and reciprocated initiatives in tension reduction (GRIT)
Guantánamo, Cuba, 3
Guarnizo, Luis, 294
Guatemala, 128, 187
Guerrilla warfare, in Bolivia, 17, 303, 304, 305, 312, 313; in Cuba, 45
Guevara, Ernesto "Che," 17–18, 249, 289, 302–13; and anti-imperialism, 303, 305–6; and audacity and creative, flexible, non-dogmatic thinking, 308; and Bolivarianism, 304–5; and Congo, 93; and Cuban Revolution, 305, 307–8, 309; and discipline, 307; and education, 304; education and transnational social justice, 303–13; and Fidel Castro, 304, 312; and *el hombre Nuevo*, 303; and honesty, truth, and self-criticism, 307–8; and love and empathy, 213, 306; and 1967 Bolivian guerrilla training mission, 17, 303, 304, 305, 312, 313; and service, sacrifice, and opposing privileges, 309–10; and transcontinentalism, 17–18, 303, 305; and Tricontinental Conference (1966), 303, 305; and Yo, Sí Puedo, 311
Guinea-Bissau, 179

Index   329

Gunn, Gillian, 155
Gutiérrez, Pedro Juan, 211, 212
Guyana, 179

Habana Blues (film), 252, 254
Haiti, 128, 129, 135, 182, 187, 267; and 2010 earthquake, 32–33, 186, 187
Haller, William, 294
Harper, Stephen, 116, 120
Havana, 13, 165, 166, 167, 168, 280, 281, 296
Havana, First Declaration of (1960), 90
Havana, University of, 100, 262
Hearn, Adrian, 155
Helg, Aline, 279
Helms-Burton Act. *See* Cuban Liberty and Democratic Solidarity Act (1996)
Henry Reeve Brigade, 184–86
Hernández, Carlos Miguel Pereira, 100
Honduras, 128, 228, 230, 236; British Honduras, 232
Hu Jintao, 97, 98, 99, 100, 103, 104
Humala, Ollanta, 134
Human rights, Cuba, 115–17; and European Union, 4
Hunt, Lee, 37
Hurricanes: Charley (2004), 30; Flora (1963), 29; Henry Reeve Brigade, 184–86; Katrina (2005), 30, 184–85; Michelle (2001), 30; Stan (2005), 185; Wilma (2005), 30
Hyndman, James, 114

Ibero-American Puente de Alcántara Award, 170
Ifá. *See* Santeria
Imperial Tobacco, 231
Independent Party of Color (Cuba), 279
India, 36
Indonesia, 228
Infante, Guillermo Cabrera, 246
Institute of Physical Planning, 171
Instituto Cubano del Arte y la Industria Cinematográficas (ICAIC), 14, 244, 246, 249, 250
Instituto Cubano del Turismo, 166
Instituto Nacional de la Industria Turística, 166
Instituto Nacional de Turismo, 165, 167
Interests Sections, 28; Cuban Interests Section (Washington, D.C.), 33; U.S. Interests Section (Havana), 31, 58, 71
International Association of Drilling Contractors, 36, 37
International Atomic Energy Agency, 35
International Book Fair, Havana, 209
International Commission of Work in Sustainable Agriculture, 201
International Film and Television School (EICTV), 254
International Monetary Fund (IMF), 144, 132, 133, 135
Interreligious Organization for Community Organization (IFCO), 182
Italy, 162; cinema, neorealism in, 244, 255
Ivens, Joris, 244, 250
Iyalocha, 149, 150

Jalisco Park (poem), 71
Jamaica, 163, 228; and cigars, 227, 231–33, 237
Jiang Zemin, 95, 96
Jimenes, León, 235
Jiménez, Antonio Núñez, 81
Jineterism, 147, 153, 155, 252, 253
Johnson, Fay Clarke, 232
Joint Committee on Scientific and Technological Cooperation (Sino-Cuban), 100
Juragua nuclear project, 53–55

Kafka, Franz, 81
Kalatozov, Mikhail, 246, 247
Karmen, Roman, 245
Kennedy, John F., 4, 47, 109, 112, 113, 118
Kent, Peter, 116
Kent v. Dulles (1958), 76
Keyishian v. Bd. of Regents of State University of New York (1967), 79
Khrushchev, Nikita, 65
Kirchner, Néstor, 132
Kirk, John, 49
Kissinger, Henry, 94
Kozak, Michael, 34
Kuroki, Kazuo, 250

La Brigadista (film), 63
Lage, Carlos, 96, 130
La lámpara azul (film), 245
Lam, Wilfredo, 90
Lambek, Michael, 258
La novia de Cuba (also known as *Más cerca de ti . . .*) (film), 250
Laos, 305
La primera carga al machete (film), 250
La Regla de Ocha. *See* Santeria
La Regla Lucumí. *See* Santeria
Las aventuras de Juan Quin Quin (film), 250
Latin America, 46
La Vía Campesina, 192, 193, 201, 203
La vivienda (film), 244

Index 331

Law No. 77, 170
Law No. 81, 171
Law No. 100, 166
Law No. 636, 166
Leary, Joy DeGruy, 282
Leavitt, Michael, 176, 188, 189
Lee, Barbara, 137
Legal issues, 7; *ABC Charters v. Bronson* (2009), 87; *ACLU v. Miami-Dade Cnty. Sch. Bd.* (2009), 88; *Board of Education v. Pico* (1982), 82–83; *Bose Corp. v. Consumers Union of the United States* (1984), 88; child custody, 84–86; Cuba and academic freedom, 78–80; *Faculty Senate of Fla. Int'l Univ. v. Florida* (2011), 87; *Faculty Senate of Fla. Int'l Univ. v. Roberts* (2008), 87; *Faculty Senate of Fla. Int'l Univ. v. Winn* (2010), 87; *Kent v. Dulles* (1958), 76; *Keyishian v. Bd. of Regents of State University of New York* (1967), 79; *New York Times Co. v. Sullivan*, 376 U.S. 254 (1964), 88; *Reagan v. Wald* (1984), 79; removal of school library books, 80–84; *Sweezy v. New Hampshire* (1957), 78, 79; *Zemel v. Rusk* (1965), 76–78, 79
Lenin, Vladimir, 63
León, Guillermo, 238
Ley de Memoria Histórica (Spain), 267
Libertad (film), 245
Literacy Campaign, 63
Liu Shaoqi, 93
López, Luis M., 247
López, Marcial, 200
López, Melina, 73
Los palacios distantes (novel), 218
Lucía (film), 250
Lula da Silva, Luiz Inácio, 135, 137, 138

Machado, Benito, 231; and B. & J.B. Machado Tobacco Company, 231
Machado, Juan, 231; and B. & J.B. Machado Tobacco Company, 231
Mack Amendment (1990), 118
Macmillan, Harold, 64–65
Madagascar, 247
Madrid, 213, 259, 260, 261, 263
Maduro, Nicolás, 129, 130, 139
Maetzig, Kurt, 246, 247
Maité (film), 252
Malaysia, 36
Malberti, Juan Carlos Cremata, 71
Malmierca, Isidoro, 95
Mao Zedong, 65, 90, 92, 93
Marcelo, J. J. de Armas, 212

March 13 Revolutionary Directorate, 93
Marcovich, Carlos, 252, 253
Mariel boat lift, 300
Marker, Chris, 245, 249, 250
Martelli, Otello, 244
Martí, José, 58, 258, 271, 306
Martin, Deborah, 253
Martínez, Mel, 68
Marxism-Leninism, 2, 64, 92, 111, 214, 308
Matanzas, 144, 152
MATASA, 237
Mauss, Marcel, 297
Mayfield, Max, 29
Medical College Admission Test (MCAT), 181
Memorias del subdesarrollo (film), 217, 218, 250
Menéndez, Rolando, 212
Mercosur, 127, 133
Mesoamerican movement, 200
Mexican Solidarity Network, 313
Mexico, 46, 133, 134, 135, 228, 230, 304
Miami, 62, 289, 295
Miami-Dade County School Board, 81
Miami Herald, 69, 236
Miel para Oshún (film), 70
Migration, 3, 6, 14, 15, 28, 34, 40, 59, 70, 71, 149, 180, 181, 194, 208, 227, 228, 230, 231, 233, 257, 259, 275, 278, 287, 290, 297
Milicias de Tropas Territoriales, 50
Milicias Nacionales Revolucionarias, 46
Mills, Cheryl, 32–33
Monreal, Pedro, 160
Morales, Evo, 131, 136, 313
Morales Domínguez, Esteban, 273, 275
Morejón, Nancy, 272
Moreno Vega, Marta, 157
Mothers of the Barrio, 128
Mulroney, Brian, 114, 119
Muñiz Varela, Carlos (Maceo Brigade member), 68

Naranjo, José, 95
Narcotics interdiction. *See* Drug interdiction
National Association of Small Farmers (ANAP), 12, 193, 196, 199, 200, 201, 203
National Bank of Cuba (NBC), 196, 309
National Council for Accreditation of Teacher Education (NCATE), 302, 311
National Farmers and Ranchers Association (UNAG), 200
National Oceanic and Atmospheric Administration (NOAA), 35, 36; National Hurricane Center, 29
National Petroleum Company of Cuba (CUPET), 98

Index

Neo-liberalism, 114, 131, 133, 192
Neto, Agostinho, 94
New Type State Farms (GENTs), 196, 202
New York Times, 35, 137
New York Times Co. v. Sullivan, 376 U.S. 254 (1964), 88
Nicaragua, 49, 54, 113, 127, 134, 228, 230, 236, 247; and Venezuela, 133
NOAA. *See* National Oceanic and Atmospheric Administration (NOAA)
Non-Aligned Movement, 47, 91
North Atlantic Treaty Organization (NATO), 8, 216
North Holguín, 168
North-South relationship, 180, 188–89
Nuclear energy, 53–55; Juragua nuclear project, 53–55
Nuez, Iván de la, 214, 217

Obama, Barack, 28, 31, 55, 136, 138, 139, 292
Olasagasti, Eneko, 252
Oliveros, Luis, 185
Operación Milagro (Operation Miracle), 128, 312
Operación Pedro Pan. *See* Operation Peter Pan
Operation Bootstrap, 230, 233
Operation Peter Pan, 6, 59–66
Oral history, 271, 280–83
Organization of American States (OAS), 104, 116, 135
Organization of Petroleum Exporting Countries (OPEC), 135
Oricha, 148, 149
Ortega, Daniel, 133, 134
Ortiz, Fernando, 208
Osgood, Charles, 27
Ouellet, André, 111

Pakistan, 182, 185
Palacio, Manuel, 252, 254
Palmer, Larry, 139
Paraguay, 133
Para quién baila La Habana (film), 245
Parrish (book), 232, 233
Partido Socialista Obrero Español (PSOE), 210
Patterson, Orlando, 276
Payne, Charles, 312
Pérez, Louis A., Jr., 64
Pérez Lopez, Jorge, 163
Pérez Roque, Felipe, 30, 130
Peru, 134, 304
Petroamerica, 135

Petrocaribe, 128, 135
Petroleum, 98, 128, 129, 130, 135, 186, 187
Philipe, Gérard, 244
Phillippines, 228, 230, 247
Piedra, Mario, 255
Piñon, Jorge, 36–37
Plasencia, Obdulia, 251
Ponte, Antonio José, 219
Popular Socialist Party, 93
Portela, Ena Lucía, 212
Portes, Alejandro, 294
Positif (magazine), 248
Postcolonialism. *See* Colonialism
Preludio 11 (film), 246, 247
Project South, 313
Prostitution. *See* Jineterism
Pueblo en armas (film), 244, 245
Puerto Rican Departamento de Trabajo División de Migración (DTDM), 233
Puerto Rican Socialist Party, 234
Puerto Rico, 208, 228, 230; and cigars, 227, 230, 233–35
Putin, Vladimir, 35

Qatar, 187
Qia Qisheng, 95
¿Quién diablos es Juliette? (film), 252, 253
Quintana, Rogelio, 164, 165
Quiroga, José, 219

Raymond, Pierre, 195
Reagan, Ronald, 40, 50, 288
Reagan v. Wald (1984), 79
Regional Marine Pollution Emergency Information and Training Center for the Wider Caribbean, 38
Reilly, William, 37
Repsol, 36, 38
Rethinking Schools organization, 313
Reynoso, Julissa, 32
Ribicoff, Abraham, 65
Richardson, Laura, 137
Riera, Carme, 212
Robaina, Tomás Fernández, 278
Robertson, Norman, 112
Rodríguez, Carlos Rafael, 95
Rodríguez, Bruno, 33
Rodríguez, Manuel Valdés, 247
Roediger, David, 277
Rojas, Rafael, 219

Roman Catholic Church, 6, 62; Miami diocese, 62, 63, 65
Roosevelt, Franklin Delano, 65, 233
Ros-Lehtinen, Ileana, 34, 35, 39, 137
Rossellini, Roberto, 255
Rousseau, Jean Jacques, 276
Routon, Kenneth, 155
Rusk, Dean, 76, 109
Russia (post-1991): and Jaragua plant, 34–35; and petroleum exploration off of Cuba, 36, 38, 39

Sabana-Camagüey, 168, 169
Salazar, Ken, 38
Saludos cubanos (film), 249
San Benito de Alcántara Foundation, 176
Sandinista movement, 129
Santeria, 10, 147; *Babalaos*, 154; Babalocha, 149; and ceremonies and rituals, 148–50, 151; and commercialization, 145, 150–55, 157; and Cuban government, 150, 154; and diplo-Santeria, 153; financial costs, 151; Iyalocha, 149, 150; initiation, 149, 150, 151; Oricha, 148, 149; *Santeros*, 148, 153, 155; and Special Period, 145; and tourists, 150, 151, 152; and transnationalism, 147, 151
Santeros. See Santeria
Santiago de Cuba, 45, 245, 251, 280, 281
Savage, Mildred, 232
Savona, David, 237
Schlesinger, Arthur, Jr., 109
School library books, removal of, 80–84
Scorsese, Martin, 247
Segal, Daniel, 277
Sex tourism, 156
Sierra, Jordi, 212
Sinopec, 98, 105
Solás, Humberto, 70, 250
Soldiers of the Soil (book), 232
Soler, Isabel, 216
Somoza, Anastasio, 236
Sonia Flew (play), 73
South Africa (Pretoria), 5, 94, 180, 187, 188, 191
South American Defense Council, 136
Soy Cuba (film), 246, 247
Spain, 230; and Cuba, 162, 208, 215, 227, 259, 266, 275; Ley de Memoria Histórica, 267; Spanish Civil War (1936–1939), 60, 208, 210, 261, 267; and United States, 230, 259, 275
—and Cuban diaspora, 257–68; before 1970, 260–64; 1970–1990, 263, 264–66; after 1990, 15, 259, 266–68

—and Cuban wars of independence: 1868–1878, 45, 184, 227, 231; 1895–1898, 16, 45, 47, 227, 229
Special Period in Time of Peace (Special Period), 3, 11–12, 51, 145, 146, 153, 160, 168, 194, 208, 209, 211, 218, 219, 290; and cinema, 243, 251–54; and race, 279
Stewart, Christine, 115, 116
St. Kitts and Nevis, 135
St. Lucia, 127
Stoler, Ann, 59
Student Farmworker Alliance, 313
St. Vincent and the Grenadines, 127
SUCRE (currency), 135
Summit of the Americas, 133, 136, 139
Suriname, 127
Sustainable tourism, 168, 169, 170–72
Sutherland, Elizabeth, 65
Sweezy v. New Hampshire (1957), 78, 79
Symposium on Sino-Cuban Biotechnology Development and Human Health, 100

Tabacalera Arturo Fuente, 237
Tabacalera de García, 237
Tarará Student City, 99
Telesur, 131
Thomas, Hugh, 63
Three Mile Island disaster (1979), 34
Tiananmen Square incident (1989), 95, 96
Time (magazine), 63
Torres, María de los Angeles, 62, 69, 71
Torricelli Act. *See* Cuban Democracy Act (1992)
Tourism in Cuba. *See* Cuba: and tourism
Transnational social justice, 305–13
Tricontinental Conference (1966), 303
Trinidad and Tobago, 136
Trudeau, Pierre Elliott, 9, 113
Trujillo, Rafael Leónidas, 235
Tsugawa, Masahiko, 251
26th of July Movement, 93, 110, 304

Uganda, 179
Ulive, Ugo, 246
Umbral, Francisco, 213
Union City, New Jersey, 289
Union of South American Nations, 136
Union of Soviet Socialist Republics, 61, 160, 168; collapse of, 50–51, 194, 197, 202; and Cuba, 33, 48, 50, 160, 168, 243, 249; and FAR, 48; Sino-Soviet schism, 49, 91. *See also* Russia (post-1991)
United Farm Workers (United States), 235

334   Index

United Kingdom. *See* Great Britain
United Nations, 188, 309
United Socialist Party of Venezuela, 130
United States, 228; and ALBA, 133, 136–38; Bay of Pigs, 47; and Canada, 110–12, 117–20; courts, 75–86; and Cuba, 27–40, 184–85, 230, 275, 293; drug interdiction, 53, 57; and embargo of Cuba, 2, 14, 109, 117–20, 188, 288; and FAR, 52–54; and Hurricane Katrina (2005), 30, 184–85; and Latin American immigration, 16, 287, 297; and missile crisis, 7, 8, 29, 48, 76, 77, 112, 218; and 1959 Cuban revolution, 45; and normalization of relations with Cuba, 27–40, 136–37, 139; and Organization of American States, 77; and Prohibition, 164–65; and race, 278; and Spain, 230, 259, 275; transnationalism, informal transnationalism, 161–17, 294–96; War on Terror, 189. *See also* Cuba: émigrés
United States Air Force, 29
United States Coast Guard, 38, 53
United States Congress, 137, 292; Black Caucus, 137
United States Constitution: first amendment, 76, 77, 78; fifth amendment, 77
United States Court of Appeals, Atlanta, 80, 81, 82, 83, 84, 88
United States Court of Appeals, District of Columbia, 79
United States Department of Commerce, 29, 38
United States Department of State, 29, 30, 31, 46; list of State Sponsors of Terrorism, 80; and travel to Cuba, 76–78
United States Department of the Interior, 38
United States Department of the Treasury, Office of Foreign Assets Control (OFAC), 37, 79, 85
United States General Accounting Office, 34
United States Geological Survey, 36
United States Immigration and Naturalization Service (INS), 85
United States Interests Section (Havana), 31, 58, 71
United States Supreme Court, 76, 77, 78–79, 82
United States Weather Bureau (Miami), 29
Uruguay, 131, 135
Urusevsky, Sergei, 247, 248

Valdés, Zoé, 212
Vamos a Cuba (book), 81–85
Varadero, 165, 166, 167, 168

Varda, Agnès, 249
Varela, Carlos (singer and poet), 71
Vega, Bernardo, 234
Venezuela, 193; and Bolivia, 132; and Hugo Chávez, 129, 130, 139; and Cuba, 9, 127–31, 186, 203; and Ecuador, 132–33; and Nicaragua, 133; and petroleum, 128, 129, 130, 187
Venezuelan Central Bank, 132
Vietnam, 92, 94, 292
Visconti, Luchino, 254
Viva Cuba (film), 71

Walsh, Father Bryan, 62, 63, 64, 68–69, 70
Wang Youping, 91, 93
Warsaw Pact (1955), 47, 48
Washington, Booker T., 312
Washington Consensus, 132, 133
Wayne, Mike, 252, 253
Wen Jiabao, 100
Westad, Odd Arne, 92
West Indian Social Club (Connecticut), 232, 233
Wilson, Jean, 66
Wilson, Michael, 119
Wirtz, Kristina, 158
Working Group on Biotechnological Cooperation (Sino-Cuba), 100
World Association of Nuclear Operators, 34
World Bank, 114
World Wildlife Fund, 171
Wu Bangguo, 101

Xu Shicheng, 91

Yang Jiechi, 101
Yemen, 174
Yo, Sí Puedo, 311
Yorùbá, 148, 154
Young Cuban Socialist Groups (Florida), 67
Yutong, 98

Zabala, Carlos, 252
Zambrano, Benito, 252, 254
Zapatero, Rodríguez, 210
Zavattini, Cesare, 244
Zelaya, Manuel, 127
Zemel, Louis, 76
Zemel v. Rusk (1965), 76–78, 79

CONTEMPORARY CUBA

Edited by John M. Kirk

Afro-Cuban Voices: On Race and Identity in Contemporary Cuba, by Pedro Pérez-Sarduy and Jean Stubbs (2000)

Cuba, the United States, and the Helms-Burton Doctrine: International Reactions, by Joaquín Roy (2000)

Cuba Today and Tomorrow: Reinventing Socialism, by Max Azicri (2000)

Cuba's Foreign Relations in a Post-Soviet World, by H. Michael Erisman (2000)

Cuba's Sugar Industry, by José Alvarez and Lázaro Peña Castellanos (2001)

Culture and the Cuban Revolution: Conversations in Havana, by John M. Kirk and Leonardo Padura Fuentes (2001)

Looking at Cuba: Essays on Culture and Civil Society, by Rafael Hernández, translated by Dick Cluster (2003)

Santería Healing: A Journey into the Afro-Cuban World of Divinities, Spirits, and Sorcery, by Johan Wedel (2004)

Cuba's Agricultural Sector, by José Alvarez (2004)

Cuban Socialism in a New Century: Adversity, Survival, and Renewal, edited by Max Azicri and Elsie Deal (2004)

Cuba, the United States, and the Post-Cold War World: The International Dimensions of the Washington-Havana Relationship, edited by Morris Morley and Chris McGillion (2005)

Redefining Cuban Foreign Policy: The Impact of the "Special Period," edited by H. Michael Erisman and John M. Kirk (2006)

Gender and Democracy in Cuba, by Ilja A. Luciak (2007)

Ritual, Discourse, and Community in Cuban Santería: Speaking a Sacred World, by Kristina Wirtz (2007)

The "New Man" in Cuba: Culture and Identity in the Revolution, by Ana Serra (2007)

U.S.-Cuban Cooperation Past, Present, and Future, by Melanie M. Ziegler (2007)

Protestants, Revolution, and the Cuba-U.S. Bond, by Theron Corse (2007)

The Changing Dynamic of Cuban Civil Society, edited by Alexander I. Gray and Antoni Kapcia (2008)

Cuba in the Shadow of Change: Daily Life in the Twilight of the Revolution, by Amelia Rosenberg Weinreb (2009)

Failed Sanctions: Why the U.S. Embargo against Cuba Could Never Work, by Paolo Spadoni (2010)

Sustainable Urban Agriculture in Cuba, by Sinan Koont (2011)

Fifty Years of Revolution: Perspectives on Cuba, the United States, and the World, edited by Soraya M. Castro Mariño and Ronald W. Pruessen (2012)

Cuban Economists on the Cuban Economy, edited by Al Campbell (2013)

Cuban Revelations: Behind the Scenes in Havana, by Marc Frank (2013; first paperback printing, 2015)

Cuba in a Global Context: International Relations, Internationalism, and Transnationalism, edited by Catherine Krull (2014; first paperback printing, 2016)

Healthcare without Borders: Understanding Cuban Medical Internationalism by John M. Kirk (2015)

Rescuing Our Roots: The African Anglo-Caribbean Diaspora in Contemporary Cuba by Andrea J. Queeley (2015)

www.ingramcontent.com/pod-product-compliance
Lightning Source LLC
Chambersburg PA
CBHW021335230426
43666CB00006B/305